THE
PRICE of
FREEDOM

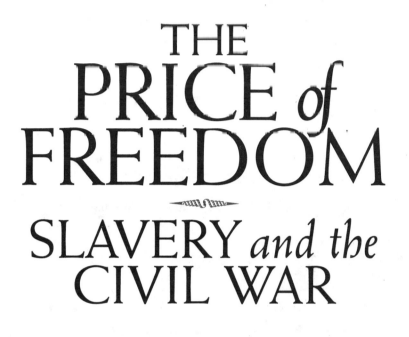

SLAVERY and the
CIVIL WAR

VOLUME TWO

The Preservation of Liberty

Edited by Martin H. Greenberg & Charles G. Waugh

with an introduction by Edna Greene Medford

CUMBERLAND HOUSE
Nashville, Tennessee

Copyright © 2000 by Martin H. Greenberg and Charles G. Waugh

Published by

CUMBERLAND HOUSE PUBLISHING
431 Harding Industrial Drive
Nashville, Tennessee 37211
www.CumberlandHouse.com

Cover design by Bateman Design, Nashville, Tennessee.

Library of Congress Cataloging-in-Publication Data

The price of freedom : slavery and the Civil War / edited by Martin H. Greenberg
and Charles G. Waugh ; introduction by Edna Greene Medford.
    p.   cm.
Includes bibliographical references and index.
Contents: v. 1. The demise of slavery — v. 2. The preservation of liberty
ISBN 1-58182-091-7 (v. 2 : pbk. : alk. paper)
  1. United States—History—Civil War, 1861–1865—Afro-Americans.
2. Slaves—Emancipation—United States. 3. Slavery—United States—History.
I. Greenberg, Martin Harry. II. Waugh, Charles.
E540.N3 P75 2000
973.7'08996073—dc21   00-056045
                                                   CIP

Printed in the United States of America

1 2 3 4 5 6 7 8 9 10—04 03 02 01 00

*To the men and women who fought for the
integrity of our nation, the ideals it was founded
on, and the liberty of all its citizens*

Contents

Introduction   *ix*
        Edna Greene Medford

Acknowledgments   *xiv*

PART 1: FREEDOM PROCLAIMED, FREEDOM SEIZED

1   "Beckoning Them to the Dreamed of Promise of
    Freedom": African-Americans and Lincoln's
    Proclamation of Emancipation   5
    Edna Greene Medford

2   The Civil War in Kentucky: The Slave Claims
    His Freedom   15
    Victor B. Howard

3   "Uncle Billy" Sherman Comes to Town: The Free
    Winter of Black Savannah   29
    William A. Byrne

4   "We'll Hang Jeff Davis on the Sour Apple Tree":
    Civil War Era Slave Resistance in Louisiana   45
    Junius P. Rodriguez

5   Emancipation in Missouri   57
    Michael Fellman

PART 2: FROM FUGITIVES TO CONTRABANDS
                TO FREEDPEOPLE

6   Being Free: Black Migration and the Civil War   73
    Allan Johnston

7   Nashville's Fort Negley: A Symbol of Blacks'
    Involvement with the Union Army   93
    Bobby L. Lovett

8   Black Violence and White Response: Louisiana, 1862   107
    William F. Messner

9   From Slavery in Missouri to Freedom in Kansas:
    The Influx of Black Fugitives and Contrabands into
    Kansas, 1854–1865   *121*
    Richard B. Sheridan

    PART 3: RACIAL ATTITUDES ON THE CIVIL WAR FRONTIER

10 Civil War Kansas and the Negro   *145*
    Albert Castel

11 The Negro in Wisconsin's Civil War Effort   *155*
    Edward Noyes

            PART 4: THE IMPACT OF WAR ON FREE
                    PEOPLE OF COLOR

12 "I Was Always a Union Man": The Dilemma of
    Free Blacks in Confederate Virginia   *171*
    Edna Greene Medford

13 Humbly They Served: The Black Brigade in the
    Defense of Cincinnati   *185*
    Edgar A. Toppin

14 Free Negroes and the Freedmen: Black Politics
    in New Orleans During the Civil War   *201*
    Ted Tunnell

            PART 5: PREPARING FOR FREEDOM

15 Union Chaplains and the Education of the Freedmen   *223*
    Warren B. Armstrong

16 Black Education in Louisiana, 1863–1865   *231*
    William F. Messner

17 Notes on the Education of Negroes at Norfolk and
    Portsmouth, Virginia, During the Civil War   *247*
    Sing-Nan Fen

18 The American Missionary Association and Black
    Education in Civil War Missouri   *259*
    Joe M. Richardson

PART 6: THE QUEST FOR SELF-DETERMINATION

19   Black Churches and the Civil War: Theological and
Ecclesiastical Significance of Black Methodist
Involvement, 1861–1865   271
     Sandy Dwayne Martin

20   Sherman Marched—and Proclaimed "Land for
the Landless"   283
     Howard C. Westwood

PART 7: AFRICAN AMERICANS AND THE LINCOLN LEGACY

21   Lincoln and Black Freedom   299
     LaWanda Cox

22   Lincoln and Race Relations   317
     Hans L. Trefousse

Notes   327

For Further Reading   393

Index   395

Introduction

In FOUR SHORT YEARS America's Civil War transformed lives, altered traditional relationships, and challenged long-held assumptions. As nearly four million enslaved people passed from legal status as chattel to human beings, they sought to exercise control over their lives and test the limits of their newfound independence. The process by which African Americans moved from bondage to freedom involved great trials, but the determination they exhibited at each stage served as testament to their belief that freedom's price was acceptable. Whether as fighting men in the field, fugitives in contraband camps, or uncooperative laborers who remained on the land, their efforts reflected a commitment to the realization of the promise guaranteed in the nation's ideological foundations.

When the conflict that pitted brothers against each other first began, few beyond the African-American community accepted its extraordinary implications for the enslaved. As free blacks in the North pressed for an unconditional assault on slavery, those in bondage—at first subtly and eventually in demonstrative ways—embraced their own cause. When their owners rode off to war, the enslaved showered them with copious tears while secretly praying for Union victory. Their declarations of unwavering loyalty dissolved as the slaveholder's image faded in the distance. Eventually, as the Confederate military siphoned off the most able-bodied white men from farms and plantations, enslaved laborers challenged the age-old practices that whites had used to exploit and subordinate them. Many took advantage of the inability of white women and of those who were left in charge of the plantations to maintain strict discipline. As they resisted efforts to adhere to the established labor regimen in house and field, insubordination became commonplace.

While the majority of enslaved people elected to experience the process of transformation within the environment of the plantation, others sought more tangible evidence of freedom. For them, nothing short of physical removal from the site of their bondage would suffice.

Hence, men and women, singly and in family units, abandoned the fields and embraced the opportunities afforded by the chaos of war.

Concern that enslaved men would fall victim to military impressment or that certain bondsmen and women would be "refugeed" sometimes influenced the timing of flight from bondage. Refugeeing involved the removal of the most valued human property farther into the interior as the Union military advanced, leaving the others behind. Black men who escaped refugeeing could expect to be forced into service for the Confederacy as military laborers. Impressment often meant that enslaved men came under the authority of those who had neither financial nor paternalistic motivations for safeguarding them from abuse. Furthermore, the nature of the work impressed laborers performed—throwing up breastworks and other fortifications, for instance—exposed black men to Union fire. The death toll convinced many enslaved men that they stood a better chance of survival if they fled.

Lincoln's issuing of the Emancipation Proclamation on January 1, 1863, provided additional incentive for bondsmen and women to abandon the Confederacy. Although congressional action had already begun the process of securing freedom for many of those whom Lincoln sought to liberate in his proclamation, no other measure of the war captured the attention of African Americans as did this one document. In the words of one contemporary, the edict was like "a pillar of flame, beckoning them to the dreamed of promise of freedom! Bidding them leap from chattelhood to manhood, from slavery to freedom!" Despite their own efforts and those of Congress, black men and women came to identify their emancipation with this single event.

Whether they fled their bondage for reasons uniquely their own or were inspired by the Emancipation Proclamation, fugitives from slavery faced uncertain and often harsh conditions. In a bid for survival, some attached themselves to advancing armies or to military posts where they provided invaluable support services. Their labor as teamsters, cooks, laundresses, hospital attendants, and as erectors of fortifications freed white soldiers for combat. When their numbers swelled into the thousands, however, most commanders who had been at best tolerant of their presence, now found the problem of caring for them problematic. Physical abuse of the contrabands and freedpeople posed a major concern as well, as Union soldiers displayed racial enmity. The hostility they showed sometimes necessitated the removal of African-American civilians from their midst.

The camps that were established to shelter the contrabands and freedpeople reflected the unhealthy conditions exacerbated by war: squalor, starvation, and exposure to the elements. For instance, many of the facilities that had been placed within and just outside of the nation's capital (such as Duff Green's Row) became notorious for the level of suffering experienced by their residents. The misery in these camps attracted the attention of philanthropic organizations and inspired the founding of additional ones. Groups such as the Contraband Relief Association and the Friends Association for the Relief of Colored Freedmen sent personnel and supplies to help alleviate the suffering. Harriet Jacobs, one of the relief agents (and herself a former bondswoman), found the contrabands were "sick with measles, diphtheria, scarlet and typhoid fever . . . a few filthy rags to lie on, others had nothing but the bare floor for a couch. . . . Each day brings the fresh additions of the hungry, naked and sick." Despite the best efforts of these philanthropic groups and their agents, many succumbed to the deplorable conditions.

Although suffering routinely characterized residence in the contraband camps, these facilities often were the first places where those making the transition from slavery to freedom took their initial steps toward self-determination. It was in the camps that many first experienced the system of free labor, began instruction in reading, and acquired skills that assisted them in providing for their families. One of these facilities, located just outside of the District of Columbia, became a model for the rest. Residents of Freedmen's Village found employment on the farms abandoned by fleeing Confederates and received instruction in useful trades such as carpentry, shoemaking, and blacksmithing. Before the war ended, the resourcefulness of its residents had produced a thriving community that benefited from the presence of a hospital, school, church, and shops.

Everywhere the contrabands and freedpeople learned to read. Having been denied access to literacy under slavery, they availed themselves of the opportunities for rudimentary instruction whenever it was offered. Teachers employed by organizations such as the American Missionary Association taught young and old, throughout the day and evening, in special Sunday schools as well as during the week. Realizing that freedom would be fleeting without the tools to understand and protect their rights, black men and women eagerly pursued instruction for themselves and their children.

The ability to read remained second only to the acquisition of land in the aspirations of men and women whose lives had heretofore been restricted by economic exploitation. African Americans felt entitled to the land they had cultivated as enslaved people. Their labor had kept it productive, even through the war, and now that freedom was at hand, they saw no reason why they should be denied its ownership. Their claim to the land was especially just, they assumed, since many of their owners had abandoned the plantations in their flight from the advancing Union army. General William T. Sherman's Special Field Order No. 15, issued in January 1865, buoyed the hopes of the freedpeople, especially the thousands who had attached themselves to his forces as he traversed the Georgia landscape in his March to the Sea. The measure allowed "possessory title" to forty acres of land per head of household on property that extended in a thirty-mile-wide band along the coast from Charleston to Jacksonville. Ultimately, forty thousand people benefited (albeit temporarily) from his actions. Elsewhere in the Union-occupied South, black men and women gained access to (if not outright ownership of) the land either with the assistance and approval of the federal government or of their own volition. But postwar actions that returned abandoned lands to their owners destroyed most freedpeople's chances of achieving economic independence.

African Americans enjoyed greater success in their efforts to control their social institutions, especially the religious ones. Restricted in their worship under slavery, they pressed during the war years for greater autonomy by withdrawing from the white churches that they had been forced to attend. Religious leaders such as James Hood of the African Methodist Episcopal Zion Church facilitated this withdrawal as they worked among the freedpeople. In the postwar years, this institution would sustain the freedpeople and their progeny as the "invisible" churches had facilitated the survival of the enslaved.

While the war years had the most profound affect on people in bondage, free men and women of color found their lives disrupted and altered as well. After the Lincoln administration embraced the twin causes of union for the nation and freedom for the bondsman and women, the ostensibly free blacks in the North witnessed personal assault and the destruction of homes and property at the hands of whites angry over the draft and competition with blacks for employment. At the same time, however, the war years afforded the residents of the African-American community in the North the opportunity to prove themselves worthy of full citizenship rights by military participation. Those who chose to stay at home supported the relief efforts for soldiers and refugees and found ways to benefit from the wartime economy.

Perhaps more than any other group, free people of color in the South found themselves in the most precarious position during the war years. Like the enslaved, free blacks trapped behind Confederate lines faced intense scrutiny from their white neighbors and military commanders, suffered impressment into Rebel service, became victims of foraging parties from both sides, and experienced the shortages that plagued the larger Southern population. Although legally free, they enjoyed fewer options than did enslaved people. While bondsmen and women could elect to run away to freedom, with little regard for anything except family ties, the need to protect what little property they had been able to acquire through years of toil sometimes complicated the decision of free people to flee or remain at home. They had favored the Union because they believed that the demise of slavery would be the prize for victory. Some were linked by blood to those still in bondage or had recently made the transition from property to free people themselves. They understood that their chances for true freedom (full citizenship rights and equality) rested with a Union victory and that a decision to remain in the Confederacy served the needs of those who sought to perpetuate a system that was to their detriment. Hence, some free people resolved their dilemma by outwardly cooperating with the Rebels while clandestinely aiding the Union. Such assistance took the form of harboring wounded Union troops, smuggling Northern sympathizers across the lines, and engaging in espionage.

In the end, the Union proved victorious, but the kind of nation that the enslaved and the free had envisioned would result from such victory never evolved. While the various congressional measures, Lincoln's proclamation of emancipation, and the actions of those who fled the plantations ultimately received constitutional sanction through passage and ratification of the Thirteenth Amendment, true freedom and equality proved illusive. In the immediate postwar years, certain northerners—although ever so briefly—attempted to continue the transformations that had commenced in 1861. But abruptly, the momentum ceased, and the freedpeople were left to fend for themselves—without economic security or adequate protection of their rights. As historians continue to debate the reasons for and the consequences of the failure to complete the changes that the Civil War initiated, we might do well to consider the price to ourselves as a nation of promises unfulfilled.

Edna Greene Medford

Acknowledgments

THE SOURCES for the selections in this volume are listed below. The original spelling and punctuation have been followed throughout with only minor typographical variations for the sake of consistency. Reference notes have been combined in a separate section following the text.

Introduction by Edna Greene Medford. Copyright © 2000 by Edna Greene Medford.

"Beckoning Them to the Dreamed of Promise of Freedom": African Americans and Lincoln's Proclamation of Emancipation by Edna Greene Medford. Copyright © 1999 by the Savas Publishing Company. First published in *The Lincoln Forum: Abraham Lincoln, Gettysburg, and the Civil War*. Reprinted by permission of the Savas Publishing Company.

The Civil War in Kentucky: The Slave Claims His Freedom by Victor Howard. Copyright © 1982 by the Association for the Study on African-American Life and History, Inc. First published in the *Journal of Negro History*, vol. 67, no. 3, 1982. Reprinted by permission of the Association for the Study on African-American Life and History, Inc.

"Uncle Billy" Sherman Comes to Town: The Free Winter of Black Savannah by William Byrne. Copyright © 1995 by the Georgia Historical Society. First published in *Georgia Historical Quarterly*, vol. 79, no. 1, 1995. Reprinted by permission of the Georgia Historical Society.

"We'll Hang Jeff Davis on the Sour Apple Tree": Civil War Era Slave Resistance in Louisiana by Junius P. Rodriguez. Copyright © 1995 by the *Gulf South Historical Review*. First published in the *Gulf South Historical Review*, vol. 10, no. 2, 1995. Reprinted by permission of the *Gulf South Historical Review*.

Emancipation in Missouri by Michael Fellman. Copyright © 1988 by the State Historical Society of Missouri. First published in *Missouri Historical Review*, vol. 83, no. 1, 1988. Reprinted by permission of the State Historical Society of Missouri.

Being Free: Black Migration and the Civil War by Allan Johnson. Copyright © 1987 by the Australian and New Zealand American Studies Association. First published in *Australasian Journal of American Studies*, vol. 6, no. 1, 1987. Reprinted by permission of the Australian and New Zealand American Studies Association.

Nashville's Fort Negley: A Symbol of Blacks' Involvement with the Union Army by Bobby Lovett. Copyright © 1982 by the Tennessee Historical Society. First published in *Tennessee Historical Society Quarterly,* vol. 41, Reprinted by permission of the Tennessee Historical Society.

Black Violence and White Response: Louisiana, 1862 by William F. Messner. Copyright © 1975 by the Southern Historical Association. First published in the *Journal of Southern History,* February 1975. Reprinted by permission of the Southern Historical Association.

From Slavery in Missouri to Freedom In Kansas: The Influx of Black Fugitives and Contrabands into Kansas, 1854–1865 by Richard B. Sheridan. Copyright © 1989 by the Kansas State Historical Society, Inc. First published in *Kansas History,* vol. 12, no. 1, 1989. Reprinted by permission of the Kansas State Historical Society, Inc.

Civil War Kansas and the Negro by Albert Castel. Copyright © 1966 by the Association for the Study on African-American Life and History, Inc. First published in the *Journal of Negro History,* vol. 51, no. 2, 1966. Reprinted by permission of the Association for the Study on African-American Life and History, Inc.

The Negro in Wisconsin's Civil War Effort by Edward Noyes. Copyright © 1967 by the Abraham Lincoln Library and Museum. First published in the *Lincoln Herald,* vol. 69, no. 2, 1967. Reprinted by permission of the Abraham Lincoln Library and Museum, Harrogate, Tennessee.

"I Was Always a Union Man": The Dilemma of Free Blacks in Confederate Virginia by Edna Greene Medford. Copyright © 1994 by Frank Cass & Company, Ltd. Reprinted by permission from *Slavery and Abolition,* vol. 15, no. 3, published by Frank Cass & Company, 900 Eastern Avenue, Ilford, Essex, England.

Free Negroes and the Freedmen: Black Politics in New Orleans During the Civil War by Ted Tunnell. Copyright © 1980 by the Southern Studies Institute. First published in *Southern Studies,* vol. 9, no. 1, 1980. Reprinted by permission of the Southern Studies Institute.

Humbly They Served: The Black Brigade in the Defense of Cincinnati by Edgar A. Toppin. Copyright © 1963 by the Association for the Study on African-American Life and History, Inc. First published in the *Journal of Negro History,* vol. 48, no. 2, 1963. Reprinted by permission of the Association for the Study on African-American Life and History, Inc.

Union Chaplains and the Education of the Freedmen by Warren Armstrong. Copyright © 1967 by the Association for the Study on African-American Life and History, Inc. First published in the *Journal of Negro History,* vol. 52, no. 2, 1967. Reprinted by permission of the Association for the Study on African-American Life and History, Inc.

Black Education in Louisiana, 1863–1865 by William F. Messner. Copyright © 1976 by the Kent State University Press. First published in *Civil War History,* vol. 22, no. 1, 1976. Reprinted by permission of the Kent State University Press.

THE
PRICE *of*
FREEDOM

<hr>

SLAVERY *and the*
CIVIL WAR

Part 1

FREEDOM PROCLAIMED, FREEDOM SEIZED

CHAPTER 1

"Beckoning Them to the Dreamed of Promise of Freedom"

African-Americans and Lincoln's Proclamation of Emancipation

Edna Greene Medford

In the nation's capital, a city noted for its majestic monuments, stands a rather modest one that commemorates the man with whom the freedpeople credited their liberation. Paid for primarily by their small donations, the memorial features a grateful slave, partly kneeling at the feet of an emancipating president. At its unveiling in 1876, Frederick Douglass, the black orator and former slave himself, thought it too suggestive of subservience and dependency since "it showed the Negro on his knees when a more manly attitude would have been indicative of freedom."[1] It is a sentiment shared by those in the African-American community today who, like Douglass and his contemporaries, understand the power of symbols for good or ill. Committed to advancing a more historically accurate image of emancipation, they have called for a reassessment of the role of Lincoln and African-Americans themselves in the destruction of slavery. The tendency has been to minimize the image of the president as "great emancipator" and to underscore the efforts of black men and women in their own liberation.[2]

The more one recognizes the centrality of enslaved and free people of color in the process of emancipation, however, the more one becomes aware of the significance of Lincoln and his historic document to the people who were most directly affected by its provisions. Despite its shortcomings (*and there were many*), contemporary African Americans saw in the Emancipation Proclamation a document with limitless possibilities. To them, it represented the promise not only of freedom and an end to their degradation, but it encouraged the hope for full citizenship and inclusion in the country of their birth as well. Although liberating in theory rather than in reality, people of color saw the proclamation as a watershed in their quest for human dignity and recognition as Americans.

From the commencement of war, African Americans recognized the significance the conflict could play in their struggle for freedom. Initially hoping to find in the president someone who would embrace the twin causes of Union and liberty, they quickly realized that Lincoln would follow neither a swift nor steady path toward emancipation. They felt compelled to denounce his insistence on preservation of the Union at all costs, especially when his actions seemingly protected the South's rights to its human property. Northern black leaders took Lincoln to task for his rejection of field commanders' acts of liberation, his refusal to back the enlistment of blacks in the army, and his preoccupation with appeasing the border states. In the months before he issued the proclamation, they chided Lincoln from the pulpit and in the press, while appealing to him to hear the cries of the enslaved. When he did move toward freedom, but with the proviso that the slaves be colonized outside the country, the black leadership intensified its criticism.[3] African Americans had no desire to increase the burdens of the president in this time of national crisis, but neither did they intend to squander this opportunity for the emancipation of nearly four million that the war afforded. Their agitation, along with that of white abolitionists, produced a climate of sentiment that helped to persuade Lincoln to move against slavery.

When he finally did embrace emancipation in September 1862, in the form of a preliminary proclamation, African Americans greeted the news with restrained optimism. Members of the black press, clergy, and other prominent leaders of the community jubilantly proclaimed that the end of slavery was near. But during the 100 days between the preliminary proclamation and the actual declaration of freedom, they fought the temptation to consider emancipation a *fait accompli*. In one of his customarily damning editorials in his monthly paper, Douglass gave voice to the apprehensions of the black community. Declaring that there was reason for "both hope and fear," his confidence was tempered by the tone of the preliminary document, whose words, Douglass charged:

. . . kindled no enthusiasm. They touched neither justice nor mercy. Had there been one expression of sound moral feeling against Slavery, one word of regret and shame that this accursed system had remained so long the disgrace and scandal of the Republic, one word of satisfac-

~~tion in the hope of burying slavery and the rebellion in one common grave, a thrill of joy would have run around the world, but no such word was said, and no such joy was kindled."~~

~~Lincoln eventually moved in the right direction, Douglass argued,~~ but his actions were born of necessity and devoid of immediatism. "~~Emancipation—is put off~~—it was made [future] and conditional—not present and absolute."[5]

~~Throughout the closing months of 1862, blacks remained fearful that Lincoln would bow to the slaveholding interests and withhold the final proclamation scheduled to become effective the first day of the new year. When the South failed to accede to his terms and Lincoln honored the promise of the preliminary document, African Americans throughout the North reacted to the news with unbridled joy.~~ Black organizations held parades and assembled in mammoth gatherings to listen to ~~prominent abolitionists extol the virtues of the president. At one such rally in New York, the Rev. Henry Highland Garnet (who like many blacks in the North had escaped southern slavery before the war) presided over the massive meeting at the Cooper Institute which had~~ been organized by the "Sons of Freedom." Conceding that African Americans had "indulged but little faith that the President would redeem his promise of September," an ecstatic Garnet nonetheless told the crowd assembled that Lincoln had always been "the man of our choice and hope."[6] One by one the speakers rose and added their voices to the praises for the man of the hour.

Celebrating Chicagoans were treated to the electrifying presence of Osborne Perry Anderson, the lone black survivor of John Brown's ill-fated raid on the federal arsenal at Harpers Ferry less than four years earlier. Anderson pronounced the proclamation "God's vindicating the principles" of the man who sacrificed his all for the cause of black freedom.[7] Numbering more than 3,000, a similar audience at Tremont Temple in Boston (site of strong abolitionist sentiment), was treated to the oratory of noted black abolitionists such as William C. Nell, Charles Lenox Remond, William Wells Brown, John S. Rock, and the ubiquitous Frederick Douglass.[8] Throughout the free states, African Americans sent prayers skyward in gratitude to God and to Lincoln.

In the Confederacy enslaved and free blacks, understandably, responded to the proclamation in a subtler fashion. News of the decree reached them through varied channels. Some, using the cover of darkness, listened outside of open windows as their owners read from letters or newspapers that told of Lincoln's actions. The literate few read the words for themselves and later rushed off to share the secret with incredulous comrades in the quarters. In some instances, the slaveholders actually learned of the proclamation from their slaves.[9] However the news arrived, the knowing was enough to alter the relationship between master and slave. Previously "faithful servants" became audacious and went about their work grudgingly, when at all. By the time the Union forces arrived in their vicinity, many enslaved people were more than ready and willing to seize the opportunity for freedom.[10]

In those areas of the South occupied by Union troops, black men and women celebrated "the day of jubilee" in much the same way as did African Americans in the North. Although not included in the emancipating provisions of the proclamation, enslaved men and women in cities such as Norfolk and New Orleans—where the Union presence had already weakened slavery's hold—welcomed the president's pronouncement as a sure sign of the inevitability of their own freedom.[11] In Norfolk thousands watched and cheered as Union troops and representatives from the black community paraded down the main streets in celebration of Lincoln's decree. Even in the border states, enslaved people recognized the significance the document held for their future liberation. In Kentucky, for instance, news of the preliminary proclamation had convinced African Americans that their freedom was imminent, despite efforts on the part of local slaveholders to dispel the belief.[12] Elation over the Emancipation Proclamation did not blind African Americans to Lincoln's other than humane motivations in declaring enslaved people free. Citing the invaluable, albeit coerced, service that blacks rendered the Confederacy, the *Anglo-African* declared the proclamation

> simply a war measure . . . an instrument for crushing, hurting, injuring, and crippling the enemy. It is per se no more humanitarian than a hundred pounder cannon. It seeks to deprive the enemy of arms and legs, muscles and sinews, used by them to procure food and raiment and to throw up fortifications.[13]

Lincoln, himself, made no secret of his motivation for issuing the document, having used the phrases "necessary war measure" and "military necessity" in the proclamation itself. From the outset of the war, the enslaved had been used to strengthen the Confederate position. Initially, the government hired them from their owners to build fortifications and perform unskilled labor that freed white soldiers for combat. Later, a slaveholding population—alarmed by the poor treatment their slaves received at the hands of the military, and fearful that their property would escape to the Union lines and freedom at the first opportunity—

made every effort to keep their laborers from the front. As a consequence, the Confederacy resorted to impressment, demanding that slaveholders commit a certain portion of their enslaved work force to the cause.[14] Black labor also kept open the South's mines, manufacturing plants, and factories. Those who remained on the plantations continued to grow cotton and other cash crops, as well as food for the army.[15] Lincoln sought to throw the Confederacy into chaos by depriving it of this indispensable labor force.

Other considerations motivated Lincoln's actions in issuing the proclamation as well. In making the emancipation of enslaved people a factor in the war, he hoped to prevent other nations, especially England, from coming to the aid of the Confederacy. Despite having ended slavery in her West Indian possessions more than two decades earlier and having been the country most solicited by abolitionists eager to gather funds for the cause, England's economic ties to the southern states led her to consider recognition of the Confederacy. Lincoln's introduction of emancipation into the equation forced England to choose between a nation of slaveholders and one committed to freedom.[16]

Neither was the Emancipation Proclamation the document that would grant the universal and unconditional freedom that African Americans expressed his intention to declare freedom only for those in the states or parts thereof still in rebellion. Apparently, military necessity precluded the need to issue a proclamation of emancipation for those enslaved persons under the control of Union forces. The excluded, hence, consisted of persons enslaved in the city of New Orleans as well as several parishes in Louisiana; the 48 northwestern counties of Virginia that now comprise West Virginia; several counties in eastern Virginia and the cities of Norfolk and Portsmouth; Tennessee; as well as the border states of Missouri, Kentucky, Maryland, and Delaware. In total, some 800,000 enslaved African Americans were excluded from the provisions of the Emancipation Proclamation.

Despite its shortcomings, however, black men and women expressed minimal criticism of the proclamation of freedom, preferring instead to see beyond its momentary limitations to its future promise. It was, as Osborne Perry Anderson declared, "no matter that the politicians say it was brought about after all other means were tried."[17] Many agreed with Douglass who considered Lincoln's failure to abolish slavery throughout the country a "blunder," but thought the final result would be positive nonetheless. "When Virginia is a free state, Maryland cannot be a slave state," Douglass asserted. "Slavery must stand or fall together. Strike it at either extreme—either on the head or at the heel, and it dies."[18]

The military necessity character of the proclamation disappointed those abolitionists who had pressed Lincoln to oppose slavery on moral grounds. Some African Americans found irony in the president's focus on military necessity because it suggested that Lincoln needed *black men* to save the Union. His authorization of the enlistment of black troops signaled, they believed, an acceptance of them as men and of his faith in their abilities. There was no small hint of pleasure and sarcasm from the pen of Thomas Hamilton, editor of the *Anglo-African*, who wrote of the impact of black men riding to the aid of the country:

> The skill of our generals [and] the bravery of our soldiers [have] been tried, the strength of our resources has been pushed to the utmost—we have in the field an army as large as that of Xerxes, and on the water, ships in thousands, and yet all these do not prevail, and our tried and trusted ruler calls upon the negro "to come to the rescue!"[19]

Hamilton urged his brethren to heed the call to arms. "What the hour demands of us is action, immediate pressing action!" he thundered. "It is a fight for freedom and we are bound to go in."[20]

Henry Highland Garnet echoed Hamilton's desire to fight for freedom, but he pressed for black men to accept military service as expressions of their patriotism as well. Recounting the rebuff of earlier attempts by African Americans to fight for the Union, Garnet believed that once the call had come, black men had little choice but to respond to it and "bequeath to future generations an heirloom in which their children and children's children would remember with pride that their fathers were not cowards when the country called them to its defense."[21]

Free men of color had other reasons for entering the conflict as well. Their own lives had been circumscribed by the prejudices and discriminations of a society that judged any man or woman of color—whether enslaved or free—unfit to lay claim to the rights and privileges reserved to white Americans. They now looked to participation in the war to secure those freedoms that had been denied to them for so long. "If freedmen are accepted as soldiers to man the forts in the Mississippi and the Southern coast, why shall not freemen be also accepted?" they argued.

> All we wanted was opportunity, and that, blessed be God, has come! Freedom is ours. And its fruit, equality, hangs temptingly on the tree beckoning our own brave arms to rise and clutch it. If we rise in tens of thousands, and say to the President, "here we are, take us!" we will secure to our children and children's children's children all that our fathers have labored and suffered and bled for![22]

Frederick Douglass also called black men to arms, but ever attuned to the possibility that African Americans would not receive fair play, he indicated that the willingness of black men to enlist in the military would be shaped by the quality of their treatment. He demanded that the government:

> assure them of protection as soldiers, and give them a fair chance of winning distinction and glory in common with other soldiers. They must not be made the mere hewers of wood and drawers of water for the army. When a man leaves home, family, and security, to risk his limbs and life in the field of battle, for God's sake let him have all the honor which he may achieve, let his color be what it may.[23]

Addressing the fear that black soldiers captured by the Confederacy would be treated as runaway slaves, Douglass insisted that the Union "hold the Confederate Government strictly responsible, as much for a black as for a white soldier. Give us fair play," he promised, "and open here your recruiting offices, and their doors shall be crowded with black recruits to fight the battles of the country. Do your part, my white fellow-countrymen, and we will do ours."[24]

A group of black leaders in Michigan, doubtless encouraged by the proclamation, tied their willingness to serve in the military to an extension of the rights of citizenship. Shortly after Lincoln issued the proclamation, the State Central Committee of Colored Men met to discuss denial to them of the elective franchise and the continued discrimination they faced from "odious and unjust laws on account of color." The committee resolved to petition the Michigan legislature to exclude the word "white" from the state constitution and to abolish all laws and statutes that made references to color. Hinting at a refusal to fight for the Union, the petitioners resolved:

> At such a time as this, when our beloved country is writhing beneath the throes of political devastation, every man, of whatever race or color, who at all values the endearing name American citizen, should be called upon and required to do his duty in upholding the General Government, and putting down the most infamous rebellion that ever distracted a country in the history of the world. Whatever may be required of others, should be required of us, and we feel willing and stand ready to obey our country's call, in a summons to arms in her defence, or in any other just capacity in which we might be required. But as residents of the State of Michigan, we cannot feel willing to serve a State while it concedes all that is due to others and denies much, if not the most, that is due to us.[25]

The Emancipation Proclamation alone may not have been enough to embolden these black men to seek the rights of other citizens, but its very existence doubtless helped to steel their resolve to do so. It gave them hope that full inclusion in American society was a dream about to be realized.

African Americans expected much from Lincoln's proclamation. In addition to it enabling them to acquire freedom and equality, they saw it as the path by which a people debased by slavery would be reconstructed. Black Civil War correspondent Thomas Morris Chester believed that in breaking the shackles of the enslaved, the Emancipation Proclamation

> . . . protects the sanctity of the marriage relationship and lays the foundation for domestic purity . . . releases from licentious restraint our cruelly treated women and defends them in the maiden chastity which instincts suggest . . . justifies the natural right of the mother over the disposition of her daughters, and gives to the father the only claim which Almighty God intended should be exercised by man over his son . . . puts an end to blasphemy and the perversion of the scriptures, and inaugurates those higher and holier influences which will prosper all the people and bless the land from the Atlantic to the Pacific . . . ends the days of oppression, cruelty and outrage, founded on complexion, and introduces an era of emancipation, humanity and virtue, founded upon the principles of unerring justice.[26]

Of course, Chester was reading a lot into a conservative, limited document. But he understood that in elevating the enslaved from property to human being, the proclamation would alter the lives of African Americans in a way that would ensure their dignity and secure for them the right of self-determination.

Recognizing that Lincoln's proclamation was "constructed of paper and ink," and that its success hinged on Union victory, African Americans resolved to provide the assistance that would secure that victory. Before Lee surrendered the battered remnants of his army at Appomattox Court House, more than 180,000 African Americans had served in defense of Union and liberty, approximately 134,000 from the South and 52,000 from the North. Untold others had aided the cause through their work as laborers for the military; as spies, scouts, nurses, and informants; and as disrupters of the institution of slavery. As the proclamation intended, many enslaved blacks fled to the Union lines and freedom at the first opportunity. By war's end, as many as 500,000 had come under Union control.[27]

But African Americans had escaped the Confederacy long before the issuing of the proclamation, and congressional action had virtually ensured the freedom of many of those Lincoln sought to liberate. Men more sympathetic to abolition had been moving the country in that direction from the earliest stages of the war. General Benjamin Butler's decision to declare as contrabands-of-war those slaves who made their way to his lines at Virginia's Fortress Monroe had been followed by congressional action that saw passage of laws that first confiscated slaves from masters who permitted them to labor for the Confederacy and later set free all those of disloyal owners who made their way to Union-held territory. In the meantime, enslaved men and women in the District of Columbia acquired their freedom through congressional action, as did those in the territories. While Lincoln supported (even championed) some of these actions, he generally followed a less radical path than did Congress, choosing instead to nudge the border states into taking the lead toward emancipation by encouraging compensation to owners of lost slave property. Yet, in the wake of the Emancipation Proclamation, African Americans—enslaved and free—credited the president with securing their freedom.

More than any other single measure of the war, the proclamation seized the attention of black people. It may have lacked the depth of feeling, the degree of moral force, that some thought the occasion demanded; yet, the recipients of its declarations recognized the power of its author to honor its promise. The proclamation had been issued by the most powerful man in the nation. For a people accustomed to power and authority vested in a single individual (in slavery, the master) Lincoln's decree was equivalent to divine law. "I never seed Mr. Lincoln, but when they told me 'bout him, I thought he was partly God," former slave Angie Garret would later recall.[28] Even before the war was over and freedom secured, before he received martyr status at the hands of John Wilkes Booth, the slaves venerated him. Lincoln was an icon, but one with whom they could communicate. Their sense of his accessibility is reflected in the letter Marylander Annie Davis sent to him less than a year before the war ended:

> Mr. President It is my Desire to be free. to go to see my people on the eastern shore. my mistress wont let me you will please let me know if we are free. and what i can do. I write to you for advice. please send me word this week. or as soon as possible.[29]

Perhaps less naively, free people of color regarded Lincoln as thoroughly approachable as well. From Buffalo, New York, Hannah Johnson wrote the president expressing her concern about mistreatment of black troops by Confederate officers. After providing him with background, which included a bit of her family history, she implored him to protect men like her son who had served with the 54th Massachusetts at Fort Wagner:

I have but poor edication . . . but I know just as well as any what is right between man and man. Now I know it is right that a colored man should go and fight for his country, and so ought to a white man. I know that a colored man ought to run no greater risques than a white, his pay is no greater his obligation to fight is the same. So why should not our enemies be compelled to treat him the same, Made to do it.[30]

Mrs. Johnson proceeded to instruct the president on the history of race relations in the South and proposed a plan of action to counter the rebel army's attack on the rights of black Union prisoners of war:

Now Mr. Lincoln dont you think you oght to stop this thing and make them do the same by the colored men they have lived in idleness all their lives on stolen labor and made savages of the colored people, but they now are so furious because they are proving themselves to be men, such as have come away and got some education. It must not be so. You must put the rebels to work in State prisons to making shoes and things, if they sell our colored soldiers, till they let them all go. And give their wounded the same treatment, it would seem cruel, but there [is] no other way, and a just man must do hard things sometimes, that shew him to be a great man. . . . Will you see that the colored men fighting now, are fairly treated. You ought to do this, and do it at once, Not let the thing run along meet it quickly and manfully, and stop this, mean cowardly cruelty.[31]

Johnson assured Lincoln that if he did the right thing "When you are dead and in Heaven, in a thousand years that action of yours will make the Angels sing your praises."[32]

These letters reflect the degree of faith people of color had in Lincoln. His image as protector and emancipator had been burned into their consciousness because the proclamation symbolized the attainability of their most fervent desires.

A contemporary observer likened the Emancipation Proclamation to "a pillar of flame, beckoning [enslaved men and women] to the dreamed of promise and freedom! Bidding them leap from chattel-hood to manhood, from slavery to freedom!"[33] Because blacks responded to that beacon, the Union won the war and secured the freedom the proclamation promised. The enslaved needed Lincoln but the president needed them as well. Union for the nation and liberty for African Americans resulted from a necessary alliance between the two. As usual, Douglass was right; a more fitting image for the freedmen's memorial to the president would have been one which depicted the slave standing triumphantly beside the equally victorious Lincoln.

CHAPTER 2

The Civil War in Kentucky

The Slave Claims His Freedom

Victor B. Howard

WHEN WILLIAM E. WOODWARD published his biography, *Meet General Grant,* in 1928, he confidently concluded that "the American negros [*sic*] are the only people in the history of the world, that ever became free without any effort of their own."[1] Although his dogmatic comment went unchallenged, it would not be accepted today, and his statement is certainly not true with reference to the blacks in Kentucky during the Civil War. From the beginning of the Civil War, the Kentucky slaves were active participants in the drama. From the moment Northern troops entered Kentucky, the objective of the slaves was to secure more self-determinism for themselves and their families.

During the spring and summer of 1861 in Kentucky, the signs of what was to come were clear. Newspaper columns carried more and more notices of runaways. Instances of insubordination increased sharply, and there were reports of work slowdowns, unruliness, and arson. In May 1861, great alarm spread across Kentucky as rumors of slave uprisings and insurrectional plots convulsed the states with fear. Slave plots were said to have exposed or uprisings undertaken in Fayette, Owen, and Gallatin Counties.[2]

The uneasiness and apprehensions concerning the effects of abolitionist ideas on the slaves led to concerted efforts to isolate the slave communities from information about the issues of the war. After the armies moved into Kentucky, many Kentucky slaveholders tried to frighten the slaves into avoiding conversation with strangers and Northern soldiers. Harry

Smith's Kentucky master told him that the Yankees would steal and sell him. "Do not pass a word with those Yankees," his master warned. The slaveholders in the region of Columbus, Kentucky, told their slaves that the Yankees had horns, and that they ate Negro "babies, and . . . lived in the North in houses built of snow and ice," and that the Yankee soldiers were fighting to take the blacks back north "where they would freeze to death." When the Northern soldiers arrived in a community, the slaves related these stories with much amusement. Despite the master's attempt to insulate the slaves from contact with the outside world, the blacks learned much about the war and spent hours discussing its effects on slavery. The slaves would eavesdrop at the door when whites were discussing the war or holding council, and sometimes the slaves induced literate yeomen to read to them about the war.[3] In Simpsonville, Kentucky, Elijah Marrs was given the task of going to town to pick up the mail for his master. As he could read, Marrs kept the other slaves in the neighborhood informed by reading newspapers mailed to his master.[4]

During his tour through Kentucky in the summer of 1861, Alan Pinkerton, an intelligence office for the United States War Department, conversed with a Bowling Green slaveholder about the knowledge slaves had acquired concerning the war. "There has been so much talk about the matter all through the State" that the blacks "know as much about it as we do . . . and too much for our safety and peace of minds," concluded the slaveholder. A Crittenden County, Kentucky, slaveholder wrote a friend that the blacks were "so free" and considered slavery "such a sin" that owners would be better off if the slaves were sold to the South.[5]

Since the whites were aware that the slaves had cause to resist continuing in bondage and that the war might furnish the occasion and resources for rebellion, the war years were an uneasy period for the Kentucky slaveholder. A delegation of citizens of Paducah protested to General E. A. Paine against arms carried by the black servants of the officers of the Ninth Illinois Regiment. The citizens were not only uneasy about the use the blacks in the Ninth Illinois Regiment might make of the weapons, but were concerned about the example they might set for the Paducah slaves. Since the servants had been armed to prevent kidnapping, they remained armed despite the protest. Whether the armed servants affected the local slaves is uncertain, but General F. Smith was called on to restore order and quiet a revolt, on a farm in McCracken County, among a dozen or more slaves, who supposed they were free because the soldiers had come.[6]

As the formation of the Kentucky military units was accelerated and the regiments from the Northwest began to move into Kentucky, it was impossible to prevent the slaves from coming in contact with the soldiers.

When the Union troops began to arrive from the Northwest in great numbers, the action of the slaves revealed that few had been so naïve as to
accept the exaggerated stories that the whites had told them. Some few
gullible slaves continued to fear the Union soldiers, but others were of the
sentiment of the slave who said to the soldier: "I thought you must be
downright heathen, but you are real good-looking people and don't seem
to do nobody no harm."[7]

In many communities, when the Northern soldiers arrived, the blacks
turned out *en masse*. The soldiers described the slaves as friendly and kind,
intelligent and "loyal to the man"[8] If the blacks lacked refined knowledge
of the issues at stake in the war, their common-sense judgment and
instincts drew them to the Union cause. As the Fifty-Eighth Indiana
Infantry moved across Kentucky in the Autumn of 1861, an old black lady
greeted them with enthusiasm and said: "God bless de soldus. I'se glad to
see 'em come." Early in November 1861, when an Ohio regiment
marched into Elizabethtown, Kentucky, it was greeted by a massive
turnout of the slaves. The attention of the soldiers was drawn toward an
old Negro woman as she paraded along the street crying, "Hurray for de
Union. Go on gemmen, I saw de Union once; it was de best Union I eber
saw." On March 5, 1862, the Twenty-Eighth Illinois Regiment left Camp
Heiman and marched along the Tennessee River. When it passed a farm
house, several blacks stood by the fence cheering the soldiers. A very
ancient woman was the center of attention. With her arms stretched
toward Heaven, she shouted over and over: "God bless Massa Lincoln!"
until her voice died out in the distance as the soldiers moved downstream.
A large number of slaves believed that God had foreordained a millennial
destruction of servitude during their lifetime. The Civil War seemed to
many slaves to be the time that was set aside for the Providential deliverance. Early in 1862 the soldiers of the Eighth Kentucky Infantry witnessed
a scene which revealed the faith the slaves had in a millennial deliverance.
As they steamed down the Cumberland River, they observed approximately fifty slaves dancing on the shore as their leader sang:

> O, praise and tanks! de Lord he come
> To set de people free an' massa tink it day of doom
> An' we of jublee.

The slaves believed that the Union army was God's instrument of
deliverance. A soldier of the Twenty-Fifth Wisconsin Infantry wrote his
family that the slaves in Kentucky could not "talk two minutes but tears
come to their eyes and they threw their arms up and down and praised de

Lord for de coming of the Lincoln soldiers." As the war wore on, the slaves became more convinced that the day of jubilee was at hand. Early in 1863 the Chaplain of the Third Minnesota Regiment who was in charge of contrabands at Fort Heiman, Kentucky, wrote the editor of the *Northwestern Christian Advocate* that the religious meetings in the camp consisted of "a general and tumultuous rejoicing at the unbound mercy of God, and the coming of the jubilee." The chaplain quoted some of their songs which were full of hope and anticipation of their deliverance by God from slavery. As the slaves sang he scribbled down parts of their hymns:

"Oh Canaan, sweet Canaan, I's boun for de lan' of Canaan"; and "Dah's a better day comin In de Army of de Lord."[9]

By the last half of 1862 the soldiers from the Northwest were often going beyond the generalization that the slaves of Kentucky were intelligent, true, and loyal to the Union. In October 1862, a soldier of the Ninth Ohio Regiment described the Kentucky slaves as being alert and "very anxious to know every step" that was taken by the Union Government in reference to slavery. "I tell you, they are not so ignorant of political matters as some suppose," he informed the editor of a Democratic journal back in northern Ohio. In November, a soldier with the Nineteenth Ohio Battery in Kentucky reported to the *Cleveland Plain Dealer* that the slaves kept informed concerning the military affairs. "They are posted on all the important battles that have taken place—particularly in their own State. They are decidedly true to the Union—every one of them," he added.[10]

When a soldier in Kentucky with Colonel James A. Garfield's regiment wrote the *Cincinnati Gazette* that the Kentucky slaves were well treated and content, a member of the Forty-First Ohio Regiment, who regularly visited Kentucky farms to buy hay, challenged the statement. "A fire of hate and hope" slumbered in the bosom of the slave and unless quenched by some means, "it would yet burst forth, and give terrible demonstration that the spirit of man, like the justice of God, will not always sleep." A chaplain with the Thirty-Eighth Ohio Regiment in Kentucky reported that the slaves were determined to secure their freedom. While the troops drilled below, the chaplain stood on a cemetery hill with an old slave, who was bent low with age and toil, and discussed the hopes of freedom for which the slaves yearned. While the old man stood in deep thought "a wild stern gleam" came from his eyes, "his lips trembled, and his breast heaved," The chaplain saw that "the spirit of freedom" had taken "possession of his soul." When the sounds of the military band faded away from below, the old man broke the silence: "I'se berry ol massa, but de little ones—dey'l see it; dey'l see it yit."[11]

The progress of events unsettled the slaves and loosened the bonds of servitude so completely that large numbers of slaves from Kentucky sought freedom north of the Ohio River. The slaves became better informed and more mobile. An informed observer of Owensboro, Kentucky, believed that the number of slaves crossing the Ohio River in a four-month period in 1861 compared favorably with the number making the journey during the last half of the century. In Henry County, Kentucky, a party of slaves belonging to both Union and Southern sympathizers fled to Indiana with a wagon supplied with provisions.[12] In January 1862, a group of about forty to sixty blacks were engaged in killing hogs at night in New Castle, Kentucky. After completing their chores, they paraded about the streets in a body for approximately two hours singing political songs and shouting for Lincoln. They seemed to take special pains to make their unusual and disorderly demonstration in front of the dwellings of one or two prominent Southern Rights citizens.[13]

The chief attraction to the Kentucky slave, however, was the Union army and the Union camps. A nucleus of a black community existed in the army from the beginning. Some Union officers from Kentucky took their personal servants with them when they entered service, and a considerable number of officers from the Northwest, particularly those from Illinois, hired free blacks as servants when they enlisted.[14]

At first the slaves who sought out Union camps came singly from adjoining farms after striking up an acquaintance with the soldiers. By the end of 1861 slaves began to come into the Union lines in large groups. A correspondent at a camp near Nolin, Kentucky, reported in November 1861, that "a batch of eight slaves arrived in camp from the Green River County." The party which included one or two who had been there before were turned over to the provost marshal, who was puzzled to know what to do with them. During the same month a group of slaves came into Camp Haycroft from southern Kentucky. They claimed their masters were in the Confederate army. In January 1862, a group of ten slaves entered the camp at Mumfordsville. They reported that they had been seized by the Confederates in Bowling Green and had made their escape. The policy of the army in Kentucky was to turn the slaves out of the camps, and although the generals sent a steady stream of orders to the regiments to keep the slaves out of the lines, the soldiers and their field officers generally refused to obey the orders. A correspondent from the camp at Paducah asserted that each company in the regiment employed five or six blacks, and the number was growing by night and day until it had reached epidemic proportions. The

slaves soon learned that they would be more freely received if they reported
that they were free blacks or that their masters were Confederates. Slaves
owned by Confederates and used for military purposes were retained by the
army. The slaves who came into the Union lines from Kentucky were often
servants of Unionists, but to the slaves it really did not matter whether their
masters were Southern or Union sympathizers as their freedom was just as
precious as that of a slave who had a rebel master.[15]

By early September 1862, the disorganizing and abrasive effects of the
war in Kentucky had all but destroyed slavery. The invasion of Kentucky by
Kirby Smith and Braxton Bragg in the Autumn of 1862 did irreparable
damage to the institution of slavery in Kentucky. The people living in the
countryside fled before the Confederate invaders. The slaves were entering
the Union army camps in an endless stream. On September 2, 1862, an
Ohio soldier reported that about six hundred slaves entered the camp at
Lebanon, Kentucky, that day.[16]

The war undermined the exclusive authority of the master over the
slave. When the master when off to war, discipline began to break down
on the plantation. Invasion of Kentucky by a Confederate cavalry or army
caused loyal Union slaveholders to flee to Union camps. Since the Union
slaveholders could not protect their slaves against the Confederate
invaders, many slaves had to look to their own safety. The slaves fled to the
protection of the army camp from all directions. The slaves quickly learned
that authority and protection resided with the army, and the control of the
slaveowner over the slave was undermined. When the Union armies
moved into areas of Kentucky which had been formerly held by Confederate forces, slaveholders who had sympathized with the Southern army fled
to the South leaving their property and slaves behind. These slaves immediately assumed the posture of free blacks.[17]

Slavery had existed as a viable institution to a large extent because the
slave did not have freedom of movement, did not receive wages for his
work, and could be subjected to corporal punishment at the will of the
master. By December 1862, the Kentucky slaves were moving about in
such numbers that it was impossible to exercise any control over them. The
mobility of slaves was almost as free as that of white laborers. It became
quite common for slaves to desert the farms and plantations because they
had been whipped by the slave owner or his agent. Many slaveholders tried
to appeal to reason as a substitute for the whip. The public jails were full of
slaves, and private slave pens were established by many whites, but the slaves
had become so mobile that it was impossible to limit their freedom of
movement. It was not uncommon for the slaves of Kentucky to insist that
they have a voice in deciding what they would plant, and frequently slaves

would ask that they be paid a wage for their labor. The Union army had paid slaves for their labor when they were impressed into labor battalions, and the slaves began to expect the payment of wages. Some of the slaveholders were obliged to pay their slaves to gather the crops in 1862. When wages were refused, the slaves often fled from the plantation. Slaveowners tried to force slaves to return by threatening to prosecute anyone who employed their slaves for wages or subsistence, but the slaves often lived on the verge of starvation rather than return to servitude. Slaveholders tried to check the growing tendency of slaves to abandon slavery by threatening to sell the slave's wife or children. A correspondent to the *Boston Journal* wrote from Cincinnati and Louisville that the slaveholders along the borderlands of the South had been obliged to hire their own slaves to gather in the crops. "The Negroes are ready to work for pay, but they refuse to work for nothing," he explained. In Louisville, he reported that a great revolution was underway, but "the change promises to be bloodless," he assured the editor. The correspondent concluded that the master's authority had been compromised. "They [the masters] have been compelled to cease flogging, for it is very easy for slaves to run away now, and not easy to catch them," he added. Peter Bruner, a slave residing in Estill County, Kentucky, fled from his owner and worked for others for wages only if they agreed to pay him by the day. In 1863 he made an agreement to work a farm for half of what he produced.[18]

When Lincoln issued his preliminary Emancipation Proclamation, September 22, 1862, it was taken as a signal by the Kentucky slaves to rush into the lines of the Union army. Mary Crane, a slave in LaRue County, Kentucky, at the time, vividly recalled the event years later. "When President Lincoln issued his proclamation, freeing the negroes [*sic*]," she recollected, "I remember that my father and most of the other younger slave men left the farms to join the Union army."[19] After the Emancipation Proclamation was issued on January 1, 1863, the steady stream of contraband slaves that had been drifting into Kentucky turned into a torrent from Tennessee, Alabama, Georgia, and Mississippi because of the abrasion resulting from the action of the military forces and the impact of the proclamation on the war. The Kentucky slave recognized no geographical limitation on the proclamation. Whether the Kentucky slaves stayed on the farm or joined the mass movement to the army camps located in the state and along the Ohio River was a personal decision made by the slave without regard for the authority of the slaveholder. By June 1863, the chaplain at Columbus, Kentucky, reported that he was in charge of about a thousand contrabands.[20] The state authorities of Kentucky tried to check the movement of slaves through the state by jailing all slaves who were found abroad without passes. County sheriffs seized the fugitives and advertised for the owner to claim the slave. The law required that slaves be sold only after confinement of eight months, but the law broke down due to the massive number of slaves who refused to adhere to the slave codes. The Kentucky legislature changed the law to limit confinement to thirty days before auction and sale. But still the law was ineffective to check the new mobility of slaves. In the larger cities the jails were filled and slaves were sent to rural counties for confinement. When slaves were sold to new owners by a sheriff's auction, many escaped again within a few hours. Many owners resorted to private pens to try to restore order, but slaves continued to roam at will.[21]

In April 1863, Kentucky's futile effort to prevent freedom of movement of the slaves was checked by a ruling of Judge Advocate General Joseph Holt that slaves from Confederate states coming into Kentucky could not be confined because they were under the Articles of War, the Second Confiscation Act of July 1862, and the Emancipation Proclamation.[22] Failing to control the movement of slaves into the state and across Kentucky's borders, the authorities could not check intrastate movement of Kentucky's slaves. The Kentucky slaves refused to recognize any distinction. By November 1863, the *Nashville Union* was informed by a Kentucky slaveholder that "a very large proportion of slave owners" in Kentucky admitted that "slavery was hopelessly destroyed" in the state. The correspondent reported that in one southern county, in the state, a hundred and fifty slaves had deserted the institution, and that trouble was increasing.[23]

Early in 1863 the War Department began to enlist slaves for military service, but when protests were carried to Washington from Kentucky, Lincoln agreed that no Kentucky slave would be enlisted in Kentucky if the state could fill her quota from whites. The Kentucky slaves effectively undermined the new policy by fleeing across Kentucky's borders to enlist in Ohio, Indiana, Illinois, and Tennessee. Since these men were lost to Kentucky's quota, the Union men in Kentucky agitated in Washington and secured a change of policy in 1864 so that Kentucky slaves were enlisted in Kentucky, and credited to the state's quota.[24]

The enlisted slaves became free men, a circumstance which in itself weakened the institution of servitude in Kentucky. Although the black recruit's family remained in servitude, the enlistment of the blacks in Kentucky set into motion a reaction which quickened the deterioration of slavery in the state. In many cases, when black Kentucky recruits entered training camps, they were accompanied or followed to the camp by the soldiers' families. In numerous cases, black families made their way to army camps after they were forced off the farm, mistreated, or threatened by the slaveholder who acted in resentment because the able-bodied males had joined the army. Occasionally, in blind anger and rage, the farmer would pull the cabin down so that the women and children would have no lodging. The refugee camps that sprang up around the army camps in Kentucky were centers of unbelievable hardship and suffering, and the black soldiers complained long and loud about the treatment of their families. Reports came to headquarters in Kentucky that large numbers of blacks had offered to enlist provided their families were freed or provided they had assurance that the army would protect their families. In November 1864, the Colonel of the Seventy-Second U.S. Colored Infantry at Covington, Kentucky, reported that a large number of slaves "offered to enlist" provided that "they had assurances" that the Government would free their families or the army would protect their families from the cruelty of their masters. The provost marshal of the first district (Paducah) in Kentucky reported to his superiors that the great obstacle in recruiting blacks was the security of the slave families. "*Attend to their wifes [sic] and families* and they will immediately rush to arms," the Colonel predicted. Individual recruiting officers permitted black recruits to bring their families along to the camp when they enlisted and promised that the army would care for them.[25]

The controversy concerning the status of black soldiers' families came to a head at Camp Nelson, Kentucky, late in November 1864, when orders were carried out to expel some four hundred women and children from the camp. The refugee camp was leveled and the half-starved, half-naked refugees were forced to wander along the highways and through the woods in a destitute condition on the coldest night of the season.[26]

The black soldiers were in a rage and it was all John Fee, and the other missionary friends of the blacks, could do to restrain them from resistance. Four months later Fee recalled that the black soldiers in Camp Nelson "were very indignant" at the treatment of their families. "I did on more than one instance use my influence . . . to induce them not to show resistance," he added.[27] The occasion was used by the missionaries to secure a change of policy which required that the dependents of the black soldiers be provided for by the War Department in refugee camps.[28] Benjamin Wade had visited Camp Nelson to investigate conditions there before the episode of November 1864, and letters had been sent to Henry Wilson, chairman of the Senate Military Affairs Committee, and to others in Washington to convince them that morale of the black soldiers in Kentucky was being destroyed by the mistreatment of their families. It was pointed out that there was a need to place black dependents in circumstances where the army could legally protect them, and the friends of the blacks in Kentucky urged the black soldiers' dependents be freed by law. Several highly placed army officers indicated that slave recruiting in Kentucky would dry up if the black recruits' families were not freed. The Camp Nelson tragedy led directly to the law granting freedom to the dependents of black soldiers.[29]

Informed military authorities in Kentucky estimated that two-thirds of the remaining slaves in Kentucky were granted freedom by the act freeing families of black soldiers. Brevet General James Brisbin, who served in Kentucky, estimated that on an average five dependents were freed each time a black soldier enlisted in Kentucky. Since the enlistment of blacks in Kentucky continued after the war had ended, until June 1, 1865, the provisions for freeing black soldiers' families enabled the Kentucky slaves to gain their freedom as well as the freedom of their families for more than six weeks after the war had come to an end. Although administrative officers and circuit judges in Kentucky declared the law freeing the families of black soldiers inoperative and unconstitutional in Kentucky, John Palmer, the Commander of the Department of Kentucky, enforced the law with vengeance.[30]

The army became actively involved in the destruction of slavery in Kentucky by the end of 1864, but the policies initiated by both General S. G. Burbridge and his successor, General John Palmer, would have come to nothing if large numbers of slaves in Kentucky had not taken the initiative by passively refusing to act the part of slaves any longer. The refusal of many slaves to work without receiving compensation for their labor was the most significant area in which the slave refused to play his traditional role. Two years of contact with the army had taught the slaves much about the wage system. When the army impressed Kentucky slaves into labor battalions for work on the railroads, the slaves of secessionists received the payment for the work they performed, and even when the slaves' wages were paid directly to loyal owners, the slaves were paid incentive wages. General William Rosecrans, Commander of the Department of the Cumberland, which covered parts of Kentucky and Tennessee, concluded in April 1863 that slavery was dead. "There is not a negro [sic] in the South who does not know he is free," he added. He wrote his father that the blacks "squatted on the plantations, and refused to work for any one but themselves. They have sown little crops of their own, and their masters have ceased to exercise any control over them."[31] Brigadier General Payne initiated a program on the Kentucky-Tennessee border to sponsor a project by which slaves would be hired to work for their former owners for wages. On June 1, 1863, Payne reported that this plan was "working admirably."[32]

The departure of slaves from Kentucky to the Northeast as wage earners, the movement of blacks to the towns and cities, and the enlistment of the Kentucky slaves in military service all combined to create an acute labor shortage in Kentucky by 1865. A farmer in Jefferson County lost sixty-three slaves during the course of the season of 1865, and his wife and daughters were forced to take up the task of farm laborers and domestics.[33] Many Kentucky farmers decided to come to terms with their slaves by using the assistance of the army. A group came to Palmer and asked for relief and he agreed to cooperate with them in securing the return of blacks to agricultural pursuits provided the farmers would declare in writing that their slaves would be regarded as hired laborers who would receive wages for their labor. The military authorities in Kentucky recognized the blacks, who returned to the soil, as liberated slaves, and agreed to furnish protection to them and to enforce wage payments. Although the army encouraged the Kentucky blacks who had abandoned slavery to enter into labor agreements with humane masters, few slaves who had broken with their former masters were willing to return to them. Returning to the supervision of the old masters seemed too much like a voluntary return to the life of a slave. The farmers had more success in retaining slaves who had not yet made a decision to leave their masters. A great number of slaveholders in Kentucky decided to recognize that slavery no longer existed. They made wage contracts with their slaves and the departure of the laborers from their farms was checked. By September 1865, three months before slavery was abolished in Kentucky by the Thirteenth Amendment, many farmers reported that the wage system was beneficial to both the white farmers and the black laborers.[34]

As the end of the war drew near, the blacks abandoned slavery in Kentucky in increased numbers. The rural areas were being depleted of laborers by the mass movement of blacks to the Kentucky cities and towns. It was impossible to determine which blacks had become legally free by the military service of a father or son. The fugitives created a crisis in the cities which local authorities hopelessly tried to resolve by filling the jails and the private pens with blacks. Finally the local authorities in desperation turned to General Palmer and urged him to remove the transient blacks from the cities to prevent an outbreak of an epidemic. Palmer insisted that the solution of the problem required that the state and local governments accept the existing reality and recognize the blacks as free men. Since potential employers feared prosecution if they employed the self-made freedmen, Palmer undertook to resolve the dilemma the Kentucky slaves had forced on the community. He published an order authorizing post commanders to issue passes to all blacks that applied for them, regardless of status, to travel abroad to find employment. The blacks chose to consider these passes as freedom papers and thus made the pass system an effective instrument to complete the destruction of slavery in Kentucky. The practical effect of the pass system was to remove the last shackles of servitude by establishing complete freedom of movement six months before the Thirteenth Amendment was ratified.[35] If the states had failed to ratify the Thirteenth Amendment, the Kentucky slaves would have still maintained their self-determinism. When the Kentucky legislature failed to ratify the amendment for the second time in May 1865, many Kentucky slaves rushed into the ranks of the army to secure their freedom and others left Kentucky for the Northwest. Since the Fugitive Slave Law had been abolished by the act of June 28, 1864, there was no federal authority to return fugitives to Kentucky. If necessary many Kentucky slaves were willing to act out the words of the folk-song sung by slaves during the Civil War:

> Before I be a slave
> I'll be buried in my grave,
> And go home to my Lord
> And be free.

Lincoln's insights were correct when he informed one of his generals that "those who shall have tasted actual freedom can never be slaves again."[36]

Slavery ceased to be a viable institution in Kentucky long before the Thirteenth Amendment was adopted. The disintegration of slavery started shortly after massive troop movements began to take place in Kentucky, and by the end of 1863 slavery in the state had suffered afflictions that left no hope for its reestablishment as it had existed in antebellum Kentucky.

The initiative taken by the masses of blacks lay at the heart of slavery's decline in Kentucky. Blacks recognized the war as an opportunity to lessen their burdens, and they began to take advantage of the situation almost from the start of the conflict. In spite of the military orders that slavery should be left alone, aided and abetted by the Northern soldiers, the slaves undermined the institution of slavery and nullified Kentucky's laws that sustained it. Large numbers of slaves abandoned the institution and rushed into the Union lines to support the Union cause, with or without the consent of the army. The bondsmen simply refused to continue to act the part of slaves and they proved to be accomplished actors who performed a critical role in the Civil War.

In spite of Lincoln's determination to support the antebellum order in Kentucky, the slaves, in Kentucky as elsewhere in the Upper South, disregarded Lincoln's slave policy. The action of the Kentucky slaves reduced Lincoln's slave policy and the Kentucky slave code to a shambles so that little effective control remained and thereby put great pressure on Lincoln to abandon his border state policy and issue his Emancipation Proclamation.

When the war ended, Kentucky still remained "a white's man's government" that was incapable of embracing either racial equality or a commitment to balance individual liberties with social justice,[37] The adoption of the Thirteenth Amendment did not fulfill the hopes for equality that was the ultimate goal of the blacks of Kentucky. Decades of determined and persistent efforts were required to move toward a fulfillment of these dreams.[38]

CHAPTER 3

"Uncle Billy" Sherman Comes to Town

The Free Winter of Black Savannah

William A. Byrne

CHRISTMAS OF 1864 FELL on a Sunday. Fanny Cohen, a young white Savannahian, wrote in her diary that it was "the saddest Christmas that I have ever spent," relieved only by the thought of "spending my next Christmas in the Confederacy." For the now-free blacks of Savannah, Georgia, however, it was as fine a Sunday, as fine a Christmas, as any could remember. On the previous Wednesday, the army of General William Tecumseh Sherman had taken the town, after its Confederate defenders had secretly evacuated it the night before. The city's whites were sometimes sullen and angry at the presence of Union soldiers. The city's blacks were not. As the Reverend James Simms recalled, "The cry went around the city from house to house among our race of people, 'Glory be to God, we are free!'"[1]

There was a kind of euphoria in black Savannah in these days, a euphoria which Union troops noticed as much as anyone. General Oliver O. Howard, who would go on to head the Freedmen's Bureau, was in the city with Sherman. He wrote in his autobiography that December 21, 1864, was "a day of manifest joy, for wasn't it a visible answer to their long-continued and importunate prayers?" "Certainly so it all appeared," he continued, "to these simple souls who met our columns of troops at every point in crowds, and with arms akimbo danced and sang their noisy welcome." Two days after the northern troops entered the city, Sherman himself mentioned that "the white people here are the worst whipped and

29

subjugated you ever saw, and the negroes are having their 'jubilee' and calling crowds to see 'Mr. Sherman.'"[2]

The enthusiastic black response to Union troops was nothing new. For about two weeks Sherman's army had been on the outskirts of town, waiting and preparing. "The darkies all seemed pleased enough," reported E. P. Burton, a surgeon with the northern troops. Dr. Burton understated the case considerably. The rural blacks of Chatham County reacted the same way that slaves elsewhere in Georgia did when Sherman came through.[3] Nothing changed when the Union army actually marched into town. When John Gould entered Savannah, swarms of black children followed his troops through the city. Another Union soldier spoke to a freed black woman who summed up her emotions by exclaiming, "It is a dream, sir—a dream!" White Savannah residents reported similar reactions to the Union presence. It was certainly apparent to them by now where black loyalties stood. One white woman saw a young black girl outside her window jumping up and down and singing as loudly as she could: "All de rebel gone to hell, Now Par Sherman come." Another woman, after vowing to a Union general that she would not walk under the United States flag outside her door, told him she would send her servants out instead. "They will not mind," she remarked correctly.[4]

This lady was extraordinarily fortunate to still have servants. Many wealthy whites now had to learn to do without the attentions they had received from blacks in the past. Richard Arnold, physician, politician, and mayor of the city when it was surrendered to Sherman, informed a northern friend in March 1865, "Almost every house servant in the city has left his or her place." Mrs. Elizabeth Mackay Stiles wrote her son, "Old Andrew stays with the Mackays & helps them nicely—so does Lizzy Rose & Peggy—all the rest took french leave." Even the most faithful slaves often deserted. Mom Jinny had been nurse and cook in the Hardee household for years. Charles Hardee had grown up listening to her stories and songs. But when Sherman came, she left.[5]

Caroline A. N. Lamar, wife of Charles A. L. Lamar of *Wanderer* fame, provides an excellent example of the problems which could befall an aristocratic white family. Already by 7:00 A.M. on the morning Sherman's troops arrived, the first slave left. "As I feared and expected," Mrs. Lamar wrote, "William proved to be a traitor." Even worse, "the wretch, William," as Mrs. Lamar referred to him, went to the Union troops themselves, informed them who his owner was, and told them there were quantities of liquor stored in his house. The Yankees promptly removed "every box of brandy, wine, ale and champagne." A week later Mrs. Lamar reported that "Harriett, Lucy Lampkin, and Nella have gone off, the former without saying a word, or having one said to her, leaving some clothes on the line, some in the tubs, and the rest in the washroom." This was not the end of it. "They said she was not willing to cook any more, so she was going. Nella said she would stay as she loved me and the children but yesterday she decamped. . . . Isetta says she *is* going, but will stay and cook for me for a time and not leave me in distress." One ex-slave was willing to remain, up to a point. "Nannie says if I go into the Confederacy she will not be willing to go with me, that she has been separated from her husband on account of my children, and will not be willing to leave him any more for them. I replied her husband could go with us, but she said, 'No.'" Mrs. Lamar's opinion for her ex-slaves was succinct: "Poor deluded creatures."[6]

Some whites solved the servant problem by becoming more self-reliant. Fanny Cohen recorded in her diary on December 30, "This morning Dr. Ballinger came to see my maid who has been sick for several days. After he left I went to my room and darned my stockings for this week for the first time I had ever done such a thing in my life. But I suppose when she leaves I shall always have it to do so I had better begin at once." Others who had long been pampered were aghast at the thought of finally having to fend for themselves. One aristocratic woman complained to George W. Nichols, a Union soldier, "It is terrible, sir! All my slaves have left me." She was poor now, in the unfortunate position of having to contemplate working for herself. This was something wholly foreign to her experience, and she was uncomfortable at the thought. "I really fear, sir," she told Nichols, "that I shall have to submit to the disgrace of giving lessons in music." Nichols, admitting he was rude, replied, "Madam, I hope so."[7]

This lady was merely pitiful. Other whites who watched their slaves of a lifetime leave without so much as a good-bye were angry and hurt. Some reacted with rage to the changes being made in the social order. "There is one thing I will never submit to," one Savannah woman said, "that the negro is our equal." Another defiant woman wrote in mid-1865, "I cannot reconcile myself to this wretched state of servitude." A third was horrified that "we southern ladies are made slaves, and our slaves made freedmen!" Some tried to maintain that the end of slavery did not really bother them. George Mercer wrote that he could accept the situation. "As I owned but one delicate negro girl, a burden and not a benefit, I do not suffer in this respect." But others who voiced the same kind of sentiments revealed more than they thought. Mrs. George J. Kollock, whose family had been reasonably decent, humane slave owners throughout the century, was clearly bitter at her slaves' leaving. She wrote her son in June 1865, "If they freed them against our will, it is all that they can do. I for one wash my hands of the race, and am obliged to the U.S. for taking off my hands the old & worthless negroes and children. To try to force me to take all mine back would be the hardest battle your Government had ever yet fought. I am relieved of all responsibility, & the care of their souls, which is now resting on the shoulder of your President." It was an odd form of bitterness which mentioned the care of souls.[8]

Richard Arnold perhaps came closest to expressing what was, to white ex-slaveholders, the poignancy of the situation. Of his seven servants, all but one left him. He claimed in March 1865 that he was not bothered thereby, that "if all had remained I would not have kept them, as each does too little and costs too much." Even so, he took the trouble to write that the one ex-slave who did stay was "born in the family, raised by my wife, nursed or rather grew up with my daughter and has nursed my grandchildren and I believe she does feel an attachment to the family." Two months later he revealed a bit more fully how he had been affected by the social changes. He wrote a northern professor at Harvard Medical School, "Our domestic institution which made us dependent on organized Slave labour renders our situation unique. That suddenly cut away, and no props or stays supplied, our whole social Fabric has fallen in an entirety from one end of the South to the other." And then he added, "Out of the fullness of the heart the mouth speaketh, and I have perhaps said too much."[9]

Whites tended to forget that once slavery had ended, it was much easier for them to be faithful to their ex-slaves than it was for blacks to be faithful to their ex-owners. Whites saw no reason not to continue a relationship based on their own brand of paternal affection. After all, whites had never been owned, and they could not fully understand why that made such a difference. And so they reacted with pain and bitterness. Their black families were leaving them not with tears in their faces but with great, broad, happy smiles on their faces. It was really, as Arnold said, a unique situation.

Blacks felt very differently. Some were amused at the way things had changed. As one put it, "Buckra wouldn't let nigger go een de park. Now nigger go and Buckra can't. Couldn't git a glass o'water for he'self, now hab to go to de pump."[10] Mostly the freed slaves accepted their freedom with a quiet dignity. They realized the solemnity of the occasion. "I'd always thought about this, and wanted this day to come, and prayed for it and knew God meant it should be here sometime," one woman said, "but I didn't believe I should ever see it." Now, though, "I bless the Lord for it." This was not a time to rampage but a time to give thanks for answered prayers. After the Confederate troops evacuated Savannah in December, poor whites and blacks engaged in some pillaging, but this was quickly halted when Sherman's men entered the city. Thereafter the freedmen remained orderly.[11]

Some blacks were bitter. One woman told a Union soldier, "All my life I have worked for them. I have given them houses and lands; they have rode in their fine carriages, sat in their nice parlors, taken voyages over the waters, and had money enough, which I and my people earned for them. I have had my back cut up. I have been sent to jail because I cried for my children, which were stolen from me." What was freedom, with her children gone? But most blacks did not seem to view their ex owners vengefully—at least they did not do so in public. As one freedman remarked, "Some of these masters have treated us shamefully, whipped, and imprisoned, and sold us about; but we don't wish to be revenged on them. The Bible says that we must forgive them."[12] Another servant told a Union soldier, "I don't feel it in my heart, sir, to go away and leave my old master, now that he is poor, and calamity has come upon him. . . . It is," he continued, "kind of ungrateful like."[13]

A large number of ex-slaves, however, used these early days of freedom to do something they had never been able to do before. They would go back to work soon enough, but now they took a vacation from a lifetime of slavery. Both southern and northern whites complained. In February 1865, Union general J. G. Foster, commander of the Department of the South, grumbled, "The streets of Savannah are full of them, lying in the sun and waiting for bread without labor." Mrs. Sarah Gordon informed her daughter-in-law, Nellie Kinzie Gordon, "I shall be thankful to get somewhere, where *Servants are Servants*. It is dreadful to see the poor negroes now, just loafing around doing nothing, when before they were active happy and always at work. They seem to think that their liberty consists in lounging around, with hands in their Pockets, looking up at the trees." Another woman was more sarcastic. "The negroes," she wrote, "with all their suffering they consider themselves in the 7th Heaven, freedom & lazyness is such a boon."[14]

In time, many of these freedmen came back to work as servants. John Middleton wrote in June 1865 that his ex-slaves were ready to return to his employ. As he put it, "They don't appreciate their freedom, on half rations." Another family had a full complement of servants by August: "We have old Hannah, the cook, Isaiah, formerly owned by Capn. Winn of Liberty, to cut wood, sweep the yard, pavement & go to market every morning with me—and one chambermaid of ours & one of Lou's, & then a little girl, white, to wait on the table." But this was now service with a difference. As William Gordon said at the end of May, "Even with money, there are many difficulties, as regards servants: whites can't be got; blacks alone can be *hired* and they are (I am told) worthless and impudent." A month later, he wrote his mother, in Macon at the time, "I really don't see . . . how you are to live if you come down here. Your servants will all expect wages when you return and will not work for your unless you pay them." The days of unremunerated labor were gone.[15]

By mid-1865, many other changes had taken place. Black Savannah had become far more independent. The black churches, always relatively autonomous, now became entirely so. In the spring of 1865, the Methodist Andrew Chapel, which had been under the control of the white Trinity Methodist Church, withdrew and attached itself to the African Methodist Church. The process of disassociation had begun less than forty-eight hours after Sherman's arrival back in December.[16] By July, Savannah's four black Baptist churches had done the same. Previously they had been a part of the Sunbury Baptist Association, composed of both white and black churches. Now they withdrew and formed the Zion Baptist Association, along with several other black churches from the Sea Islands.[17]

Other important changes were occurring simultaneously. A few days after Sherman arrived, a meeting was held at the First African Baptist Church. The church was filled to overflowing. It was an emotional evening, complete with speeches, sermons, and songs. By the end of the meeting, the Savannah Educational Association had been formed and money had been raised to start a school for black children. A few days later, some five hundred black boys and girls gathered at the church and marched through the streets of Savannah to the building which was to be their new schoolhouse. The Reverend W. J. Richardson, of the American Missionary Association, described the scene: "Such a gathering of Freedmen's Sons, and daughters, that proud city had never seen before. Many of the people rushed to the doors and windows of their houses wondering what these things could mean! *This* they were told, is the onward *march of Freedom*." One of the two AMA schoolhouses in the city, it had been built some fifteen years before by John S. Montmollin, a Savannah slave trader. Ironically it had been a slave mart throughout its existence, most lately under the ownership of Alexander Bryan. Now, with bars still on the windows and slave bills of sale still in evidence, it was turned into a school.[18]

Predictably, some whites were grossly offended by this turn of events. One old gentleman, described by Whitelaw Reid as being "of rubicund visage and silvery hair," felt that education for blacks was positively indecent. "Sir," he told Reid, "we accept the death of slavery; but, sir, surely there are some things that are not tolerable." Such opinions counted for little in black Savannah, and the schools continued their work. There would be many problems ahead, but by summer 1865 black education in Savannah was doing well. The 1,200 children in school represented about 75 percent of the black children in the city. For the first time, truly substantial numbers of blacks were being taught to read and write.[19]

Political desires were expanding as well. Sometime during the first half of 1865, the Colored Union League was formed. At its June meeting, the league resolved that "we will cherish no enmity towards those who held us in bondage, and sought to destroy the Union, but will welcome them to their homes, to the Union, and to the peaceful pursuits of life." More significantly, the league further resolved "that we do expect, and ask, not as a reward, but as a right, that the government will allow us not only to pay taxes for its support, but to vote for its maintenance, and to help elect our representatives who make the laws of the State and nation that we are to obey." Slaves six months before, Savannah's blacks were now demanding the franchise. A few months later, they would be further demanding the impeachment of Andrew Johnson for committing a multitude of sins, crimes, and indiscretions. The elixir of freedom was doing its work.[20]

Blacks were also able to progress economically. S. W. Magill, of the American Missionary Association, wrote in February that the blacks were "picking up a great deal of money" working about the city. "It is most interesting & encouraging to see how soon [the] negro gets upon his feet & begins to earn a living." Magill perhaps did not realize that many of Savannah's blacks had been earning their own livings for years. Many continued to do so in the same way they had before the war. Whitelaw Reid pointed out that "there is a general air of intelligence and independence among them, here, which comes only from education and knowledge of the ways of the world." And he continued, "No one, who saw or conversed with leading Savannah negroes, would doubt their entire capacity to support themselves."[21]

In other ways, however, life for the freedmen changed less than might be expected. White northerners may have freed black Savannah, but they tried to retain control over the freedmen in a number of areas. They may not have been generally vicious or even blatantly racist, but they were certainly racist in more subtle ways and were by turns patronizing or callous or imperious.

Some of the changes in black labor demonstrate the point. The major employer of freedmen in the winter of 1864–1865 was the Union army. Its opinion of its laborers was ambivalent. As soon as the army reached Savannah, it began to employ local people. The army needed teamsters, carpenters, blacksmiths, and laborers, regardless of their race. But sometimes army orders sounded almost like those of an overseer on an antebellum plantation. Consider the following, issued January 4: "All unemployed negroes in this city will report immediately to the office of the Post Quartermaster, for the purpose of obtaining wood for the city." As early as December 24, 1864, an order was issued which stated, "Recruiting agents are forbid recruiting negroes for military services as all are wanted for labor." Army officials seemed to assume that blacks and menial labor were made for each other and were perfectly willing to coerce those who did not volunteer.[22]

At the same time that the army as an institution sometimes seemed biased against blacks, many individual Union troops exhibited their own kind of bias even more offensively. Blacks viewed the northern soldiers as heroes, but the compliment was often not returned. Mrs. Jane Wallace Howard wrote in her diary on December 27, "The Yankees and negroes appear to be on the most intimate terms, a perfect equality prevails." The equality, if it ever existed at all, was short-lived. In March, a woman told a Union officer that if the town were not cleaned many would die during the summer. "We'll be away long before then," the officer replied. "Only niggers and rebel women will be left, and it doesn't matter what becomes of them." When blacks were convicted of crime, the Union military authorities often put them to work in the streets wearing a ball and chain. Whites were not treated in such a fashion, a fact which blacks resented. By June one woman noted, concerning the freedmen, "Many officers already own the U.S. government had made a great mistake in freeing them."[23]

Another woman, filled with dislike of Yankee troops, reported in her diary that they had been less than just to the newly freed slaves. She said disapprovingly that the soldiers had been "stealing from them, searching their houses, cursing & abusing & insulting their wives & daughters." She may have been biased, but she was not mistaken. This kind of activity was common, especially in December and early January, when conditions were still relatively unsettled. Edward S. Allen, a Union soldier in Savannah with Sherman, informed his parents that troops in need of lumber had dismantled a house lived in by blacks. "Why I tell you," he continued, "a small house empty, stands no more show than does a fat cow, if she came near the Regt. while in camp." A Union chaplain reported that one group of freedmen, living almost entirely on rice, had much of their food stolen by soldiers. Union troops foraging outside the city took food from blacks quite as easily as they took it from whites. As an example, in December Union troops descended upon Mary Jess's house a few miles from the city. By the time they left they had relieved the woman of 2 cows, 10 hogs, 20 turkeys, 60 chickens, 300 pounds of honey, 15 gallons of syrup, 50 pounds of lard, 100 pounds of coffee, 2 sacks of flour, 75 pounds of sugar, 50 pounds of tobacco, 5 gallons of Port wine, and all her furniture, utensils, and clothing.[24]

Foragers of another kind tried to force blacks to serve in the army as substitutes for northern whites. Immediately after Sherman reached Savannah, the city was, in his words, "beset by ravenous State agents." They came from Hilton Head, South Carolina, eager to steal as much black manpower as they could. As one of Sherman's soldiers observed, "It is shameful that the negro, even in a state of freedom, cannot escape the cupidity and persecution of the white man." On one occasion Sherman's aide-de-camp found over a hundred freedmen locked up in a pen, put there by recruiting agents who were waiting for the cover of darkness to spirit them to Hilton Head. After complaints from local blacks, Sherman prohibited the use of violence or coercion in enlisting troops. He explained himself in a mid-January letter: "I have said that slavery is dead and the Negro free, and want him treated as free, and not hunted and badgered to make a soldier of, when his family is left back on the plantations. I am right and won't change."[25]

Although Sherman allowed the enlistment of freedmen, he did not want black troops in his own army. Neither did he want to impose black troops on Savannah's whites. He wrote General Ulysses S. Grant on New Year's Eve, "The people are dreadfully alarmed lest we garrison the place with negroes. Now, no matter what the negro soldiers are, you know that people have prejudices which must be regarded. Prejudice, like religion, cannot be discussed."[26]

He still thought his conduct toward blacks exemplary. "As regards kindness to the race, encouraging them to patience and forbearance, procuring them food and clothing, and providing them with land whereon to labor," he wrote in his memoirs, "I assert that no army ever did more for that race than the one I commanded in Savannah." Black Savannahians would have agreed with Sherman's assessment. They knew only that he had freed them, and consequently they came to see him by the hundreds. One of Sherman's men wrote that "there were a constant stream of them, old and young, men, women, and children, uncouth and well-bred, bashful and talkative—but always respectful and well-behaved." Sherman, in a half-contemptuous, half-patronizing way, thought them almost comical. "It would amuse you to see the negroes," he wrote home on Christmas day. "They flock to me, old and young, they pray and shout and mix up my name with that of Moses, and Simon and other scriptural ones as well as 'Abram Linkon,' the Great Messiah of 'Dis Jubilee.'"[27]

Black Savannahians visited other Union officials as well, and were treated far more cynically by them than they were by Sherman. Chief Justice Salmon P. Chase came to the city in the spring. In his one meeting with local blacks, he spent the whole session asking them political questions, seemingly trying to convince himself that the freedmen really were able to tell who their friends were. "Suppose you *were* permitted to vote," the Chief Justice asked, "what guarantee would the Government have that you would know how to vote, or that your influence would not be cast on the side of bad morals and bad politics." The rest of the meeting was conducted as self-interestedly, with Chase's concern for the blacks rising in direct proportion to their willingness to vote the Republican ticker.[28]

Rather similar was a meeting held in January between Lincoln's secretary of war, Edwin M. Stanton, and a delegation of twenty local black leaders. In truth, it was not a meeting at all—it was a catechism class. Stanton arrived with written questions, which were asked in a completely formal manner. "State what your understanding is in regard to the acts of Congress and President Lincoln's proclamation touching the condition of the colored people in the rebel States" was the first of twelve long interrogations. They were led by Garrison Frazier, who provided the answers to Stanton's questions. Frazier, who had been the pastor of the Third African Baptist Church through most of the 1850s, was sixty-seven years old and had been a slave until shortly before the war, when he bought himself and his wife for $1,000. He was typical of the group, many of whom had been manumitted long before Sherman arrived. They tolerated Stanton's attitude, and Stanton condescendingly tolerated them. Reportedly, he was surprised at their intelligence and good sense, and now had, according to one informant, "new hopes for the future of the colored race."[29]

One group of Unionists in Savannah got along well with the city's black population. Regardless of how Sherman felt about the matter, Savannah was in time garrisoned by black Union troops. At one time or another during the spring of 1865, four black regiments were in the city. In March, the 1st South Carolina Volunteers—renamed the 33d United States Colored Troops the year before—arrived in the city, as did the equally famous 54th Massachusetts. By the middle of the month Savannah was the temporary home of 2,300 black soldiers.[30]

Even though these were perhaps the best black regiments which the Union army had to offer, the reaction of native white Savannahians was decidedly mixed. One man wrote sarcastically in June 1865 from the city, "Some of the troops stationed here are negroes, which adds to my comfort." Perhaps inevitably, there was occasional friction. The blacks were sometimes jostled and sneered at as they walked down the streets. Relations between black and white Union troops were no better. William Washington Gordon commented that "the feeling between them is not good." The *Savannah Republican* agreed, for it wrote disapprovingly of "the animosity that is cherished by some of our best soldiers and many citizens, against the colored soldiers." The newspapers warned that "all parties are bound to respect their uniform . . . no matter what their complexion may be."[31]

By and large, the black troops were better behaved than the whites who disliked them.[32] The *Republican* continued its lecture on race relations by remarking, "The colored troops, since their arrival in the city, have behaved in a soldierly manner, never seemingly forgetting that they are placed here to preserve, rather than disturb the order and quietude of our city." They were described as exhibiting a "high state of perfection" at military reviews. Even ex-Confederates were sometimes impressed. Jane Wallace Howard, who roundly despised many more Unionists than she liked, nonetheless wrote admiringly of one black soldier. He was on guard duty when passed by Commodore Josiah Tattnall, late of the Confederate navy. Mrs. Howard was afraid that the guard would insult the old gentleman. But instead the guard saluted respectfully and stood at attention. Mrs. Howard remarked that he was "more decent than his white comrades," quite a spectacular compliment for her."[33]

It would be a mistake to paint the Union army in wholly negative terms. Many individual soldiers were sympathetic to the problems faced by the freedmen. With all of their faults, northerners had still abolished slavery and given black Savannah some small measure of hope. On a more pragmatic level, the army and other northerners did take some important steps to help those who were impoverished by the war. Conditions were particularly severe for blacks in early 1865 because of the large number of black refugees who crowded into the city. A week before Sherman took Savannah, one Union soldier on the outskirts wrote, "Our horses and mules are living on rice straw, and the Lord only knows how the ten or twelve thousand fugitive negroes within our lines are living." The correspondent of the *New York Times* was, if anything, understating the case when he wrote that those who followed Sherman to the coast arrived "weary, famished, sick, and almost naked." Sherman had tried to discourage the slaves from following him through Georgia, feeling they would impede his progress. But they came anyway, by the thousands. "The black followers seemed to me more numerous than the army," one Union civilian wrote from Savannah. The town was full of refugees and continued so.[34]

As a result of the extremely crowded conditions, hunger, disease, and death were common. Rations of only unhulled rice were far from unknown. One observer wrote that "hundreds" of blacks had "already died in and about Savannah of actual starvation." He exaggerated, but there was still much suffering in the city[35] A campaign was initiated in New York and Boston to send food for the relief of the hungry and destitute.

By the end of January, a large quantity of provisions had arrived and was being distributed to the city's poor.[36]

The relief line was supposed to be for all who were hungry, regardless of color. Many blacks were helped, but several people charged that the Union army discriminated against the freedmen. One black woman, speaking of the provisions sent by the North, said to Charles Coffin, "I 'spect you intended that black and white folks would have them alike." Upon being told that was indeed the intention, she bitterly remarked, "Not a mouthful have I had." General Rufus Saxton noticed the same turn of events. He reported in his diary in early January, after having visited Savannah from Beaufort, South Carolina, "Charities from the North are given to rank secesh women in silks, while poor whites & destitute negroes are turned away, and told to go to work."[37]

It was soon obvious that a more permanent solution to the problems of freed black refugees was needed. Savannah could not support them all. As a consequence, many were shipped to the South Carolina Sea Islands. This course of action had been decided upon even before Sherman arrived in the city. On December 19, a large group of refugees was sent to Hilton Head. "It was a strange spectacle," wrote one observer, "to see those negroes of all ages, sizes, and both sexes, with their bundles on their heads and in their hands trudging along, they know not whither." The Hilton Head area was already packed with refugees. General Saxton wrote Sherman on December 22, "Every cabin and house on these islands is filled to overflowing—I have some 15,000." But more would be forthcoming. On Christmas night, 700 arrived, described by the *New York Times* correspondent as being "in a state of misery which would have moved to pity a heart of stone."[38]

Making an already overcrowded situation worse was clearly no answer to the refugee problem. A much more enlightened and effective solution was to give the freedmen land. One of the points which Savannah's black leaders made in their conference with Stanton in January was that "the way we can best take care of ourselves is to have land and turn it and till it by our labor . . . and we can soon maintain ourselves and have something to spare." Significantly, all but one agreed that it would be better for the freedmen to live by themselves, away from whites, "for there is a prejudice against us in the South that will take years to get over." As it turned out, both points were well taken.[39]

James T. Ayers, a perceptive but delightfully subliterate Union soldier, wrote in his diary in early February, "I Really think this whole South, or that part called South Carlina with A large Portion of Georgia and Florida will be gave to the niggers for A possession. I Say give it to them." Good that Ayers felt so, for on January 16, Sherman had issued Special

Order Number 15. It began: "The islands from Charleston south, the abandoned ricefields along the rivers for thirty miles back from the sea, and the country bordering the Saint John's River, Fla., are reserved and set apart for the settlement of the negroes now made free by the acts of war and the proclamation of the President of the United States." Each family could have forty acres of tillable ground. Blacks were to have complete control over their own affairs. Whites, except for the military, would not be permitted to reside among them.[40]

It was a bold move, not only permitting but encouraging blacks to work out their own destiny. It is ironic that Sherman, who was never particularly radical in his thinking, should have been the one to issue the order. It is unclear whether the general's motives were to protect the freedmen or only to get unwanted blacks out of his way. The *New York Tribune* thought the latter. "Gen. Sherman assumes that the negro is a race apart and different from the white, and, if intrusted with freedom, must be isolated and left entirely to itself." This, the newspaper maintained, was "a vicious principle of prejudice against color." Still, in reality Sherman was only acceding to the wishes of Savannah's black leaders themselves, in phrasing the order the way he did.[41]

Special Order 15 was the principle theme of conversation in black Savannah for days. On February 2, a meeting was held in the Second African Baptist Church between the freedmen and General Saxton, whom Sherman had placed in charge of the land distribution program. A thousand people were there. The building was packed to capacity, with hundreds turned away. The meeting was emotional, almost passionate. S. W. Magill was right when he wrote that it was "one of the most remarkable meetings ever held in the city of Savannah." "I have come to tell you what the President of the United States has done for you," Saxton began. "God bless Massa Linkum," came the reply from the audience. "You are all free," Saxton exclaimed. "Glory to God! Hallelujah! Amen!" the ex-slaves shouted back. Saxton and a member of his staff, the Reverend Mansfield French, explained Sherman's order and exhorted the freedmen to "be good citizens, truthful and honest." "You ought to show your late masters that you can take care of yourselves," said French. "If I were in your place, I would go, if I had to live on roots and water, and take possession of the islands." The response was unanimously enthusiastic. Hymns were sung, tears were shed, prayers and thanks were given to God, and people began preparing for a life on their own land. The city had truly never seen anything like this before.[42]

The enthusiasm did not dim, but it did become more critical. A few days later, another meeting was held in the old slave mart which was now a schoolhouse. The freedmen were concerned about what kind of deeds they would have to their new holdings. "I have a house in the city," one man said. "I can get a good living here, and I don't want to go to the islands unless I can be assured of a title to the land." Most in the room agreed. They were answered by Mansfield French that, while the government could not give them deeds, Sherman's order would be carried out. "You will have the faith and honor of the United States," French insisted. This was good enough for one man who stood up and said, simply, but effectively, "My bredren, I want to raise cotton, and I'm gwine."[43]

And so off they went. Between Charleston and Florida there were 435,000 acres available for cultivation. Altogether, 20,000 freedmen had established themselves on the islands by April, double that by June. Of these, a sizable number came from Savannah. Just in the areas east of the city, there was enough abandoned land to provide new lives for many. One group, under the leadership of the Reverend Ulysses L. Houston, pastor of the Third African Baptist Church and himself an ex-slave, went to Skidaway Island, a few miles southeast of the city. They were over a thousand strong, controlling almost 3,000 acres. They planned farm lots and laid out a village. One central lot was set aside for a church, another for a school. "We shall build our cabins and organized our town government," said the Reverend Mr. Houston. Indeed, by summer several hundred acres of vegetables and cotton were under cultivation. They were confident of a prosperous future.[44]

The winter of 1864–1865 was a period in which black optimists could smile. Certainly not all problems were solved, but freedom would solve problems. So would land. It was a good winter, all in all. There were still irritants aplenty, but irritants can be destroyed when people are free. Black Savannah could not know, at that point, that the freedom would end and the land would be lost. The government had said that the land would be guaranteed by the faith and honor of the United States. That faith and honor lasted only a few months. By summer, the new president, Andrew Johnson, was issuing pardons to ex-Confederates, and those pardons entitled them to their old lands. They returned to claim those lands and had the power—if not the faith and honor—of the United States to back them up. By and large, blacks were given a choice: Sign work contracts, which would effectively reduce the signers to the status of peons, or leave. It was a choice which blacks fought, sometimes with force. But the government which had destroyed the white South would find the black South little problem.[45]

In the end, there was nothing to do but obey the orders of the government. People like Oliver O. Howard and Rufus Saxton of the

Freedmen's Bureau helped the freedmen however they could, but Howard was consistently overridden by President Johnson, and Saxton was simply fired. A few blacks, perhaps two thousands, were able to stay on the land, but they were mostly from South Carolina, around Beaufort. A few others secured valid leases of five or ten acres from the restored property owners allowing them to stay for a year anyway, so long as they paid their rent on time. Mostly, though, the freedmen got nothing except the crops they had planted in 1865, and sometimes they did not even get those. Sometimes the restored owners took them all, in an early version of the crop-lien system. Sometimes the freedmen were removed forcibly from the land by United States soldiers. Some restored owners waited until the freedmen had harvested all the crops and then kicked them off the land empty-handed. In one case, a group of freedmen sold their cotton crop for cash, only to see the government actually expropriate 80 percent of the money, since, after all, the freedmen did not have title to the land they were farming. Little wonder that most blacks signed work contracts in the end. There were no other options.[46]

Even some white southerners realized how sorry the state of affairs had become. One who did was Mrs. George J. Kolluck, embittered by the changes in the southern social order, but still a decent woman. She was told by a Yankee officer that the ex-slaves were to be forced to return to their ex-owners, with the old owners paying the blacks a small wage and charging them all their expenses. After all, he said, the blacks must be controlled. "I answered very quietly," Mrs. Kollock wrote her son, "this is what your Government calls 'Freedom.' The *injustice* to us in robbing us of our property does not begin to compare to the cruelty to the negro himself." If Mrs. Kollock understood this, so did the freedmen themselves. One group on Edisto Island, South Carolina, composed a petition to President Johnson. "This is our home," they said. "We have made these lands what they are. We were the only true and loyal people that were found in possession of lands. . . . Are not our rights as a free people and good citizens of these United States to be considered before the rights of those who were found in rebellion against this good and just government? . . . And now after what has been done will the good and just government take from us as this right and make us subject to the will of those who cheated and oppressed us for many years?" The answer was yes, it would.[47]

By the end of the year the affair was mostly over. Many freedmen came back to town. Eighty came in early November, from St. Simons, St. Catherines and Ossabaw Islands, with all their furniture and crops in tow. They left when they learned that their land had been given back to its former owners by the government. They were not the only ones. One group of blacks went to Skidaway Island in the spring of 1865. There were ten families, farming 270 acres. Another family joined them in September. They did not make it. The notation in the Freedmen's Bureau records is simple and poignant: "All left and gone to Savannah Ga." Rather quickly, 90 percent of the land on Skidaway was restored. Statewide, of the several hundred thousand acres available to freedmen in early 1865, less than 32,000 remained in January 1866. By the summer of 1868, only 650 acres remained. The rest had all been restored to the previous owners.[48]

But the winter of 1864 1865 black Savannah did not yet know that this would happen. In winter, black Savannah could still dream. The end of Reconstruction in Georgia killed the dream, but the dream had already begun to die when winter turned into spring. The Union army freed Savannah's black and left them in a kind of limbo. It took slaves and made them, perhaps, free persons of color, but it did not really make them free human beings. Black Savannahians were given their freedom, which was worth much, but which was increasingly little in a white world which soon began to try to negate that freedom wherever possible. Besides their freedom they were given scarcely anything at all, and were not allowed to take.

CHAPTER 4

"We'll Hang Jeff Davis on the Sour Apple Tree"

Civil War Era Slave Resistance in Louisiana

Junius P. Rodriguez

I N A LETTER WRITTEN shortly before the 1860 election, Supreme Court Chief Justice Roger Brooke Taney speculated upon the South, its institution of slavery, and the grave prospects that Republican victory might have upon both. The aged jurist wrote, "I am old enough to remember the horrors at St. Domingo, and a few days will determine whether anything like it is to be visited upon any portion of our own southern countrymen." Stirred by the passionate intensity of painful remembrance, Taney mused, "I can only pray that it may be averted and that my fears will prove to be nothing more than the timidity of an old man."[1] Justice Taney's words, tinged with the grace of reflective eloquence, convey the weariness of an observer concerned that a generation, unacquainted with history, might precipitate actions that could invite servile war. Yet among those who experienced life amidst a black majority and lived in fear of slave unrest, the portent of Republican victory and the triumph of abolitionism were concomitant evils of the highest order. The "only wish" that one Baton Rouge resident mentioned in an October 1860 letter was that "black republican candidate Lincon [*sic*] will be *beat*."[2]

Despite southern efforts to avert the abolitionists' political assault and its anticipated social consequences, the Republican Party triumphed by plurality and elected an avowed "free soiler" as president. For southern states with black majorities, Abraham Lincoln's election on November 6, 1860, was the catalyst for secession. Prompted by South Carolina and Mississippi's decision to secede from the Union, Florida, Alabama, and Georgia, in rapid succession, also withdrew allegiance to the United States Constitution and laws. On January 26, 1861, Louisiana became the sixth state to secede, joining the other seceded states in forming the Confederate States of America on February 18, 1861.[3]

Louisiana Senator John Slidell shared concerns about secession, civil war, and the inherent danger of slave rebellion with President James Buchanan in hopes that reason and compassion might prevail. This conversation influenced the tone of Buchanan's annual message to Congress on December 3, 1860. The President said, "no political union . . . can long continue if the necessary consequence be to render the homes and the firesides of nearly half the parties to it habitually and hopelessly insecure."[4] In early January 1861, shortly before the state's decision to secede, Slidell addressed colleagues again cautioning against any invasion of the South for fear that it might induce a massive slave rebellion. The northern press admonished Slidell for using such inflammatory rhetoric, but the senator recognized Louisiana's previous pattern of slave unrest and could easily speculate what the advance of an invading army might do to stir that rebellious tradition.[5] Mississippi Senator Jefferson Davis defended Slidell's stand, calling it courageous, and noting similarities between the French army's foray into Santo Domingo and a potential northern invasion of southern territory. Remarking that "history does not chronicle a case of negro insurrection," Davis argued that insurrection was not an act of spontaneous slave resistance, but rather, a response engendered by governments "sending troops among them [slaves]" to inspire unrest.[6]

Jefferson Davis's vision of slave rebellion did not correlate with views of Louisiana planters living in black-majority parishes. Understanding that war pressures would further dilute population by removing young white males for military service, residents suddenly realized that slave rebellion was a real and immediate danger. C. J. Mitchell, a Madison Parish cotton planter, wrote Davis to express common concerns about the domestic security crisis that civil war entailed. Mitchell informed the Confederate president that on the home front the threat of slave revolt "has produced a sense of insecurity here which has already brought men to think of their women and children." The planter speculated, "should even a John Brown raid occur, what with the sparse population and deep seated anxiety in regard to Negroes, such a panic would ensue as would be ruinous to our cause."[7]

While internal developments were alarming, the constant threat of importing slaves tainted with a rebellious spirit continued to plague the state. When Texas planters discovered dangerous conspiracies, many chose to sell their unmanageable slaves at New Orleans rather than "risk them in the scales of justice at home." Apparently the lure of compensation was greater than any ethical constraints for immediate justice since both sellers and buyers negotiated for the best bargains, regardless of social consequences in either state. An anonymous Texan, recognizing the dangers of *caveat emptor,* warned, "I would caution planters and others purchasing negroes not to touch any from the tainted district of this State at any price." The writer cautioned, "many of them have been so tampered with that it would be folly to place them in a position to contaminate others."[8] Yet the opportunity to purchase cheap slaves during an expensive market period convinced many to forego security considerations and bargain with the Texas traders.

The April 1861 attack upon Fort Sumter marked an epiphany of unrest across Louisiana as signs of servile disorder soon began to appear. Officially, the southern attitude remained optimistic, focusing on a short war with no real problems of internal security. An editorial in the *Daily Picayune* acknowledged, "The civilized world has not ceased shuddering at the recollection of the infernal massacre of St. Domingo. It will not allow the age to be disgraced by one in the Confederate States of America."[9] Yet, signs of tension manifested themselves as the specter of slave violence, both real and imaginary, emerged and white society responded.[10] In May 1861 New Orleans police arrested Dr. Thomas Jinnings, a free black physician who attended a charity bazaar sponsored by the local white Episcopal Church. Officials charged the doctor with "intrading [*sic*] himself among the white congregation . . . and conducting hisself [*sic*] in a manner unbecoming the free colored population of this city." The arrest report also mentioned the unforgivable transgression, that Jinnings planned these actions "to create insubordination among the servile population."[11] Although such an incident appears trivial and almost amusing by modern standards, it was a serious affair in the emotionally charged wartime atmosphere of 1861.

The day of Dr. Jinnings's arrest at New Orleans, a rural newspaper reported, "Our servile population remains perfectly quiet, happy, and contented, with plenty to eat, drink, and wear, and nothing to disturb their thoughts by day, or dreams by night."[12] Taken at face value, the report suggests an idyllic setting where contented servants labored happily in a land of plenty, but closer inspection, suggested by the revealing article title "Keep Your Eye on Your Neighbors," exposes a region fearing itself to be on the brink of massive slave insurrection. In June 1861 Louisiana's coastal residents in St. Mary, Iberia, and St. Martin Parishes prepared to defend themselves against an expected invasion by abolitionist mercenaries. Public hysteria rose as the local press mentioned "rumored gatherings of slaves in considerable numbers on the banks of a certain bayou between sea marsh and main land, soidisant [it is said], to be drilled for unrighteous work." Iberia Parish officials ordered Charley Miller, a German immigrant suspected of abolitionist leanings, to leave the community and warned that "Lincoln sympathisers" might become "a different flower" swinging from the boughs of local magnolia trees. Swift actions taken by the parish patrol prevented the spreading of the conspiracy, but the imprudent reporting of slaves' misdeeds to owners probably tempered the dispensation of justice. The *Attakapas Register* criticized the "improper step" that "to advise the owners of the slaves, of the deeds of the latter" meant "to put a man's interest in direct opposition to the course of legal proceedings in such cases."[13]

Despite suspicion of any moderating influences, local magistrates imparted punishment upon many slaves believed guilty of a role in a St. Martin Parish conspiracy. Those slaveowners who felt financially victimized by the execution or imprisonment of their slaves submitted requests to the state's compensatory fund for monetary redress. Ten slaveowners received a total of $8,500 in compensation for seventeen slaves implicated in the conspiracy. St. Martin Parish officials hanged six slaves on June 24, 1861, and the remaining eleven received sentences of imprisonment for life at hard labor.[14]

Residents of north Louisiana parishes were not immune to conspiracies and threats of slave rebellion like those that plagued the state's southern parishes. In May 1861 Isaac Harrison, a Tensas Parish planter, hid in the crawl space beneath a slave cabin to overhear a conspiratorial meeting. Assuming the rapid advance of federal forces, several slaves, supported by five local abolitionists, planned a revolt to begin on July 4, 1861, when they would "march up the River to meet Mr. Linkum." Early detection of the plot prevented any disturbance from occurring, but one observer noted "there are many who live in great fear."[15]

Tensas Parish officials used the heightened state of public anxiety as the perfect occasion to remedy an annoying problem. Having free persons of color living within a slave society was generally considered dangerous, since the presence of free blacks might encourage slaves to seek their own liberty. Many assumed that free blacks could provide a leadership role usually missing from most slave conspiracies and that this fact alone justified social separation of slaves from free blacks. Within weeks of the failed conspiracy, Tensas Parish officials arrested three free men of color on horse-stealing and larceny charges and set excessive bonds to guarantee their lasting imprisonment. Since Tensas Parish recorded only eight persons of color in the Eighth Census, the imprisonment of Judson Hardin, Daniel

Gaiter, and Frank Lockett, Tensas Parish's only free black males, eliminated them as a leadership source should other conspiracies arise.[16]

Both Concordia Parish, Louisiana, and Adams County, Mississippi,
experienced a coordinated slave disturbance in the summer of 1861.[17]
Planters organized a patrol to capture the slave conspirators and then
established an extralegal planters' court at Jacob Surgets's Ashley Plantation in Concordia Parish to try the accused.[18] As one planter who was
serving as clerk transcribed the incident, those sitting in judgment
allowed each slave to testify and confess involvement before sentencing
the accused to death. The planters, sitting as judges, sentenced ten slaves
from three plantations to death by hanging. They cited the authority of
"orders of the committee." One Louisiana planter who witnessed the
trial remarked, "from what I learned, I think the testimony was sufficient
to justify the action of the committee."[19]

The testimony of the ten convicted slaves is quite revealing since their
gallows confessions show no remorse, but rather indicate a passionate,
albeit convoluted, hatred of white society. Boasting "if the black folks were
turned loose with hoes and axes they would whip the country," one par-
ticipant's naivety proved the insurrectionist's simple logic. The slave Harry
Scott's testimony mentioned a threefold strategy among conspirators to
"kill old master and take the ladies for wives and ride [with] the leaders" as
the insurrection progressed. The slave Orange's statement suggested that
conspirators also intended to steal their masters' money after killing them.
The testimony of certain conspirators showed that sexual fantasy was a significant motivating factor in uniting the plotters. The slave George Bush
predicted that "white women would run to the black men to hold them"
once the rebellion began, and another slave's assertion, "Simon be
damned if he don't have one too," reflects the societal taboo that sexual
conquest epitomized the ultimate upheaval of white society.

Besides the stereotypical words and phrases that usually outraged
southern whites, the confessions included occasional germs of revolutionary rhetoric and suggested that slaves had rudimentary understanding of sectional politics. The plotters convinced a runaway slave with a
double-barreled gun to join the conspiracy and this convert's fierce loyalty showed in a pledge to be "kicking ass" when the rebellion commenced. Unshaken by the terror of vigilant justice and inescapable death,
the slave Simon exposed the fallacy of southern manhood with the crude
assertion that "Northerners make the South shit behind their asses." The
testimony suggested a martial spirit among the plotters that encouraged
the recognition of compatibility between goals of northern armies and
insurrectionists. Equating their conspiracy with formation of a strike force

to "help old Lincoln out," the plotters predicted that joint operations between the regular army and slave rebels could speed the day when General Winfield Scott "would eat his breakfast in New Orleans." Additionally, the conspirators mentioned that encouraging news from Kingston [Jamaica], where "the negroes had got up an army" set into motion the original plans for an armed insurrection in Louisiana.[20]

Under normal circumstances, blacks constituted 90.9 percent of the Concordia Parish population, but the exigencies of civil war, especially the insatiable demands for troops, would only exacerbate fears among the remaining white minority. White residents gloomily noticed the steady population decline and prayed that slaves would not seize the opportunity to rebel. Yet Bill Postlewaite, one of the convicted slave conspirators, mentioned the population differential during the testimony and confided that insurrection was "an easy job now as so many men had gone away."[21] Southern governors understood this danger and purposefully withheld local troops to defend against possible internal slave violence. Historian Armstead L. Robinson noted that one-half of the Confederacy's forces were unavailable to commanders in July 1861 since local officials, preoccupied with preventing slave revolts, demanded their services at home.[22] For southern field commanders, soldiers' preoccupation with maintaining domestic security at the homefront created a morale problem of immense proportions. News about incidents of slave unrest at home did little to encourage military order, but rather, made soldiers reconsider their commitment to states' rights when self-preservation and individual rights appeared endangered.[23]

Even the northern press recognized that slave rebellion, either provoked or spontaneous, was a distinct possibility as the war progressed. A New York journalist wrote, "I see the Inevitable Horror—awful to me as to the South—creeping up sluggishly from the swampy poison-land—the dim devil-spectre of SERVILE REBELLION!" The knowledge that many slaveowners in upper-South states like Virginia had sent slaves southward to avoid the financial loss that capture and liberation entailed, only heightened confidence and focused speculation among Northerners as to when and where the inevitable outbreak would occur. Although northern Virginia was the focus of battlefield action, many realized that "the devil is raising his head away down South in Dixie."[24]

In April 1862 as federal gunboats steamed past the Forts Jackson and St. Philip guarding the Mississippi River's mouth, the impending capture of New Orleans excited servile passions to heretofore unparalleled heights. On several Louisiana plantations, anticipation of liberation prevailed as slave intransigence predated the arrival of federal troops. Local commanders warned Confederate military headquarters of a "very marked sign of discontent" among Louisiana slaves and predicted inevitable disturbances of public security.[25] Describing a region burdened by "pillage and desolation," an observer echoed these apprehensions by acknowledging "the negroes, for more than fifty miles up the river, are in a state of insubordination."[26] At one plantation above New Orleans, slaves constructed a gallows and then issued the ominous warning that former masters and drivers would eventually swing from its gibbet. As these disturbing signs became manifest and the future appeared uncertain, one New Orleans diarist felt compelled to admit "there was a peck of servile war in the lower part of the city."[27]

Slaves abandoned the plantations and flocked to join their liberators so rapidly that Union forces, unaccustomed to detaining large numbers of refugees, were powerless to stop the exodus and ill-prepared to handle the growing crisis of the newly dispossessed. Unable to feed, clothe, house, or employ the multitude seeking succor at Union lines, federal military commanders contemplated the vengeful fury that such an unruly mob might release upon former oppressors unless conditions improved immediately. This alarming prospect positioned federal forces in a curious dilemma in which they found themselves protecting Louisiana's slaveowners against the anticipated wrath of liberated slaves.

General Benjamin F. Butler, federal commander of occupied New Orleans, recognized the precipitous danger of servile war in Louisiana and used all commissioned powers to prevent racial hostilities from developing. Butler informed Secretary of the Treasury Salmon P. Chase that "a single whistle from me would cause every white mans [sic] throat to be cut in this city."[28] In a letter to his wife, the general stated that a risk of impending slave insurrection prevailed in Louisiana and that the uncertainty of time or place only exacerbated the anguish, making one unsure "whether he wished it more than he feared it."[29]

Butler, who had advanced active abolitionist sentiments before arriving at New Orleans, allowed the pressures of maintaining public order to direct military policy, thus modifying long-standing personal antislavery views. The general understood the military's twofold role in occupied Louisiana and recognized that "to have every species of disorder quelled" was not inconsistent with the other basic directive "to restore order out of chaos."[30] Butler's new conservative racial attitude often clashed with the active abolitionist sentiments championed by some federal officers. General John Wolcott Phelps, assigned to help Butler in the Gulf Department, was an early proponent of arming blacks as a preemptive measure to avoid the potential rebellion that idle, unemployed blacks might incite. Viewing labor as a redeeming social force, Phelps warned, "the danger of a violent revolution, over which we can have no control, must become more imminent every day," and asserted that the rigorous demands of military training, with its inculcated patriotic fervor, would prevent any manifestation of insurrection. He was decried as an "outlaw" by the Confederate Congress for "arming and training slaves for warfare against their masters." Phelps's ideas produced an expected chorus of criticism from Confederate circles, but also engendered reproach from General Butler. Calling Phelps "mad as a March Hare on the 'nigger question,'" Butler refused to adopt the "vexed question of arming the slaves," thereby giving tacit support to Louisiana's slaveholders who feared the consequences of such actions. This ideological rift produced no clear winners as Phelps resigned from the Army on August 21, 1862, and on December 16, 1862, the War Department reassigned General Butler to other duties in Virginia.[31]

As civil war progressed and southern will stiffened, the exigencies of political reality forced Abraham Lincoln to redirect the war's aims by focusing the conflict as a liberating crusade to end slavery in the United States. With the Emancipation Proclamation's promulgation on September 22, 1862, Lincoln finally grasped the moral momentum of the abolitionist movement and tried to make that cause's fervor unify northern resolve to continue the increasingly unpopular struggle. Yet, by declaring the intention to free all slaves in areas in rebellion on January 1, 1863, Lincoln inadvertently heightened southern resistance by raising the ugly spectre of slave rebellion.[32]

General Daniel Ruggles, Confederate chief of staff, had warned political leaders that the unending demand for white males to fill Confederate armies produced situations where absence of "the ordinary and necessary control of the white man" created "pernicious influences" among slaves.[33] The Confederate Congress reacted swiftly to the threat that notions of emancipation might ignite a latent spirit of rebelliousness among slaves by passing a controversial measure to expand police protection on southern plantations. On October 11, 1862, Confederate President Jefferson Davis signed "An Act to Exempt Certain Persons from Enrollment for Service in the Army of the Confederate States," ignominiously dubbed the "Twenty Nigger Law," enacted as a wartime measure designed to protect certain plantation districts against threatened slave insurrection by augmenting white population in those regions. The new military exemption act's most controversial aspect was a clause excusing masters and overseers who supervised twenty or more slaves from active service in the Confederate army, an indiscreet admission that many plantations faced great danger.[34]

Facing the related crises of conscription demands and insurrection anxieties, most people agreed that the pressures of impending emancipation would ignite servile war in certain parts of the Confederacy. *The Times* of London predicted that in places like Louisiana, "where the negro race is numerous," slave insurrections "would extirpate the white population as completely as in St. Domingo."[35] The activities of Louisiana's delegates within the Confederate Congress suggest their understanding of the potential disaster to befall their state if massive slave unrest prevailed. Representatives Duncan F. Kenner and Lucien J. Dupré, apparently recognizing the significance of their efforts to Louisiana, worked tirelessly to enact the military exemption bill that allowed greater policing of plantations. President Davis, immediately after signing this measure, responded negatively to a supplementary request by Confederate Congressman Dupré asking for special permission that some Louisiana regiments return to their home state to increase domestic defenses against possible disturbances.[36]

Within Louisiana, white residents at all levels of public and private life anticipated slave disturbances in the final months of 1862. Count Mejan, French consul at New Orleans, reported noticing "unmistakable signs" of upcoming slave unrest in Louisiana.[37] Confederate General Daniel Ruggles raised the issue of war crimes by accusing Federal General Benjamin F. Butler of encouraging "war on human nature" by "inaugurating, deliberately, servile war, by stimulating the half civilized African to raise his hand against . . . the Anglo-Saxon race."[38] Robert R. Barrow, a Terrebonne Parish planter, political leader, and prolific letter writer, attempted to rally fellow citizens to "expose and drive out from our country all sulking enemies who are here but to betray us."[39] New Orleans matron Julia LeGrand, acknowledging that "many are in great alarm," understood the immediate cause of public concern and admitted "it is scarcely human to be without fear." A neighbor named Mrs. Norton nervously awaited New Year's Day 1863, the announced arrival of emancipation, by waiting with "a hatchet, a tomahawk, and a vial of some kind of spirits" in dire expectation of an outbreak of hideous crimes against white residents.[40]

The uneventful passing of January 1, 1863, did not calm Louisiana residents' fears of slave insurrection. One resident commented that the tenuous and often indefensible position of white society's public safety generally required "Machiavellian diplomacy" toward Louisiana's blacks.[41] The promise of emancipation encouraged slaves to take a more active role in achieving their own liberation. One observer noticed that Louisiana slaves often gathered in canebreaks at night and "talked of the Yankees, and prayed for them and for the flag of the free."[42] Patrols prevented local conspiracies from expanding in Madison, Rapides, and Tangipahoa Parishes, but brazen attempts at servile revolt only became more freqent.[43]

In April 1863, a force of forty armed blacks marched upon the town of St. Martinville. These insurrectionists battled sixty white residents near a bridge at the town's entrance in full view of the 52d Massachusetts Infantry. After killing four blacks and capturing several others, the victorious whites offered the captives to the federal regiment's provost marshal who refused to accept the prisoners. Interpreting this refusal as an invitation for vigilante justice, local residents hanged the captured slaves from the Bayou Teche bridge in hopes of discouraging future slave unrest. Within a few days, the town again faced attack by insurrectionists, and a combined force of residents and federal troops dispersed the motley army that disbanded and fled to nearby swamps.[44]

Unable to discount news of any conspiracy from the ridiculous to the substantive, Louisiana's white residents suffered a precarious existence in a world where anything could occur. Accordingly, citizens responded both to rumors and actual violent outbreaks by honing local defenses and remaining vigilant. The St. Landry Parish Police Jury, responding to an incident in nearby Cheneyville, revised its slave patrol ordinance to provide greater security against possible plantation restlessness.[45] In July 1863 James A. Seddon, Confederate secretary of war, alerted Louisiana Governor Thomas O. Moore to recently discovered intelligence suggesting a massive federal scheme to foment slave revolt across the South on the night of August 1, 1863. Such a conspiracy seemed realistic to Governor Moore who received coincident details from Confederate commanders that Union advances in north Louisiana "turned the negroes crazy."[46] Evidence suggests that servile loyalty was a mere chimeric hope of white society since most slaves made "preparations for immediate skedaddling [*sic*]" when given an opportunity to escape.[47]

During the final months of the Civil War, thousands of Louisiana slaves abandoned their plantations and made the treacherous journey to the safety of Union lines. This final exodus, often misunderstood in the simplistic expression of the "jubilee spirit," represents the slaves' ultimate revolutionary sentiment, the manifestation of self-worth. Moved perhaps by religious fervor and imbibed with biblical notions of deliverance, these self-emancipated slaves were radicals—as evidenced by the lyrics "we'll hang Jeff Davis on the sour apple tree" sung to the tune of a Methodist anthem. Recognizing that the plantation South could not survive without their labor, these economic insurrectionists made the leap of faith necessary to achieve freedom and in so doing, hastened the fall of the Southern Confederacy.[48]

In *The Wretched of the Earth,* psychiatrist Frantz Fanon argued that "the oppressed, in order to prevent themselves becoming total victims, lashed out against their oppressors and in doing so, created their humanity."[49] The Civil War presented Louisiana slaves with the opportunity to employ their revolutionary tradition of insurrection, thereby proving their humanity. These slaves did not sit by as passive recipients of emancipation, but rather, they shared an active participatory role in gaining freedom. These men and women struggled together, planned work slowdowns together, conspired together, escaped together, revolted together, and fought and died together. They created their own humanity and recognized their own self-worth out of the formidable legacy of intolerance and subjugation that was their reward for misfortunate birth and they proved that a people ripe for revolt could endure in the social tinderbox of Louisiana.

CHAPTER 5

Emancipation in Missouri

Michael Fellman

T HE DAILY DEGRADATION DURING the segregation era of American race relations has led historians to discount the importance of slavery's destruction during the Civil War. Certainly the brutalities of postwar racial oppression should not be downplayed. During the war and the decade of Reconstruction, however, blacks obtained a measure of freedom which they had not had as slaves and of which they were deprived during the segregation era.

In Missouri, blacks gained more freedom by seizing opportunities during the war than Republican politicians later granted them.[1] The widespread guerrilla conflict enabled blacks to participate in the war in many locales, particularly as informers against Confederate guerrillas. This role proved beneficial to an army fighting against bushwhackers hiding in the midst of civilian sympathizers. Reliable black informants deeply and positively influenced the attitudes of beleaguered Union soldiers towards them. Discovering islands of black truthfulness in a sea of white deceit contradicted one of the underlying racist premises of slavery, that slaves never could be trusted. This realization led many whites to reconsider their attitudes towards blacks in general. One can examine this shift further by looking at white attitudes toward black women and families, the main social building blocks in a yeoman society. In addition, the appearance of black troops helped modify white attitudes. One also must stress, however, that contempt for blacks continued during the war, even among whites who began to rethink their images of blacks.

Many blacks quickly understood the opportunities freedom offered them. They learned to manipulate the politics of war to their advantage. As the war deepened and lengthened, and as abolitionism became the chief Union goal, blacks increased their acts of liberation. Blacks took their freedom from a society designed for their total oppression.[2] Non-slaveholding southern whites as well as slaveholders attempted to keep blacks in their place. With slaveholders a shrinking minority in Missouri by 1860, the state nevertheless held distinctively southern attitudes. This was not surprising, because in the 1850s, approximately 75 percent of Missourians claimed southern origins, and many more came from Ohio, Indiana and Illinois where Southerners had settled earlier in the nineteenth century.[3] Data from the 1860 census show 431,397 Missourians born outside the state; of these, 273,500 came from slaveholding states, nearly all of whom had migrated from the Upper South states of Kentucky, Tennessee, Virginia and North Carolina.[4]

Most of these southern migrants, who brought slaves with them, settled along the Missouri River, in the west-central, hemp-growing areas and in the east-central tobacco-growing regions. Missouri became the second largest hemp producing state, after Kentucky, and the sixth largest tobacco raiser. The market for hemp lay in the South, because planters and ginners used it to bag and bind cotton bales.[5] However, a high federal tariff on hemp protected this market and bound producers to the Union despite the free trade philosophy of most Southerners. In the central portion of the state, the Missouri River counties formed a slaveholding island cut off from the South by free states to the North, East and West, and by the nonslaveholding, thinly populated hill region in southern Missouri. Many southern mountain whites who settled there disliked both blacks and the planter class.

Despite their pretensions, Missouri slaveholders were not landed gentry. They held an average of only 4.66 slaves each in 1860. About one Missourian in eight (as opposed to one in two in the Lower South) held slaves; nearly 75 percent owned fewer than five, while 540 had twenty or more; thirty-eight owned more than fifty.[6] Furthermore, slavery diminished in importance during the 1850s. By 1860, slaves made up only 9.8 percent of the population, as the proportion of nonslaveholding whites increased yearly.

Yet, if slavery was decreasing in importance, few challenged it. Little antislavery sentiment existed outside the German population of St. Louis. Slaveholders and their merchant allies dominated the ruling faction of the

Democratic party. In 1861, slavery represented an organic and accepted, if increasingly marginal, part of Missouri society; four years later it died. Put more positively, by 1865 the slaves had been liberated. Emancipation became the most politically and socially revolutionary aspect of the Civil War, one marker of Missouri's rapid social transformation from a traditional, localist southern economy to a northern market-oriented one. After emancipation, which stripped the slaveholders of their labor force, white Missourians in general had to adjust to a new set of race relations.

Attitudes toward slavery divided Missourians at the start of the Civil War. Conservative Unionists as well as secessionists supported slavery, while Unconditional Unionists opposed both slavery and secession. At the start of the war, Abraham Lincoln, in many respects a Conservative Unionist, sought to placate the majority party in the border states by allowing slavery where it existed. By that action, Lincoln hoped to retain loyalty of the border states and preserve the Union. Although he hated slavery, Lincoln resisted joining forces with Radical Unionists, who attempted to make antislavery the test of true Unionism. This bitter division between the political camps in Missouri caused Unionists to expend much energy in internecine fighting. J. H. Ellis of Chillicothe in north-central Missouri, for example, complained bitterly in 1863 that Brigadier General Odon Guitar, the local district commander, enforced slavery by halting blacks who attempted to cross the border into Kansas, sending them back to their masters. Guitar also had a black shot who had free papers. If the slavehound Guitar presumed to "dictate" for the district, Ellis concluded, "there are some people would prefer removing to that America whereof Mr. Lincoln is President." Ellis represented a growing number of Unionists in 1863, emboldened by the Emancipation Proclamation, who believed that actively defending slavery was tantamount to

Year	Total Population	Whites	Free Colored	Slaves	Percentage of slaves/blacks of entire population	Percentage of increase of slaves/ slaves
1810	20,845	17,277	607	3,011	14.5	. . .
1820	66,586	54,903	376	9,797	15.4	239.4
1830	140,455	115,364	569	25,091	17.8	145.4
1840	383,702	322,295	1,478	57,891	15.5	132.1
1850	682,044	592,004	2,618	87,412	12.8	50.1
1860	1,182,012	1,063,489	3,572	114,931	9.8	31.0
1870	1,721,295	1,603,724	118,071		6.8	0.3

Adapted from Walter H. Ryle, *Missouri: Union or Secession* (Nashville: George Peabody College for Teachers, 1931), 25.

fighting for the South. Guitar continued to hold a traditional and, by then, anachronistic position on slavery. Ellis, on the other hand, wished to align north-central Missouri with the emerging, national aim of emancipation.[7] In 1861, the vast majority of Missouri Unionists supported slavery without question. By the 1864 state elections, the Radicals had won a majority of the white population. As hatred for the South grew, antislavery became a more widely accepted test of Unionism.

From the beginning of the war, military action and self-emancipation undermined the institution of slavery. On August 30, 1861, General John C. Frémont, the Union commander headquartered in St. Louis, declared all slaves free. Lincoln, however, compelled Frémont to rescind the order and soon removed him from command. The Unionist Provisional Governor Hamilton R. Gamble declared subsequently that no Union action would interfere with slavery. Nevertheless, Frémont's action expressed a previously unthinkable proposition concerning slavery in Missouri.[8]

In addition, Kansas troops raided the western border counties of Missouri to encourage slaves to follow them back to free soil. On November 15, 1861, in Kansas City, Illinois Private Dan Holmes recorded in a letter the speech John Brown Jr. gave to Kansan Charles R. Jennison's regiment. Holmes wrote that Brown "was going to take all the negroes he could from the secessionists, arm them and form regiments of them and set them fighting, and if the government won't sustain him he will go on his own hook. He is a bold, rash, impetuous desperado. He has a flag being made at Boston with a life size portrait of Old John Brown upon it." Ushered by Kansas troops, some 2,000 male slaves fled to Kansas within six months. These free blacks filled two Colored Regiments. The First Kansas Colored Infantry, commissioned on January 13,1862, became one of the initial black regiments in the Union Army. Thousands of other slaves ran off, wandering the country, often accompanying Union troops who both cared for and exploited them.[9]

In general, Union officers and men, even negrophobic ones, believed that because slaveholders were their enemies, depriving them of their labor force would cause economic and psychological injury. Furthermore, black actions could be of direct aid to Union troops. In the context of Missouri's guerrilla war, bushwhackers blended into the citizenry, and few whites would help fight bushwhackers. Therefore, Union soldiers learned that blacks provided the most trustworthy military information. In exchange, soldiers often granted black informers freedom and protection. Because Union soldiers trusted the freedmen rather than white southern sympathizers, they raised their estimate of the black character. This was a lesson in practical abolitionism for many Union troops.

A. J. McRoberts, a Saline County Unionist, wrote in April 1863, that his neighbor, a Mr. Manfrew, "came very close to losing his scalp." Northern General Benjamin Loan's men "would have killed him if they would have found him. He caught a negro that was on his way to Loan to report on the rebels, and gave him a thrashing, he must have hit the negro a hundred licks & they said you'll tell the damn feds will you, & Loan's men got hear of it and it made them desperate mad."[10] Many slaves realized that information, their most valuable possession, provided the route of self-liberation. As the war progressed, more and more Union commanders automatically provided protection to black informers, and thereby institutionalized the exchange of information for freedom. On March 10, 1862, for example, Lieutenant Colonel Arnold Krekel destroyed a guerrilla band, killing three, including "the notorious Tid Sharp." Krekel reported to his commander, "A negro boy gave valuable information in conducting the command, and I would ask permission to retain him until the war is over, as he cannot safely return."[11] Later in the war, field commanders like Krekel assumed authority to free helpful slaves.

As the war deepened, increasing numbers of Union soldiers viewed slaveholding as treason and supported emancipation. Ephram J. Wilson, a slaveholding farmer near Palmyra in Northeast Missouri, complained in the summer of 1863 that: "About ten days ago a hired negro man in my employ left my premises without any cause whatsoever and carried away with him by force a small boy, a slave belonging to me." Wilson took his revolver, a family keepsake, and unsuccessfully pursued his property, whom he heard had fled to Colonel Edward A. Kutzner's camp. A few days later, about one hundred federal troops rode to Wilson's house, demanding his pistol, "threatening to search my wife's person unless the pistol was produced," and ransacked his house. He felt certain, probably with reason, that the blacks had informed on him. Outraged at this violation of his property rights and wanting the return of his pistol and slave, Wilson called on the provost marshal in Hannibal "to make complaint." The provost marshal, however, bluntly remarked that "any man who would hold a slave with very few exceptions is neither a Christian, a patriot or a loyal citizen."[12] Wilson then complained to the district commander, hoping for redress from a higher Union authority. He still believed that any honorable man would share his outrage at theft of his private property. Wilson did not comprehend the shift in Union soldiers' attitudes from seeing blacks as property to valued informants.

Union troops found it difficult to stand by and watch the return of escaped slaves who sought their protection. In July 1862, Wisconsin infantryman Stanley Lathrop wrote his parents from northern Arkansas. "We are the first Federal troops who have ever been in this part of the state. Almost all the rich plantation owners have fled as usual, and their negroes are beginning to come to us, often riding to us, often riding a mule or horse of their master. Some of the owners have tried to get them back but it was no go. Col. [Edward] Daniels says he did not persuade them to run away and he will not return them as the Fugitive Slave law privilege of *habeas corpus* etc. are suspended."[13] For this Union colonel, secessionist slaveholders had forfeited the protection of the law. When escaped slaves came to the Union lines they acted freely, and he would not return them as property against their wills.

Relatively early in the war, Charles E. Cunningham, sheriff of Johnson County in west-central Missouri, also learned that a large number of slaves planned to accompany Federal troops when they withdrew from Warrensburg. Cunningham notified Major Charles Baunzhaf, the local Union commander. Baunzhaf told Cunningham to retrieve the slaves by coming to the train stop, four miles from town. Cunningham gathered a posse and rode out to the train. Accompanied by Baunzhaf, the sheriff collected the slaves, left his posse as their guard, and rode on looking for more. "I found one more," he wrote, "and was taking her back to the others, when I met them released from the guard . . . I undertook to catch one of them when a large number of guns were drawn on me and the negroes released, with threats made against my life as well as that of my men with me. This was done without the Major attempting to quiet the men although I had gone out at his own request."[14]

In a straightforward, traditional manner, Sheriff Cunningham represented the citizens of Johnson County. Many were slaveholders, and he simply tried to protect their property. He later appealed, without success, to Gamble, the provisional governor and Conservative Unionist who had claimed in his official pronouncements to protect both the Union and the institution of slavery. Cunningham had encountered military forces, more organized than local militias and more committed to antislavery than the general populace and the provisional governor. In this case, the enlisted men also opposed slavery more than did their major. Baunzhaf possibly sought to prevent a riot in Warrensburg. By misleading Sheriff Cunningham and inviting him to reclaim the slaves four miles out of town, the Union major would have a monopoly of armed forces. Baunzhaf might have entrapped Cunningham with a plan to deceive him and hurt him. More likely, if Cunningham's report was accurate, Baunzhaf responded to the opinion of his men and changed his mind about returning the slaves. Certainly, the troops responded with vigor against the sheriff; when they witnessed the event, they drew their guns and stopped the slaves' return, regardless of the major's intention.

As these cases demonstrate, the Civil War led many whites to change their attitudes toward blacks. Blacks no longer remained private chattel of whites, and they could not be punished with complete impunity. Physical punishment, formerly a disciplinary norm, and murder became crimes, at least in the opinion of some whites. This new respect for blacks in large part resulted from the reliability of blacks who provided information to Union troops about secessionist activities. The impact of the black regiments fighting for the Union also contributed to the new attitude. White Union soldiers sensed the comradeship of black soldiers; they came to understand that black soldiers sought to protect their women in the same way whites wished to shelter their own. Revised attitudes toward black women and black families indicated the general reconsideration of racial beliefs which accompanied emancipation.

Raping and beating black women had been intrinsic parts of slavery, an institution which gave superhuman powers to the owners. Some owners avoided excessive brutality, and decried the viciousness of harsh masters. Yet, few masters refrained from whipping, and many used their enormous power over slave women to coerce them sexually. White men were not punished for raping black women.

Although many accounts make general allusions to rape and abuse of black women in Missouri during the war, particularly "contraband" who followed the army, few direct reports exist. One concrete example came in the court-martial of guerrilla James Johnson of Platte County. Frances Kean testified that Johnson, John Nichols and another bushwhacker had seized her eighteen-year-old slave girl. Kean reported the girl's account. "They rode on a piece and said to her, God damn you we will punish you. Nichols then got off his horse and said now ride boys and she told me they done with her what they wanted to—she said they violated her person."[15]

In March 1864, a slaveowner named Tapley, of Pike County, recaptured his escaping slave woman. Because she would not tell him where she had hidden her three children, she reportedly was "stripped and beaten on the bare back with a band saw until large blisters formed, and then the wretch sawed them open, under which treatment the poor woman died." Mrs. J. R. Roberts, secretary of the Freedmen's Relief Society of Quincy, Illinois, clipped this newspaper story from the *Chicago Tribune* and sent it to the provost marshal of Missouri. The story also reported that Lincoln's proclamation freeing wives and children of black soldiers had enraged Missouri slaveholders. This woman had run off to join her soldier husband when her owner caught her.[16]

Although Tapley's fate remains unknown, James Johnson was sentenced to death, in part for his crime against a black woman.

In February 1863, while the First Iowa Cavalry foraged on the farm of an Arkansas rebel, they asked a slave woman if her master had a gun hidden away. "She denied knowing anything about it but being threatened she owned that it would be death to her if she told anything," Private Timothy Phillips recorded in his diary. "Our boys promised to rescue her and take her along with them." The Iowa troops found the gun and placed her on a horse in the baggage train. Later, the owner caught up with the column and offered anyone who would return his slave twenty dollars in gold. Upon her return, he paid the $20. "The whole thing was got up so quick that few in the train know anything about it," Phillips wrote in his diary that evening. Lieutenant Edward A. Dunham, head of Phillips's squad, was blamed and forced to turn the money over to the colonel. Phillips concluded, "There is considerable excitement in the regiment about this matter and if the boys had it in their power they would make short work of Lieut. Dunham."[17] Obviously, Lieutenant Dunham had no qualms about returning the woman for $20. However, Phillips, unlike his lieutenant, thought it criminal to break an official promise to the black woman if only because other slaves might be less forthcoming in the future.

For many Kansas regiments, freeing slaves remained central to their agenda. Perhaps they felt less racial sympathy than desire for revenge against their long-time enemies, the Missouri slaveholders. In May 1862, Surgeon Joseph H. Trego reported that two captains had resigned from the Fifth Kansas Cavalry regiment when Colonel Powell Clayton ordered the return of fugitive slaves. "This case was particularly agrivating [sic] because the fugitives were wenches and one of them was whipped severely when her master got her home." Although Trego used racist language, he sympathized with the female victims whom he sought to free and to protect.[18]

In 1864, General James A. Pile organized black regiments at Benton Barracks in St. Louis. He sought assurance from the commander of the military district that wives and children of his new troops would be protected. Pile particularly was concerned about the wife and six children of Richard Glover. They had been treated cruelly by owner George Caldwell, from whom Glover had escaped. Caldwell had beaten the wife with a buggy whip, "and this when she is *Pregnant* and nearing *confinement,*" in order to procure her consent to be taken to Kentucky. Pile added, "This is not an isolated case, but only a sample." He protested, "This *infamy* in the name of *God—Justice—and Humanity* . . . against these Sable patriots and true heroes."[19] Pile wished to recruit more troops, and that success appeared contingent, in part, on aid to their families. Because he sought black men he had more reason to be sympathetic toward their stories about beatings of their wives.

Captain Louis F. Green wrote to the former owner of "Ed Payton colored boy," who had just joined the black regiment he was recruiting. Green told the master to send Payton's wife and children. "*I have promised him that he shall have them and he shall*." Failure to comply would mean "your *life* or property. When that black man Ed Payton enlisted here yesterday, he purchased his wife and children from you and from now on he is fighting for the government, and is entitled to the privileges it now gives—*freedom to all*."[20]

If paternalistic and condescending to their charges, white officers in black regiments responded to such pleas of recruits for their families. Other whites maintained more traditional racism, or indifference to blacks. In many parts of Missouri, guerrillas turned against free blacks at the end of the war. Timothy Phillips reported seeing many black bodies floating on a river in southern Missouri at the end of the war.[21] Lynching also became common in Missouri in the spring of 1865. Generally, during and after the war, black women were violated far more frequently than whites. Yet amidst the mayhem blacks came to be more nearly accepted as humans, which included respect for black women.

For the slaveholders, the world turned upside down. They lost their property and their means to wealth; they lost their traditional means of control over blacks whom they regarded as potentially dangerous insurrectionaries; they lost much of their community standing as men of station and property. With a combination of exasperation, resignation, fear and anger, they responded to this social upheaval.

Exasperation and bitter humor characterized the manner in which James L. Morgan, a tobacco merchant in Glasgow, dealt with the loss of his slaves. He had come to Missouri from Virginia in 1859. In 1863, he wrote back to an old friend, encouraging him to pay a visit. "We have plenty to feed you on—and at present have servants enough to wait upon you. Don't know how long we will have them, however, we had 8 to run off last week—the negroes are leaving this section fast—when I came to this state I sold most of my negroes and of course my Father thought it a very bad move—I am satisfied now that the only bad part was that I did not sell them all."[22] Morgan expressed pride that he had been shrewd enough to have cut his losses in slaves before the war. He regretted that soon he might not have enough "servants" to guarantee his Virginia visitor a gracious reception. He dealt with his loss in a refined manner, using humor rather than outright anger.

In 1861, Margaret J. Hayes described the plundering of her property in Westport in a similar tone. The Kansans filled her carriage with loot and her slaves and drove off west. "It was very aggravating to see [the carriage] driven up to the door and to see [my slaves] jump into it and drive off."[23] That they departed so eagerly seemed particularly irritating.

Some slaveholders feared retaliation from their ex-slaves. Rumors of impending raids caused some to panic. In October 1862, J. B. Henderson, from Louisiana, Missouri, wrote to Conservative Unionist James O. Broadhead, U.S. district attorney in St. Louis: "Many people are shuddering over negro insurrections and the terrible outrages of negro freedom." In 1863, Richard C. Vaughan, in Lafayette County, wrote to Broadhead about widespread fear of black regiments forming in Kansas to invade and devastate slaveholding areas. "Our wives and daughters are panic stricken, and a reign of terror as black as hell itself envelops our county." Fear of slave rebellion and the violation of white women greeted the march of black Union regiments.[24]

Some former slaveholders reacted by taking revenge on their former slaves. On January 28, 1864, Jim, a Union soldier with a squad of six men, approached William C. Reynolds, his mother's former master. He asked for her clothing and for tobacco due her. According to white witnesses, "Mr. Reynolds talked very friendly," and then, without provocation, seized his gun and called out to his three sons. They stepped from the house and began firing their shotguns. The other black soldiers fled, but Jim fell. Reynolds and his sons then went up to him and shot him twice in the head.[25]

Lynching blacks commenced in Missouri at the end of the war. If blacks were freed, they had to leave the region or be hanged, many whites believed. The bushwhacker James H. Jackson sent "general orders" to one farmer in Ralls County, "my garrilis is heard that you have a cople of famellely of negroes settle on your plase . . . and if you dont make dam negroes leve there ride away i will hadn the last negro on the plase and you will fair wors for we cant stand the dutch and negros both."[26] Generally considered the worst "nigger lovers," Germans also represented foreign elements to be purged from the American community. But free blacks appeared the greatest threat, and lynching offered one immediate response to their appearance.

Whites attempted to maintain clear color lines in public places, particularly in cities, as another means to reassign black freemen to a subordinate place in society. On the morning of November 16, 1864, S. F. Aglar, a railroad agent, boarded a St. Louis streetcar with his wife and the wife and daughter of a Union colonel, all on their way to attend an Orphan's

Fair. "We found a squad of soldiers on the platform and several negro women in the car. The ladies of course objected to ride in the same car with negroes." They upbraided the conductor who agreed to make them ride on the platform. However, the captain of the troops, characterized as a drunken German by Aglar, did not consent, "saying that the colored women had as much right in the car as white people." The captain finally agreed to make them ride on the rear platform, but "appeared greatly exasperated at us because our ladies objected to ride with colored women." Arriving at the corner of Broadway and Franklin, the captain suddenly ordered his men off the car, dragged Aglar down to the street by his collar, took his name and threatened him with arrest. Aglar reported the incident to General Williams S. Rosecrans, commander in St. Louis, expecting him to punish this offensive German.[27]

Segregation, reinforced with physical intimidation and lynching, would triumph in the long run. However, in 1864, no consensus existed that segregation would be the appropriate form of racial control. Former slaveholders and many negrophobic whites had not yet put blacks firmly in their "place."

Whatever the postwar outcome, blacks, fleeing their masters and joining the Union cause during the war, found their liberation both frightening and exhilarating. With pleasure, sixty-seven-year-old escaped slave Paris Bass swore out a deposition to Union authorities against his longtime master, Eli Bass. He reported that notorious outlaw Bill Anderson many times had spent the night on the Bass farm in Callaway County. "He always rode a sable horse. I knew the horse & could tell his nicker."[28]

Slaveowners feared the worst revenge if a slave joined the army. For example, in 1864, Private Spottswood Rice, in St. Louis, wrote his former master in Glasgow: "the longor you keep my Child from me the longor you will have to burn in hell and the qwicer you will get their for we are now makeing up a bout one thoughsand blacke troops to Come up thorough and wont to come through Glasgow and when we come wo be to Copperood rabbels and to the Slaveholding rebbels for we dont expect to leave them root neor branch." Concerning black family rights, Rice emphasized that his children were his own and not a slaveholder's property. Rice, now free, would show his former master who had the power to establish social relations. "When I get ready to come . . . I will have bout a powrer and autherity to bring hear away and to execute vengencens on them that holds my child you will then know how to talke to me I will assure that and you will know how to talk rite too."[29] Spottswood Rice intended to go from the bottom to the top of the social ladder and to place his master several rungs beneath.

In at least one case, an ex-slave had the opportunity to shoot his former master from behind Union lines. After the 1861 engagement at Boonville, where Union forces routed the pro-Southern state militia, one northern soldier reported the death of a wealthy Confederate leader: "Five negroes brought the news of the intended attack and were inside the entrenchment during the engagement. Among them was a slave of Col. William O. Brown's. Whilst fighting he took hold of a gun and shot his master who fell and soon after expired. The darky is tickled almost to death."[30]

On August 8, 1864, at Jefferson City, a slave named Jackson took the stand as the sole witness for the state in the court-martial of his former mistress, Fanny Houx, of Lafayette County. The army charged her with entertaining and feeding guerrillas. On a July morning five weeks earlier, Jackson had been plowing when he noticed "a parcel of horses around the well." When he went to the house for breakfast he observed "some wash pans and a couple of towels in the yard." As he sat waiting for his meal, his mistress "come down the steps out of the dining room and observed to me that I had better go and watch for the feds. She said they might come and get to fighting and some one or other get killed. Says I to her I don't care if they do. She says you don't? I says no Madam I don't. She (the accused) says I will tell the bushwhackers directly . . . what you said right before their face. I said I don't care if you do, tell them." The twelve bushwhackers then came up to the house, and Fanny Houx told them what Jackson had said. "One stepped up and said God damn your black soul what do you mean talking that away. I said nothing." A second guerrilla said, "who is talking that talk. The other says the old nigger setting there, the Lady says. So he stepped up and drew his pistol and struck me on the head, and the first thing you know you will be taken out and have your brains blown out." Fanny Houx then sent her son up on the hill to watch for Feds, "and said to the bushwhackers come up to breakfast." After breakfast, one of the guerrillas dragged Jackson to the yard, stripped off his shirt and took a hickory pole in both hands. "He just tip toed to it and come down on me the same as if he was beating an ox. He said to the others standing around, boys you've got nothing to do but cut hickories and fetch them to me as fast as I can wear them out." After the hickories, the guerrilla continued beating Jackson with a lap board. "He wore that out on me. He turned me loose [saying] I want you to go to the feds now, God Damn you so that I can slip in at the dead hour of the night and shoot you."

Jackson remained steadfast in his story under cross-examination by Fanny Houx's lawyer. In her deposition to the court, Houx claimed that Jackson harbored a "malicious spirit of revenge" toward her for interceding earlier when Jackson was beating his wife. Houx's lawyer asked if "you and your wife had not had some serious difficulties before those bushwhackers came . . . and whether Mrs. Fanny Houx did not interfere in favor of your wife." Jackson answered, "Yes sir, we had some words four or five weeks before. I slapped her twice with my hand. I thought she needed it. There were not bushwhackers there then and that had nothing to do with the bushwhacking scrape." Did Jackson bear hatred towards Mrs. Houx for her interference? "No, Sir." Houx claimed she opposed bushwhacking and had only fed the guerrillas when compelled to do so. In Houx's defense, Jacob A. Price, the sheriff of Lafayette County, testified that he had known Jackson for eighteen years and would not believe him under oath. He regarded Houx as a vocal opponent of bushwhacking. However, Price was Houx's brother.

The panel of seven Federal officers believed Jackson and convicted Houx. They took the word of a black man, who five weeks before had been a slave, against a well-bred white lady and an elected law enforcement officer.

Jackson's testimony revealed the traditional manner of disciplining a slave who had sassed his owner, and the white assumption that beating would reinforce subordination and prevent further repercussions. Jackson surely knew he would be beaten by the guerrillas, who were arriving when he sassed his mistress. Why then did he do so? Perhaps in desperation, he refused to help proslavery guerrillas out of principle. Perhaps in anger, he forgot himself, or saw the chance to turn on his mistress. In any event, he went about thirty miles to the nearest Union post and within weeks, upon his word alone, caused a court-martial to be convened. The court convicted his mistress, challenged her brother's reputation and believed him to be a truthful free man. He ably manipulated the military justice system to his own ends. Adroit in his testimony and convincing in his narration, he cleverly avoided being trapped on the question of animosity to his mistress. To testify in such a case, much less be believed, would have been impossible before the war or twenty years after it. Jackson gained revenge, employing the court against his former mistress while guaranteeing his own freedom. Stripping off the mask of servitude, Jackson turned his world upside down.[31]

The importance of such victories, which occurred when blacks went to Union military authorities, should neither be downplayed nor romanticized. Jackson and other slaves believed they would receive equal justice. Segregation soon would become the common method of race control among whites. But for a tantalizing historical moment, under the pressures of guerrilla war, the white community in Missouri disagreed on the race issue. Slaves like Jackson could deploy one party against the other. The destruction of the slave system was the most revolutionary social change in the war. Many slaves took their freedom in immediate acts of self liberation. This action often debased and punished their former masters, while temporary white allies sympathized with them and urged them on. Because whites were not certain how to deal with freed blacks, and because blacks could participate in public life during the war, a tantalizing hint of genuine freedom accompanied emancipation in Missouri.

Part 2

FROM FUGITIVES TO CONTRABANDS TO FREEDPEOPLE

CHAPTER 6

— ⊸⊸⊸⊸ —

Being Free

Black Migration and the Civil War

Allan Johnston

SOME OF THE FIRST and most fundamental decisions facing newly freed men and women during and after the Civil War concerned the question of whether, and if so when and where, to move from the plantations and farms on which they had lived and worked as slaves. Yet that aspect of Afro-American history has been relatively neglected by historians. This neglect is all the more regrettable because the choices black Americans made in answer to those questions contribute to our understanding, not only of the wartime experience and its impact on the lives of former slaves, but also of the nature and strength of Afro-American culture. This paper begins an exploration of those issues by analysing the broad outlines of black migration in the 1860s and through a case study of the wartime migration of large numbers of former slaves into Washington, D.C.—the largest city-ward movement of blacks in the nineteenth century. It highlights the complex range of alternatives facing former slaves and the importance of local conditions and opportunities in shaping the decisions which saw some find their way to cities like Washington while others chose the more predictable future of life with their former masters.

It is not altogether surprising that the wartime migration has been relatively neglected by historians. As a study of the black migration experience it has been overshadowed by interest in the northward diaspora of the early twentieth century, not only because of the much larger scale of that later movement, but also because of the relative ease in recognizing, analyzing and explaining broad movements across state and regional boundaries compared with the more localized moves which character-ized this earlier period. Similarly the relative paucity of sources for deter-mining the movements and motives of individual black migrants in the mid-nineteenth century has contributed to a reluctance to undertake the study of earlier migrations.

The fact that blacks left the plantations in large numbers during the Civil War and Reconstruction has been well documented in the historical literature, but our understanding of the magnitude and nature of that migration has advanced relatively little beyond the general outline pre-sented in Carter G. Woodson's "classic" history of black migration first published in 1918.[1] The most recent analysis, Daniel Johnson and Rex Campbell's *Black Migration in America* (1981) is largely a re-statement of previous work, and a poor one at that.[2] Johnson and Campbell derive their account of wartime migration largely from Woodson and from Bell Wiley's 1938 study and ignore more recent histories of black migration by Peter Kolchin, Nell Painter and others.[3] Despite the promise of a "social demographic history" Johnson and Campbell's account adds little to our understanding of the processes which shaped the movement of blacks in the war and post-war years. It is only through a closer examina-tion of individual migrations of the type undertaken by Peter Kolchin of blacks in Alabama and Nell Irwin Painter's study of black migration to Kansas after Reconstruction that we can hope to understand the complex sets of actions, motives and means which saw some individuals and groups abandon their former homes for life elsewhere.

The issues raised in this paper contribute not only to the history of black migration, but also to a more general argument about the strength of Afro-American culture and its ability to survive in slavery and in free-dom. More particularly, the impulse to study the wartime migration flows in part from questions raised by the debate over the strength of Afro-American culture and the long-term effects of slavery. This arose in the political context of the Civil Rights movement, was fueled by the Moyni-han Report in the early '60s, and continues today.[4] Broadly speaking, one approach in that debate concentrated on the supposed weaknesses of Afro-American culture and its inability, at least initially, to withstand the stresses of urban life. The focus, in the work of Moynihan and others, was on such things as the rural origin of twentieth century urban blacks and the initial shocks of urban life in uprooting old patterns. In particular, the impact of slavery in destroying African culture, community and family patterns was singled out as the primary basis for an ongoing pathological situation in the black community. An alternative view has stressed the existence of a stronger slave culture created from a synthesis of African and white values on the plantation. The move to the city was, in this view, merely an extension of the original migration from Africa and one in which traditional customs were preserved. The problems of unemployment and social dislocation which undoubtedly faced urban blacks in the 1960s and 70s were explained by destructive forces operating in the city itself—poverty, discrimination and institutionalized racism.

The political implications of those two divergent approaches ought to be obvious: if the malaise in the black community was the product of inherent weaknesses in black culture, then civil rights anti-poverty programs and the like could do little to redress the "black problem." If, on the other hand, the real "problem" was "the city" those same measures might be effective. A generation of historians was drawn into this debate and the challenges it posed for finding ways to better understanding of black culture in America. They concentrated initially on two aspects of the Afro-American past. In the late '60s and early '70s a number of scholars, utilizing black sources on a large scale for the first time, examined slavery, and particularly the behavior of blacks on the plantations and in the slave community, in an attempt to examine its impact on African culture and the formation of an Afro-American hybrid.[5] At the same time other historians, also utilizing black sources for the first time and with the aid of computer techniques which enabled the analysis of large volumes of social data, conducted studies on black communities in a number of late-nineteenth- and early-twentieth-century cities.[6]

In the late 1970s and early 1980s the focus of analysis shifted to the neglected period immediately following the slave experience. The moment of freedom, it is argued, offers an ideal point at which to examine the legacy of slavery before the impact of the modern urban economy and any attendant problems could have a major influence. Herbert Gutman's work on the black family, Lawrence Levine's analysis of "expressive culture" and Leon Litwack's majestic overview, *Been in the Storm So Long,* all focus, in whole or in part, on that crucial time in which black and white Americans were forced to create new institutions governing both their own lives and the regulation of social, economic and political relations between the races to replace those abolished along with slavery.[7] This paper carries the analysis of that transition period further by focusing on an important element of black behavior at the time of emancipation.

For most of the nation's four and a half million blacks the most far reaching effect of the Civil War was that it brought an end to over 250 years of servitude. In a real sense that freedom turned out to be illusory. The Thirteenth Amendment abolishing slavery in the United States was no temporal River Jordan across which lay the Promised Land. It did not take long for blacks to see that they had been betrayed, but in the interim they savored the illusion of their freedom and sought ways of expressing it. It was a time for learning new ways and adapting to a new life. As Litwack has stated

> for the black men and women who lived to experience the Civil War, there would be the moment where they learned a complex of new truths: they were no longer slaves, they were free to leave the families they had served, and they could aspire to the same rights and privileges enjoyed by their former owners.[8]

Perhaps the most fundamental decision former slaves had to make was whether or not to leave their former masters and to strike out on their own. Former slaves knew that, among other things, free men and women exercised the right to move in search of work or higher wages, or merely because they felt like doing so. Movement was an integral part of being free. Blacks insisted on behaving as they understood free men and women to behave, and so they too became people in motion.[9]

Geographic mobility was not new to black Americans. Their distribution had changed radically since the first national census in 1790. By 1850 the center of black population had shifted from Virginia to South Carolina and by the time war broke out it had begun to move west into Georgia. The shifting center of population reflected the movement of slaves with their owners, or with slave traders who sold them to new masters carrying the "peculiar institution" into the fertile lands of the old Southwest.[10] Some free blacks, and slaves who managed to escape from bondage, made their way north, but they were no more than a trickle against the main tide.

With the onset of war both the volume of movement and the nature of the forces behind it changed. Some slaves moved with their masters in flight from the advancing Union armies, but more took advantage of the turmoil and confusion of war to flee their old plantations in search of freedom and new means of survival. As we shall see some unwittingly acquired new masters in place of the old as they were taken up and moved about as pawns in the hands of Union and Confederate army officers, but eventually many could exercise a greater degree of freedom to decide for themselves where and how they would live and work.

In the context of national and international trends in migration this new mobility is easily overlooked. On a national scale the net result was a continuation of trends established in the antebellum period. The shift of black farmers and farm laborers to the Southwest continued as did the lesser migration to the farms and cities of the North and Northwest, but in neither case was the volume of movement remarkable.[11] Consequently the authors of one study of this migration have concluded that, given the size of the black population of the United States at the end of the nineteenth century, the amount of lifetime interregional movement of blacks in the post-war years indicates a low level of geographic mobility.[12] Blacks remained predominantly rural and southern throughout the nineteenth century. The black share of the total southern population reached its maximum point in 1880. In that year the South still housed 89 percent of the nation's blacks and 80 percent of Southern blacks lived in rural areas.[13]

But the concentration of interregional migration obscures extremely divergent trends within the South and ignores significant local movements. A number of states exhibited quite different population characteristics from others with which they were linked in census tabulations. While the period from 1860 to 1910 was one of relatively weak interregional black migration, coming as it did between westward expansion in the antebelleum South and the great shift northward in the twentieth century, those seemingly quiet years saw a substantial movement, both in terms of volume and importance, at the inter- and intra-state levels.[14]

The absence of large-scale, long-distance black migration in the second half of the nineteenth century is not difficult to explain. The relative absence of capital, both in material resources and knowledge, severely restricted the distances over which nineteenth century blacks could or would migrate.[15] Moreover, long-distance migration tends to take place within well-defined streams, along well-defined routes to specific destinations.[16] The movement of Southern blacks to northern cities has been found to be strongly influenced by the prior movement of relatives and friends who provide both information and aid to new arrivals.[17] Clearly that pattern is dependent on the existence of lines of communication between established and potential migrants, either through letters or cheap and frequent visits "home." The high level of illiteracy among former slaves and the relative absence of low cost passenger rail transport, especially in the South where many existing lines were destroyed during the war, severely limited the "relatives and friends" effect. Finally, officials of the Bureau of Refugees, Freedmen and Abandoned Lands (Freedmen's Bureau) found that in the years immediately after the war freedmen were very reluctant to move to areas they knew little about or of which they had formed negative opinions. Even in the midst of economic hardship, and with the promise of jobs elsewhere, former slaves in the border states, who had once been threatened with sale "down South," were reluctant to move to the Deep South. Similarly the propaganda of slave owners, especially during the war, fostered a fear of the cold climate and "devil Yankees" of the North that was not easily dispelled.[18]

Despite the absence of evidence of dramatic shifts in population between North and South in the second half of the nineteenth century there was a substantial migration of blacks in the very first decade after the war. Map 1, indicating the percentage change in the black population for the various states and territories between the federal census years of 1860 and 1870, shows the beginnings of a recognizable trend. Most notably, a band of border states, from Virginia in the east to Missouri in the west, actually had fewer black inhabitants in 1870 than ten years before. Over a period in which the nation's black population rose by 9.9 percent, among the Southern states only Florida and Texas, two areas of rapid expansion, had black population increases appreciably above the national average. In part the lower rate of growth in the South can be attributed to lower fertility and higher mortality rates in areas ravaged by war. However, the discrepancies are too great to be explained by those factors alone, especially as states with similar war experience had quite different growth rates. The pattern was largely the product of migration. Border states, it appears, suffered the heaviest losses because migrants from those areas moved both north and south.[19]

At the intra-state level the movement of blacks was even more pronounced. Reduced to its most basic concept migration is no more than a permanent or semi-permanent change of residence.[20] Movement from one part of a city or state to another may have widespread social and economic implications for those involved in the move and for the wider community. Evidence of a great deal of black mobility in the years during and shortly after the Civil War can be seen in a number of local areas, including the counties in Maryland and eastern Virginia depicted in Map 2. The large volume of movement in that area is highlighted by the fact that of the eighty-nine counties represented on the map, twenty experienced a change of more than 30 percent, plus or minus, in their black population between the census years of 1860 and 1870. Most counties shown on the map experienced a loss of black residents in the decade. That loss coincided with three other trends: the overall decline in the black population of Virginia and very slight increase in Maryland; the general shift of blacks to the western counties of Virginia where slavery had been less entrenched before the war; and the movement of blacks to urban areas within the region itself.[21]

The clearest trend (Map 2) was the movement of blacks to the cities and towns of Virginia, Maryland and the District of Columbia in the 1860s. With the exception of Kent County in Maryland, all those coun-

ties with the greatest percentage increase in black population were counties which contained, or were adjacent to, major urban centers.[22] In those
cities in the region with more than 10,000 inhabitants in 1870 (Baltimore, Washington, Richmond, Norfolk, Petersburg, Alexandria, George-
town and Portsmouth) the white population grew by an average 23
percent (from 302,583 to 371,915) from 1860 while their combined
black populations increased from 72,623 to 129,262 (a growth of 78
percent) over the same period. Numerical increase, as well as percentage
change, was greater for blacks than for whites. Three of the cities (Petersburg, Alexandria and Portsmouth) actually had smaller white populations
in 1870 than ten years before. The growth of the urban black population
in Maryland, Virginia and the District of Columbia took place at a time
when the black population for the area as a whole declined slightly.[23]
Aggregate patterns revealed in maps and tables can suggest certain trends
and tentative interpretations of them can be offered. However, a fuller
understanding of the processes of migration requires analysis at a level
where the individual motives and aspirations of black migrants are
revealed. While the range of sources which enable this "behavioral"
approach to migration is extremely limited, government records and individual diaries, letters and memoirs of former slaves provide some clues.
The many volumes of narratives and interviews with former slaves are a
useful starting point for the historian of wartime migration.[24] They form
the bulk of evidence relating to the behavior of slaves and former slaves
and, fortunately, have been subjected to close analysis by Leon Litwack,
Paul Escott and others already.[25]

Litwack's analysis of those sources and what they have to say about
black behavior during and immediately after the Civil War confirms the
fact that migration reflected the most basic expression of the slaves' new
status as freedmen and women.

> Walking off the plantation remained the surest, the quickest way to
> demonstrate to themselves that their old masters and mistresses no
> longer owned or controlled them, that they were now free to make their
> own decisions.[26]

But, as he also notes, "walking off the plantation" frequently represented much more than just a way of experiencing the sensation of freedom. It was often purposeful: reflecting the slaves' determination to
improve their economic position, or locate family members, or return to
homes from which they had been removed during the war.[27] Another
dominant motive for those who moved was the desire to relocate where
newly won rights could be more readily secured. For many that place was

the town or city. According to Litwack the "size of the city or town to which many blacks flocked after emancipation mattered less than the freedom, the opportunities, the protection and the camaraderie they expected to find there."[28] The idea that "freedom was free-er" in the towns was widespread.[29] For some former slaves the promise of freedom and safety was enough to attract them to a city occupied by Union troops, for others an added advantage lay in the opportunities that urban centers afforded for work, especially semi or unskilled work. Marrinda Jane Singleton, a former slave who had found her way to Norfolk, Virginia, described the expectations of her contemporaries who "found wurk in cities 'round ducks, on boats as cooks, waiters etc. As a rule dar was very few slaves whar didn't know how to cook and do dat house wurk."[30]

Paul D. Escott has analysed this evidence of slave behavior during and after the war in a more systematic way than Litwack. In his *Slavery Remembered* Escott tabulated the experiences of former slaves, as revealed in the series of WPA slave narratives (collected in the 1930s) both during and after slavery.[31] The results of his work, in so far as they relate to the subject of migration and the decision to leave the plantation or stay on after emancipation, are summarized in tables 1 and 2.

Table 1: Reported Reasons for Staying or Leaving (Percentages)[32]
(N=745)

Reason for Staying or Leaving	Percentage
Left to join the U.S. Army	3.2
Left to reunite family	20.4
Left because disliked master	19.0
Left to seek opportunity	3.9
Left to marry	2.1
Master forced them to leave	2.1
Left to rejoin good master	0.5
Left for other reasons	1.5
Liked master, stayed	27.8
Had good job, stayed	3.8
No alternative, stayed	4.0
Stayed for promised reward	0.7
Kept by master	0.7
Stayed for other reasons	0.5
Circumstances forced decision	9.8

Escott's analysis underlines the point made by Litwack that there were many reasons for leaving the plantation (or staying) and that "former slaves chose to manifest their freedom in many different ways, with each individual acting on his or her own set of priorities."[33]

It is also clear that there were just as many variations in the timing of the decision to leave.

Table 2: Timing of Decision to Stay with or Leave Master at End of War by Race of Interviewer

(Percentages)

Decision	White Interviewer (N=816)	Black Interviewer (N=248)
Left during the war	4.4	13.3
Left immediately	6.6	11.3
Left within one year	28.5	26.2
Left, time uncertain	9.9	13.3
Stayed 1 to 5 years	14.4	11.7
Stayed several years more	25.0	15.7
Stayed, time uncertain	9.9	5.6
Left, but returned	1.3	2.8

The figures in Table 2 must be treated with some caution, not least because they tend to suggest that former slaves were more likely to reveal negative feelings about their masters and their willingness to act upon those feelings to black interviewers. There was almost certainly a wide variation in the exact time at which individuals assumed they were free. For some it was the moment Yankee soldiers entered the vicinity of their plantations; for others it was the time of the Emancipation Proclamation, and so on.[34] Nevertheless, and importantly, Escott's analysis indicates that slaves weighed the decision to leave carefully before acting upon it.

The advantages of the approaches adopted by Litwack and Escott are that they enable us to see the range of individual motives which determined slave behavior during and after the Civil War and add a "behavioral" dimension to the study of black migration in that period. But each also has its limitations. The weaknesses of a broad brush approach are evident in the inability to distinguish between actions which took place in widely different circumstances, and in the lack of specific links between the size, timing and composition of particular migrant streams and those same circumstances. For example, they make little allowance for the presence or absence of Union or Confederate troops in different areas; or the different size and nature of plantations between areas; or differences in the age and sex composition of the migrants; or any number of factors which are not easily measured at such a general level. For a more inclusive and more accurate analysis of black migration we need to supplement those general

and aggregate pictures with more detailed case studies of specific migrations. Only then can we begin to offer answers to specific questions of
interest to historians of migration: who moved, when, how, and from
where? The remainder of this paper takes up those questions in the context of a case study of the migration of blacks into Washington, D.C., from
neighboring counties in Virginia and Maryland.[35]

Among the cities of the region depicted in Map 2 Washington, D.C.,
was the preeminent mecca for black migrants. In the decade after 1860
Washington's black population rose by 223 percent, outstripping the
numerical growth of the larger city of Baltimore. By century's end Washington's black population was the largest of any city in the United States.
Migration into Washington in the 1860s was crucial in shaping its black
community for decades to come. In the 1850s, as a result of repressive
measures against free blacks, the rate of growth of the black population
was markedly lower than that of the white population. The following
decade, however, saw a significantly greater growth rate among the blacks
that was also unique for the century. By 1870 blacks formed a major element in the population of the city. Washington's population in that year
was 32.5 percent black. With some minor fluctuations it remained at
approximately that level through to the end of the nineteenth century.[36]

In the 1860s Washington's black population grew at a steady rate in
both war and peacetime until about 1867, after which it slowed down.
The first attempt at an accurate estimate of the city's population after the
war was made in March 1866 when a census conducted by officials of the
Freedmen's Bureau placed the number of blacks then in the city at
27,287—up 16,304, or 148 percent, from the 1860 figure.[37] A more
detailed census taken in November the following year arrived at a total of
31,937 and the federal census enumerators in 1870 counted 35,455
blacks in the city of Washington.[38] Of those present in 1867, an average
of more than three and a half thousand had arrived each year between
1862 and 1865.[39] Despite a high rate of retention of antebellum residents, perhaps as few as 25 percent, and no more than 30 percent, of
blacks living in Washington in 1867 had been there seven years earlier.
The overwhelming majority of these newcomers to the city came from
the counties of Virginia and Maryland depicted in Map 2 and the fullest
record we have of who they were is contained in the records of the several
refugee or "contraband camps" that were set up in and around the city of
Washington to shelter them.[40]

The first and most obvious fact arising from an analysis of arrivals at
the camps is the extent to which the volume and point of origin of black
refugees was tied to military events in the surrounding countryside. There

were, of course, many circumstances under which former slaves made their way into the Washington area. Some stories were a testament to the determination and courage of individuals like Sarah Johnson, a seventy-year-old woman who walked alone from Leesburg, Virginia, in search of freedom. To avoid capture by Lee's troops she traveled thirty miles to Washington at night and hid out during the day.[41] Other migrants, most notably a group of 408 emigrants from the island of La Vache near Haiti who arrived at Camp Springdale in March 1864, seem to have found their way to the camps for reasons unrelated to the war.[42] For most, however, migration was a direct response to wartime events and this paper concentrates on the years 1863 and 1864 when the records of the refugee camps are most detailed. Maps 5 and 6 depict the county of origin of arrivals at the camps in those years. When taken together with the information in Figure 1 on the following page, which indicates the number of arrivals in each month, a fairly comprehensive picture of migration emerges.

In each year both the volume and source of migration were tied unmistakably to military events in the surrounding countryside. Map 4 illustrates the path of the Union army and the location of major battles in 1863 and other years. By comparing it with Map 5 it is clear that the same counties in northern Virginia where hostilities were concentrated were the major generators of migrants into the Washington area. The heaviest fighting occurred in May and June with the defeat of the Army of the Potomac at Chancellorsville and Lee's advance on to Gettysburg. That activity was matched by an upsurge in the number of new arrivals in May and June. They came primarily from those areas through which the Union armies marched in retreat—Culpeper, Madison, Fauquier and Loudon Counties. The largest number from any single county, 261 came from Culpeper County. Chancellorsville is located at the southeastern tip of Culpeper County. Sizeable numbers of newcomers continued to arrive from Maryland counties along the Potomac (Prince George, Charles and St Mary's) and smaller numbers came from similarly situated counties in Virginia (King George, Westmoreland and Northumberland). But for the most part the army remained the major influence on black migration from Virginia.

The year 1864 duplicates the 1863 pattern. Following a seasonal lull in migration in the winter of 1863–4 the number of new arrivals increased again in the Spring of 1864. Most of the early arrivals came from Maryland, particularly from neighboring Prince George County, but in June military events assumed a central role once more. The greatest influx of refugees occurred in that month when 1,466 persons entered the camps. Of those 1,466, over three-quarters came from Hanover, King William and Caroline Counties in Virginia. Between Wilderness and Spotsylvania in mid-May and Cold Harbor in June, Grant forced Lee back towards Richmond and the James River in one of the most decisive actions of the war. Following the influx associated with that campaign the number of new arrivals fell away dramatically in the three remaining months for which figures are available.

The key to understanding this migration lies in the complex evolution of United States Army policy relating to the employment of former slaves as laborers, and later soldiers in the Union war effort.[43] The impact of those policies, and particularly the decisions to conscript former slaves into army service, also helped determine who would come to Washington. This impact on migration can be seen in a comparison of the age distribution of those entering the camps in 1863 and 1864 with that of slaves in the major counties of origin in 1860. The similarity between the two distributions is striking—striking because it contradicts theories of migration which predict that migrants are usually single or young adults with fewer family ties than those at other stages of the life cycle.[44] The differences between the expected and actual patterns occur because the theory assumes a basically free migration. In fact, migration into Washington, particularly from Virginia, was subject to extensive control by the United States Army which increasingly "siphoned off" able-bodied men and either directed or left women and children to find their way to the refugee camps.[45]

Figure 1: Contraband Camp Arrivals
June 1862–September 1864

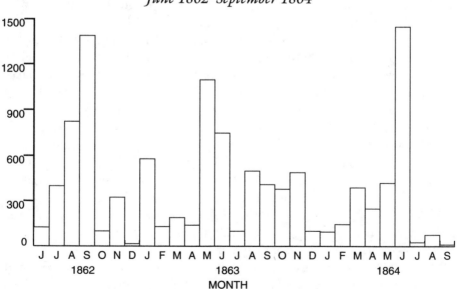

The camp records for 1862, before the service of blacks in or with the Union armies became widespread, indicate that the patterns of migration at that time more closely matched the expected pattern. Single men predominated among adult arrivals (17.7 percent of all arrivals), followed by married men (15.3 percent) and married women (13.8 percent). Children were the largest single group (44.1 percent) but formed a smaller proportion of total arrivals than they would in the months to follow. Adult males outnumbered women by three to two.[46] By mid-1863, after passage of the Conscription Act, the ratio of men to women had been reversed. Adult males had dropped to 22.6 percent of arrivals, and women had risen to 29 percent. The biggest drop was among single men, from 17.7 percent to 7.7 percent of total arrivals. The changes clearly reflected the evolution of the United States Army policies which altered the pattern and composition of black migration. A comparison of the age structure of 1863 and 1864 immigrants suggests that this pattern was accentuated in the latter year. As adult men were pressed into service in greater numbers the proportion of migrants of military age decreased and the proportion of children and older adults increased. It seems likely that the stream of migrants from Hanover and Caroline Counties in mid-1864 was composed of women and children whose husbands, fathers and brothers had been drafted into the army. The effects of this imbalance and others resulting from the particular form and process of migration into Washington were felt by the black community for many years and were reflected in a variety of economic and social problems which they fought to overcome.

The story of wartime migration into Washington is wider than the process revealed in the records of the refugee camps dotted around the city. It is impossible to determine exactly how many men and women passed through the city in search of freedom and security or how closely the experience of those who did not come under the umbrella of the "contraband" camps matched that of the eleven thousand or so who did. The evidence drawn from official government sources is largely silent on the movement of blacks around the countryside, save for the many letters and telegrams from army officers in the field reporting the large number of freedmen flocking into their lines. That evidence which is available, then, seems to confirm that for many migration was a two-stage process: slaves and former slaves who chose to exercise their freedom by leaving the plantation flocked in increasing numbers to Union army lines. Their subsequent destination was often the subject of a later decision and was not always one in which they had a major say.

Ultimately the story outlined here should be seen in the context of the wider picture painted by Litwack, Escott and others. Washington's "contraband" refugees highlight the central importance of migration in the transition to freedom and at the same time remind us of the range and complexity of motives and opportunities it reflects. In the final analysis the process of black migration can only be understood fully in the context of the specific set of circumstances which shaped and directed each of the many streams of movement across the country. Washington's migrants demonstrated that the decision to move was a positive one closely linked with concepts of freedom. They took advantage of opportunities to make freedom a reality when those opportunities arose. But unfortunately their story also demonstrates that they were deceived: that freedom was still an illusion and its limits were often still determined by others.

Map 1: Change in Black Population

Eastern United States, 1860–1870 (By State)

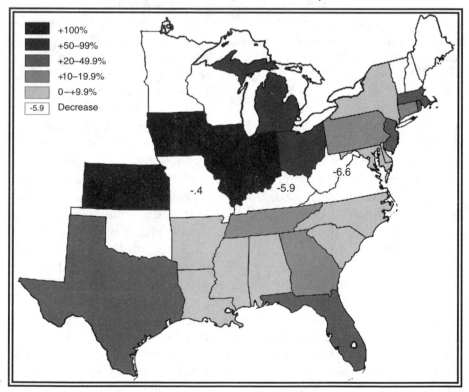

Map 2: Change in Black Population

Maryland and Eastern Virginia, 1860–1870 (By County)

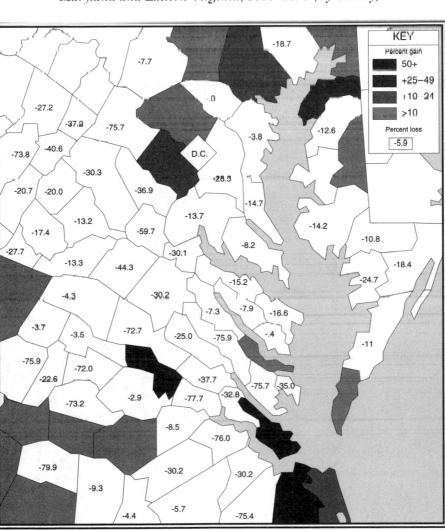

Map 3: Location Map

Maryland and Eastern Virginia

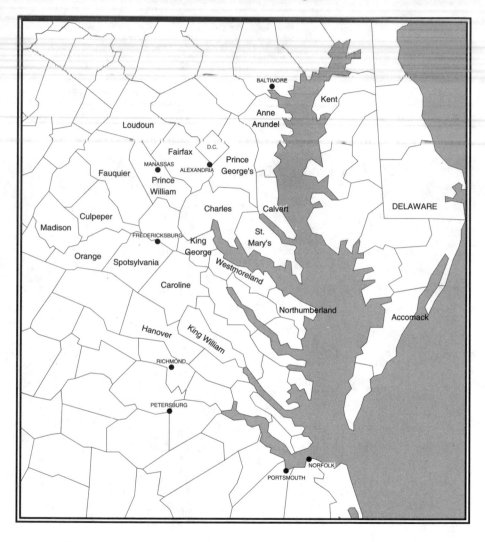

Map 4: Major Military Campaigns, 1862–1865

Maryland and Virginia

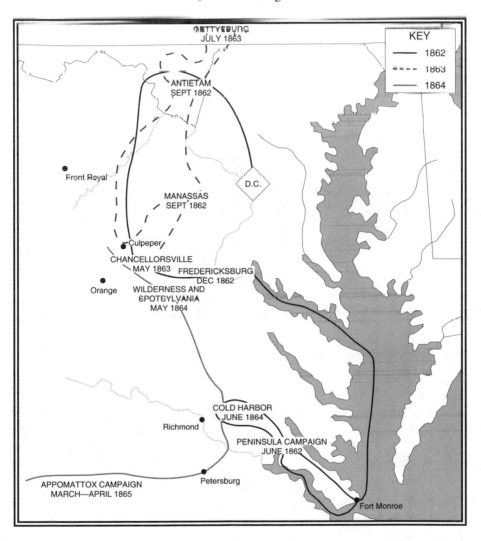

KEY

——	1862
- - -	1863
——	1864

GETTYSBURG
JULY 1863

ANTIETAM
SEPT 1862

Front Royal

D.C.

MANASSAS
SEPT 1862

Culpeper

CHANCELLORSVILLE
MAY 1863   FREDERICKSBURG
DEC 1862

Orange   WILDERNESS AND
SPOTSYLVANIA
MAY 1864

COLD HARBOR
JUNE 1864

Richmond

PENINSULA CAMPAIGN
JUNE 1862

APPOMATTOX CAMPAIGN   Petersburg
MARCH—APRIL 1865

Fort Monroe

Map 5: Contraband Camp Arrivals, 1863

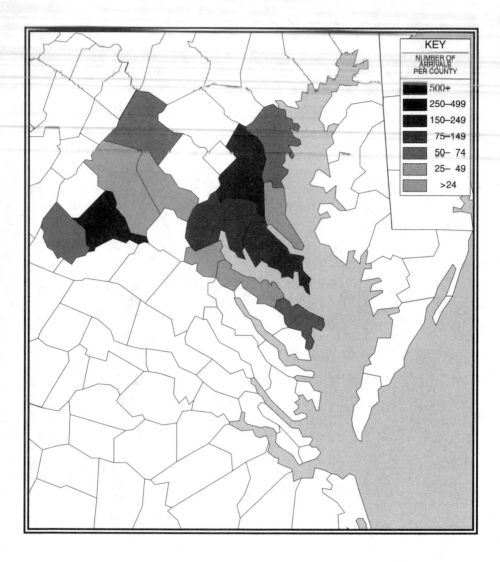

Map 6: Contraband Camp Arrivals, 1864

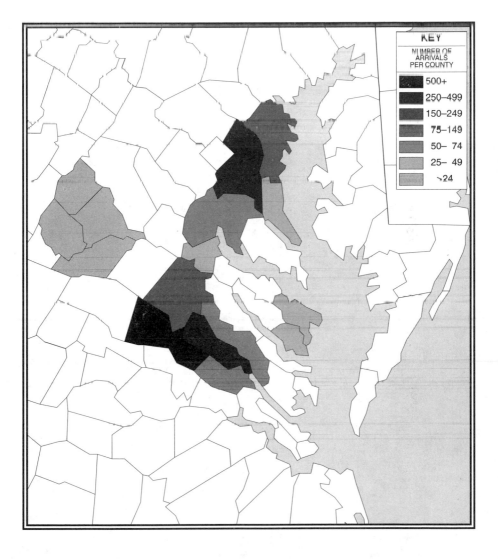

CHAPTER 7

━━━━━

Nashville's Fort Negley

A Symbol of Blacks' Involvement
with the Union Army

Bobby L. Lovett

TO TELL THE HISTORY of Fort Negley, the historian must relate the story of the Union Army's occupation of Nashville, the building of numerous fortifications and the involvement of local blacks in the building of the forts and filling of vital positions in the Union Army. Soon after the fall of forts Donelson and Henry, the Confederate Army of Tennessee retreated to Nashville. Upon the advice of engineers, however, the Confederate Army command and Governor Isham G. Harris gave orders to abandon Nashville. On February 22, 1862, the Army of Tennessee retreated southeastward to Murfreesboro. Confusion set in as citizens rushed to evacuate their belongings before the Yankees arrived in Nashville. The town's Negroes hid in order to avoid being forced to load and drive supply wagons; however, a few unlucky black residents were discovered in their hiding places and taken to Murfreesboro.[1]

During the earlier stages of the Civil War, the Confederate Army of Tennessee had attempted to use Negro labor from Kentucky and Middle Tennessee. But slave masters generally resisted the efforts to impress their expensive slaves for dangerous military duty. In June 1862, the Tennessee General Assembly tried to obtain military laborers by passing an Act to Draft Free Negroes as laborers; but Tennessee only had 7,300 free blacks, most of whom were too old, crippled, too young, or too unwilling to serve the Confederate military. Chief Engineer for the Army of Tennessee, J. F. Gilmer, attempted to "procure Negroes from their [Kentucky] masters to work on the entrenchments for defending the city of Nashville against land approach. . . .," but failed.[2]

At last, General Ulysses S. Grant's Union Army of the Ohio began to occupy Nashville on February 23, when the gunboat *Diana* docked at the foot of Broad Street. On February 25, the Sixth Ohio Volunteers' regimental band paraded down Broad playing "Hail Columbia," as slaves and Unionist residents danced in the street. In March 1862, President Abraham Lincoln appointed Senator Andrew Johnson of Tennessee as the Military Governor of occupied Tennessee. Johnson, a former tailor and East Tennessee slave master, assume the rank of Brigadier General for Tennessee Volunteer Forces. Elias Polk, a free Negro, went with a delegation of pro-Union citizens to Murfreesboro in order to accompany Johnson on the train to Nashville. Upon the Military Governor's arrival, crowds of Negroes, Unionists, and Federal soldiers cheered and lined the streets as Johnson led a parade in his honor. Those pro-Confederate citizens who had not fled the city watched in utter disgust as Yankees and runaway slaves took over their town.[3]

Governor Johnson was nervous and quite apprehensive of being kidnapped and hanged as a southern traitor. He began to pressure the Union Army and Secretary of War Edwin Stanton to fortify the town heavily with an enclosure of forts. Unlike their enemy predecessors, the Union Army engineers believed that Nashville could be defended against great odds with a ring of forts and a garrison of at least 6,000 men. The city was undulating, rocky, with beautiful, picturesque scenery, and surrounded, lying like a vast amphitheater, by a range of hills. It occupied six square miles, three miles long by two miles wide.[4] During the late summer of 1862, General Don Carlos Buell took his army out of Nashville in pursuit of the Confederate Army into Kentucky, leaving 6,000 troops under General James S. Negley to hold Nashville.[5] Johnson now began to demand immediate erection of fortifications for the city. He tried to convince Lincoln and Stanton that he was better able to command and position Nashville's troops than was General Negley. However, neither Buell nor any other Federal official was about to risk the charge of a Union Army garrison in Johnson's hands. Yet, General Buell did respond to the Governor's sense of urgency and also realized that the Confederate Army could double back and take the city. To make matters worse, indeed, it was rumored that Confederate cavalry units under Nathan Bedford Forrest might attack the city during the late summer of 1862. Buell ordered Captain James Sinclair Morton, a West Point graduate of 1851, from Philadelphia, to take a detachment of men and go to Nashville to help Negley fortify the city. Buell told Morton: "We should be in the edge of the city to command the principal throughfares and other prominent points"; Buell also sought to quiet Johnson's fears by ordering Morton, to "devise some defenses also around the capitol building."[6]

Captain Morton was born in 1829, the son of Dr. Samuel G. Morton of Philadelphia. He was among the best of Civil War military engineers and was later promoted to Brigadier General. His command was called the Pioneer Brigade, which was equipped with its own arms, ammunition, clothing, axes, hatchets, saws, files, spades, shovels, picks, hammers, augers, nails, spikes, rope, wagons, mules, and whatever was needed to go in advance of the army in order to prepare or repair bridges, fortifications, railroads, and roads.[7]

After forcing the Confederate Army to retreat from Kentucky toward Murfreesboro, Buell wired the Nashville command on August 6, 1862, and ordered them to call upon local slave masters for hands to be employed in Morton's Fort Negley project. With the Confederate Army less than 100 miles to the east, Morton assured General Buell that the planned fort would be secure "against any attack except regular approaches and investments."[8] Of course, the Union Army under General Buell was supposed to catch the Confederate Army before it could attack Nashville. But the Confederate Army commanders were masters of deception and well-schooled in the tactics of evading the clutches of the numerically superior Union Army.[9]

For this reason, among others, the completion of Nashville's military fortifications was rushed ahead with all deliberate speed. Morton wired Buell: "I lost 48 hours trying to get Negroes, teams, tools, cooking utensils, and provisions. Only 150 Negroes so far, no tools, teams, etc. I wanted to employ 825 Negroes by the 11th." But Morton found that he needed about 2,000 blacks, including local free Negroes, to complete Fort Negley. On August 12, Colonel John F. Miller, Post Commander, ordered the Nashville *Daily Union* and the Nashville *Dispatch* newspapers to print notices that rebel slaveholders of Davidson County were to supply 1,000 slaves with "daily subsistence and axes, spades or picks with terms of payment to be made known by Certificates of Labor, which will be furnished after the service shall have been performed."[10] Part of Morton's problem was that he had no money to pay the local blacks who wanted to be paid by the day; whereas, ironically, they had worked for nothing as slaves. In order to pay the laborers and keep them on the project, General Negley issued Special Orders No. 17 (October 17, 1862), which ordered "a known contributor to the rebel cause to be required to advance the money to Captain Morton."[11] Unionist citizens, a minority in Nashville, cheered the Negley decision and hoped that all rebel sympathizers would be similarly punished.

It was known, indeed, that local slave masters tried every trick in the book to keep slaves from coming into contact with the Union Army. The slaves were told that the Yankees were cannibals who would eat them alive. Until blacks learned better, Yankee cavalry often had to run some rural slaves down and force them to walk to the Nashville labor camps.[12]

Notwithstanding, Nashville was an ideal place to find skilled blacksmiths, carpenters, coopers, shoemakers, stone masons, and wagonmakers. In spite of slavery, local blacks resided in the center of town, mostly integrated amongst their masters and patrons. A small concentration of prosperous free blacks resided east of Spruce Street (8th Avenue), between Crawford and Cedar (Charlotte) streets. Nashville had the largest free black population of any Tennessee town and three semi-independent black church congregations including First Colored Baptist Church which was pastored by a free black named Nelson Merry.

Meanwhile, Morton designed some temporary defenses for the city. General Negley positioned some regiments of cavalry, which were sent to the city for that purpose, around the town along with several batteries of artillery. Siege guns and rifle pits occupied South Nashville, and the fires of Federal camps lit up the night sky in every direction. To feed the growing number of Negro laborers and soldiers, Negley took his army south to Franklin, Tennessee, and foraged 18,000 bushes of corn, as well as bacon, cattle, flour, hams, and horses. It took twenty railroad cars to transport the loot.[13]

Morton forged ahead with the construction of Fort Negley, designed to be the pivot point of Nashville's defenses. On November 7, the 1st Michigan Engineer Corps made their way into the city to build three bridges over Mill Creek in order to reopen the Nashville-Chattanooga Railroad, allowing additional supplies to flow into the city. Nashville now had 11,000 troops in town, enough to provide detachments of cavalry to round up more black laborers and to guard them against Confederate raiders. The Union cavalry surrounded the Colored Baptist Church during its services and marched the able-bodied members of the congregation off to the Fort Negley construction site on St. Cloud Hill.[14] Julius Casey, a former slave, recalled that the Federals took two of his older brothers and one sister. Another former slave, Francis Batson, remembered that the Union Army's constant raiding and labor impressment caused the young black children to become frightened and to run when they saw the "blue mans" (Union soldiers) coming.[15]

During the course of construction, long, impressive lines of wagons went back and forth carrying away felled trees and blasted rock. The blacks chopped St. Cloud Hill completely bare of trees in order to give the fort's guns an unimpaired view of the surrounding terrain and to provide no places for the enemy to hide. Children fourteen to fifteen years old, women, and men were camped on the St. Cloud Hill, some living in tents and others sleeping out in the open. Women and young adults pushed wheelbarrows, cooked the food for the laborers, washed clothes, and frequently served as teamsters for wagons. Black stone masons blasted the rock, fashioned the stone, laid the walls, and dug the underground magazines.[16] Curious citizens could clearly see the construction site from a point near the Murfreesboro Pike.

Although the blacks were often forced to labor without adequate food, warm clothing, shelter, or pay, they were willing to defend their creation with their lives. On November 5, 1862, before the fort was completed, General Nathan Bedford Forrest ordered the city to surrender. With approximately 3,000 men, he attacked the city near the Lebanon and Murfreesboro pikes, east of Fort Negley. The Negro laborers sent a delegation to the officer of the day and asked to be armed for the protection of themselves and the fort. Their request for guns was denied; but the Army allowed them to make a symbolical stand armed with axes, shovels, and spades.[17]

The Federals, nevertheless, had sufficient forces to defeat the Confederates. Rachel Carter, a pro-Confederate resident, wrote in her diary on November 5, 1862, that one of the artillery shells from the fight "struck Mrs. Trimble's smokehouse."[18] In fact, Mrs. Trimble's smokehouse was east of the guns of Fort Negley and in the general vicinity of today's Cameron-Trimble Bottom, Nashville's oldest black neighborhood. As night came and a drizzling rain fell on November 5, Forrest's cavalry fled to the east, leaving the city in the hands of the Union Army and its black allies. Some 23 Confederate soldiers were captured, and the Union Army suffered 26 men wounded and 19 men missing.[19]

At the least, this demonstration convinced the Union Army's Nashville command that black labor was vital for the release of white soldiers from time-consuming labor chores. By using Negro laborers, the Army could put more white soldiers *Au fort du combat*. Before, the Army allowed slave masters to search the camps and reclaim their runaway slaves. As late as August 7, 1862, for example, the Nashville *Daily Union,* a pro-Union newspaper, published a notice for two twenty-three-year-old runaways named Foster and Edmund who belonged to Dr. John L. Cheatham and his brother, William S. Cheatham. Slaves were yet worth $300 to $1,000 a piece. A short time earlier, Davidson County Sheriff Jim Hinton ran an advertisement in the local papers that read as follows:

July 18, 1862. A Negro man, who says his name is Henry and belongs to Matt Scruggs, Bedford County, Tennessee, age about 28, 5 feet 7 inches high, weighs 155 pounds, color black. The owner is requested to come forward, prove property and pay charges as the law requires.[20]

On February 27, 1863, the Nashville Union Army command issued an order prohibiting the return of fugitive slaves to their masters. Further, the Nashville Provost Marshall threatened to arrest any law officer caught arresting Negroes to be sold or transported to masters.[21]

Nearly a year later, on February 4, 1864, the Union Army ordered Captain Ralph Hunt of the 1st Kentucky Volunteers to establish a contraband camp in the area of the Chattanooga-Nashville Railroad Depot.[22] A larger contraband camp was built on the east side of the Cumberland River, north of Edgefield and near the Louisville-Nashville Railroad tracks; it initially held over 2,000 Negroes. A third contraband camp was located south of Broad Street, between Front and Cherry streets; it was called "Black Bottom." A former slave, Joseph Fowley, recalled that "they had contraband camps, and men, women and children had to be guarded to keep the rebels from carrying them back to the white folks."[23]

After a short time, the Federal government investigated the notoriously inhuman conditions of Nashville's contraband camps. Although camp superintendent Ralph Hunt was accused of stealing supplies meant for the blacks and selling them in his downtown store, nothing ever came of the charges. Attempts were made to "colonize surplus Negroes" on locally abandoned farms. This colonization effort was similar to the Freedmen's Bureau's 1865 relocation program in Memphis which was designed to force thousands of unemployed blacks to leave the urban camps and relocate in the countryside where the cotton crop was suffering from lack of pickers. Undoubtedly, such a relocation effort accounted, in part, for Nashville's Negro population not rising above 10,000 during the war years.

At any rate, the contraband camps and the influx of black laborers into town served the Union Army's purposes by 1865 and at little cost to the government. Between August 1862 and April 1863, for example, the Army paid black workers only $13,648.00 of the $85,858.50 that was owed to them. One author, Peter Maslowski, who has studied Union military occupation of Nashville, estimates that between 600 and 800 blacks died working on fortifications in the Nashville area during the whole occupation period.[24]

By December 7, 1862,[25] Fort Negley was completed. Captain Morton's report included praise for the blacks:

To the credit of the colored population be it said, they worked manfully and cheerfully, with hardly an exception, and yet lay out upon the works at night under armed guard, without blankets and eating only army rations. They worked in squads, each gang choosing their own officers; one was often amused to hear the Negro captains call out: 'You boys over there, let them picks fall easy, or they might hurt somebody.'[76]

The creation of the Negro laborers and the Union Army engineers was impressive. The topmost structure was constructed of twelve-foot erect timbers. On the parapet surrounding the outside of the stockade, the artillery rested on carriages which rolled about on smooth planked flooring. This flat area for the artillery operations was protected by three-foot-high ramparts, nine-foot-thick embankments of earth walled with stone. The ramparts on the east and west side of the stockade had projected redans. Below the east and west ramparts and parapets were scarps, steep slopes, which were in turn protected by a glacis, a smooth, gentle slope. At the bottom of these hills on the left and right side of the south section of the fort were two groups of four blockhouses, which were really bombproofs topped with railroad iron, timbers, and dirt. Each blockhouse had embrasures or openings for riflemen's guns. The bastioned blockhouses were protected by a salient system that projected out from the fortification. Above the bastion was a stoned scarp, protecting the first two blockhouses, an entrenchment connecting the two parallel blockhouses, another stoned scarp rising above the entrenchment, and the other two blockhouses rising above the scarp, with a passage way between the blockhouses. The fort's entrance was on the north side with a gentle slope; visitors passed a sharp salient, a gateway, a timber-structured guardhouse, and a loop-holed bombproof flanking the gate. And on top of each corner of the wooden stockade were rounded gun turrets.

Adapted to the local situation, Fort Negley was a copy of an old European architectural system, a repeat of the Castillo de San Marcos, built by the Spaniards of St. Augustine, Florida. San Marcos used a bastion system which was developed by sixteenth-century European military engineers. The fort was polygonal. Eight lower salients, four on the east and west sides, projected from the fort; each of these salients had broad parapets apparently for infantrymen, stone scarps, and glacis. Again, each set of four blockhouses had a salient; thus the fort resembled a many-sided star. There was no "dead" space in the design, and every inch of ground could be covered by defenders. The enemy had to climb the bastions, scale the glacis, jump over the ramparts, cross the parapets, climb another glacis, scale a scarp, jump over another rampart and fight the defenders behind the main parapets and ramparts, before setting siege to the troops and horses behind the stockade. But if the enemy chose to come in from the south side, he had to face the murderous rifle fire from the blockhouses as well.

The entire fort consumed a staggering 62,500 cubic feet of stone and 18,000 cubic yards of dirt. It occupied a space of 600 by 300 feet and claimed 51 acres of St. Cloud Hill. It was 620 feet above sea level, some 150 feet above the surrounding terrain, and two miles south of the city limits.[27] A typical garrison for Fort Negley was described in 1864 as the "12th Indiana Battery and Battery C of the 1st Tennessee Light Artillery Volunteers." Occasionally, various infantry regiments camped on the lower part of the hill, including the 105th Illinois Volunteers and the 33rd Indiana Volunteers.[28]

Fort Negley's first major military role was in the Battle of Nashville, December 15–17, 1864. After taking Atlanta, General William T. Sherman sent General George H. Thomas and 20,000 troops hurrying back to Tennessee to set up a defense against the Confederate Army of Tennessee which was moving across Northern Georgia and Northern Alabama. Inevitably it was headed for Nashville, in hopes of drawing Sherman back from his intended march through Georgia. Fort Negley became the pivot point of Thomas' defense at Nashville. Thousands of soldiers from Wisconsin, Illinois, Indiana, Ohio, and other northern states camped near St. Cloud Hill while dining on boiled beef, beans, baker's bread, coffee, and occasionally some rabbits, squirrels, turkeys, and other wild game. Some of the soldiers thought that Nashville was "quite a nice place for the South."[29] Thomas collected nearly 50,000 troops by obtaining reinforcements from Chattanooga, Missouri, and some 13,000 black troops.

Thomas made heavy use of local blacks as forced laborers. He used the labor organization techniques that had been perfected by the building of Fort Negley and the building of the Northwestern Military Railroad. Between August 1863 and March 1864, Governor Johnson and the Union Army impressed thousands of blacks into labor battalions of 98 persons each—with white officers, a cavalry escort, and Negro labor captains—to build a railroad from Nashville seventy-five miles to Johnsonville on the east bank of the Tennessee River. Fully 20 percent of the black laborers were women, and the ages of the black laborers ranged from 14 to 55. The completion of the Northwestern Railroad made it logistically possible for Sherman to launch his famous march through Georgia. Union steamers brought supplies to Johnsonville, where they were shipped on cars to Nashville warehouses, and on to Sherman's staging area at Chattanooga. Thomas sought to resurrect this system in order to expand Nashville's fortifications. One former slave remembered being captured by the Federals as he made his escape from a Murfreesboro plantation. He recalled that General Thomas seldom was able to provide the black laborers with sufficient rations, and he added:

> We would kill a beef, cut off the head, take out the insides, skin it, and cut the meat into big chunks. Then we would put our meat on a long-forked pole, one end buried in the ground and the other slanting up and pointing towards the fire. It would make me awful sick at times, and I would throw up a lot.[30]

General Thomas' engineers had a problem in recruiting an adequate supply of black labor. For instance, many of Middle Tennessee's black males between the age of eighteen and forty-five were mustered into the military, leaving few able-bodied Negroes for labor duties. On September 10, 1863, a Bureau for the Recruitment of United States Colored Troops was established at 38 Cedar Street (Charlotte Street). Similarly, recruitment stations were established at Clarksville, Columbia, Lynneville, Murfreesboro, Pulaski, Shelbyville, Tullahoma, and Wartrace. Even the black laborers who had completed the Northwestern Railroad project were marched to their camps, sworn in to Federal service, armed, and trained as soldiers. Consequently, the Davidson County area contributed to the filling of five infantry and two artillery units, including the 2nd U.S. Colored Light Artillery Battery A and the 9th U.S. Colored Heavy Artillery Battalion, which used 380 free black Ohioans to complete the organization. Additionally, two infantry regiments were organized at the Clarksville contraband camps; the units relied heavily on recruiting runaway slaves from Kentucky. The 14th U.S. Colored Infantry Regiment was organized at the Gallatin contraband camp and recruited slaves from Robertson, Sumner, and Wilson counties. Four infantry regiments were organized at Pulaski's contraband camps and consisted of so many runaways from Northern Alabama that the regiments were at first named the 1st, 2nd, 3rd, and 4th Alabama Infantry Regiments of African Descent; but they were later renamed the 101st, 106th, 110th, and 111th regiments of the United States Colored Troops.[31]

Equally important, after finding the local agricultural economy to be devastated because of the scarcity of black labor and pro-Union citizens lustily protesting their financial ruin, on November 10, 1863, the army command at Nashville issued orders to prevent this growing economic-political disaster by directing Union officers to take no more than "one-half of any loyal master's slaves."[32] For even Sherman took two Middle

Tennessee black regiments and black laborers to be used as supply troops and teamsters during his long march through Georgia. Therefore, Thomas' engineers found few black laborers for impressment. As a result, on November 1, 1864, General Thomas issued orders to recall black soldiers and white garrisons from their Middle Tennessee posts. These troops, along with available black laborers, worked on the fortifications.[88]

Thomas' job was made easier because of the existing fortifications that had been built by Captain Morton in 1862. These fortifications included the capitol building which had been fortified and named Fort Johnson, Fort Casino which overlooked Fort Negley, and Fort Morton which in turn protected Fort Casino. In contrast to Fort Negley, these forts were smaller and consisted of earth parapets, timber-reinforced blockhouses, crushed stone glacis, and dozens of light artillery pieces. Nevertheless, the area these forts would help to defend was very important to the Union. The District of Nashville included the defense of the Nashville-Chattanooga Railroad as far as the Duck River, the Nashville-Decatur Railroad as far south as Columbia, the Northwestern Railroad southwest to the Tennessee River, the Louisville-Nashville Railroad to the Kentucky state line, and the posts of McMinnville, Clarksville, Fort Donelson, and Nashville—the apex of the iron quadrangle.

From November 1 to December 1, 1864, the black workers and the Union Army soldiers struggled through heavy rains to complete the ring of forts. Fort Morton, situated on Curry's Hill near Granny White Pike and Jackson Street, was reinforced. Next in line to the north, Fort Houston was built near Belmont and Broad streets, and named after Russell Houston, a strong Union supporter, who allowed his home to be blown up to make way for the fort. Fort Houston was designed to hold over 35 guns and to protect the Charlotte Pike. A small fort was built on Hill 210 by the 182nd Ohio Volunteers in an octagon shape, with blockhouses and underground magazines to protect the Northwestern Railroad and warehouses in West Nashville. Fort Dan McCook was built just east of Fort Negley; it held 26 guns for the cover of the main fort and the Nashville-Decatur Railroad. On the present site of Fisk University's Jubilee Hall, Fort Gillem was constructed (later named Fort Sill). Fort Gillem was built by a native of Jackson County, Tennessee, General Alvin Gillem, and the 10th Tennessee Volunteer Regiment. Fort Gillem was about 120 feet square with narrow ditches, walled with stone, 6 feet high, with emplacements for 8 artillery pieces. North of Fort Gillem was Fort W. D. Whipple (Redoubt Donaldson); between Forts Gillem and Whipple was Hyde's Ferry Fort (Fort Garesche) on the south bank of the Cumberland River, and built by the 82nd Ohio Volunteers in November 1864. The 15th Illinois Volunteer Regiment built a small redoubt on the north side of the Cumberland River in order to cover the Louisville-Nashville Railroad. Fort Negley was expanded at a cost of $20,000 by adding the interior double-cased blockhouses and entrenchments. The Inspector of fortifications, General Z. B. Tower, wrote to Thomas with this request: "If I can secure a black regiment, some 200 men, which have been promised, it will be a great gain."[34] By November 30, over 10,000 black troops were working on the fortifications and carrying out reconnaisance patrols on alternate days beginning December 1 and ending December 13. The entire fortifications project cost an estimated $300,000 and $130,000 for Fort Negley. The city of Nashville was enclosed within a ring of twenty-three forts, redoubts, and fortified bridges.[35]

From September to October 1864, Hood's army encountered much resistance from the black and white Union garrisons at Decatur and Sulphur Trestle, Alabama, and Pulaski and Johnsonville, Tennessee. Many black soldiers lost their lives and hundreds more were shipped as prisoners to Mobile, Alabama. Further, Hood's army of 36,000 caught General John Schofield's Union Army of 23,000 at Franklin and forced it to fight. Although the federals lost 2,000 men, the Confederates lost 6,000 men and 6 of their best generals; moveover, while the enemy slept on that night of November 30, 1864, Schofield abandoned his dead and wounded and sneaked across the Harpeth River and arrived safely in Nashville, thirty miles away, on December 1. After receiving Schofield's reinforcements, General Thomas had nearly twice Hood's troop strength.

And yet, General Hood unwisely turned his battered army toward Nashville instead of retreating into the deep South. Hood could not turn back because he had slept on too many dreams and had made a personal pledge to President Jefferson Davis to carry out a successful campaign. As the Army of Tennessee approached Nashville on December 2, they saw a formidable fortress gleaming with new forts, behind which more than 50,000 Union troops waited. The gods cursed the Confederates by blasting the Nashville area with a winter storm that left glistening ice. A Maury County Confederate soldier said: "being in range of the guns of Fort Negley, we were not allowed to have fires at night." During the day, however, an unspoken truce allowed both sides to gather firewood.[36]

On the cold, foggy morning of December 15, 1864, the ice melted and the guns of Fort Negley came alive to signal the start of the Battle of Nashville. Out of mist came the dark, shining faces of seven regiments of Colored Troops, who advanced on the enemy's right flank near Brown's Creek—east of the guns of Fort Negley. Patsy Hyde, a former slave, recalled the moment: "When dey wuz fighting at Fort Negley, de cannons would jar our house. The soldiers' band played on Capitol Hill: 'Rally round the flag boys, rally round the flag.'" Another slave remembered "when the Yankees on Capitol Hill gave the signal—God bless your soul— it sounded like the cannons would tear the world to pieces. I could hear the big shells humming as they came; they cut off trees like a man cutting woods with a scythe."[37]

Two days later, the Confederate Army was in mass retreat. They left behind 10,000 prisoners and 68 pieces of artillery. One Negro soldier, Joseph Fowley [Farley], who joined the Union Army along with his father at the Clarksville contraband camp, recalled the Confederate soldiers were captured just as bare-footed "as they could be." He said: "I brought my gun from Nashville right here to Clarksville and kept it for 25 years."[38] The Negro troops took part in the pursuit of Hood's army as far south as central Alabama. Nashville's 17th Colored Troops Regiment won personal recognition for bravery from General Thomas and the New York *Times* (December 19, 1864). The Battle of Nashville was one of the last major military actions of a dying Confederacy that surrendered in April 1865.

What some men create, other men let weather and die. In short, Fort Negley and its sister forts were not monuments that a defeated South wanted to preserve. The forts were gradually forgotten and allowed to go into ruins. In 1865, Fort Negley was renamed Fort Harker; and in 1867, the Union Army abandoned the fort. Fort Harker became the secret meeting place for the Nashville Den of the Ku Klux Klan, which was active until 1869. In that year the Nashville Klan defied a government ban against public demonstrations, marched through the streets to Fort Negley where they burned their robes and officially disbanded.[39] Until the late 1890s, citizens took wagons and streetcars out to the fort at Chestnut and Ridley streets and held Sunday picnics just as in prewar days.

Years later, during the Great Depression, Fort Negley was restored and opened to the public. The Works Progress Administration provided funds to put Davidson County's unemployed to work in a restoration project. According to the Nashville *Tennessean* (January 31, 1936), the Fort Negley restoration project became one of the top WPA programs in the state. When the WPA workers finished the project in 1937, they left a crudely chiseled stone at the entrance, which read: "Fort Negley, Restored by the WPA, 1936." The Tennessee WPA Federal Writers' Project, which was designed to put unemployed writers to work, compiled histories of the state's forts, including a two-page overview of the history of Fort Negley.[40] The restored fort was a city park until 1941, with a "museum." The WPA workers attempted also to restore the subterranean magazines; they built some stone walkways to make the fort and the "museum" more accessible to visitors. A drainage ditch, covered the natural stone, encircled the bottom of the hill. Air photographs that were taken in 1941 and preserved by the Tennessee Department of Conservation revealed a road of rough gravel and a parking lot on the north side near the entrance of the fort.[41]

With the coming of World War II the fort was forgotten and allowed to be overgrown by weeds and other vegetation. Not until the Civil War Centennial celebration of 1964 did the Nashville Committee for the Civil War Centennial include a tour of the old fort, and local college professors came out to speak on the history of the fort. In 1975, the Metro Historical Commission made application to have the fort placed on the National Historic Register.[42] On May 14, 1979, according to the Nashville *Tennessean*, the Metro Historical Commission and the Council on Abandoned Military Posts jointly suggested that the city restore the fort. In August 1980, a feasibility study was completed for the Metro Historical Commission with the recommendation that the fort be made into a recreational historic park at a projected cost of $145,521.38.[43]

Though covered with vines and trees, and hidden from easy view, Fort Negley continued to serve as a monument to local Afro-American and Civil War history. The fortress and it sister forts served as symbols of the uneasy alliance between the Union Army and local blacks in their successful campaign to preserve the Union and destroy slavery. Consequently, much history was hidden beneath Fort Negley and its sister fortifications, including the lost histories of thousands of black laborers, the contributions of 13,000 black Union soldiers, and the blood and tears of thousands of black women.

In brief, the Fort Negley project was the Union Army's first heavy use of local black labor. It set the precedent for using black laborers on all large Middle Tennessee Union military projects. Such use, one might reflect, made the Union officers realize the utility value of maintaining contraband camps—ready sources of black laborers and Negro soldiers. Indeed, the Union Army fully utilized both in winning the war. Hence, the influx of Negroes into Nashville doubled the black population between 1862 and 1865.

Finally, one might argue that the Union Army's labor system, which was first induced by the need to build Fort Negley, the Northwestern Railroad, and other military projects, acted as a catalyst for the development of black Nashville communities. Ironically, the Union Army's efforts to control the local Negro population for military purposes caused a disintegration of antebellum controls over slaves and free blacks. Freed at last from the legal restraints of black codes and slave codes, the free blacks and the former slaves built communities in Nashville and Edgefield that were complete with economic, political, and social institutions including a black-owned drugstore, a black-edited newspaper (the *Colored Tennessean,* 1865–1866), and a branch of the Freedmen's Savings and Trust Company bank. In 1865 the Union Army and the Freedmen's Bureau attempted to force thousands of Negroes to relocate on rural farms; however, the black migration into Nashville continued into the twentieth century. On the whole, although the Union Army occupied Nashville in 1862 without any intention of becoming involved in the social and political questions of slavery and Negro affairs, the Union Army and its agencies served as grudging agents for social change in Nashville and paradoxically were responsible for the genesis of ghettozing blacks due to segregating and concentrating them into local contraband camps.

CHAPTER 8

Black Violence and White Response

Louisiana, 1862

William F. Messner

A CURIOUS DUALITY MARKED ANTEBELLUM thought regarding the black slave: the black image was a mixture of Sambo and Nat Turner, fawning simpleton and flaming revolutionary. White Americans explained this apparent anomaly in terms of the acculturation process which the plantation regimen imposed upon all slaves. By nature blacks were savage brutes, but through contact with the higher civilization of the white South the African had been domesticated. As long as the discipline of the white man was secure, the slave would remain a Sambo; but remove the authority of the master and blacks would revert to type as bloodthirsty savages.[1] Although this pattern of thought was not peculiar to the South, in that region its influence was particularly pervasive, for the southerner's belief in the black man's violent potential tended to reinforce the widely held opinion that a profitable production of staples could only be accomplished through the maintenance of a stable labor force. Slavery, therefore, had the complementary functions of ensuring white control over a potentially subversive minority population and of maximizing profits by the stabilization of labor.

The outbreak of civil war in 1861 sparked among whites a fear of imminent black violence, and in southern war zones the exodus of slaves from plantations accompanied by sporadic acts of servile violence only sharpened in the white mind the image of the manic Afro-American. In Louisiana especially the racial stability secured by the slave system shattered beneath the weight of the Federal assault on New Orleans in the spring of 1862, and the resulting turmoil convinced both native whites and Federal military officials of the necessity for establishing mechanisms to check the black threat to law and order. While most southerners favored a reinstitution of the slavery regime, Federal military officials during 1862 devised a series of contraband programs which stabilized the racial situation by placing blacks under white control and which also aided the Union war effort. Prompted initially by the white fear of black violence, these programs served as precursors for future Federal efforts among the freedmen of the Southwest during the Civil War and Reconstruction.[2]

As soon as Federal warships appeared at the mouth of the Mississippi River early in 1862 plantation owners along the coast of Louisiana and Mississippi began to take precautions against the feared uprising of their slaves. Whites increased security measures, issued fewer passes for travel, and resorted more often to the whip. So fearful were planters of black violence that they refused to allow their slaves to congregate in large numbers even for such vital functions as repairing crevasses in the levee.[3] White fears were seemingly justified as blacks began to escape from their owners and to make their way by rowboat to the Federal staging area on Ship Island.[4] Other slaves bided their time until the Union assault on New Orleans was completed in May 1862. Believing the Union army had come to free them, slaves in the immediate vicinity of the city fled from their plantations and flocked into Union camps surrounding New Orleans. At Camp Parapet, just north of the city, 450 black refugees resided less than a month after the arrival of Union troops, and their number swelled to over a thousand by the end of the summer.[5]

Federal military officials were perplexed by the black exodus. "What shall I do with my niggers?" asked the hard-pressed commander at Fort Macomb.[6] "I am placed in an awkward dilemma," complained the commander at Fort Saint Philip; "I have no authority to feed them [the slaves] . . . or send them away. I cannot have them in the fort, and know not what to do."[7] A New Hampshire officer noted in his diary that the blacks were "coming into camp by the hundred and are a costly curse. They should be kept out or set at work, or freed or colonized or sunk or something."[8] The sentiments of an enlisted man were expressed in a letter from a private in the Fourth Wisconsin Volunteers. "Potatoes are knee high, & beans to the top of the poles," he wrote from Baton Rouge. "It is a nice country if it were not for the negroes."[9]

Accompanying the exodus of blacks from plantations were incidents of black violence which solidified in the white mind the image of the barbaric black man freed from the restraints of white discipline. During the summer reports abounded concerning black unrest in the parishes of southern Louisiana. "[T]here is an uneasy feeling among the slaves," reported a correspondent of the New York *Times* in late July; "they are undoubtedly becoming insubordinate, and I cannot think that another sixty days can pass away without some sort of demonstration."[10] Three weeks later the same reporter wrote that the slaves in two nearby parishes were in a state of "semi-insurrection."[11] The correspondent of the New York *Herald* concurred in these conclusions. "There is no doubt that the negroes, for more than fifty miles up the river, are in a state of insubordination," he reported from New Orleans. "The country is given to pillage and desolation. . . . The slaves refuse obedience and cannot be compelled to labor."[12] On a Plaquemines Parish estate the owner recorded the following disturbing scene: "We have a terrible state of affairs here negroes refusing to work and women all in their houses. The negroes have erected a gallows in the quarters and give as an excuse for it that they are told they must drive their master . . . off the plantation . . . and that then they will be free."[13] On a neighboring plantation the slaves had already driven off the overseer and taken over the estate for their own use, and on another place blacks killed an overseer who had beaten slaves for refusing to work.[14] Frustrated in their own attempts at quelling the racial turmoil, slaveowners turned to the Union army as the only means for restoring order in the parishes.[15]

The tide of racial turmoil extended even into New Orleans. On the outskirts of the city violent confrontations often occurred between police and black refugees attempting to enter Union lines. Disgusted with such militant actions, the New Orleans *Daily Picayune* declared in July 1862 that the slaves had "become impudent, disobedient and reckless. This morning fifteen, armed with clubs and cane knives, came up from a plantation below the city."[16] Two weeks later a New Orleans citizen noted in his diary that "late last night & early this morning there was a speck of servile war in the lower part of the city." Forty slaves had overpowered the police and were only routed when Federal troops arrived on the scene.[17] Once inside the city the behavior of blacks improved very little. Police reports for the Third District of New Orleans reflect the racial instability which gripped the city. Arrests of slaves accused of impudent and violent behavior were daily occurrences during the summer, and a constant stream of fugitive bondsmen flowed in and out of the city's jails.[18] Especially disturbing to whites was the frequency with which police arrested slaves for insulting and even assaulting their owners. One such incident was recorded by the *Picayune:* "A savage old nigger named Ben, forgetting all past benefits conferred upon him, was brought into court for insulting his mistress. Among other disloyal expressions the old rascal said that he wanted to get arrested, for then he could become a soldier, fight his mistress, and do what he pleased. He was sent to prison for three months."[19] Disturbances such as this confirmed the *Picayune*'s opinion that "Recent events have made many of the negroes in this city and neighborhood almost unmanageable."[20]

The Union commander charged with the responsibility for restoring order to the Gulf Department was Major General Benjamin Franklin Butler.[21] At first glance Butler appears to have been an unlikely choice for the command of the Union expedition against New Orleans. A professional politician, he had no military experience prior to 1861 save for the command of a brigade of Massachusetts militia. As a lifelong Democrat, the general had supported the Buchanan administration throughout its tumultuous term of office, and in 1860 he had campaigned for the election of John Cabell Breckinridge, the one Democratic candidate whom Butler believed had a chance of defeating Abraham Lincoln for the Presidency. But with the secession of South Carolina the Massachusetts politician decided to divest himself of the robes of Hunker Democracy and took up the cause of the national government. In attempting to rid himself of the stigma of his Democratic past, Butler informed Massachusetts governor John Albion Andrew well before the outbreak of hostilities that he was ready to serve with the militia in case of an emergency. Eager to gain Democratic support for the Union war effort, Governor Andrew was only too glad to appoint the willing Butler commanding general of the state militia in the field. Only a month after Fort Sumter, Butler evoked the public's notice when, in response to severe criticism from the radical wing of the Massachusetts Republican party for having returned slaves to their master, he labeled three fugitive slaves who came into his lines at Fort Monroe, Virginia, contraband of war and refused to return them to their owners. Butler justified his politic maneuver on the basis of military necessity. The slaves had previously been aiding the Confederate war effort, and Butler's actions simply shifted their energies to support the cause of the Union.[22]

Despite having earned the reputation of a foe of slavery during his command at Fort Monroe, Butler was initially disinclined to tamper with the peculiar institution in southern Louisiana. His goal in the Gulf Department was to restore Louisiana to the Union by assuaging the fears of the planting and propertied interests who were "well-disposed toward the Union, only fearing lest their negroes should not be let alone. . . ."[23] Confiscation of slaves would have been, in Butler's opinion, an "injustice to the bona fide loyal creditor, whose interest the Government will doubtless consider."[24] Contributing to his determination to ensure that slaves remained under the control of their masters was his dread of the blacks' potential for violence. Deeply disturbed by the racial instability he met in New Orleans, Butler outlined his thoughts on slavery in a letter to Secretary of the Treasury Salmon Portland Chase: "Be sure that I shall treat the negro with as much tenderness as possible but I assure you it is quite impossible to free him here and now without a San Domingo. A single whistle from me would cause ever white mans throat to be cut in this city. Accumulated hate has been piled up here between master and servant, until it is fearful. . . . There is no doubt that an insurrection is only prevented by our *Bayonets*."[25]

Convinced of the necessity for maintaining civil order, Butler attempted to reassure the native white population that the Union army would not tolerate further racial unrest. During the first week of the Federal occupation he publicly declared that "All rights of property, of whatever kind, will be held inviolate, subject only to the laws of the United States." The object of the military in Louisiana was "to restore order out of chaos . . ." and "to have every species of disorder quelled." He also promised that all persons aiding this cause would not be disturbed in either their persons or property.[26] Determined to fulfill these promises, Butler directed his troops to confiscate only those slaves whose owners had committed an overtly treasonable act. All other black refugees who could not be employed by the army were to be excluded from Union lines.[27]

Butler delegated primary responsibility for implementing his slave-exclusion policy in New Orleans to the city police, for War Department orders prohibited military authorities from returning slaves to their owners. Throughout the summer of 1862 police officers gathered and imprisoned fugitive slaves from the streets of New Orleans and delivered them to their owners on demand.[28] Outside the confines of the city, however, the task of restraining blacks from leaving their owners belonged by default to the Federal army. Contrary to both national law and military orders, the army not only excluded slaves from its lines during the summer but also returned slaves to their owners and disciplined recalcitrant black workers.[29] Even the navy became involved in maintaining civil order. During the unsuccessful naval assault on Vicksburg in June blacks succeeded in boarding Union vessels despite the efforts of ship commanders to exclude them. Naval regulations required that these slaves be hired as laborers on the flotilla, but many were returned to owners who claimed loyalty to the Union.[30]

Although most officers in the Gulf Department agreed with Bulter's contention regarding the slaves' potential for violence, not all concurred in his methods for controlling blacks. The most notable critic of the commander's contraband policy was Brigadier General John Wolcott Phelps, a regular army officer who first articulated much of the thinking which would later shape Federal efforts among the freedmen of the Southwest. An outspoken proponent of the primacy of the Anglo-Saxon race and the efficacy of free labor, Phelps believed that the presence of the black slave thwarted the extension of northern laborers and institutions throughout the South. He hoped the war would result in the abolition of slavery and the exportation of the slaves, but he believed special measures had to be taken during the war to care for blacks who, left to shift for themselves, would either initiate a race war or align with the rebels in response to native white promises of protection. In order to stabilize and control the black population Phelps proposed the organization of blacks into military units and the establishment of a rigorous educational program for all slaves. At the end of hostilities he hoped to utilize his troops as the vanguard of a black exodus to Africa for exploiting the "underdeveloped riches" of the Dark Continent.[31]

Immediately upon his arrival in the Gulf Department Phelps began implementing his antislavery beliefs despite General Butler's policy of buttressing the slave system. During the first weeks of Federal occupation slaveowners besieged the commander with complaints that their chattels were being given refuge at Camp Parapet, the headquarters of General Phelps. Butler attempted to cajole and then to scold his balky subordinate into submission, but all his efforts proved unavailing. Phelps believed that if the army continued to support slavery, "the danger of a violent revolution, over which we can have no control, must become more imminent every day," and therefore he continued to accept fugitive slaves into his camp and subsequently began a system of rudimentary black education and military training.[32]

Phelps's utilization of black troops placed him on a direct collision course with his commander. By writing department headquarters in late July and requesting provisions for his new troops, he precipitated the final confrontation with General Butler. As justification for the enlistment of slaves, Phelps argued that his program was "the best way of preventing the African from becoming instrumental in a general state of anarchy."[33] Butler reacted heatedly to this latest provocation. He wrote to his wife that Phelps was "mad as a March Hare on the 'nigger question.'"[34] Not even deigning to consider Phelps's proposal, Butler directed his subordinate to employ his "contrabands" in cutting down the trees around his camp. Regarding Butler's orders as an affront and unwilling to perform the functions of a "slave-driver," Phelps tendered his resignation.[35] By the end of the summer he had left the Gulf Department and the army, but his ideas lingered on. Through his efforts Phelps popularized the notion that programs could be established for transforming blacks into a positive element in the war effort and for eliminating the slaves' disruptive potential.[36] Even before his departure from the Gulf Department, Phelps's beliefs were beginning to replace the more conservative practices of General Butler.

The necessity for a basic alteration in the army's confiscation program was impressed upon Butler by a combination of local and national developments. Within the Gulf Department, despite the best efforts of the military, blacks continued to manifest their discontent with the institution of slavery, and black insubordination remained as the leitmotif of labor relations on sugar plantations. In Butler's opinion, the continuing racial instability threatened to make his department a "Sodom & Gomorrah," with the slaves acting as the "fire and brimstone" of God. At his wits' end concerning the unruly blacks, the commander exclaimed to his wife, "we shall have a negro insurrection here I fancy. If something is not done soon, God help us all. The negroes are getting saucy and troublesome, and who blames them?"[37]

At this juncture in the late summer of 1862, although Butler was still convinced of the necessity of maintaining control over the black population, he was no longer certain that this goal could be accomplished through the medium of slavery. Rather, over the last three months of the year Butler instituted programs which simultaneously signaled the demise of slavery in southern Louisiana and the reinstitution of white control over blacks. The final impetus for this change came from the national level. Administration spokesmen, such as Secretary of War Edwin McMasters Stanton and Secretary of the Treasury Salmon Chase, informed Butler during the late summer of a shift in national sentiment toward the abolition of slavery. They suggested that he place himself at the head of this movement by acting decisively against the peculiar institution in the Gulf Department.[38] Their opinion was confirmed by the passage of the Second Confiscation Act on July 17, which freed all slaves of rebel masters as soon as they came within Union lines.[39] Butler's politically astute wife analyzed the growth of antislavery sentiment for her husband in early August. She wrote: "Emancipation, and arming the negroes is held in check for a little . . . [as] soon as there is a plausible hope of success it will be brought forward again. . . . Phelps' policy prevails instead of yours. The abolitionists will have this a war to free the slaves at once if possible, nothing else is thought of. The Administration will assent to it just as fast and as far as the country will sustain it."[40] Butler was ever responsive to shifts in the political winds, and this information, coupled with the army's inability to control blacks as slaves, prodded him into a more radical direction regarding slavery.

The first action by General Butler which marked a movement away from his former policy of buttressing the institution of slavery was the enlistment of blacks into the Union army. Although he had been initially disinclined to utilize black soldiers, by the end of the summer Butler was faced with a dire need for more soldiers to bolster his increasingly diffused command. His need for additional troops, combined with his awareness of favorable administration sentiment and the necessity to discipline blacks, convinced him to "call on Africa to intervene . . ." in the war effort. On August 14 he informed Secretary of War Stanton that he was enlisting into the Union service a brigade of free black men raised the year before by the Confederates.[41] Butler's action was a reflection of his political astuteness. The Rebel regiment, entitled the Native Guards, was composed of New Orleans freemen and had originally been organized in May 1861 by Louisiana governor Thomas Overton Moore. Because of the Confederate origin of his new soldiers and their free status, Butler believed he had insulated himself from criticism. "I have kept clear of the vexed question of arming the slaves," he explained to Henry Wager Halleck, general in chief of the Union army. "I am fortified by precedents of a half century's standing, acted upon by the Confederate authorities within six months, and I believe I have done nothing of which the most fastidious member of Jefferson Davis' household political can rightfully complain . . ."[42]

Butler's black military organization was an immediate success. Within two weeks after its founding over eighteen hundred black men had enlisted in the Native Guards, and by the end of the year Butler had formed three infantry regiments and two batteries of heavy artillery from his black recruits.[43] The reason for Butler's phenomenal success in locating recruits for his new organization was explained by a Native Guard officer: "Any negro who could swear that he was free, if physically good, was accepted. . . ."[44] Utilizing this tactic, the army was able to recruit slaves as well as free blacks for the Native Guards. Indeed, by the end of 1862 the overwhelming majority of enlisted men in the black organization were former slaves. For Butler to have followed any other practice would have been foolish, since the army desperately needed troops and fugitive slaves needed the discipline which only the military could provide. George S. Denison, customs collector for the port of New Orleans and Butler's political colleague, recognized this rationale for arming slaves: "One individual can control 50,000 disciplined men," he wrote Secretary Chase, "but cannot control a mob of fifty."[45] Blacks were not only utilized as enlisted men by Butler but were also given commissions in the Native Guards. Sixty-six black men, most of them "free men of color," received commissions as captains and lieutenants during 1862. The military's desire for racial stability also played a role in the decision to utilize free blacks as officers. Butler believed that the enthusiasm and intelligence of the freemen made them prime officer material and that their presence as Native Guards officers would have a stabilizing effect on the enlisted men. Racial hostility could be avoided if the slaves were treated fairly by being armed and given officers of their own color. Any other policy, according to Butler, would not only be unfair to the black man but would also be "an injustice which is pregnant with dangerous consequences."[46]

Butler's emphasis upon controlling the dangerous proclivities of Afro-Americans and inculcating them with the essentials of military discipline was reflected by the use which the army made of its black auxiliaries. Very rarely were black troops in the Gulf Department permitted to assume combat roles. Rather, military efficiency and discipline, combined with the supposed immunity of blacks to climatic diseases, dictated that the Native Guards be placed in the role of a fatigue and garrison force. The army's utilization of the first three Native Guard regiments during 1862 was indicative of this pattern of thought. The first regiment spent two weeks repairing railroad track and bridges and then devoted the rest of the year to foraging. The second regiment guarded the railroad at Opelousas for the whole of 1862 and then traveled to desolate Ship Island, where it spent the next three years on prison guard duty. In late November the third regiment saw its first military duty clearing the sugar-cane fields in the Teche district for the next year's crop. After many weeks of this arduous labor the regiment closed out the year foraging the surrounding countryside.[47] The vaunted servility of the black man when placed firmly under white control made the Native Guards perfectly suited for these labor details, and Butler's utilization of black troops during 1862 established a pattern which would be uniformly followed in the Gulf Department for the remainder of the war.[48]

The second phase of General Butler's program for stabilizing the black population of the Gulf Department was the establishment of a wage-labor system on the sugar plantations of southern Louisiana. Sugar was the mainstay of Louisiana's economy, and the commander realized that the revitalization of this most important industry was an integral part of the reconstruction process in his department. But before any progress could be made in the restoration of the industry, sugar producers first had to acquire a reliable labor force. In the past slaves had assumed this role, but during the summer of 1862 blacks manifested an increasing reluctance to continue laboring as chattels. The situation was doubly irritating to planters because the sugar crop then reaching maturity was even more promising than it had been in record-setting 1861. Butler was aware of the planters' plight, if only because he was the unwelcome recipient of many slaves who had formerly composed the work force of the sugar plantations. On September 1 he reported to the War Department that his commissary was issuing twice as many rations to black refugees as it was to the troops of his command. "They are now coming in by the hundreds nay thousands almost daily," he lamented to General Halleck. "Many of the plantations are deserted along the 'coast.' . . . Crops of sugar cane are left standing to waste which would make millions of dollars worth of sugar."[49]

Prohibited by the Second Confiscation Act from excluding slaves any longer from his lines, Butler turned to wage labor as a means for placing blacks back on plantations, where they could aid in the development of the Gulf Department's agricultural resources. Secretary of the Treasury Chase had been urging the general throughout the summer to institute a wage-labor program, and Butler had received similar advice from Edward Lillie Pierce, who had established a comparable program in the Sea Islands of South Carolina.[50] In addition, many planters had become convinced that wage labor was the only means by which blacks could be induced to work once again on sugar plantations. According to a New York *Times* correspondent, the planters of southern Louisiana were convinced that "so utterly disorganized have the slaves become, that the institution, under its old order, is forever destroyed and worthless, no matter what Mr. LINCOLN or anyone else may say on the subject."[51] While this sentiment was by no means universal among sugar planters, there were many businessmen in the Gulf Department willing to utilize black wage labor if they could be reasonably assured of making a profit from sugar production.

By December the military in conjunction with sugar planters had developed the framework of a wage-labor program to be utilized on Gulf Department sugar plantations. The army's standard wage-labor contract provided a ten-dollar monthly wage for all black workers, with three dollars to be deducted for clothing. Employers also were required to provide their laborers with food and medicine as well as protection for the immediate relatives of workers incapacitated by sickness or old age. In return, the military required all blacks to return to plantations and to labor ten hours a day, twenty-six days a month. Butler forbade "cruel or corporal punishment" but promised to punish refusal to work or insubordination by "imprisonment in darkness on bread and water." The army guaranteed to provide each planter with an adequate supply of laborers as well as guards and patrols to "preserve order and prevent crime."[52] General supervision of the labor contract was placed in the hands of a three-man Sequestration Commission. This body was to supply laborers to planters and also to work for the government any plantations which had been abandoned by their owners. Because of the need for laborers and the army's desire to establish white control over black workers, the commissioners required that all black refugees return to plantations under the stipulations of Butler's wage contract. The commission placed its workers under military guard and delivered them on request to planters and private businessmen leasing abandoned plantations from the army.[53]

Despite the seemingly liberal compensation called for in Butler's wage contract, few workers profited from the wage-labor program. Anxious to rid themselves of their black burden, many military commanders simply delivered blacks to planters with little or no regard for the wages promised to the laborers. Concurrently, many refugees, equally anxious to escape the drab and often unhealthy environs of the contraband camp, signed on with planters despite the meager recompense offered to them.[54] Even in those situations where workers were promised full wages, many employers simply turned off their employees after the harvest without paying them. On the Star Plantation, leased by Charles Weed from the army in the fall of 1862, the workers were still waiting for their first wages in July 1863.[55] The 330 workers on the David Pugh Plantation, hired at ten dollars a month, harvested a crop for their employer valued at $36,000, for which they received shoes and rations totaling $1,500. Sixty percent of the workers received no pay at all.[56] Cases such as these were by no means unique. In January 1863 General William Helmsby Emory reported to department headquarters that "it appears that those who have been working for their own profit the abandoned plantations have in many cases turned off the hands without payment, food or clothing." As a result, blacks in a "wretched and destitute condition" were once again flocking into military posts and contraband camps.[57]

Although the army gave only perfunctory attention to the payment of workers, great care was taken to ensure the subordination of black laborers to white employers. General Butler had promised planters that the military would "preserve order" on sugar plantations by providing guards and patrols to "prevent abuse on one side and insubordination on the other." These military guards generally construed their role to be that of overseers for the plantation owner, and employers found it an easy matter to enlist the sympathy, and police powers, of Union soldiers on their behalf. Numerous incidents of plantation guards aiding planters in cheating workers were referred to Superintendent of Contrabands George H. Hanks, who reported to his commander that he had "no doubt of their truth . . . and that many other cases of like injustices will be brought to light."[58] The military's emphasis on black subordination did not end with the termination of General Butler's command in the

Gulf Department at the end of 1862. Although his successor, General Nathaniel Prentiss Banks, eliminated some of the grosser inequities from the wage-labor program, the military continued to stress, in Banks's words, the need to "induce" blacks to return to plantations and the necessity of requiring them to "work diligently and maintain respectful deportment to their employers, and perfect subordination to their duties."[59] Under Banks the anomaly of a system of compulsory free labor reached its zenith in the Gulf Department, for only through such a program was the military confident that the "necessity of toil" could be impressed upon the black man.[60]

By the end of 1862 most Federal officials and northern observers considered General Butler's wage-labor program an unqualified success. True, only one-third of the plantations within Federal lines had been worked and the harvest was only a fraction of the record total of the year before, but these debits were offset by the experiment's clear evidence that staples could be grown at a profit by free black labor. On plantations where the experiment was tried, "sugar was manufactured more rapidly than during any previous season," reported a correspondent for the *Times,* ". . . the same number of negroes, with the same machinery, producing a hogshead and a half more of sugar each day than under the old system."[61] The wage-labor program successfully refuted the theories by which southerners had justified slavery. "The labour necessary to the Working of Sugar Plantations can be done without the Aid of the Slave Drivers Whip," John Wilson Shaffer, Butler's chief quartermaster, reported to President Abraham Lincoln. "Free labour on Sugar Plantations. Thank God, [it] is no longer an Experiment, it has been tried and found to be the better System."[62] The magnitude of the program's success was not lost on its founder. In late November Butler reported to the President that his program had proven that "Black labor can be as well governed, used, and made as profitable in a state of freedom as in slavery. . . ." Despite the opposition of some planters who refused to give up the use of the lash, Butler predicted the program would show enough profit to finance the department's relief measures for at least a half year. Although he believed that gradual emancipation was the most effective means for controlling blacks and restructuring the social institutions of the South, he thought it "quite feasible" for free blacks to be put to work immediately "with profit and safety to the white," but he asserted that it could "be best done when under military supervision."[63]

Two weeks after reporting the success of his wage-labor program to the President, Butler was relieved of his command and replaced by General Nathaniel Banks, another Massachusetts political general. But the removal of Butler did not imply administration disapproval of his contra-

band programs.[64] Rather, the military utilized Butler's attempts at controlling blacks as the basis of its efforts among blacks in the Gulf Department
during the remainder of the war and even into the period of Reconstruction. Specifically, the commander's emphasis upon "military supervision"
was at the core of his successor's publicized efforts among the freedmen.
Under Banks's leadership Gulf Department officials between 1863 and
1865 established an extensive series of contraband programs, including
the institution of black wage labor throughout all of southern Louisiana,
further black military enlistment, educational programs for the freedmen,
and various relief measures for unemployed blacks. In all these programs
the army stressed the necessity for maintaining firm control of its black
wards. Soon after Banks's arrival in the Gulf Department the military
developed the technique of the police dragnet, which it used with great
success throughout the remainder of the war as a means of eliminating
black vagrants from the towns and cities of southern Louisiana. Banks
eliminated the black officer corps of the Native Guards because of white
dissatisfaction with this administrative innovation. Compulsion became
the watchword under the new commander in the army's efforts to recruit
blacks for military and plantation labor. Even the efforts of the military to
provide for black education and relief were utilized by Banks as a means of
controlling the anarchic tendencies of the freedmen and of shaping them
into productive farm workers.[65]

By the end of the war freedmen in the Gulf Department were the
objects of a wide variety of contraband programs and were probably more
secure physically than in any other area of the South. But the freedmen's
security was purchased at a price. Under both Butler and Banks the fear
of black violence played a role in shaping the army's contraband programs. Both commands considered strict white control to be essential in
structuring freedmen's activities. Gulf Department officials considered
independent thoughts and actions on the part of blacks as threatening to
the reconstruction process, and the military's contraband programs
therefore de-emphasized and even discouraged the growth of black economic and political autonomy.[66] The goal of Federal officials relative to
the freedmen was the development of an efficient and stable plantation
labor force, and within this framework there was little room for the
uncurbed, and potentially subversive, gropings of black individuals.

A final result of the army's institution of contraband programs was a
reshaping of the black image in the white mind. Just as the outbreak of war
had given emphasis to the image of the black man as manic revolutionary,
so had the reimposition of order by the Union military signaled a reversion
to the Sambo image of the Afro-American. In explaining the success of

blacks as wage laborers and soldiers, military officials in the Gulf Department never tired of emphasizing the innate docility of the black man. In the summer of 1863 General Banks appointed two former abolitionists to assess the progress made in the implementation of a wage-labor program in southern Louisiana.[67] The conclusion reached by these inspectors was that on those plantations where the army's experiment had been faithfully carried out the black workers were "docile, industrious, & quiet."[68] A year later Banks's superintendent of Negro labor reported that the blacks were "more willing to work, and more patient than any set of human beings I ever saw. . . . The negroes willingly accept the condition of labor for their own maintenance. . . ."[69] A similar line of thinking characterized white explanations of the freedmen's success as soldiers. A Massachusetts soldier characterized the suitability of the black man for the army in the following terms: "Their docility, their habits of unquestioning obedience, pre-eminently fit them for soldiers. To a negro an order means obedience in spirit as well as letter."[70] In the estimation of General Daniel Ullmann, a commander of black troops in the Gulf Department, the freedman's outstanding qualification as a soldier was his "habit of subordination."[71] According to General Butler black soldiers were "more exact, inasmuch as they are more obedient."[72]

Even before the conclusion of the war, then, the black image in the white mind had come full circle, and blacks who in 1861 had been feared for their violent potential were now praised for their docile behavior. This development is of more than passing interest, for the reimposition of white control over blacks significantly diminished the need felt by whites for instituting new programs for southern freedmen. Just as fear had been the catalyst for many of the military's contraband programs, so had the abatement of the white man's violent racial fantasies marked the end of the army's innovation in the field of freedmen's affairs. By 1865 the Union army had successfully reestablished racial order by putting young black males under military discipline and by placing the remainder of the Gulf Department's black population back on plantations as wage laborers under white control. These programs, first inaugurated under General Butler, checked the black threat to law and order and transformed the slave population into a positive element in the Union war effort. Having thus stabilized the racial situation in Louisiana, federal authorities during the period of Reconstruction felt little compulsion to move beyond the wartime experiences of the army in expanding upon the meaning of freedom for the former slave.

CHAPTER 9

From Slavery in Missouri to Freedom in Kansas

The Influx of Black Fugitives and Contrabands into Kansas, 1854–1865

Richard B. Sheridan

A S IS WELL KNOWN to students of American history, the passage of the Kansas-Nebraska bill in 1854 repealed the Missouri Compromise of 1820 and built upon the Compromise of 1850. It created two new territories, Nebraska and Kansas, in place of one. It led to the negotiation of cession treaties whereby some Native Americans, or portions thereof, were allowed to remain within Kansas, but the greater number were relocated in territories outside Kansas. Moreover, the principle of squatter sovereignty which had been established by the Compromise of 1850 was extended to both territories, in which the majority of white settlers were authorized to form and regulate their domestic institutions, especially the institution of chattel slavery.

Missourians first pushed across the border to claim choice lands under the terms of the Preemption Act of 1841. Their proslavery leaders perceived the necessity of flooding Kansas with slaves and establishing a slave state. Settlers from New England and the Ohio Valley followed, motivated by the same land hunger as the Missourians but determined to withstand slavery and found a free state. For a time the struggle resulted in victory of proslavery forces who waged guerrilla warfare throughout Kansas Territory and sacked free-soil Lawrence. Reprisals were led by John Brown, James Lane, and others, whose forces plundered and killed pro-slavery settlers, running off their slaves to freedom in Canada. Kansas

121

was born in a struggle for liberty and freedom, a struggle that raised the curtain on the Civil War and sounded the death knell of slavery.[1]

The contest for possession of the Territory of Kansas has been told many times from the standpoint of white Americans who were involved in the struggle. On the other hand, much less is known regarding the black people and their role in overturning slavery, both in the antebellum and Civil War years. This paper, in five parts, is concerned with the blacks of Missouri and Kansas. The first section deals with the growth of slavery in Missouri and the flight of fugitives to Kansas Territory especially the free-state stronghold at Lawrence. Part two takes up the problems of disposing of the contraband slaves who flocked to Union army camps throughout the South, and especially in the state of Missouri. The third section examines evidence regarding the size and geographical distribution of contraband populations of Kansas, their work, education and social life, and part four deals with the recruitment and deployment of black soldiers from Kansas in the Civil War. The last section summarizes and concludes with a brief examination of the plight of the black people of Kansas in the postbellum period. Much of the evidence regarding the contrabands and black soldiers was generated by the colorful exploits of James Henry Lane, who was both U.S. senator from Kansas and a military commander in Kansas and Missouri during the territorial and Civil War periods.

I

THE SLAVE economy of the western counties of Missouri, which was a small affair in the early decades of the nineteenth century, became of increasing importance in the years leading up to the Civil War. According to John G. Haskell, a resident of Lawrence, Kansas, who had seen military service in Missouri, the early western Missouri slaveholder was a poor man; his wealth at the time of settlement "consisted mainly in one small family of negro slaves, with limited equipment necessary to open up a farm in a new country." Owing to such factors as poor transportation facilities and limited market outlets, the typical farm was small when compared with the cotton plantations of the deep South, agricultural production was diversified, and almost all food, clothing, and shelter was of local production. Slavery in these circumstances was much more a domestic than a commercial institution. "The white owner, with his sons, labored in the same field with the negro, both old and young. The mistress guided the industries in the house in both colors. Both colors worshipped at the same time, in the same meeting-house, ministered to by the same pastor."[2]

From its near-subsistence stage, the farm economy of western Missouri grew slowly at first, but more rapidly as the Civil War approached. New markets were opened with the growth of steamboat traffic on the Missouri River, the relocation of Indian tribes from east of the Mississippi River to the territory west of Missouri, the establishment of new military posts, railroad construction, and the opening of Kansas to white settlement. Besides a variety of foodstuffs, Missouri farmers supplied these new markets with transport animals—oxen, horses, and mules. Rising farm profits led, in turn, to in-migration, land settlements, and lively markets for farming tools and implements and especially black slaves. By the eve of the Civil War there were a considerable number of medium to large slaveholdings. Hemp, which was used in ropemaking, came to be grown on slave plantations of some size, although its culture was mostly restricted to the Missouri River counties.[3]

The slave population of Missouri increased from 3,011 in 1810, to 9,797 in 1820, and to 25,091 in 1830. It then more than doubled to 57,891 in 1840, grew to 87,422 in 1850, and reached 114,931 in 1860. That a disproportionate number of these slaves were concentrated in the Missouri River and western border counties is the finding of Harrison A. Trexler. He writes that

> The large and excessively rich Missouri River counties from Callaway and Cole to the Kansas line—Boone, Howard, Chariton, Cooper, Saline, Lafayette, Ray, Clay, Jackson, and Manitou—contained 34,135 slaves in 1850 and 45,530 ten years later. The whole series of counties along the Kansas border from Iowa to Arkansas—Atchison, Buchanan, Platte, Jackson, Cass, Jasper, and the rest—had 20,805 bondsmen in 1850, while in 1860 they contained 29,577.

The total of the Missouri River and western border counties was 54,940 in 1850 and 75,107 in 1860, or 62.8 percent and 65.3 percent, respectively, of all slaves in the state.[4]

Slaves who planned to permanently abscond from their masters in Missouri had several modes and courses of escape. They might be aided by relatives or friends who had successfully escaped from slavery and returned to aid others. They might be aided by white people in Missouri and elsewhere who held strong views against slavery. Free coloreds are reported to have taken fugitives under their protection, written passes, given instructions and directions, and provided temporary board and lodging. The so-called Underground Railroad was a secret system to aid fugitives bent on flight to Canada, by transporting them from station to station along well-defined trails or routes. Some slaves managed successful flight solely by their wits and luck. Slaves escaped as stowaways on steamboats. Others stole small boats or built rafts to speed their flight to freedom. The coming of the railroad furnished a new means of escape. Prior to the passage of the Kansas-Nebraska Act, the runaway slaves from Missouri headed for the two contiguous free states of Iowa and Illinois, and thence northward to Canada.[5]

Much greater opportunities for escape came with the filling of Kansas with free-soil settlers. By 1857 the problem was so great that both the federal and state governments were appealed to for protection of slave property in Missouri. Bills were introduced into the Missouri General Assembly to provide special patrols in the counties on the Illinois, Iowa, and Kansas borders. After the Kansas struggle had resulted in a victory for the antislavery forces, writes Trexler,

> the golden age of slave absconding opened. Escapes apparently increased each year till the Civil War caused a general exodus of slave property from the State. The enterprising abolition fraternity of Kansas—Brown, Lane, Doy, and the rest—seemingly made it their religious duty to reduce the sins of the Missouri slaveholder by relieving him of all the slave property possible.

In 1855 one editorial writer asserted that "ten slaves are now stolen from Missouri to every one that was spirited off before the Douglas bill."[6]

The raids into Missouri to free slaves struck terror into the minds of slaveholders and contributed indirectly to black flight from bondage. John Brown is known to have made several such raids and to have escorted a group of fugitives from Kansas to Canada in 1859. Less well known are the guerrilla chieftains James Montgomery and Dr. Charles R. Jennison whose bands of "jayhawkers" terrorized proslavery settlers in southern Kansas and made raids across the border into Missouri. According to George M. Beebe, acting governor of Kansas Territory, it was the purpose of these guerrilla chieftains

> to shelter fugitives owing service to southern states, and to kill any who should assist in attempting to enforce the fugitive-slave law; stating that they acted upon a settled conviction of duty and obedience to God. In short, their professions were the exact counterpart of those of the late notorious John Brown, in conjunction with whom they formerly acted.[7]

In the years immediately preceding the Civil War, the Underground Railroad was increasingly active in helping slaves escape from Missouri. The Rev. Richard Cordley, Congregational minister and historian of Lawrence, Kansas, said that the Underground Railroad line ran directly through Lawrence and Topeka, then on through Nebraska and Iowa. He had been told by people who ought to know "that not less than one hundred thousand dollars' worth of slaves passed through Lawrence on their way to liberty during the territorial period." Cordley, himself, together with his wife and members of his congregation, harbored a slave named "Lizzie," about whom he wrote an interesting account of their efforts to secrete her from a federal marshal and his deputies and see her safely on the road to Canada.[8]

James B. Abbott, who was active in the antislavery movement in Kansas, said that fear of being sold to planters in the deep South prompted the slaves of Missouri

> to secure their freedom before the difficulties were increased and the opportunities were gone, and so it is not at all strange that hardly a week passed that some way-torn bondman did not find his way into Lawrence, the best advertised anti-slavery town in the world, and where the slave was sure to receive sympathy and encouragement, and was sent on his way rejoicing either by himself or with others, as the circumstances seemed to suggest was most wise.

Abbott asserted that the slaves across the border were far from the least interested party in the Kansas conflict. Indeed, they were early taught "the places and men to shun, as well as the places and men to trust."[9]

Col. J. Bowles was another Lawrence resident actively engaged in the Underground Railroad. On April 4, 1859, he wrote a long letter to Franklin S. Sanborn, a leading abolitionist at Concord, Massachusetts. Bowles claimed that during the previous four years he personally knew of "nearly three hundred fugitives having passed through and received assistance from the abolitionists here at Lawrence."[10]

The Underground Railroad intensified the Missouri slaveowners' resentment toward the free-state settlers of Kansas. Moreover, it carried a growing number of passengers through Lawrence and other stations in Kansas because of the fears of both masters and slaves. Indeed, it has been asserted by Wilbur H. Siebert "that the Underground Railroad was one of the greatest forces which brought on the Civil War, and thus destroyed slavery."[11]

II

OPPORTUNITIES FOR blacks to escape slavery increased during the Civil War as Union armies invaded the South. Although some Union generals returned slaves when they escaped to Union camps, on grounds that the

Fugitive Slave Law of 1850 required that the fugitives be returned to their masters, other commanders refused such surrender lest the slave property contribute to the armed rebellion. Declaring the slaves who escaped to his camp contraband and liable to confiscation by the laws of war, Gen. Benjamin F. Butler, whose forces occupied Confederate territory in Tidewater Virginia in 1861, established a precedent which was followed by other Union generals as the war expanded into the South. In March 1862 an act of the Union government "declared contraband slaves—those belonging to persons in rebellion—henceforth and forever free," and on January 1, 1863, President Abraham Lincoln issued his Emancipation Proclamation which declared forever free the slaves in rebellious states.

Blacks who first escaped to the Federal lines were eagerly recruited for a variety of occupations. They built fortifications, served as teamsters, wheelwrights, blacksmiths, hospital attendants, officers' servants, and employees of the commissary and quartermaster departments. Many of those who had skills settled in cities as barbers, draymen, carpenters, blacksmiths, servants, seamstresses, nurses and cooks, of whom a large number conducted businesses of their own. In rural areas they became tenant farmers or were employed as farm laborers and woodchoppers.[12]

The influx of contrabands into Kansas must be seen against the background of the Civil War on the Western Border. In Missouri the question of secession was decided by an elected convention that voted eighty to one against immediate secession. When Gov. Claiborne F. Jackson repudiated President Lincoln's call for troops and intrigued to gain control of the federal arsenal at St. Louis, he and the legislature were ousted and Hamilton F. Gamble, a Lincoln supporter, was elected provisional governor. Meanwhile, Jackson, Sterling Price, another former governor, and other southern loyalists formed a breakaway government. After an ordinance of secession was adopted, the breakaway government was admitted to the Confederate States of America.[13]

In Kansas, after years of political rivalry between proslavery and free-state factions, free-state delegates framed an antislavery constitution at the Wyandotte Convention. It was ratified by a large majority on October 4, 1859. After Lincoln's victory, Kansas entered the Union under the Wyandotte Constitution on January 29, 1861. Charles Robinson was elected governor, and Martin F. Conway congressman. On April 4 of the same year the Kansas legislature elected Samuel C. Pomeroy and James H. Lane to the U.S. Senate.[14]

James Henry Lane (1814–1866) was a remarkable leader whose actions as a military commander and politician were responsible for the influx of large numbers of slaves into Kansas and their recruitment into black regiments. It is uncertain whether he was born in Kentucky or Indiana, but the latter state is usually given as his birthplace. He studied law and went into politics at an early age. He served as colonel of a regiment in the Mexican War, after which he was elected lieutenant governor of Indiana and later represented that state in the U.S. Congress. In 1855 he went to Kansas Territory where he soon became a leading politician and military leader of the free-state forces. Lane was a man of boundless energy, great tenacity of purpose and personal magnetism, and possessed of oratorical powers of a high order. Wendell Holmes Stephenson characterizes Lane as "a radical, an enthusiast, a direct-actionist, who tolerated no halfway measures." Moreover, "he was rash, hot-headed, daring, persistent, subtle, provocative, warm-hearted, magnetic." He was called the "Grim Chieftain," a tall, thin, stern-visaged man, who, like Cassius, bore "a lean and hungry look." It was said of Lane that no man ever had firmer friends or more bitter enemies. Lane was an ardent supporter of Abraham Lincoln for the presidency, and, as a U.S. Senator, a close personal friend of the wartime President. He took his own life, in 1866, in a fit of depression after losing political support in Kansas and being accused of involvement in fraudulent Indian contracts.[15]

Lane was appointed a brigadier general of volunteers by President Lincoln in June 1861. He proceeded from Washington, D.C., to Kansas to raise volunteer regiments under the authority of Congress, at a time when Confederate armies had won several important battles. In Missouri, Gen. Sterling Price and his Missouri National Guard secession army had defeated Gen. Nathaniel Lyon and his Union army at the Battle of Wilson's Creek on August 10, 1861. The Grim Chieftain worked fast to meet the threatened invasion of Kansas by a force some ten thousand strong under General Price. Lane marched with his hastily gathered troops to Fort Scott, Kansas, near the Missouri border, where Price was expected to attack. On September 2, Lane sent twelve hundred mounted men to Dry Wood Creek, twelve miles east of Fort Scott, where a brisk skirmish was fought with Price's advance-guard. Price decided to discontinue his advance into Kansas upon learning that Lane was waiting to give battle, and turned north toward Lexington, Missouri.[16]

"As Lane's 'Kansas brigade' marched through Missouri," writes Stephenson, "a 'black brigade' marched into Kansas." Two of Lane's chaplains wrote long accounts of the slaves who flocked to Lane's brigade and of their march into Kansas. In his *The Gun and the Gospel*, Chaplain Hugh Dunn Fisher tells of the trek of the black brigade. While the Kansas brigade rested at Springfield and on the march to Lamar, Lane's camp was "the center of attraction to multitudes of 'contrabands' and refugees." Lane sent for Fisher the second day out of Springfield, explaining the imminent danger of attack and the helpless condition of the great multitude of blacks. He asked Fisher, "Chaplain, what can we do to relieve the army of these contrabands, without exposing them to their enemies?" Whereupon, Fisher replied that "all the men were in the army, and the women and children in Kansas needed help to save the crop and provide fuel for winter, and I advised to send the negroes to Kansas to help the women and children." Lane's laconic reply was, "I'll do it."[17]

When the Grim Chieftain's brigade arrived at Lamar, forty miles southeast of Fort Scott, he directed his three chaplains, Fisher, Moore, and Fish, to take charge of the refugees and escort them to Fort Scott.

> Next morning early there was a stir in the camp. Fourteen men were detailed as an escort to save us from falling into the hands of the guerrillas. We had a wagon load of almost useless guns. I picked out about thirty negroes and armed them, the first negroes armed during the rebellion. We divided this company, and also the white escort, and placed half as an advance guard with orders to "scout well," and the other half as a rear guard with orders to keep well up, and by no means to allow a surprise. Such a caravan had not moved since the days of Moses.

It was a nondescript emigration. They traveled day and night, eating only cold food until they came upon a small herd of cattle, of which three were killed and hastily broiled and eaten.

When they reached Kansas, Fisher halted the caravan and drew the refugees up in a line. He raised himself to his full height on his war horse, "commanded silence, and there under the open heavens, on the sacred soil of freedom, in the name of the Constitution of the United States, the Declaration of Independence, and by the authority of General James H. Lane, I proclaimed that they were 'forever free.'" Immediately the blacks "jumped, cried, sang and laughed for joy." Fisher claimed that they were the first slaves formally set free. He said it occurred in September 1861, long before Lincoln's Emancipation Proclamation was issued.[18]

Fisher's account was largely substantiated by that of Chaplain H. H. Moore. In a letter to John Speer, editor of the *Lawrence Republican,* Moore told of the motives and circumstances of individual slaves who came into the camp, some of them bringing valuable mules and wagons. "Our colored teamsters and servants act as so many missionaries among their brethren," he wrote, "and induce a great many to come into camp. It cannot be denied that some of our officers and soldiers take great delight in this work, and that by personal effort and otherwise, they do much towards carrying it on. None but such as are decided in their wishes to obtain freedom, are brought into camp." Moore went on to say that there were 218 fugitives, including several children, forming a train a mile long. The train camped on Dry Wood Creek for the night, when some members of the party stole grain from a "traitor's" cornfield and "killed one of his cattle of beef." The blacks became excited when they sighted the distant hills and bluffs of Kansas. When they crossed the line they gave "three hearty cheers for Gen. Lane, the Liberator."[19]

After he returned to Washington, Lane told the Senate of the success of his policies and actions in Missouri and Arkansas. In a speech on May 15, 1862, he claimed that 4,000 fugitive slaves from Missouri and Arkansas were then being fed in Kansas, and two months later he said the number had increased to 6,400. In a speech to the New York Emancipation League in June he said that he had himself "aided 2,500 slaves to emigrate" during the year, and a month later he told the Senate that at one time he had 1,200 blacks in his brigade.[20]

Later in the Civil War several groups of contrabands were brought from Arkansas to Leavenworth on steamboats. After the victory of the Federals at Helena, Arkansas, on July 4, 1863, the camps were overrun with blacks seeking freedom. Chaplain Fisher was ordered to take control of large numbers of contrabands, who left that port and neighboring ports in three steamboats, and scatter them "throughout Missouri, Illinois, Iowa, and Kansas, sending some of them as far as Ohio." Fisher said he had intended to go in charge of the slaves on the *Sam Gaty,* but at the last minute decided to go by rail instead to prepare for their reception at Leavenworth. Unfortunately, the *Sam Gaty* was captured by a band of guerrillas or bushwhackers at Napoleon, Missouri. Nine black men were killed and seven black women were shot, but none killed. The guerrillas searched the boat for Chaplain Fisher and would not be satisfied that he was not on board until they had killed three white men in his stead. When the *Sam Gaty* arrived at Leavenworth, hundreds of people assembled on the levee to welcome the survivors. Fisher said that the whole party of contrabands was promptly provided with homes in good families.[21] Among the contrabands who arrived by boat, one Lieutenant Colonel Bassett is said to have returned to Kansas from a military campaign in Arkansas with over six hundred black refugees on board four steamboats.[22]

It would be misleading to leave the impression that all of the contrabands entered Kansas under the auspices of Union military units. Many of them, perhaps the greater number, came of their own volition, either crossing along the land border or the approximately seventy-five-mile stretch of the Missouri River which separates Missouri from Kansas.

Writing in February 1862, the editor of the Atchison *Freedom's Champion* adopted an attitude of mock sympathy for Missouri slaveowners whose property walked away, saying

> The beloved darkies, the cherished possession of the secesh, are constantly arriving in Kansas from Missouri—they come singly, by pairs, and by dozens. . . . We acknowledge that it must be very trying to the feelings of our Missouri brethren to have those which they have brought up from infancy, or in whom they expended large sums of money, to thus forsake them at the first opportunity, and frequently not only take themselves away, but also a valuable horse or mule. We repeat that all this must be very trying, but all the consolation we can give them is that "such are the fortunes of war," and we trust that hereafter they will learn wisdom and not invest large sums of money in property of this description, for every day's experience only tends to convince us that it is a very uncertain species of riches, and although not taking "wings," nevertheless frequently take "legs" and is lost forever.[23]

Slaves even walked across the Missouri River to freedom in Kansas when the ice was thick enough to support their weight, as was reported to be the case in February 1863 when contrabands in considerable number crossed over on the frozen river and enlisted in the Union army.[24] A few reportedly swam across the river at some peril to their lives, while others came on skiffs and ferries. One group that arrived by ferry at Wyandotte was said to consist of "poor, frightened half-starved negroes . . . men and women with little children clinging to them, and carrying all of their earthly possessions in little bags or bundles, sometimes in red bandana handkerchiefs."[25]

The exodus continued at a rapid pace until the end of hostilities. Writing from Glasgow, Missouri, to Gov. Thomas Carney of Kansas, on August 24, 1863, B. W. Lewis said that hardly a night passed but what from two to a dozen slaves left their masters. Having incurred heavy costs in policing his own slaves, Lewis proposed to sett [*sic*] all our Negroes free who may desire it and put them on a Boat and pay their way to some point in your State." Those who preferred to stay, he said, would be paid wages. Lewis asked the governor to advise him if there would be any objection to his sending the slaves to Kansas. Though Lewis's proposal was no doubt unique, it was symptomatic of the despair of Missouri slaveholders regarding the viability of the peculiar institution. That the slave population of Missouri was seriously eroded by the flight of blacks during the turmoil and destruction of the Civil War can be demonstrated by population statistics. In fact, only 73,811 slaves remained in the state in 1863, as compared with 114,931 in 1860, or a decline of 35 percent. The loss was probably greater in a qualitative sense than the statistics indicate, since the greater part of the fugitives were reportedly able-bodied males and females capable of performing heavy field labor.[26]

III

THE INFLUX of contrabands was significant from the standpoint of the numbers involved and their impact on the economy and society of wartime Kansas. Table 1 shows that the black population increased from 627 in 1860 to 12,527 in 1865, or from 0.6 percent to 8.8 percent of the Kansas population. The influx may have been as great as 15,000, since many black soldiers from Kansas were out of the state when the census of 1865 was taken. Although blacks came to Kansas in growing numbers after the Civil War, and especially in the late 1870s and early 1880s, when the "Exodusters" arrived from the South, the white population increased even more rapidly. Thus, the blacks declined as a percentage of the total population—to 4.7 in 1870, 4.3 in 1880, and 3.5 in both 1890 and 1900. In the twentieth century the black population of Kansas increased from 3.5 percent of the total in 1900 to 5.4 percent in 1980. It is therefore noteworthy that the influx during the Civil War years raised the black population of Kansas to its highest level in relation to whites and Indians.

Not only did the blacks constitute a larger proportion of the total population of Kansas; they were also highly concentrated in certain towns and counties, as shown in Table 2. Eight of the thirty-seven counties that were enumerated in 1865, contained 77.5 percent of the black population, and the three leading counties—Leavenworth, Douglas, and Wyandotte—contained 55.5 percent of the blacks. Although it lacked a town of any consequence, Wyandotte County had the third largest black population in 1865, with nearly half as many blacks as whites.[27] The Kansas census of 1865 shows that seven towns contained 37.6 percent of all blacks in the state, and that four towns—Leavenworth, Lawrence, Atchison, and Fort Scott—contained 33.4 percent. There was one black to every three whites in Fort Scott, a ratio of one to four in Osawatomie, one to five in Leavenworth, Lawrence, and Mound City, and one to seven in Atchison and Topeka. In the eight most populous counties, females accounted for 52.3 percent and males for 47.7 percent of all blacks in 1865. It is significant that four of the leading towns—Lawrence, Topeka, Mound City, and Osawatomie—had been stations on the Underground Railroad. More or less protection was afforded the contrabands who came to Kansas by the Missouri River, the Union military establishments at Fort Scott and Fort Leavenworth, and the antislavery and abolitionist sentiments of the townspeople and rural inhabitants.[28]

Table 1

Growth of Kansas Population, 1860–1900
Distinguishing Whites, Blacks, and Indians

RACE	1860	1865	1870	1880	1890	1900
White	106,390	127,261	346,377	952,155	1,376,619	1,416,319
Black	627	12,527	17,108	43,107	49,710	52,003
Indian and other races	189	382	914	834	1,679	2,173
Total Population	107,206	140,170	364,399	996,096	1,428,108	1,470,495
Percentage White	99.2	90.7	95.1	95.6	96.4	96.3
Percentage Black	0.6	8.8	4.7	4.3	3.5	3.5

SOURCE: U.S. Censuses, 1860, 1870, 1880, 1890, 1900; Kansas 1865 MS, Census, vol. 10, Compendium of Statistics Reported to the Legislature, Archives Department, Kansas State Historical Society

Table 2

Blacks in the Leading Kansas Towns and Counties,
1865, Compared with the Total Population

	BLACKS IN TOWN POPULATION	ALL BLACKS IN COUNTY	TOTAL TOWN POPULATION	TOTAL COUNTY POPULATION
Leavenworth (Leavenworth County)	2,455	3,374	15,409	24,256
Lawrence and North Lawrence (Douglas County)	933	2,078	5,401	15,814
Wyandotte County	—	1,504	—	4,827
Atchison (Atchison County)	432	613	3,318	8,909
Fort Scott (Bourbon County)	359	787	1,382	7,961
Mound City (Linn County)	270	690	1,494	6,543
Osawatomie (Miami County)	138	409	750	6,151
Topeka (Shawnee County)	118	257	958	3,458
Toyals	4,705	9,712	28,712	77,919

SOURCE: Kansas 1865 MS, Census.

The "Black Brigade" was brought to Kansas chiefly to supply much needed farm labor. As more and more contrabands arrived in the state, many were dispersed over the countryside and employed as rural wage laborers. After several wagons loaded with contrabands had passed through two of the border towns in January 1862, one editorial writer predicted that the coming crop season would find "Kansas better provided with free labor than any of the Western States." Later in the same year the editor of the *Fort Scott Bulletin* made a tour of the Neosho River valley. He observed that cultivated farms were springing up on all sides, and "almost every farm was supplied with labor in the shape of a good healthy thousand dollar Contraband, to do the work while the husbands, fathers and brothers are doing the fighting."[29] Another journalist noted that black labor, mostly that of fugitives from Missouri, was largely responsible for producing the bountiful Kansas harvest of 1863. He said that large quantities of labor were needed to harvest the wheat, since very little machinery was used on Kansas farms and the crop needed to be taken off quickly once it had ripened. Even Senator Lane was reported to have used contrabands to build a fence around his Douglas County farm and to experiment with the growing of cotton with free black labor.[30]

Whether or not the contrabands settled on farms or in the towns depended upon several circumstances. Relatively few arrived with sufficient wealth and experience to begin as farmers. The overwhelming majority depended upon wage employment, and as the demand for farm labor was to a large extent seasonal, the contrabands' chances of obtaining work was contingent upon their arrival in Kansas during the crop season. If they arrived in the winter months the towns were most likely to supply the means of subsistence.

"Contrabands in large numbers are fleeing from Missouri into Kansas and especially into Lawrence: 131 came into Lawrence in ten days, yesterday 27 had arrived by 2 P.M.," wrote John B. Wood of Lawrence to George Stearns in Boston on November 19, 1861. Continuing, he said, "thus far they have been taken care of, as the farmers needed help." He warned, however, that the hundreds, if not thousands, who were employed in harvesting the crops would soon be unemployed, and they would gather in Lawrence for the inhabitants to feed and clothe with the assistance of the "friends of humanity at the East." The contrabands came to Lawrence by the scores and hundreds, according to Richard Cordley. For a time their numbers and needs threatened to overwhelm the inhabitants. "But they were strong and industrious, and by a little effort work was found for them, and very few, if any of them, became objects of charity," said Cordley.[31]

Recalling her girlhood experiences with the contrabands of Lawrence, Agnes Emery wrote that at the beginning and through the years of the Civil War "a veritable army of slaves drifted into Lawrence as if by instinct, to a sort of haven." She told of the contrabands who worked for the Emery family on their hilltop farm near Lawrence as follows:

> "Old Mary" could get up a breakfast that we did not know was possible. She could cook in such a manner as to make food of many plants that we did not know existed. "George" who lived in our barn was trustworthy and devoted to our interests. We always felt perfectly safe to know that he was near enough [to] protect us if the need arose. . . . Emily Taylor came two days each week, for years and years, to do our laundry. She also helped in sickness and in deaths. I will remember the day she came to tell us of the death of President Lincoln. Everyone in our family was depressed by the news.[32]

Besides helping the contraband secure a livelihood, Lawrence citizens made a concerted effort to teach the newcomers to read and write. While the children attended the public schools, adults were encouraged to join classes after working hours. S. N. Simpson, who started the first Sunday school in Lawrence in 1855, established a night school for contrabands which met five or six nights a week for two hours in the courthouse. Classes were taught by a corps of volunteer teachers who were described as women and men of culture, character, and consecration. About one hundred adults, entirely ignorant of their letters, applied themselves earnestly to the simple lessons given in the spelling books. Study and recitation were interspersed with the singing of familiar hymns. In the course of a few weeks several of the blacks were able to read with some fluency and were ready to commence with figures.[33]

The contrabands who came to Lawrence were a church-going people. Cordley said that a Sunday school was organized and Sunday evening services were conducted for them at the Congregational Church. They outgrew this facility, and, about one year after their arrival, the new Freedmen's Church was dedicated on September 28, 1862. It was described as "a fine comfortable brick Church," believed to be the first one ever erected in the United States for fugitive slaves. Cordley said the church was "filled with an attentive congregation of 'freedmen'—all lately from bondage, and all neatly dressed as a result of their short experience of free labor."[34]

After the difficult period of first arrival when white paternalism was most conspicuous in the adjustment to freedom, the contrabands encountered racial hostility and reacted by drawing on their own latent but slender resources in an effort to build a viable black community. Agnes Emery recalled that the freedmen did their share in becoming good citizens. "They were kind to each other in times of illness and misfortune, their demands were few, they were strong, eager, and willing to work, and soon made themselves useful in the community." After meeting in white churches and then in the inter-denominational Freedmen's Church, the blacks "divided into various ecclesiastical camps" with their own preachers. They met together to celebrate such anniversaries as the Fourth of July, slave emancipation in the British West Indies, and, beginning in 1864, Lincoln's Emancipation Proclamation. In 1864 the black women of Lawrence organized the Ladies Refugee Aid Society to collect food, clothing, and money to assist freedmen who had fallen on hard times.[35]

The occupations of 624 blacks in Douglas County are shown in the 1865 census, of which 349 lived in Lawrence and North Lawrence, and 275 in rural parts of the country. Soldiering was the leading occupation of the blacks in Lawrence and North Lawrence, where 95 were so designated. Following behind the soldiers were 85 day laborers. Of the 92 female workers, 49 were domestics, 27 employed at washing and ironing or as washerwomen, 7 worked as housekeepers, 6 as servants, and 3 as cooks. In all, some 270 blacks or four-fifths of the town total were unskilled laborers. The other one-fifth consisted of skilled and semiskilled workers. There were 23 teamsters, 8 blacksmiths, 6 porters, 4 barbers, 3 hostlers, 3 woodcutters, 2 stonemasons, 2 draymen, 2 rock quarriers, and one each of distiller, saloonkeeper, miner, harnessmaker, brick moulder, coachman, carpenter, shoemaker, printer, and preacher.[36]

The high ratio of rural to urban workers, or 44.0 percent of all workers, may possibly be explained by the fact that the census was taken on May 1, 1865, when much farm labor was needed. There were 145 blacks designated as farmers, 59 as laborers or day laborers, and 31 as farm laborers. Although these occupations are not defined clearly, it seems reasonable to assume that almost all of the blacks so designated performed agricultural wage labor. Thirteen other farmers and one other farm laborer were residents in Lawrence and North Lawrence. The remaining rural males consisted of 10 teamsters, 6 soldiers, 4 brickmakers, and one each of porter, blacksmith, and schoolteacher. The rural females consisted of 9 domestics, 5 servants, 1 washerwoman, and 1 employed at washing and ironing.[37]

As the oldest town in Kansas, Leavenworth and the nearby federal fort by the same name was the largest population center in Kansas in 1865. Its growth was largely a result of its steamboat and overland wagon transport facilities and its place as a mobilization and supply center. The towns of Atchison and Leavenworth were first settled primarily by Missourians whose sympathies were proslavery. By 1858, however, Leavenworth had a free-state majority and the town hosted a state convention that adopted a radical antislavery constitution, which, although nominally approved by popular vote, was defeated by the U.S. Congress. Within months of the outbreak of the Civil War, Leavenworth had become a cosmopolitan town with inhabitants from all quarters of the Union and refugees and fugitives from the rebel states. A soldier from Wisconsin wrote home in February 1862, saying, "The city is full of 'contrabands,' alias runaway negroes from Missouri; of whom it is said there are a thousand in the neighborhood.— They are of all ages and characters, pious Uncle Toms and half-ape Topscys."[38] Five months later, in an editorial entitled "Our Colored Population," the black population of Leavenworth was estimated at fifteen hundred, almost all of whom were newcomers and the great majority fugitive slaves from Missouri. These people, with scarcely a single exception, had arrived at Leavenworth "wholly destitute of the means of living." As they came in large numbers, and many of them in mid-winter, suffering among them was inevitable.[39]

Compared with Lawrence, Leavenworth had a more formal and extensive organization to provide for the contrabands' welfare. On February 5, 1862, some of the town's white leaders met with their black counterparts at the First Colored Baptist Church to "take into consideration measures for the amelioration of the condition of the colored people of Kansas." Prominent white leaders in attendance were Col. Daniel R. Anthony, Dr. R. C. Anderson, and Richard J. Hinton. The black community was represented by the Rev. Robert Caldwell of the Baptist church, Lewis Overton, a teacher in a black school, and Capt. William D. Mathews, a free mulatto military officer. Several months later, Charles H. Langston, a free mulatto schoolteacher, became a prominent leader in the black community. Hinton, a prominent journalist and abolitionist, had interviewed John Brown and his chief aide, John Henrie Kagi, during their stay in Kansas in 1858. At the Leavenworth meeting Hinton presented a plan of organization for the Kansas Emancipation League, which was approved. Anthony was elected president, Dr. Anderson, treasurer, Hinton, chief secretary, Overton and Caldwell, members of the executive committee, and Mathews, superintendent of contrabands. Dr. Anderson told the audience of the origin of the scheme for sending an agent east to lay before the public the condition of the contrabands and to solicit aid. Before the meeting adjourned, a committee submitted a skeleton constitution and by-laws which were adopted.[40]

The Kansas Emancipation League's second meeting was held on February 10, 1862. After the minutes of the preceding meeting and the formal constitution and bylaws were read and approved, Richard Hinton "brought to the attention of the League the constant attempts at kidnapping which occur daily in this city." This matter was taken into consideration by a committee that was directed to work with police and military officials to provide protection to the black residents of Leavenworth and the state of Kansas. The object of the league, it was agreed, should be to "assist all efforts to destroy slavery, but more especially to take supervision and control of the contraband element so freely coming to our State." Furthermore, it was "the object of the League to encourage Industry, education and morality among these people, to find them employment and thus make them a benefit and not a burden to the State which shelters them." As superintendent of contrabands, Captain Mathews was instructed "to take charge and provide for their temporary wants and in every way look after their interests."[41]

Beginning on February 13, 1862, and continuing for several months, the *Leavenworth Daily Conservative* ran an advertisement of the Labor Exchange and Intelligence Office established by the Kansas Emancipation League at the drugstore of Dr. R. C. Anderson on Shawnee Street. All persons in need of black workers, including hotel waiters, porters, cooks, and chambermaids were asked to apply at this office. Furthermore, laborers were supplied for such jobs as woodsawing, whitewashing, teaming, etc., at the same office. About a month after the first advertisement was printed the Labor Exchange general agent reported that good work had already been accomplished, and that "over one hundred colored men have been sent from our city to labor on farms and that the demand for this kind of labor is still constant and pressing."[42]

Although the Labor Exchange and Intelligence Office helped to reduce the number of contrabands who were dependent upon the league, it by no means eliminated unemployment since many of the laboring men not only had large families but were unable to work as a result of sickness and exposure. For these people the league appealed for assistance in Leavenworth and elsewhere. Early in May 1862, Richard Hinton authored a printed circular which stated the problems encountered by the league and appealed to "friends in other states" for material support. One copy of this circular at the Kansas State Historical Society has a handwritten note, probably appended by Hinton, that states that the first money contributed to the league came from George L. Stearns, the Boston merchant who supplied John Brown with money for his abolitionist crusade.[43]

IV

SOLDIERING WAS the chief occupation of able-bodied male contrabands in the war years from 1862 to 1865, and it was General Lane who led the campaign in Kansas to organize black regiments and recruit black soldiers. In a speech at Leavenworth in January 1862, Lane recalled that contrabands who came into his camps in Missouri had played at soldiering after their evening meal; he said they took to military drill as a child takes to its mother's milk. "They soon learn the step, soon learn the position of the soldier and the manual of arms." He urged the government to arm the blacks, citing as precedents the use of black soldiers in the armies of George Washington and Andrew Jackson.[44] At a time when President Lincoln was calling for 300,000 volunteers, Lane was appointed commissioner of recruitment for the Department of Kansas. He was authorized to appoint recruiting officers, arm and equip volunteers, establish camps of instruction, and arrange for the procurement and transportation of supplies. Lane assumed that his recruiting commission, issued by the War Department in July 1862, entitled him to enlist blacks as well as whites.[45]

Arriving at Leavenworth on the 3d of August, Lane appointed recruiting agents and disposed of related matters. That he took speedy action is indicated by a *Leavenworth Daily Conservative* advertisement that appeared three days later. It announced that all able-bodied colored men between the ages of eighteen and forty-five had an opportunity to serve in the First Kansas Regiment of the "Liberating Army," and said that one thousand such men were wanted. It went on to say that "Ten Dollars Per Month will be paid, and good quarters, rations and clothing provided." A similar advertisement in an Atchison newspaper promised that, in addition to the pay and rations, a certificate of freedom would be issued to each black volunteer, as well as freedom for his mother, wife, and children.[46]

Recruiting and training proceeded at a fast pace in the weeks following Lane's initial appeal for black volunteers. An item in a Leavenworth newspaper on August 28, said the colored regiment had received one hundred recruits within the previous twenty-four hours. At Mound City some one hundred fifty black recruits were drilling daily, and more were reported to be on their way to the camp adjoining that town. North of the Kansas River approximately five hundred blacks had been enlisted within a short time. They were instructed to rendezvous by September 10 at Camp Jim Lane, near Wyandotte bridge. Capt. George J. Martin returned from Wyandotte to Atchison on September 12, and reported the regiment to be six hundred strong, with daily additions from Missouri. "The men learn their duties with great ease and rapidity," he said, "and are delighted with the prospect of fighting for their freedom, and give good earnest of making valiant soldiers." On October 17, 1862, the First Kansas Colored Infantry was organized near Fort Lincoln, in Bourbon County.[47]

There is evidence that not all of the blacks recruited into the regiment entered voluntarily. One Missourian wrote to President Lincoln, complaining that a party of some fifteen Kansans had entered Missouri to "recruit Negroes for General Lane's Negro brigade." They forcibly took possession of some twenty-five blacks and about forty horses. Another incident involved a recruiter for a contraband regiment at Hiawatha, in the northeast corner of Kansas. On August 21, 1862, he announced that he would pay "two dollars per head for buck niggers—that is, for every negro man brought over from Missouri, he will pay two dollars to the person bringing him across."[48]

That the black regiment's fighting qualities brought honor to Afro-Americans in Kansas and elsewhere is well documented. Writing from Fort Africa, Bates County, Missouri, on October 30, 1862, a *Leavenworth Daily Conservative* correspondent told of a campaign against a notorious band of bushwhackers. In a sharp engagement in which some two hundred thirty black troops were pitted against about six hundred bushwhackers, "The men fought like tigers, each and every one of them, and the main difficulty was to hold them well in hand. . . . We have the guerrillas hemmed in, and will clean them and the county out," said the correspondent. Gen. James G. Blunt wrote an account of the Battle of Honey Springs, near Fort Gibson in Indian Territory, on July 25, 1863. Soldiers of the First Colored Regiment "fought like veterans, with a coolness and valor that unsurpassed," he wrote. "They preserved their line perfect throughout the whole engagement and, although in the hottest of the fight, they never once faltered. Too much praise can not be awarded them for their gallantry." The general, who was battle-hardened from long campaigns, judged the blacks to be "better soldiers in every respect than any troops I have ever had under my command." General Lane, who continued to support the enlistment of blacks, often paid tribute to their fighting ability.[49]

Beginning in June 1863, a second Kansas black regiment was recruited and molded into an effective fighting unit by Col. Samuel J. Crawford, afterwards governor of Kansas. Besides the Kansas regiments, a black brigade was recruited and sent into action. Altogether, a total of 2,083 black soldiers were recruited, or approximately one-sixth of the black population of Kansas in 1865. Kansas lived up to its radical tradition by recruiting the first black troops to engage in military action against Confederate forces.[50]

The black military achievement was even more remarkable when it is considered that the soldiers faced great obstacles in the form of race prejudice and bureaucratic procrastination and delay. General Lane received blacks into the First Kansas Colored Regiment under what he thought was congressional authority, only to be informed that such recruitment had to have presidential authority which was not forthcoming for several months. As a result, this regiment was not mustered into service until January 13, 1863. Instead of soldiering, the troops were first put to work building fortifications and in fatigue duty. This led to anger, disillusionment, and for a time, numerous desertions. Lane had promised his black recruiting officers that they would be commissioned as officers of the companies they recruited, but this was denied and white officers were appointed in their place. Even after the regiment was mustered in, payment of the troops was delayed until June 1863. Furthermore, the Union government defaulted on its pledge to pay black recruits at the same rate as whites—actually three dollars less per month than white soldiers and a deduction of three dollars for clothing. "Not until 1864," writes Dudley Taylor Cornish, "and then only after furious debate in the army, in the press and in congress, did Negro soldiers finally get what amounted to equal pay for equal work." Race prejudice raised its ugly head, as is indicated by the advice given by an editorial writer for the *Fort Scott Bulletin*. He advised that the black regiment be kept away from Kansas troops which were then in the field, for "with one exception, there is not a Kansas regiment from which they would not have as much to fear as from the rebels."[51]

While the black soldiers felt insulted and betrayed by the government's delay and discrimination in matters of mustering into service and pay, the dependents they left behind in Kansas suffered real hardships. In Leavenworth, the public was urged to subscribe clothing, food, and money to the wives and children of the men in service. When it was discovered that a group of blacks planned to hold a bazaar to raise money for a charitable cause outside the town, a public meeting of colored citizens was called. It was resolved, that since the great majority of the black population was poor, and that many continued to arrive in Kansas "destitute of money, clothing and bedding," that the blacks should be urged *not* to send money out of town but "to do all within their power to relieve the poor and suffering among us, and urge our friends here and elsewhere to aid us in this good work."[52]

V

KANSAS TERRITORY attracted a small group of ardent abolitionists who, with moral and material support from the East, established stations and conducted "passengers" on the Underground Railroad to freedom. When the Civil War commenced, contrabands from Missouri made straight for these stations and other places for refuge and opportunity for employment. As the editorial writer of the *Leavenworth Daily Conservative* pointed out, "These freed men settled in various parts of the State guided by their interest, inclination or supposed safety, our city and Lawrence being the principle [*sic*] points of location."[53]

Kansas became more Negrophilic during the Civil War when the contrabands supplied much needed labor to harvest crops and perform a variety of tasks in rural and urban areas. Most importantly, black men volunteered for military service and made a notable contribution. Unfortunately, race prejudice and bureaucratic delay and discrimination brought great hardships to the families of black servicemen and proved to be a serious obstacle to progress on the road toward racial integration.

Before the Civil War had ended, much of the cooperative effort that had characterized the Kansas Emancipation League and other organizations broke down and the black and white communities tended to go their separate ways. In Leavenworth, for example, the black community held public meetings to protest the treatment accorded black soldiers; the Suffrage Club was organized to agitate for an amendment to the Kansas Constitution which would extend the franchise to black males. Beginning in October 1863, the Kansas State Colored Convention met annually in the leading cities to debate and act upon such issues as equal suffrage, the right to serve in the state militia, the right of trial by a jury of political equals, and the abolition of discriminatory practices by the proprietors of stages, railroad cars, barber shops, hotels, saloons, and other public institutions.[54]

In the face of an overpowering Negrophobic white majority, the blacks of Kansas turned more and more to their own cultural heritage, to their schools, churches, lodges, mutual aid societies, and the celebration of anniversaries that marked their progress from slavery to freedom. One such celebration was the emancipation of slaves in the British West Indies on August 1, 1864. On August 1, 1864, the black community of Leavenworth and vicinity began their celebration of West Indian emancipation with a procession headed by the Colored Battery of Capt. William D. Mathews, followed by the Sabbath schools, and the Suffrage Club. Not less than two thousand people met at Fackler's Grove where a fine dinner, interesting speeches, and splendid music were enjoyed.[55]

It is ironic that when the U.S. Supreme Court came to consider race discrimination a century after Kansas Territory had been a staging ground for civil war on the issue of chattel slavery, it was a case brought by a black Kansan against the school board in the state's capital city that overturned court-enforced segregation and ushered in the Civil Rights Movement.

Part 3

RACIAL ATTITUDES ON THE CIVIL WAR FRONTIER

CHAPTER 10

Civil War Kansas and the Negro

Albert Castel

K
ANSAS," DECLARED THE CHICAGO *Tribune* in 1866, "is the most
radical of the States."[1] By this it meant that Kansas surpassed all
other states in a desire to punish the South for the sins of slavery and
secession, and to advance the legal, political, and social position of the
Negro. Underlying the statement was the belief, widespread then and
persisting to this day, that Kansas had been settled by zealous New England abolitionists engaged in a crusade against slavery. Indeed, Northerners and Southerners alike thought of the state as a hotbed of
antislavery fanaticism, with the result that "Kansan" and "abolitionist"
were practically synonymous terms during the Civil War era.

To an extent this reputation was well-deserved. "Bleeding Kansas"
had played a key role in defeating the South's attempt to expand slavery
into the western territories; antislavery New Englanders were prominent
in the state's affairs; and practically all of its major officials were outspoken abolitionists—men such as Governor Charles Robinson, Senators
James H. Lane and Samuel C. Pomeroy, and Representative Martin
Conway, the last of whom advocated the Wendell Phillips doctrine of letting the South secede in order to rid the nation of slavery![2] But in a more
fundamental sense Kansas' radicalism was essentially a myth, or at least
greatly exaggerated. In the first place, the vast majority of Kansans hailed
from the Midwest, not New England.[3] Secondly, only a few of them

settled in Kansas solely or even primarily for the purpose of combatting slavery. As one of them put it in later years, "We came to Kansas to better our conditions, incidentally expecting to make it a free State."[4] And finally, while the bulk of the population opposed slavery, full-fledged abolitionists constituted at most only a small minority—a vocal, active, and influential minority, to be sure, but still a minority. In fact, according to one highly qualified observer, many Kansans had a "deadly terror of being termed 'abolitionists,'" and were "frightened by the mere mention of that mysterious specter, 'negro equality.'"[5]

Basically the people of Kansas held the same attitudes on the Negro and slavery as most other midwesterners of the time. They considered the Negro naturally inferior, believed that his proper status in society was one of subordination to the white, and objected to slavery not for idealistic or moralistic reasons but because they feared its social and economic effect on the small white farmer. Paradoxical as it may seem, they were almost as much anti-Negro as they were antislavery, and in large part they were antislavery precisely because they were anti-Negro: i.e., by keeping slavery out of Kansas they also kept out the Negro, whose presence in large numbers they considered a threat to the community.[6]

When the Civil War broke out the majority of Kansans shared the prevailing Northern belief that the sole purpose of the struggle should be preservation of the Union. Only a handful of radical abolitionists proclaimed slavery as the "basic issue" and proposed freeing the slaves of "rebel masters."[7] The leaders of this group were James Montgomery, who had served with John Brown and who had financial support from the same New England abolitionists who had backed Brown's Harpers Ferry raid; Charles R. Jennison, a twenty-six-year-old adventurer whose hatred of slavery was exceeded only by his love of plunder; and Daniel R. Anthony, brother of Susan B. and publisher of the Leavenworth *Daily Conservative*, which despite its name was the most radical paper in the state. Closely associated with them were a number of influential journalists, preachers, and politicians headed by Senator James H. Lane, the "Grim Chieftain" of the Republican Party and the "King" of Kansas politics. A master demagogue, hypnotic orator, and utterly unscrupulous, Lane exploited antislavery radicalism as a means of advancing his political ambitions—at the same time always being careful never to offend the anti-Negro prejudices of his constituents. All of these men, for a variety of motives, sincere and cynical, selfish and altruistic, welcomed the war as a golden opportunity to strike a death-blow at slavery.[8]

Nor were they slow in taking advantage of this opportunity, and in the most direct fashion possible. During the summer and fall of 1861 bands of

Kansas "jayhawkers" led by Montgomery, Jennison, and Anthony swept across the border into Missouri and "liberated" hundreds of slaves in the name of suppressing rebellion. The climax to these raids came in September, when Lane at the head of the "Kansas Brigade" marched through western Missouri, burning and looting, and distributing copies of General John C. Frémont's recent proclamation freeing the slaves of all rebels— blithely ignoring, as he did so, the fact that President Lincoln had repudiated the proclamation shortly after its appearance. By the time the raid ended his troops were accompanied by hundreds of Negroes, many of whom were serving as teamsters, cooks, and even soldiers. In November he joined Frémont's army in an expedition to Springfield, Missouri, from which region he sent back to Kansas six hundred Negroes in a "Black Brigade" led by two Methodist chaplains. As they entered the "Happy Land of Canaan" the ex-slaves gave forth with cheers for "Jim Lane, the liberator." The chaplains then distributed them as laborers among the farms and villages of southern Kansas.[9]

Even greater numbers of Negroes poured into Kansas on their own, attracted by the state's abolitionist reputation. Most of the refugees, naturally, were from Missouri, but a few were from Arkansas, the Indiana Territory, and Texas. They came singly, in small groups, or sometimes in parties of several dozen. Often they brought with them the mules, horses, wagons, furniture, and other property of their erstwhile masters. In September 1861, the Leavenworth *Daily Conservative* reported that according to information gathered from citizens living along the border "at least one hundred slaves leave Missouri each day for Kansas."[10] A month later George W. Collamore, Mayor of Lawrence, Kansas, wrote the prominent Boston abolitionist George L. Stearns that "Slavery is fast disappearing in Missouri" as Negroes fled into Kansas "in no small numbers."[11] And in November another of Stearns's Kansas correspondents testified that 131 Negroes had arrived in Lawrence during the past ten days alone, and that 56 of them had come in one group the previous evening.[12] By 1863 8,000 former slaves had refugeed to Kansas, and by the end of the war the state's colored population had swollen from a mere 816 in 1860 to almost 13,000.[13]

Missouri slaveholders, as might be expected, greatly resented the jayhawking and flight of their valuable chattels. At first they endeavored to prevent them from escaping, or to recover them if they did succeed in getting to Kansas. But their efforts along these lines proved utterly futile, even dangerous, and eventually large numbers of them gave their slaves freedom, with the choice of remaining to work for wages or going to Kansas. Some Missourians were so terrorized by the jayhawkers that in self-defense they told their slaves to leave, considering "no course safe but to urge, even to force, the last house servant to leave."[14]

The majority of the former slaves congregated at Leavenworth, Lawrence, Wyandotte, and Fort Scott, in that order.[15] Leavenworth, then Kansas' most populous city, had in the summer of 1862 about 1,500 colored residents, two Negro churches (one Baptist, the other Methodist), and a Negro school with 128 students.[16] Lawrence attracted a great many fugitives because of its fame as an "abolition center." Its citizens, although strongly antislavery, were somewhat dismayed by the influx and "almost regretted the reputation their history had given them." But their fear that the Negroes would become a burden on the community proved unfounded. "By a little systematic planning work was found for them as fast as they came, and . . . the freedmen were self-sustaining almost from the start." In December 1861, the night school which had been established for the illiterate ex-slaves had 83 pupils ranging from old men to young children, and 27 volunteer teachers.[17] Wyandotte (now part of present-day Kansas City, Kansas) by 1865 possessed 1,504 Negro inhabitants—approximately one-half of its total population, and the much smaller town of Fort Scott had about 500 "citizens of color."[18]

The refugee Negroes were welcomed for their labor, as a severe manpower shortage existed in Kansas because of heavy enlistments in the army. "A great many farms are not cultivated in this section," wrote a farmer who lived near Topeka to a relative back East, "for want of working men. . . ." "It would be a great blessing," he added, "if more darkies would understand their rights and come to our aid."[19] Kansas farmers eagerly sought the services of the Negroes brought out of Missouri by Lane in the autumn of 1861, and Lane's political enemies accused him of asking and accepting money for them.[20] Lane himself employed Negro laborers, and in 1863 boasted that he had "made nine miles of fence this spring," and planted all of his cotton with the aid of Negroes who "were slaves in Missouri but a short time since."[21] The bountiful harvest of 1863, affirmed the Leavenworth *Daily Conservative,* was made possible only by Negro help: "Almost every farm is supplied with labor in the shape of one or two large, healthy negroes . . ."[22] Thus economics reinforced abolitionism and weakened prejudice in Kansas; otherwise it is doubtful if the state would have been so hospitable to the fugitives.

Some of the freedmen, however, proved reluctant to work. To them slavery and work were (understandably enough) synonymous, and initially at least they adopted the attitude that when one ended so should the other. A woman who spent her childhood in Civil War Kansas later recalled seeing young white children in the fields hoeing corn while the "negroes who abounded in the neighborhood . . . would not work, no matter what pay was offered."[23] A newspaper correspondent from Illinois described a colony of "contrabands" near Fort Scott, its members sprawled out on the ground in "squads," completely unconcerned about the future, and declining to accept any of the jobs offered them. They preferred, stated the correspondent, to exist on the hospitality of their fellows who had erected "little shanties and were earning a living."[24] Eventually, of course, dire necessity if nothing else forced even the most reluctant ex-slave to realize that "freedom" did not mean freedom from work.

As the war progressed, antislavery feeling in Kansas rapidly increased. The editor of the Oskaloosa *Independent* ably summed up this develop-ment in September of 1861:[25]

> When the present rebellion first broke out, there was but one senti-ment among loyal citizens—that of maintaining the government against the rebels, and of avoiding the Slavery issue, as such, in the contest . . . But of late . . . there is an evident change in public feeling on the sub-ject of Slavery. . . .
> While no one, or at least none but a mere handfull [*sic*] of rabid abolitionists, wishes the war to assume the Slavery issue as the leading feature or the main end to attain, yet there is a growing desire to have the institution, which is either the real cause of the rebellion, or the instrumentality used by ambitious demagogues to carry out their trea-son, put out of the way.

When Frémont issued his "premature" emancipation proclamation of 1861, previously mentioned, the state's newspapers praised it as "striking at the root and cause of the war," and later expressed regret when Lin-coln revoked it.[26] In this instance Kansas was indeed "radical," being far in advance of prevailing Northern opinion, which was not prepared to support emancipation until a year later.

Not only did Kansans come to favor freeing the slaves, but as 1861 gave way to 1862 a small but growing number of them began to advo-cate enlisting Negroes in the army, another pet project of the abolition-ists, who believed that nothing would do more to subdue the South than the spectacle of black men in blue uniforms. The arguments put forward by the Kansas proponents of Negro troops, however, had little in common with abolitionist idealism, but were strictly utilitarian in charac-ter—probably deliberately so. Thus the Emporia *News* maintained that if the South insisted on using Negroes "to shoot down our brave boys, ought we not to retaliate by using them to subdue the enemies of the government?"[27] The Leavenworth *Conservative,* as part of a prearranged propaganda campaign designed to build up support for recruiting Negroes, argued that they were needed to help defend the long frontiers of Kansas against guerrillas and Indians.[28] And Lane, in a speech early in 1862, asserted bluntly that the Negro might "just as well become food for powder" as the white man.[29]

It was Lane who brought about the enlistment of the first Negro troops in the state. In August 1862, he came from Washington wearing the title of "commissioner for recruiting in the Department of Kansas" and established an "office of recruiting" in Leavenworth. He then proceeded to raise four infantry regiments—three of whites and one of Negroes. In doing the latter he acted under the terms of the recently passed Confiscation Act, which empowered the President "to employ as many persons of African descent as he may deem necessary and proper for the suppression of this rebellion. . . ."[30] Although he had no official authorization from the President to enlist Negroes, he did possess Lincoln's verbal promise that he would have the tacit sanction of the Government. By raising the Negro regiment he hoped to become the hero of the Northern radicals and so ride the abolitionist horse into the White House.[31]

Despite the campaign of the *Conservative* and other radical newspapers, enlistment of Negroes encountered strong opposition in the state. A Fort Scott editor advised Lane to keep his colored soldiers away from the "Kansas troops in the field," for "with one exception, there is not a Kansas regiment from which they would not have as much to fear as from the rebels."[32] Lane himself later admitted in the Senate that it required four months of propaganda to prepare the "antislavery people" of his state for the great innovation of armed Negroes, and that the prejudice against the black recruits was so intense that they had to be kept out of sight and drilled in seclusion.[33]

Indications are that the Negroes themselves were not overly anxious to become soldiers. In a recruiting speech at Leavenworth, Lane felt it necessary to declare that "the negroes are mistaken if they think white men can fight for them while they stay at home. We have opened the pathway. We don't want to threaten, but we have been saying that you would fight, and if you won't fight we will make you."[34] The reluctance of Negroes to enlist stemmed mainly from a fear that they would be badly treated by the white troops and the Government, and from concern over the welfare of their families who would be left at home. Furthermore, the terms offered by Lane to Negro recruits—ten dollars a month and a "certificate of freedom"—were deemed unjust and unfair by Negro leaders, who pointed out that white soldiers received much higher pay and who argued that the certificate was of no consequence since Negroes in Kansas were free anyway.[35]

Additional obstacles to Negro recruitment came from the unexpected quarter of Jennison, who resented Lane being in charge of it. For awhile Lane conciliated Jennison, who was very popular among Western radicals, by appointing him a special recruiting commissioner for Negroes, but aroused his enmity again by refusing to make him colonel of the Negro regiment, a position which that other arch-abolitionist and jayhawker James Montgomery also wanted, but which went instead to an obscure character named James M. Williams—a man the Senator could easily control. Calling Lane a "great humbug," Jennison and his friend George Hoyt (who was head of a jayhawker gang known as the Red Legs) tried to break up the regiment's encampment near Wyandotte, with the result that 200 of the 600 recruits present deserted, most of them going to Leavenworth.[36] Their white officers followed and arrested them, and also forced freedmen who had not enlisted to join up. "Radical Leavenworth," as the *Daily Conservative* rather wishfully called the town, became greatly angered over these arrests and forced enlistments, for they took away valuable workers, and the mayor attempted unsuccessfully to arrest Colonel Williams.[37]

Lane's agents even resorted to kidnapping in order to fill the ranks of the Negro regiment. On August 22 a gang of fifteen jayhawkers under "Lieutenant Swain," alias "Jeff Davis," crossed over from Wyandotte to Kansas City to "make converts" among the colored population there. They collected twenty-five Negroes and forty horses, but before they could recross the river they were intercepted by a force of the Missouri State Militia, which captured eight of the band, wounded one, and recovered the Negroes and horses. The captives were jailed at Liberty, Missouri, and kept there despite Jennison's threats (this happened before his break with Lane) to free them by force. However, they soon escaped and returned to Kansas. The citizens of Wyandotte held a meeting, condemned the raid, and disassociated themselves from it. But some of the inhabitants of the Missouri counties near Kansas City were greatly alarmed by the affair, and petitioned Lincoln to disband the Negro regiment and punish Lane and Jennison for raising it. Otherwise, they warned, there would be "most serious difficulties" between Kansas and Missouri.[38]

Late in October a detachment of Lane's Negro soldiers under the command of Major H. C. Seaman entered Missouri and camped near Butler. The purpose of the expedition most likely was to obtain additional recruits. On the 28th a force of Confederate irregulars attacked Seaman's men. According to the official Kansas account they beat off the Confederates "with considerable loss" while suffering casualties of ten killed and twelve wounded themselves. They then retreated to Kansas. The only importance of this skirmish was that it was the first action of the Civil War fought by a Negro unit.[39]

About a month later five companies of the colored regiment re-entered Missouri and near Island Mound had another clash with Confederates, after which they captured "a large amount stock" and marched on to Fort Scott. Here, early in 1863, Lane's Negro regiment was mustered into United States service under the designation of the First Kansas Colored Volunteers.[40] It was the fourth colored regiment officially to enter the Union Army, three Negro regiments having been enrolled by Ben Butler at New Orleans in the fall of 1862.[41] Kansas, however, could rightly claim to be the first Northern state to enlist Negroes. Individual honors in this matter must go to Major General David Hunter, who anticipated Lane by about four months while commanding in South Carolina.[42] However, as noted previously, Lane had armed Negroes in his Kansas Brigade in September of 1861, and Jennison's Seventh Kansas Regiment was reported by the famous artist George Caleb Bingham to have had an entire company of Negro soldiers under a Negro officer during the raid through Missouri in November 1861. [43]

Before the war ended Kansas raised (with Lane again taking the lead) another Negro regiment, which was mustered into Federal service late in 1863 as the 83rd United States Colored Infantry. This unit performed well in the Union campaign in Arkansas in 1864, especially at the Battle of Jenkins' Ferry, where it repulsed several times its numbers of Confederates, captured a battery, and took no prisoners in retaliation for a Confederate massacre of Negro soldiers of the First Kansas Colored at the Battle of Poison Spring a short time before. Its commander, Colonel Samuel J. Crawford, became the third Governor of Kansas in 1865.[44]

By being the first Northern state to raise Negro troops Kansas no doubt enhanced its reputation for radicalism. This reputation was in no way diminished as the state enthusiastically applauded the Emancipation Proclamation and was among the first to ratify the Thirteenth Amendment, which passed the legislature by unanimous vote.[45] But all the while anti-Negro prejudice remained strong. The majority of Kansans, all evidences indicate, continued to consider the Negro, in the words of one editor, "greatly inferior to the white man,"[46] and to regard him with that mixture of contemptuous amusement and distrustful apprehension characteristic of whites in general during that era. A few of the more fervent abolitionists, to be sure, were "proud to show the new element in their population undisguised marks of respect and esteem," but the rest of the populace were determined to keep the freedmen "in their place."[47]

An incident illustrative of this last can be found in the journal of Samuel J. Reader, a young farmer who lived in Indianola, near Topeka. In the fall of 1864 some of the Negro children in Indianola attended the same school as the white. The parents of the latter immediately withdrew their children from the school, and the white pupils threw stones at the colored. Reader protested this action to one of the white parents, whose reply, as recorded by Reader, is quite revealing:

> He told me that the Darkies coming to school was breaking it up, and thinks they ought to leave, and Mrs. Jones will teach them. I told him that did not look like a Christian spirit; that it was the prejudice against having them educated, for fear they could not be kept slaves! "Well," said he, "it's not that so much but because they will get SASSY. . . ."

Reader found himself in the minority, and a separate school was established for the Negro children.[48] Not until ninety years later, as a result of the Supreme Court's historic Brown v. Topeka Board of Education decision did schools in the Topeka area cease to be segregated.

Kansas manifested their non-radical attitude not only in respect to schools, but also by their stand on the question of Negro suffrage. In 1863 the legislature overwhelmingly rejected a proposal to eliminate the word "white" from the voting provisions of the state constitution. It repeated this action three years later, and in 1867 the citizens of the "most radical of the States" voted two to one against Negro suffrage in an election in which it figured as the main issue.[49] Kansas did ratify the Fourteenth and Fifteenth Amendments without any undue delay (although there was strong opposition to them), but not until 1884 did it get around to removing the word "white" from the constitution, despite the fact that it had been meaningless legally ever since the Fifteenth Amendment went into effect nationally in 1870![50]

Yet so well-established, widespread, and persisting was Kansas' radical reputation that fifteen years after the Civil War it became the object of one of the most dramatic events in the history of the Negro race in America, namely the great "Exodus" of 1879–80. In those years thousands of Southern Negroes, in a seemingly spontaneous mass movement, abandoned their homes and began trekking northward and westward into Kansas where, they firmly believed, they would not only escape the systematic oppression of the South but find free land and a new and better life. Kansans drew back in mingled fear and bewilderment as the hordes of tattered, hungry, and penniless immigrants poured into the state, and there were some who advocated using guns if need be to keep them out. Fortunately, however, the counsels of common sense and decency prevailed. The governor set up a special commission to deal with the problem, and eventually the "Exo-dusters" either established farm settlements in the southern part of the state or else moved into the Negro sections of such towns as Leavenworth, Kansas City, Topeka, Lawrence, Wichita, and Pittsburg.[51] Here they and their descendants experienced a life which in most ways was probably supe-rior to the one left behind, but which fell far short of any dreams of the "promised land."

To sum up and conclude: Kansas deserved its Civil War reputation of radicalism to the extent that it did take a leading part in the struggle against slavery, especially prior to 1861. Also, owing to the activities of a dynamic minority of abolitionists and radical politicians, it was generally ahead of other Northern states during the war in advocating and carrying out measures designed to promote the freedom of the slaves. But at all times the rank and file of its citizens remained basically anti-Negro, sup-porting such policies as emancipation and the enlistment of colored troops essentially for reasons of expediency, self-interest, and out of a desire to win the war, preserve the Union, and punish the South, not because of any intrinsic sympathy for the Negro as such. When the war was over and slavery destroyed, Kansas backed the Radical Republican Reconstruction program nationally, but within its own borders showed itself less progres-sive on the subject of race than many other Northern states, particularly in New England. In fact, if anything, it more resembled the border states on this matter than it did New England—which perhaps simply reflected the origin of most of its population as well as its geographic situation. Yet, so strongly established was its reputation for radicalism that Negroes fled to the state as a refuge, and many people to this day believe that John Brown was the incarnation of the spirit of early Kansas.

CHAPTER 11

The Negro in Wisconsin's Civil War Effort

Edward Noyes

H ISTORICAL LITERATURE PERTAINING TO Wisconsin in the Civil War has all but ignored the Negro in the state's military effort. This may be due to the fact that Negroes serving in Wisconsin's behalf did so largely under classification as United States Colored Troops.[1] Besides, it has been easy to overlook the Negro in Civil-War Wisconsin because his numbers were few. In 1860 the state's colored population was only 1,171; a decade later it was but 2,113. Nevertheless, the Wisconsin Adjutant General's records contain names of 353 Negroes credited to the state's war roster. This number is modest in comparison with the total of troops Wisconsin furnished the Union, but it represents a proportion to the state's Negro population greater than that of white soldiers to their segment.[2]

To achieve perspective concerning circumstances under which the Negro rendered service to Wisconsin's Civil War effort, it is appropriate first to define his position as an individual in the community and to examine popular wartime attitudes toward him as a potential soldier. Generally, the status of the Wisconsin Negro in 1861 was that of uncertain sufferance accorded him by his white neighbors. His image was one hardly to be envied; he possessed few rights to rouse anger or jealousy. Underprivileged economically and unaccepted socially, the Negro in Civil-War Wisconsin could hope for little truly serious regard in the life of the state or in its military affairs.

The Wisconsin Negro of 1861 might be described politically as a friendly alien. If he owned property, he contributed to cost of government as a taxpayer. He could testify equally with white men before the courts, but he lacked the ballot and so was not a citizen.[3] The war years saw no change in this condition. Indeed, many war-time Wisconsinites agreed with the principle enunciated in 1862 by Democratic Party leader Edward G. Ryan that in America, government was "instituted by white men for white men"[4] To such believers, any hint of enfranchising the Negro was alarming. For example, in 1864 the anti-administration Madison *Patriot* professed to see in Negro suffrage an abolitionist scheme for seizing power and warned that if ever the slaves became free they would

> vote down Americans of Caucasian descent, and . . . as soon as the war is over (they dare not try it now) the Germans, Irish, Norwegians &c., will be shut out. The Abolitionists cannot control, but the negroes they can; hence their bold push for the negroes vote. White men, how like you the picture before you now?[5]

Hostilities found the Wisconsin Negro in modest economic condition. For example, a survey of occupations and property ownership listed by twenty-four Negro residents of Milwaukee in the manuscript census of 1860 reveals that they held jobs mostly as barbers, whitewashers, cooks, or domestics. Milwaukee Negroes did not own valuable property. Only seven possessed real estate, the highest value being $5,000 declared by a mason aged eighty-five. Fifteen owned personal property of modest worth, but nine of the twenty-four had no property at all.[6]

The Wisconsin Negro's social status in 1861 was akin to his political and economic condition. Although John Nelson Davidson, a distinguished Wisconsin clergyman, averred in 1896 that "the men who made Wisconsin an abolition state believed themselves . . . agents to do a revealed will of God,"[7] evidence indicates that during the war not all Wisconsinites responded to the Christian impulse with sympathy for the Negro. If the colored man appeared in newspaper reports, it was usual for him to be depicted as lacking in manners, morals, and resolution, or to be made the butt of crude reference and coarse jest.[8] He was often an object of suspicion or hatred. And in 1861 a mob from Milwaukee's Third Ward lynched a Negro whom it mistakenly held responsible for the fatal stabbing of an Irishman.[9]

But this was not all. The Negro migrant, who entered Wisconsin in greater frequency as the war continued, was by no means entirely welcome. True, in 1863, Trempeleau County farmers facing a labor shortage caused by heavy enlistments expressed interest in obtaining Negro workmen, and there were other neighborhoods in which Negro labor was utilized.[10] Even so, vigorous opposition to colored immigration developed in many Wisconsin communities. Typical of more vociferous opponents was Peter V. Deuster whose editorials in the Milwaukee *See Bote* flayed Union war policies and likened Lincoln to the "spiked helmet" Kings of the Germans. Deuster, himself a migrant to Wisconsin from Germany in 1847, asserted: "The North belongs to the free white man, not to the Negro."[11] To those sharing Deuster's opinions, colored migration was likely to become a black tide engulfing Wisconsin and usurping places of her white people in workshop or field. In 1862 the arrival of 75 Alabama Negroes in Fond du Lac, where they were employed as servants, prompted the anti-abolitionist *Daily Wisconsin News* to assert that this occurred because black labor was cheaper than white, and hence it would "not be many months before the state will be swarming with this black population."[12] Similarly, the West Bend *Post* charged that immigration of "free blacks into the free states, to mix with . . . and compete with . . . free white labor . . . is . . . most outrageous."[13] And, there were attempts to impose statutory prohibition upon Negro settlement in Wisconsin. Although one such effort failed in 1862, it happened that following Emancipation in 1863 the state legislature received over a hundred petitions seeking laws to prevent Negroes from becoming residents. But every petition was rejected. The reporting committees contended that Wisconsin's borders were open to all and that colored immigration was hardly a problem because the Negro would incline toward remaining in the South once that region became more hospitable to him. Among petitioners were Peter V. Deuster and Frederick W. Horn, a former Wisconsin Immigration Commissioner who migrated to the state from Germany in 1836.[14]

If examination of the Negro's status in the civilian life of Civil-War Wisconsin reveals conditions of insecurity and inequality, it may be stated that his situation in terms of military service was one of rejection during many months of the struggle. In 1861, neither federal nor state authorities accepted him as a soldier. True, Negroes fought creditably in the Revolution and the War of 1812, but the Civil War was different from those conflicts because it arose partly from the slavery controversy. Thus, "prudent and political rather than legal" considerations led Lincoln's administration to refuse official admission of colored men into the United States Military establishment until 1862.[15] As for service in the Wisconsin militia, the Negro was ineligible under terms of the first territorial militia law enacted in 1838, and because succeeding statutes brought no change, he remained so from the beginning of the rebellion to its close.[16]

But if in 1861 the Wisconsin Negro was ineligible for military service, there is evidence that he was willing to fight for the Union. Lincoln's call of April 15 for 75,000 militiamen put upon Wisconsin responsibility of furnishing one regiment, and on the next day Governor Randall invited companies of state militia to volunteer for duty, urging "All good citizens, everywhere, [to] join in making common cause against a common enemy."[17] This would have excluded Negroes who were not citizens, but on April 18, W. H. Noland, a Negro clothes cleaner of Madison, and usually known as "Professor" Noland because of his interest in public affairs, wrote to Randall inquiring if he would accept a company of colored men for either state or federal service on a footing equal with other soldiers. Noland expected such recruits to fight, asserting that many a colored man was eager to "hurl back . . . the charge that Negroes . . . are neither brave or loyal, and not reliable in an emergency like the present." "Professor" Noland recognized limitations in the Negro's status, but did not consider them as hindrances in his willingness to defend the Union. He wrote:

> Notwithstanding they are deprived of the Election Francize [*sic*] and many other Civil Rights they are not unmindful of the fact that they enjoy the protection of the laws in their persons and property, and that their Alters [*sic*] and firesides are held sacred, and to maintain a government guaranteeing these rights, and defend it against such wicked attempts as the present, they would pledge their lives, their Fortunes, and their sacred honor.[18]

Diligent search has not discovered a reply from Randall to Noland, but after more than a century, Noland's letter appears as an earnest plea of a man lacking rights of the citizen, yet eager even so to make himself and his fellows worthy Americans through honorable service in a just cause.

Noland's inquiry could hardly have had serious consideration in view of the Negro's ineligibility for military service, but this detracts nowise from the motivation behind it. It is of interest to note that the letter came to the Governor just as that officer was being forced to disband and disarm certain Wisconsin militia units which had shown much less patriotism by refusing to volunteer in response to his call for troops.[19] And, another letter which came to Randall under the same date as that of Noland's, but far different in content and purpose, was that of former Wisconsin Immigration Commissioner Frederick W. Horn. At long length, Horn explained that federal policies were not to his liking, and he was therefore resigning his captaincy in the state militia. Besides, Horn remarked, his life insurance policy would become "null and void" if he went into active service.[20]

Although Noland's attempt to rouse interest in Negro soldiers for the Wisconsin war effort was foredoomed to failure, Congress took an important step affecting the military status of American Negroes in July, 1862, when it authorized the President to accept Negroes into the United States service as laborers or in whatever military capacity they were competent. This action became an important basis for raising all Negro troops "until well into 1864," but it denied colored recruits equal pay with others and subordinated them militarily.[21]

Nevertheless, the nation was beginning to show interest in arming Negro soldiers and in this Wisconsinites shared. In mid-1862 the government was conducting a great drive for troops, and among a population past its first enthusiasm for war, there was growing conviction that the conflict was being waged for the black man, and thus he should help fight it. To be sure, not every Wisconsin observer was certain of this, but in discussion of the July 17 law, Wisconsin Senator James R. Doolittle thought a place for the Negro in the army justifiable because the Southerners were already so using him. Doolittle was careful to explain, however, that although he was "last to sanction a departure from the rules of civilized warfare," he believed the North could in good conscience "employ the same class of person to fight against the rebels which they employ against us."[22] The West Bend *Post,* however, regarded use of Negro troops as too great a humiliation upon white Americans by putting preservation of their institutions in the hands of colored soldiers. On the other hand, the Oshkosh *Northwestern* urged use of all loyal men in the war effort, and in reporting presence of hostile guerrillas at Newburg, Indiana, remarked on July 24, 1862, "We shall soon find it well not to reject even the assistance of the blacks, if we want to put down this rebellion." But the Madison *Patriot* ridiculed proposals to raise a Negro regiment in Rhode Island, and suggested that Sherman Booth, Wisconsin abolitionist of controversial reputation, should command it "if the negroes do not object."[23]

If a sampling of opinions about arming the Negro reveals differences among Wisconsin observers in 1862, talk of conscription, which was in fact announced on August 4, may have been causative to feeling that the Negro should bear arms and thereby lessen effects of drafting on the white community.[24] Of such feeling the Madison *Patriot* remarked: "A great many may be diddled into the cry of arm the Negroes [*sic*] because they think . . . there might be less need of their services, and less liability of being called on. This to say the least, is cowardly."[25]

Nonetheless, passing events may have stirred hope among Wisconsin Negroes that they might become combat soldiers as is disclosed in a letter of Cornelius Butler to Edward Salomon then serving his fourth month as governor. Butler, a colored cook who lived in Kenosha, wrote Salomon on July 29:

> I wish to lay before your excellency the hope and desire of the colored men of this State to do something to aid the government at this time. If it shall meet your approbation and receive the cooperation of the public authorities we can raise a company perhaps two in the State to be joined to any regiment of our race to fight for the country.[26]

Although the Governor seems not to have replied to Cornelius Butler, he soon informed Edwin M. Stanton of offers to raise troops from the state's Negro "citizenry" and asked if encouragement might be given them. Lincoln had not yet determined to arm Negroes, however, and on August 6, Salomon learned that they were not acceptable as troops.[27]

That these developments were closely watched by some members of Wisconsin's white community and that Lincoln's attitude was frustrating to them may be noted from statements by a resident of Rock County which possessed the third heaviest Negro population among Wisconsin counties. This Rock County resident wrote Edward Salomon on August 7:

> Our community were very much disappointed & displeased when the word came yesterday that the President refuses to arm the Negroes. We think that he should receive them. . . . A great many express the hope that the Govs of the North will refuse to send [any] troops unless they receive all *Black* as well as *White* & Force the Pres. to receive them or resign. . . . I wish all the means to force that upon him as the best means of putting down this cursed rebellion. The Negroes freedom is what the war is for & why not have them help in all the ways possible.[28]

But 1862 closed with no change in the military status of the Negro in Wisconsin.

In early 1863 the Union government took steps which brought all Negroes closer to combat duty. One was inauguration of active recruitment for colored regiments in both North and South: this was systematized under a Bureau of Colored Troops established in May. Only individuals or agencies authorized by the Bureau might recruit among the Negro population, and any men procured were to be designated as United States Colored Troops. Another development was that terms of the National Enrollment Act of March 3, 1863, which declared liable for drafting all male citizens between the ages of twenty and forty-five as well as foreigners swearing intent to become citizens, did not exempt the Negro, and the law was applied to those who where free. Therefore, the Wisconsin Negro became subject to national conscription equally with the state's white citizenry, and the draft of November in 1863 included him.[29] This seemed wrong to a Negro conscript who had tried previously without success to enlist. The conscript, Andrew Pratt by name, wrote Salomon:

> Now will you permit a poor Fugitive from Bondage, to ask you some questions,—am I by the laws of Wis. a Citizen of the State, and if not, and am not allowed to inlist [*sic*] in the Army to fight for our Country which you know was my wish to do . . . , am I by the Laws of the United States subject to be drafted the same as a white man who has rights under the Constitution. Other men . . . who where drafted the same day I was have been allowed to inlist [*sic*] and received the Bounty, and I think it is a hard case, for me to be Compell,d [*sic*] to fight for a country whose Laws does [*sic*] not recognize me as a man.[30]

Salomon quickly assured Pratt that even though he lacked rights of white citizens, he was indeed subject to conscription. The Governor explained, "Young men under 21 years of age are also subject to draft, although they have not all the rights of white citizens yet. . . ."[31] But Salomon overlooked the basic question by confusing race with age, and Pratt's complaint was not fairly answered.

Although the draft law of 1863 was applied to free Negroes and the amendatory Enrollment Act of February 24, 1864, held able-bodied American Negroes liable to conscription, it was mostly as volunteers that colored men were credited to Wisconsin's Civil War effort. Under vigorous measures taken by the Bureau of Colored Troops, over 37,000 Negro men entered the ranks by October 31, 1863. There was, however, no material progress made in Wisconsin, although the Bureau had authorized Salomon to initiate such enlistments on July 31.[32]

This should not be construed as evidence of lack of interest on the part of the Governor in procuring men from the state's colored community. Shortly before issuance of the July 31 directive, the authorities received inquiries concerning Negro recruitment in the state; one of these came from Captain Orrin T. Maxson of the Twelfth Wisconsin who remarked that if properly officered the Negro "would compare favorably with new men being forced into service." Maxson explained that Wisconsin would have credit for such personnel—that Governor Andrews had accomplished this for Massachusetts.

Salomon seems to have been seriously impressed, and on August 25, following a conference with the officer, asked Adjutant General Lorenzo Thomas to consider Maxson's proposal that soldiers he selected be released from duty to recruit in Wisconsin. Weeks passed without results, but the Governor did not hurry. Thus, when an Illinois pastor expressed hope to Salomon that his son would be commissioned to enlist Negroes in several states including Wisconsin, he was informed that the Governor would gladly help but "did not see the way clear to do it." The minister reasoned that enlistment of Negroes would "diminish the need of white men to fight our battle," but Salomon regarded as a major obstacle the apparent refusal of federal authorities to release a man from active duty for the purpose of recruiting. Besides, he was reluctant to act until he had waited "a reasonable time" to hear from Captain Maxson whom he regarded highly.

Finally, on October 19, Maxson informed Salomon that Thomas was not entertaining plans for recruiting colored men in the loyal states, "not even in Missouri." Furthermore, the officer stated that the army must appoint recruiting officers, or if they came from the citizenry, the Governor would do so.[33] A week afterward, and in what may have been reference to the directive of July 31, the Wisconsin authorities announced authorization for raising a "regiment, battalion, or company of colored troops" with intention to form one or two companies.[34] The announcement testified to the likelihood of only modest results in obtaining enlistments from Wisconsin's sparse Negro population. Indeed, the state's three counties with the greatest colored population in 1860 possessed but 75 Negro males of military age and in 1863 the Census Director reported only 292 in the entire state.[35]

From available records, it is not possible to determine with accuracy how many Negro soldiers credited to Wisconsin actually lived there. About 20 percent of those designated as residents were recruited in other states, both North and South. Whatever their origins, colored troops credited to Wisconsin served with the Fifth, Twelfth, Fourteenth, Twenty-First, Twenty-Ninth, and Forty-Ninth United States Colored Troops. Four enlisted in the Twelfth United States Heavy Artillery, and a handful may have served in the Navy. Others were unassigned. The only organized unit credited to Wisconsin was Company F of the Twenty-Ninth United States Colored Troops.[36]

Company F owed its origin partly to Salomon's authorization to recruit Negroes in Wisconsin and partly to a movement to raise a Negro regiment in Illinois. A vigorous supporter of the Illinois effort was William Bross, Chicago civic leader and journalist. Chicago's colored community also assisted in the undertaking as did the *Tribune* with which Bross was associated. John Bross, brother of William and lieutenant-colonel-elect of the proposed unit, directed personnel recruitment and it was he who obtained permission to enlist Wisconsin Negroes for it. Lewis

Isbell, a colored barber of Chicago, served capably as recruiter in Wisconsin, his appointment being dated April 7, 1864.[37] An interested observer of these developments was the Milwaukee *Sentinel* which may have stated the wishes of many when it expressed hope that Wisconsin would help fill the Negro regiment "thereby diminishing our quota."[38] For this there was good reason. On February 1, Lincoln had called for 500,000 volunteers, and on March 14 for 200,000 more.

Company F was mustered into federal service on July 8, 1864, at Quincy, Illinois, for three years of service. On July 22 the unit joined Burnside's Corps with the Army of the Potomac in the trenches before Petersburg.[39] There, Union sappers had nearly completed mining operations for blowing a gap in the Confederate lines opposite Burnside's position and protecting high ground commanding the town. Once the break was made and before the enemy recovered from surprise, national troops would rush through to seize the elevation thereby forcing evacuation of Petersburg, the key to Richmond. On July 30 the mine was detonated, but Burnside's attack broke in the crater left by the explosion and ended in failure which Grant termed "the saddest affair" he had witnessed in the war.[40]

From testimony given before the Committee on the Conduct of the War and from participants' accounts, Union plans for the battle of July 30 were but poorly executed. A major flaw was claimed to be that of not permitting unjaded Negro units to head the attack as Burnside had intended within hours of its beginning. Burnside believed that white troops used in the assault were lacking in nerve because for six weeks previous they had been under fire almost continuously and had acquired the habit of "covering themselves by every method within their reach." Because the Negro units had not been so exposed, it seemed reasonable that in their uninhibited state they would rush ahead and win the objective.[41] *The West Point Atlas of the Civil War* remarks that Burnside wished to use the colored personnel because they were his only "fresh" troops,[42] and with this there can be no disagreement with regard to Company F. Only twenty-two days had elapsed since its muster at Quincy until the battle of July 30.

Union casualties at the Crater numbered 3,798, and Negro troops suffered greatly from the enemy. Some may also have been murdered by white Union soldiers thinking this would render counterattacking Confederates less vindictive.[43] Be this as it may, Company F sustained heavy losses. Of eighty-five men comprising the company, ten were killed and one later died from wounds. Eight of the slain were credited to Milwaukee and the others to towns in Kewaunee and Kenosha Counties. It might be noted, however, that striking as these battle losses were, Company F also lost twenty-one men by death from disease during its sixteen months of existence. One of those to die was Andrew Witherspoon, musician, aged sixteen, and credited to Milwaukee.[44]

There was another aspect of the Negro's role in Wisconsin's Civil War effort beyond his service in the ranks. In later months of the war and as demands upon manpower grew heavier, the colored man became to many Wisconsinites a means of filling required quotas. One way of accomplishing this was to enlist Negroes in the South under a law of July 4, 1864, authorizing Northern states to send recruiting agents into rebellious areas. Men so obtained were credited to the procuring state and to any subdivision thereof. The law assumed greater significance when, on July 18, Lincoln called for 500,000 volunteers for one, two, or three years' service. Fifty days were allowed for volunteering, and if the call was not completed, a draft would follow.[45]

Under this summons, which one Wisconsin citizen termed a "buster," the state's quota was originally set at 19,032, and the Negro in the South quickly appeared an instrument for helping to meet it. Sundry proposals to tap this source of manpower came to James Lewis, Salomon's successor in office. Governor Lewis offered no objections and appointed some recruiting agents with the reminder that the state could supply them no funds. This meant that interested communities would have to tax themselves to carry on the effort. An example of one to do so was the Seventh Ward of Milwaukee where each enrolled man was assessed twenty dollars to defray costs of the work.[46]

But recruitment of Negroes in the South had little effect on helping Wisconsin meet its quotas. From the first, both the Madison *State Journal* and the Milwaukee *Sentinel* doubted that the plan would succeed. The *Journal* described it as "a very Utopian" idea; the *Sentinel* remarked that with advance of Union arms the Southern whites would drive Negroes into the interior, thereby defeating the scheme.[47] Another hindrance was that Wisconsin offered no state bounty to colored enlistees, whereas some states gave as much as $500 over federal inducements.[48] There were other problems. Harrison Reed, one-time Wisconsin entrepreneur, informed Lewis from Washington that he was willing to try to raise Negroes in South Carolina and Florida, but he warned the Governor that the military authorities quickly "gobbled up" those available. Reed stressed quick action to offset such competition, indicating that he needed $10,000 to begin.[49] This was not all. One E. L. Brockway, who had been recruiting Negroes as far south as Georgia, wrote Lewis that he discovered "Our forces need all the darkies they can get to do work on fortifications," and so he thought it prudent to avoid taking Negroes inside the lines of William T. Sherman.

Brockway did indeed obtain eleven recruits at Adairsville, Georgia, but when Joe Wheeler's Cavalry raided the train on which he and the Negroes were riding, all fled to the woods. The hapless agent finally brought five recruits to Nashville only to witness their seizure by the army.[50] Nor did Governor Lewis enjoy better success when he proposed organizing a new Negro regiment in the rebel states with himself to appoint its officers. Lewis soon learned from the Bureau of Colored Troops that any soldiers so obtained would go into old regiments, and this precluded granting the request.[51]

Although recruitment of Southern blacks ended in disappointment for Wisconsin, some resident Negroes contributed to the state's war effort as substitutes for those seeking thus to discharge an obligation described by Justice Dixon of the Wisconsin Supreme Court as "the highest . . . the citizen [is] called to . . . bear."[52] Until July 20, 1864, a Negro could be a replacement only for a Negro, but an announcement of that date certified colored males to be acceptable as substitutes for all.[53] This development followed Lincoln's call of July 18 for 500,000 men by two days and brought a search for Negroes as replacements in Wisconsin. The demand could not have been lessened when the July levy ended in a draft and when in December of 1864 the government summoned 300,000 volunteers for terms of service ranging from one to three years. Results may be seen in registry of 97 substitutes on the roster of 176 Unassigned Colored Troops credited to Wisconsin. Most of these men were obtained from late summer of 1864 onward; the last Negro recruited in the state was Manual Raynolds who enrolled at Fond du Lac on April 10, 1865. He was a substitute.[54]

Procuring substitutes had become an established business in Wisconsin as wartime demands on manpower accelerated. By 1863 a soldier there had as "quotable value as a horse," especially during drafting periods, and heavy calls of 1864 caused high prices for replacements with length of service determining procurement cost.[55] In August the *Sentinel* quoted substitute prices at Prairie du Chien as running from $250 to $400; at Milwaukee, where the newspaper reported a demand in excess of supply, figures ranged from $500 to $1,000.[56]

For persons whose means permitted, procurement of a substitute was an entirely honorable method of discharging the military responsibility. So doing was considered far more patriotic than paying an allowable but impersonal commutation fee. It was a matter for the individual to decide, and if he chose to engage another to take his place in the ranks, his judgment was not a subject of reproach. In fact, while supplementary drafting was taking place in Milwaukee during the fall of 1864, the *Sentinel* quoted a local procurer to the effect that "quite a number" of the city's "most sagacious business men" had "wisely taken time by the forelock" by hiring so-called representative recruits with the objective of escaping conscription. Records reveal that not a few Milwaukeeans, some of whom were prominent figures in the city banking and brewing circles, obtained Negro substitutes. There were those in other Wisconsin communities who availed themselves of the same opportunity.[57]

If Wisconsin derived benefits from the Negro militarily, it cannot be said that the Negro received benefits in return. Because he was enrolled in the national service, the colored soldier credited to Wisconsin suffered exclusion from benefits the state provided its armed personnel. True, in 1864 a legislative committee reported that family aid laws could be applied to the Negro, and in the same year the Adjutant General urged this as "a simple act of justice." Nonetheless, it was not until 1866 that Wisconsin granted the Negro soldier family aid.[58] With regard to boun-ties, Negroes recruited for Company F were declared ineligible from the first, but a law of June 15, 1864, extended federal premiums to most col-ored troops. There was no state bounty for any Wisconsin soldier; this was a community responsibility. Search has not discovered any record of local bounty payments made to Negroes.[59] As for wages, the state had no voice, but the federal law of June 15 equalized pay of all Negro troops free before April 19, 1861, with that of other soldiers. One supporter of this step was the Milwaukee *Sentinel* which asserted that persons per-forming identical tasks should have the same pay. The enrollment law of March 3, 1865, brought still further improvements, but this affected only those Negroes mustered after that date.[60]

The Negro credited to Wisconsin also faced the challenge of proving himself as a soldier. There were no black heroes to appear individually in the newspapers, and Company F of the Twenty-Ninth United States Col-ored Troops provides the single example by which organizational appraisal is possible from official records. If judgment may be based on its losses at the Crater, the Company was capable of sacrifice. Moreover, its total death roll was heavier proportionately than that of the combined state units. Twelve men, it is true, deserted Company F by the time of its muster out at Brownsville, Texas, in November 1865, but this was much less in degree than the experience of the 34th Wisconsin which lost by desertion 283 of its original strength of 961 in only nine months of duty.[61] Company F was only a small organization, but its performance was such as to aid in bettering the Negro soldier's image before his fellow Americans. And in this respect the Negro had far to go. To compare him thus with Wisconsin's other non-white soldier, the Indian, it was usual for both black and red man to suffer much the same inequities in civilian life, but as a potential fighter, the Indian's courage was not questioned as that of the Negro's often was.[62]

It would be exaggerative to say that the Negro exerted great or crucial effect on Wisconsin's Civil War effort. It is likely that most Wisconsinites forgot him once he became a number in filling a quota or as soon as he left the substitute broker for camp. He was, so to speak, a stepson of the state.[63] Nevertheless, the Negro soldier performed much as did others in Wisconsin's Civil War effort, and from his station contributed to the military history of the state and to that of his people.

Part 4

THE IMPACT OF
WAR ON
FREE PEOPLE
OF COLOR

CHAPTER 12

"I Was Always a Union Man"

The Dilemma of Free Blacks in Confederate Virginia

Edna Greene Medford

FREE PEOPLE OF COLOR were an anomaly in the antebellum South. Their very presence ran counter to the white idea of the proper role of the African American in society. Both planters and non-slaveholders feared them for their potential to incite revolt among those in bondage, and hence, white Southerners attempted to regulate nearly every facet of their lives. The exploitation of free black labor and the denial of full enjoyment of basic liberties reflected the attempt on the part of whites to reduce them as much as possible to the level of the slaves.

Perhaps at no time was the complexity of the position of free people of color more evident than during the Civil War. The wartime needs of the Confederacy expanded free black economic opportunities. By taking advantage of the labor shortage created by the loss of white men off at war and slave laborers who made their escape from the plantations, free people managed to improve their economic circumstances in a way that had been denied to them previously. Contemporaneously, however, certain Confederate policies placed free people in danger, and threatened their liberty and property. Free blacks were keenly aware that any support they gave the Confederacy would give tacit consent to the continuation of their own oppression (perhaps even intensifying it) and that of the millions of African Americans in bondage. Conversely, support for the Union could result in serious if not fatal immediate consequences for individuals, as well as jeopardize the continued freedom of all free people of color if the North lost the war. Ultimately, a combination of self-interest and a shared racial heritage with those in bondage led most free blacks to embrace the Union cause.[1]

The role of free blacks as soldiers and as noncombatants within Union lines has been well-documented.[2] Less is known about the attitudes, actions, and circumstances of free men and women of color who lent support to the Northern effort from inside the Confederacy. To the degree that historians have concerned themselves with this matter, they have focused their attention on the elite free people of New Orleans, Mobile, and Charleston. Nothing of substance has been written of the free blacks in the tidewater Virginia counties of Charles City and New Kent, where the wartime experiences of free blacks were shaped by their close proximity to Richmond and the consequent advances and retreats of both the Union and Confederate armies. Hence, this essay addresses those people. Like other Unionists, these free blacks were subject to the same consequences suffered by anyone whose disloyalty to the Confederacy was uncovered. Their race, however, made them even more vulnerable to disclosure and punishment. Moreover, their Unionism was generally motivated by a deep concern for their personal freedom and future liberty rather than by ideological or philosophical factors, as was evident among white Southern loyalists.[3] In essence, black Unionists had more to lose from Northern defeat. Their actions during the war reveal their recognition of this reality.[4]

Table 1

Population of Charles City and New Kent, 1860

COUNTY	FREE BLACK	SLAVE	WHITE	TOTAL
Charles City	856	2,947	1,806	5,609
New Kent	364	3,374	2,145	5,884

SOURCE: U.S. Bureau of the Census, Eighth Census, 1860.

In 1860, the free African-American community was well established in Charles City and New Kent, two wholly rural counties that occupied the northern end of the Virginia Peninsula.[5] Slightly more than 1,200 free people of color lived and labored in this part of Virginia's "Black Belt." Free people constituted over 10 percent of the overall population and nearly one-fifth of the African-American (see Table 1). Within this free population were people who had descended from venerable families whose histories dated back as far as the late seventeenth century.[6] Despite residence whose longevity rivaled that of some of the first white families of Virginia, free people endured the same denial of basic rights as African Americans elsewhere in the state. Virginia law denied them access to an education, restricted their movement, prevented them from bearing arms or congregating beyond the watchful eyes of whites, and otherwise limited their rights as a free people.' At the same time, they were required to contribute to the community and the state by paying taxes and rendering any other service deemed necessary and appropriate. Failure to do so invited arrest and the possibility of temporarily being subjected to forced servitude. Their children suffered the indignities visited upon the parents as well. A parent's indigence subjected the child to forced apprenticeship to local planters, farmers, and craftsmen, thereby reducing them to the status of quasi-slaves.[8]

Although oppressed by laws that circumscribed their liberty, free people of color in Charles City and New Kent benefited from an economy that enabled most to gain a modest subsistence and allowed some to enjoy a certain measure of economic independence. The mixed farming economy provided ample opportunities for employment. The vast majority of free blacks became farm laborers, tending the fields of middling white planters and farmers. The few who worked their own land had modest holdings. A handful, however, were distinguished for the large size of their farms. In New Kent, four free men—Robert Burgoine, Carter Lewis, Thomas Pearman, and George Fox—owned over 100 acres each. They were joined in Charles City by Samuel Hampton, William Turner and Samuel Brown. Hampton was clearly the wealthiest free man of color in either county with 360 acres of land.[9]

Free people in the two counties engaged in non-agricultural labor as well. They worked at sawmills and chopped wood independently, fished extensively in the James and Pamunkey rivers, and pursued other unskilled specialized labor like well digging and teamstering. A small percentage made their living principally as craftsmen: blacksmiths, wheelwrights, and carpenters. A handful of women owned and farmed their land; some labored beside men as farm laborers, while others contributed to the family economy as carders, spinners, and weavers.[10]

What is most striking about the economic activity of these free people is the extent to which they combined occupations. Farm laborers and farmers (renters and landowners alike) supplemented income most frequently by fishing or cutting wood. Blacksmiths and carpenters, although they considered their craft to be the primary source of their livelihood, used the money earned from those occupations to buy land which they farmed as well.[11] For the most part, free blacks remained poor people, but the nature of the economy allowed many to live in comfortable circumstances and gave them greater control over their labor.

Free blacks in Charles City and New Kent also managed to develop a sense of community by establishing a religious institution which became central to their community life. In 1810, Charles City free people built their own church. Elam Baptist became the spiritual and social center for African Americans in the county, free and slave—until Nat Turner's rebellion escalated white fears—and attracted congregants from neighboring New Kent as well. After the Turner rebellion, Virginia law required them to accept nominal supervision by a white pastor, but free people continued to find a relative independence that was denied to them in the white churches.[12]

Hence, on the eve of the war, the free black population of Charles City and New Kent consisted of people who, although accustomed to hardship and oppression, had managed to gain some degree of control over their lives; some had even known prosperity. The war threatened that. As the conflict escalated, free blacks struggled to maintain this relative independence and economic security. Believing that their future stability depended on Northern victory, a few eagerly joined the Union army after the federal government approved the enlistment of black men; others who fled the Confederacy served the Northern forces in some noncombatant capacity. They left behind people who were equally committed to the Union cause, but who did not see flight or soldiering as a viable option for themselves. As one free man put it, "I was willing at all times to do all in my power to help the Union, but I didn't want to leave my home—I had a wife and family dependent on me."[13] One suspects that these free men who stayed were equally motivated by a desire to protect property for which they had struggled so long. By clandestinely supporting the Union at home, these free blacks could safeguard their possessions while undermining the society that limited their freedom. Their actions during the war reflected their commitment to that end.

War came to Virginia's lower peninsula in May 1861, when Union troops reinforced the federal contingent already in possession of Fortress Monroe in Hampton Roads. Confederate forces assisted in the evacuation of white residents from their homes and bore them to secured territory north of the Hampton-Newport News area. Some were forced to leave their slaves behind as bondsmen and women resisted attempts to remove them from the area by fleeing to the fort.[14] During the first year of the war, Union forces expanded outward from Fortress Monroe and eventually claimed and occupied much of the territory at the southern end of the Peninsula. There, the wartime experiences of free blacks and slaves were shaped by Northern troops who despised and exploited them, and by the federal government's attempt to grapple with the monumental problems associated with managing and caring for the large number of displaced and fugitive peoples.[15]

By the spring of 1862 the Union launched its Peninsula campaign—a northwestward advance of forces over 100,000 strong—in an ambitious attempt to capture Richmond. Led by General George McClellan, Union forces marched up the Peninsula and crossed through both Charles City and New Kent counties. Whites fled the Union advance, and their slaves seized upon the opportunity provided by the Northern presence to liberate themselves.[16] On the great estates that stretched out along the James River, bondsmen and women took advantage of their access to the waterway and fled in large numbers. Escapes increased dramatically as Union forces cut a path of retreat through Charles City. Over two-thirds of the 63 people enslaved on the Westover Estate sought freedom when the Northern army camped near the plantation in the summer of 1862. John Selden, the owner of Westover, would have lost even more of his property had he not removed 17 of his slaves beyond the reach of the Union lines. Despite this precaution, however, three of the 17 managed to escape.[17] Slaves fled the other plantations in the area as well: 85 ran away from Shirley, the estate of the Carters; the Sherwood Forest Plantation of former U.S. president John Tyler lost 15 laborers; and 50 escaped the Wilcox estate. An observer of the times noted that "nearly, if not fully one-half of the negro men" in Charles City County fled the Union during the war.[18] Many of them were transported to the southern tip of the Peninsula where they swelled the ranks of those already settled in the over-crowded contraband camps in York and Elizabeth City counties.

Shifting lines of defense bewildered Charles City and New Kent residents who could not always be sure of who was in control of their area. In fact, both the Confederacy and the Union claimed the two countries throughout the war. This complicated the lives of free blacks even more, as they could not feel secure in their property or personal freedom with such fluidity in the lines.

While the slaves made their escape to freedom, free people of color contemplated their options: leave home and perhaps join the Union forces or remain in the Confederacy where they might be able to protect family and property and still support the Union. Both options entailed some risks, and those who chose to stay at home soon realized the difficulty of conducting daily activities and supporting Union victory while being compelled to respond to the demands of the Confederacy. As the war deepened, free people found themselves involuntarily drawn into the struggle both directly and indirectly. As residents of the state, they were expected to surrender a proportion of crops requisitioned by the Confederacy. Rebel forces also seized the property of free blacks illegally, taking poultry, livestock, and farm implements and tools. Years later a free man complained that the Confederates "took little things from us . . . and threatened us in all sorts of ways . . ."[19]

The greatest threat to free people of color, however, was the exploitation of their labor. At first Confederate authorities encouraged free blacks to volunteer their services to the cause. When volunteerism failed to meet adequately the demands for labor, however, African Americans—slave and free—suffered impressment at the hands of rebel commanders.[20] In February 1862, the Virginia legislature took steps that made it easier to compel free blacks to labor for the Confederacy, requiring all free black men between 18 and 50 years of age to register with the local courts. When Confederate commanders needed laborers, they simply submitted a requisition to the court, which then selected the specified number of laborers. Such involuntary service could extend for up to 180 days. Laborers thus impressed were entitled to monetary compensation, medical care, food and quarters.[21]

Free blacks from Charles City and New Kent were impressed in the first year of the war to assist in the building of entrenchments in Yorktown and Mulberry Island near Jamestown.[22] In December 1861, at least 600 African Americans, "many of them free negroes," labored to construct batteries and earthworks around Yorktown. The rate of compensation for the labor amounted to $10 per month.[23] Again, in January 1862, General John Bankhead Magruder, commanding Confederate forces on the Peninsula, sought to replace troop labor with black slave and free—because "the sickly season came and the army could no longer work."[24] The extent to which free blacks were impressed is evident in a March 19, 1863, requisition for labor that drew 100 free blacks from Charles City County and 20 from New Kent's much smaller population.[25] Given the size of the requisition, however, it must have been devastation to the free African-American community. The use of free black laborers to build defenses and perform other military labor for the Confederacy only intensified as the war dragged on.

Black laborers found the erection of breastworks and other defenses to be arduous. Trees had to be felled to obstruct rivers, tons of earth dug up and hauled into place, and revetments constructed. Laborers worked in all manner of inclement weather and were made to stand waist deep in water and mud. Despite assurances of adequate food and medical care, many suffered lasting physical disabilities from their experiences in erecting Virginia's defenses.[26]

The Confederacy employed slave labor extensively as well—at first on a voluntary basis; but as illness and death from overwork, poor care, and abuse turned the cooperation of planters into alarm over the well-being and survival of their bondsmen, coercion was necessary. Resistance from slaveholders forced the state legislature to compel them to surrender their slaves between the ages of 18 and 45 upon the demand of Confederate authorities. The law allowed the Confederacy to employ these bondsmen for up to 60 days.[27] Planters reluctantly sent their laborers to the front; others defied the requisition orders altogether, and wrote letters of protest to any official whom they held had the authority to redress their grievances.[28]

Failing to obtain exemption for their bondsmen who had been conscripted for service on Confederate fortifications, planters attempted to hire free black substitutes. John Selden, for instance, hired free black men for that purpose in July, August, and again in December 1861. He contracted to pay the men 75 cents per day. Apparently Selden experienced some difficulty in procuring the labor of free black men from his county, since he had to send to Petersburg to find substitutes for his slaves.[29]

While planters moved to protect their property in slaves, free blacks were left to devise their own methods of circumventing the Confederacy's demand for labor. Some went to extraordinary lengths. Most commonly, they fled, dodging the impressment officials who sought to carry them away, or making their escape upon reaching the work site. The case of Riley Jones was fairly typical. Jones, a 40–year-old Charles City County farmer, was impressed in the first year of the war to work on fortifications at Mulberry Island. After working there for two months, Jones left without authorization and returned home. Fearing that the Confederate forces would arrest him and compel him once again to labor for them, he hid out in the woods on several occasions, once for a period of three weeks.[30] Other free black men from the county took similar action. After working for eight days on breastworks at Mulberry Island, Edmund Jones also returned home without being released by the rebel authorities. Doubtless to his amazement and delight, impressment forces did not pursue him or attempt to conscript him again.[31] His good fortune eluded County resident Albert Brown, however. After Brown escaped from that same island, Confederate officials impressed him a second time and compelled him to assist in constructing defenses around Richmond. Eventually, he made his escape from there as well. From that point on, Brown and several other free black men in the county began to lie out in the roads at night to avoid the "conscript guards who would come for us to do some kind of work for the Confederates, which we were determined if possible not to do."[32]

Free men of color used whatever tactics were at their disposal to escape impressment. When running away failed to solve their problem, they appealed to white patrons to intercede for them. Warren Cumber, a prominent farmer whose family had lived in New Kent County as free people for generations (perhaps as early as the late seventeenth century), appealed to an old lawyer friend of his when the Confederates sent him to work on fortifications at Yorktown in June 1862. The lawyer managed to get Cumber released and sent him on his way. That favor, however, did not extend to his 19–year–old son who was forced by the rebels to serve as a wagoner.[33]

Legitimate and feigned illness spared some free black men from the impressment ranks or cut short their terms at labor. After serving ten days on fortifications at Williamsburg, Joseph Brown of New Kent received a furlough because he had sickened. On several subsequent occasions, Confederate officials attempted to impress him for work in Richmond, but each time Brown managed to avoid service by acquiring a certificate from the Quartermaster Department attesting to his unfitness for labor.[34] His "condition," however, did not appear to hamper his cultivation of the farm he owned during the war.

Beyond the threat of impressment, black men found themselves subjected to the suspicions and fears of local whites and Confederate officials. From the perspective of whites, Southern victory required the complete loyalty of every member of the society and participation that aided the rebel cause. Despite tolerance and even acceptance of the free black presence before the war, whites recognized the contradiction of black freedom within a slave society. Few believed that black men could be fully trusted. Thus, an ill-advised comment in the presence of the wrong persons could bring an involuntary visit to the rebel camp, if not more serious consequences. Warren Cumber must have considered himself fortunate to have escaped serious repercussions for voicing the opinion that "the northern army would win the day."[35] As a consequence of his comment Confederate soldiers arrested him and carried him before General Fitzhugh Lee, whose forces were camped not far from Cumber's home. Lee apparently saw nothing gained in making an example of the free man, but soldiers under his command took the matter more seriously and, ignoring Lee's order that Cumber be released, took him to another commander instead. Fortunately for Cumber, he encountered a Confederate officer who knew him and had him released.[36]

At least one free man of color in Charles City attracted unwelcome attention to himself as well. County authorities arrested Edmund Collier Brown early in the war and charged him with being in possession of a New York paper that encouraged African Americans to rebel.[37] Brown was eventually acquitted, but the experience doubtless convinced him and other free people of the necessity for increased circumspection during the course of the war.

Confederate officials had good reason to suspect and fear disloyalty from free people of color. All over the Peninsula African Americans—slave and free—lent support to the Union cause by serving as guides, spies, messengers, and agents for those attempting to escape to federal lines. The Union consistently relied on information supplied or corroborated by "intelligent negroes" and "mulatto informants."[38] Free blacks reported troop movement and the strength of units and the degree of fortifications the Confederate Army had erected. For instance, when Union Lieutenant Franklin Ellis was sent out across Charles City County in June 1862 to ascertain the feasibility of establishing signal communications between headquarters and gunboats, he encountered a free black man who informed him of his imminent capture by the Charles City Troop, a home-based group of Confederates. Undoubtedly because of this help, and perhaps owing to the assistance of other like-minded blacks, Ellis and his unit were able to "pass through more than 30 miles of the enemy's country, none of which had ever been traversed by a federal soldier before . . ."[39] Ellis' reconnaissance convinced him that although it was "impracticable to signal across this country by the usual method . . . many free negroes can be found who could be fully trusted with the transmission of messages in cipher."[40]

Support for the Union did not preclude free blacks from advancing their economic interests during the war. The close proximity to Richmond of Charles City and New Kent made the city accessible to trade. Hence, free black farmers and fishermen traveled the 25 miles to Richmond weekly by mule cart. While there they sold agricultural products and marketed shad and other fish caught from the James and Pamunkey rivers. Given the food shortages that plagued Richmond during the war, free blacks doubtless found a ready market for most of their goods. Generally, they traveled unmolested by the Confederates. There is no indication, however, that they established a direct commercial relationship with Confederate soldiers, as occurred in some areas of Virginia, but their weekly trips to Richmond unmistakably aided the Confederate cause.[41]

If free blacks were troubled by this indirect aid to the Confederacy, they could assuage their consciences by reflecting on the non-economic byproducts of those weekly trips to Richmond. The business activities of black farmers and fishermen allowed them to acquire passes from the clerk of the market, and hence enabled them to move freely in and out of Richmond. This access to the Confederate capital enabled them to provide an invaluable service to the Union. On the return trip home from market they carried out messages and letters and transmitted military information to the federal forces. In a more dangerous action, they smuggled out Northern sympathizers and Union soldiers who had been imprisoned by the Confederacy.

William Henry Brisby was perhaps the most notable of these smugglers of human cargo. Early in the war, apparently fearing impressment (and doubtless wishing to remain close to his substantial property), Brisby had yielded to pressure to render blacksmithing services to a Confederate cavalry unit camped near his home. For several months, he shod their horses and, when the Confederates finally released him, Brisby began his crusade for the Union cause. He was credited with orchestrating and executing the escape of several Unionists from Richmond and transporting them to federal lines. His escapees included Union soldiers (three of whom had escaped from Libby Prison), white women whose husbands had already left Richmond, and African Americans (presumably slaves) who wished to leave the Confederacy. Brisby sometimes hid these fugitives on his property and transported them to within reach of the Union lines after dark.[42] The Confederates twice imprisoned him in Castle Thunder on suspicion of spying for the Union, but each time he won release because his accusers failed to prove him guilty.

Free people of color who were less daring or who did not have the opportunities presented to Brisby on his market days assisted the Union by aiding injured soldiers who were the casualties of the many skirmishes in and near the two counties. After General Philip Sheridan's forces were engaged in fighting near William Adkins' home in 1864, Adkins persuaded a small group of his neighbors to assist him in gathering together a few of the wounded Union troops. The free black men put the soldiers in a house nearby where Adkins oversaw their recovery. Once the soldiers gained enough strength to allow safe transport, he carried them to a nearby federal gunboat.[43]

The resolve of free people of color within the Confederate lines to support the Union never wavered, but the attitudes and actions of the Northern army sometimes tested even the staunchest Union men and women. For much of the war, Union forces were in striking distance of Charles City and New Kent. When federal soldiers were not marching through the counties to attack Richmond, they sent out foraging parties that appropriated anything (sometimes even property that had been nailed down) that they believed to be useful to the military. In some instances, soldiers took property presumably for their own personal use. White planters and farmers expected such incursions and prepared for Northern arrival. Free blacks doubtless assumed they would be spared because of their loyalty and assistance to the Union, but their faith in the Northern army proved ill-advised. Many lost provisions that had been stored for the use of their families or were destined for sale in the Richmond market, and they suffered the loss of livestock and other agricultural products essential to their livelihood as farmers. The barely subsisting, as well as the most prosperous among them, fell victim to these foragers. The industrious William Brisby suffered a significant loss when Union troops took his blacksmith and carpentry tools and pulled down his shop. The army used the planks from the structure for firewood and to build quarters. Before they left his place, Brisby lost 1,000 pounds of iron, oak timber, a variety of agricultural goods (including fodder, oats, cornmeal, flour, several boxes of tobacco, over 300 pounds of bacon, and over a dozen hogs), two horses, a cart, several barrels of fish and three fishing boats.[44] In contrast, the army only appropriated a three-year-old mule from William Charity. But its loss doubtless made it more difficult for Charity to gain a subsistence on the rented land he farmed.[45]

Not content to appropriate only stored goods, Union troops turned out their horses to graze in oat and corn fields. Harris Miles gave voice to the frustrations of free blacks when he complained that the army "grazed down and utterly destroyed" the crop for which he had so diligently labored. Miles had been the unfortunate recipient of two Union visits, and as a consequence, he had lost most of his livestock and all of the fencing that enclosed 18 of the 20 acres he had rented from John Selden.[46]

Foraging parties did not limit their activities to preying on able-bodied free men, and black women did not escape their raids, either. Lucy Green a 52–year-old free black widow of Charles City, lost nearly all her property when Union soldiers camped near her 50–acre farm in 1863 and again in 1865. As they had at other farms, the army tore down her fences for firewood, carried off the cow, calves, and poultry, killed her pigs, and stripped her garden of vegetables. The army took household items as well, including blankets, pillows, a teakettle and water bucket. When she refused to surrender her horse, which she had locked in the stable, Union troops bore a hole through the structure and senselessly killed the horse with a bayonet.[47]

Lucy Green's experience with the Union army parallelled that of the other free people of color in Charles City and New Kent. When they protested at the appropriation of their property they were answered with gruff retorts and admonishments that the Union was fighting for the freedom of black people and that the free people "ought not to grudge them" use of the property.[48] On occasion, commanders showed some compassion and returned a horse or a cow, but usually they merely assured free blacks that they would eventually be compensated for their loses.[49]

While both armies consumed the resources (both physical and material) of free black men and women, people of color continued their struggle to make a living. Generally, they attempted to reach a subsistence in the ways they had before the war. During the antebellum period they had readily found employment on the farms and plantations of the two counties. Now, with so many slaves escaping from the area, free black labor proved even more valuable. Local whites complained, however, that free people were unwilling to work for them in the fields. In the spring of 1862, former Virginia acting governor and resident of Charles City County, John M. Gregory, complained about the possible loss of the wheat crop because "the free negroes refuse to work, and the demand for labor is so great in consequence of the great number of negroes who have gone from this County to the Yankees that no labor can be hired."[50]

Contrary to Gregory's assertions, free blacks did continue to work for whites. But they did so with the recognition that the conditions of war allowed them a large measure of control over the terms of their labor. Perhaps at no other time in their lives did they possess the degree of control over private (civilian) labor contracts as during the war years. Just as the relationship between master and slave was transformed during the war, so too was that between white employers and free people of color. Free black labor was deemed valuable enough by 1864 to prompt Charles City planters—who had complained of the impressment of their slaves in the early part of the war—to seek to have the county exempted from free black requisitions.[51] By this time, of course, the slaves had departed for the Union lines, and planters were compelled to negotiate terms of employment with those laborers who remained.

Indeed, despite the hardships of war, some free people of color managed to better their conditions by taking advantage of the opportunities made available to them during this period. Robert Brown, for instance, owned ten acres of land when the war commenced. In 1863, his improving economic circumstance allowed him to purchase an additional 40 acres and erect a house on the site.[52] William Brisby, already the owner of 32 acres of land in 1857, used the war years to expand his fishing business and enlarge his carpentry and blacksmithing operations. In April 1863, Brisby purchased a net, and with this and his three boats, he "caught large quantities of fish which he sold to the people who came for them to the shore and shipped some away."[53] Brisby also erected a fish house on the Pamunkey where he stored barrels of salted fish; he marketed some of his catch n Richmond. The war gave industrious and ambitious free men like Brisby and Brown the opportunity to increase their income by responding to the needs of neighbors and the larger market at

Richmond. Clashing armies and military movements occasionally disrupted weekly trips to the market, but free black entrepreneurs resumed trade when conditions improved. African Americans who had benefited from the varied ways of making a living before the war capitalized on the ability to do so in the midst of the chaos.

Postbellum statements of free people of color revealed the extent to which they had feared a worsening of their circumstances should the North suffer defeat. Some of these men and women voiced the concern of those who lent support to the Union because of the belief that Northern victory would ensure the destruction of slavery as well as ensure better conditions for the race in general.[54] But what is most apparent in their statements is the extent to which free people were motivated by dissatisfaction with their limited freedom and concern over greater loss of status. They complained that before the war they had been treated badly and had few liberties. They especially lamented the denial of education and believed that Union victory would increase their rights. Moreover, free blacks were motivated by the assumption that if the Confederacy had won, they would have been reduced to slavery. A few of them believed that any money accumulated from selling free people into bondage had been promised to the wives of Confederate soldiers.[55] According to William Brisby, local magistrate Edward Pollard had even warned him that he "meant to have me certain if the Confederacy succeeded."[56] Perhaps Riley Jones best summed up the sentiments of free people when he stated: "We believed that if the southern people succeeded all of us free people would be made slaves of; and we believed that if the yankees succeeded we should remain free and have a better chance for our living."[57]

Free black men and women in Charles City and New Kent saw their economic positions strengthened in the postbellum era and benefited from the inclusion of African Americans in the political process during Reconstruction and for several years beyond. They became leaders of the African-American communities, founding churches, establishing schools, winning election to office, acquiring land and starting businesses. William Brisby, for instance, represented New Kent County as a member of the House of Delegates in the first legislative session after Virginia's restoration to the Union. After serving one term there, he returned to the county where he was repeatedly elected to local office either as a supervisor or as a justice of the peace. He held office and was a powerful political force in the district until the turn of the century. Warren Cumber won election as a Commissioner of Roads and served as a judge of elections for the Republican Party in New Kent. In Charles City, Harris Miles became the first black man to serve as clerk of the court. Others, like Thomas Cotman and Robert Brown, played active roles in the church and community. The economic advantage that generations of freedom permitted them enabled these free men to acquire additional property in the postbellum era. Their acquisitions dominate land transactions among African Americans in the first decade after the war, and their role as grantors of deeds reflects the extent to which the landholdings of free men and women enabled freedpeople to become property owners as well.[58] By staying home free people of color provided the continuity that facilitated the transition of freedpeople from slavery.[59]

Free people of color in Charles City and New Kent counties experienced the war from a perspective that differed from that of both planter and slave. They were forced to reconcile three different components of themselves: African American, free person, resident of the Confederacy. Their actions during the war were shaped by their own unique needs and ambitions. Self-interest kept them at home, but it made them supporters of the Union as well. They saw no contradiction in the two. Without antagonizing Confederate officials, they could safeguard their freedom, expand their liberties, and protect their property. Once they had associated these goals with Northern victory, "They were all Union people— They were colored free born and couldn't be anything else."[60]

CHAPTER 13

Humbly They Served

The Black Brigade in the Defense of Cincinnati

Edgar A. Toppin

T HE EXPERIENCE OF THE Black Brigade during the "siege" of Cincinnati, September 2–20, 1862, epitomizes the role of the free Negro
of the North during the Civil war. Eager to serve despite rebuffs, cheerfully toiling despite mistreatment, the members of the Brigade won respect
for their downtrodden race. While only a civilian laboring battalion and
never officially mustered into state or federal service, these valiant men
foreshadowed the subsequent courageous service of the Negro soldier.
That Negroes were not bystanders in the war can be seen in their role in a
key city threatened by invasion prior to the general acceptance of colored
troops. The story of the little known Black Brigade deserves re-tellings.[1]

The threat to Cincinnati came at a time of ebb in Union fortunes. President Lincoln, concluding that "Things had gone from bad to worse, until
. . . we . . . must change our tactics, or lose," had in desperation "determined upon the adoption of the emancipation policy . . ." He hungrily
awaited a victory, any victory, so that the emancipation would not appear a
"last *shriek* on the retreat."[2] But Union triumphs then were rare. In the
east, McClellan had abandoned the Peninsula campaign and Pope had
failed at Second Manassas, while in the west Grant was bogged down
before Vicksburg. The impending danger to Cincinnati, however, was a
product of Buell's supine retreat from Chattanooga to Nashville that
cleared the way for Confederate forces under Braxton Bragg, John Morgan,
and Kirby Smith to invade Kentucky and menace Cincinnati.[3]

Judge William Martin Dickson, a prominent citizen of Cincinnati and commander of the Black Brigade, complained of the Union mismanagement that made possible this threat to the city. He deplored the "fatal mistakes" that "scattered our armies everywhere" and that caused us to focus on "holding places instead of checking the Enemy's army," so that "the more places we took the weaker our armies becam [sic], having . . . to protect the captured territory." Following Shiloh, he went on, our army spread itself along a line from Memphis to Chattanooga, instead of pursuing the enemy. It also left a gap in east Tennessee beyond Chattanooga, "leaving the enemy a clear road" northward. While Buell watched his portion of this line, "the enemy . . . unmolested marched around to Knoxville, thence . . . into the heart of Ky., hundreds of miles into the rear of our arrmies [sic]."[4]

Cincinnati was an inviting and exposed target. The nation's seventh largest city was extremely prosperous with an annual trade of about $175,000,000 and a yearly manufacturing output of $112,254,000, in 1859. Confederate commanders enticed their columns with visions of the cash and supplies it held; Gen. Heth planned to demand a ransom of $14,000,000 to spare the "Queen City" from destruction.[5] Cincinnati was also of strategic importance, situated midway the length of the Ohio River about 440 miles by water from its termini, Pittsburgh and Cairo. Stretching six miles along the river, the city was in the center of a vast natural bowl formed by hills three hundred feet high that surround it and continue on the south side of the river, embracing the Kentucky cities of Newport and Covington as well. An enemy reaching the hills overlooking Newport and Covington could command defenseless Cincinnati with his batteries.[6]

Cincinnati had an ambivalent attitude toward the Negro. Many residents were from the slave states and related to plantation families. The Black Brigade's commander, Judge Dickson, was married to a Kentucky belle who was a cousin of Mrs. Lincoln; Lincoln stayed with them on a visit to the city in 1857. This gateway to the South had such a prosperous southern trade that city fathers, fearful of offending slave state customers, tried to repress abolitionists. Antislavery sentiments, however, easily developed in a city that harbored runaways and that was so close to the horrors of slavery. Lane Seminary, under Lyman Beecher and Calvin Stowe, was a hotbed of abolitionism in the early 1830's, Harriet Beecher Stowe gathered impressions for *Uncle Tom's Cabin* during two decades in the city, James G. Birney moved his antislavery *Philanthropist* there in 1836, and Levi Coffin came there in 1847 to become "national president" of the Underground Railroad. Most citizens disagreed with those abolitionists. A resolution passed by Lane Seminary's trustees in 1834 stifled student discussion of slavery and led to an exodus to Oberlin. In 1836 a mass meeting of prominent citizens resolved that "no abolition paper be published or distributed in the town"; a mob followed up by wrecking Birney's office and press when he refused to desist. Likewise, William L. Yancey's pro-slavery harangue in Pike's Opera House in 1860 went unchallenged. This pro-slavery bent was still seen in April, 1861, with the election of an ardently pro-South Democrat as mayor on the 1st, in the return of a fugitive slave on the 4th, and in unmolested transit of cannon for the Confederacy on the 5th.[7]

Public hostility and mob violence imperiled Cincinnati's colored people frequently, despite the substantial contributions of this abused fortieth of the citizenry.[8] As early as 1840, Negroes had $228,000 of real estate there. Samuel T. Wilcox was a prominent merchant worth $60,000 by 1859. Henry Boyd invented a corded bed that proved so popular that he employed twenty-five white and colored people in his factory. And former slave Robert Gordon made a small fortune as a coal dealer that enabled him to invest heavily in United States bonds during the war and to buy real estate on fashionable Walnut Hill in the postwar period.[9] Nonetheless, anti-negro riots began as early as 1829 when the people of Cincinnati realized that the 2,258 black inhabitants were one-twentieth of the population: severe mob attacks caused over half to migrate then. In July, 1836, the mob that destroyed Birney's press also demolished Negro residences in Church Alley. In September, 1841, after well-armed Negroes halted a destructive mob, the white toughs secured a 6-pounder cannon, planted it at the corner of Sixth and Broadway, and pounded away at the negro settlement. This riot, which brought Governor Corwin to the city, was not ended until the Negroes, under military escort, reached a haven in the city's jails. In the 1860s a Negro leader proclaimed bitterly, "Nowhere has the prejudice against colored people been more cruelly manifested than here."[10]

Cincinnati's ambivalent attitude continued in wartime. Upon learning of the attack on Sumter, the people of Cincinnati ignored their financial ties with the South, squashed rebel sympathizers, volunteered for the colors, appropriated $200,000 to raise Union troops, and resolved at a mass meeting that any one shipping provisions, arms, or contraband "to any person or any state which has not declared its firm determination to sustain the Government in the present crisis, is a traitor." Nevertheless, the mayor and police made no effort to protect abolitionist lecturer Wendell Phillips from a riotous mob bent on lynching him 11 months after Sumter, and Henry Ward Beecher was not allowed to lecture for fear this would provoke anti-abolitionist rioting. While the police were distracted by Morgan's Confederate raiders approaching through Kentucky in July, 1862, a mob launched a murderous assault upon the colored people; this riot did not end until fears of secessionist Kentucky river toughs joining Morgan's cavalry to capture the city caused the better element to exert pressure to stop the violence.[11] Thus, although residents of Cincinnati heeded Lincoln's call and eagerly flocked to enroll, their crusade was to save the Union, not to free the slaves or dignify the blacks; this reaction typified sentiment throughout the North.

Hence it was no surprise that the citizens reacted adversely to the offer of Cincinnati's Negroes in 1861 to aid in defending the Union. When the war began, the city's colored element held a meeting "to organize a company of 'Home Guards.'" Anticipating sensitivity concerning Negroes firing at whites, even Confederate rebels, "They did not propose to invade the South, but merely desired to aid in the defense of the city. . . ." The police, nonetheless, rudely seized the keys of the schoolhouse where the Negroes planned a second meeting, ordered the American flag removed from a place serving as a recruiting station for the blacks, and also informed Negroes "to keep out of this; this is a white man's war."[12] Similarly, throughout the North, Negroes who formed units and volunteered for service were turned down by the Lincoln Administration. With four slave states on the Union's side, Lincoln was not anxious to make the war an abolitionist crusade or to enroll Negroes to invade the rebelling states.[13] Despite their humiliating rejection in 1861, the Negroes were still ready to do their part to defend Cincinnati when it seemed endangered by Smith's army in September, 1862.

The storm cloud that cast a shadow over Cincinnati's sunny war prosperity arose from the Union disaster at Richmond, Kentucky. Confederate General Kirby Smith, in coordination with Bragg, had advanced in mid-August into Kentucky where Morgan had reported there were few federal forces, ample supplies, and many rebel sympathizers. At Richmond, Smith's seasoned veterans were attacked on August 30, 1862, by a smaller force of raw Union troops under Gen. Manson; this foolhardy assault saw the Unionists overwhelmed with 206 killed, 844 wounded, and 4,303 captured or missing, while the Confederates had only 451 casualties. On September 2nd, Smith took Lexington without a fight and now was only 75 miles from defenseless Cincinnati.[14] With Smith at Lexington and Bragg's even larger army advancing through Kentucky, Cincinnati's placid days were over and the people scurried for shelter.

The Federal rout at Richmond shocked Kentucky's Unionists and the people of Ohio. Reports described residents of Covington and Cincinnati as being "greatly agitated," exhibiting "alarm," and in a state of "intense excitement" at the danger. Governor James F. Robinson, proclaiming that Kentucky "has been invaded by an insolent foe," called upon the people of the state to "rush to the rescue." Governor David Tod of Ohio hastened to Cincinnati and issued an appeal to the loyal people of the Ohio River counties to form "military companies and regiments to beat back the enemy at any and all points he may attempt to invade our State." A *Commercial* editorial warned solemnly: "The people of Cincinnati must prepare to defend themselves. . . . We are very seriously menaced. . . . Four days of forced marching would bring [Smith's army] to the banks of the Ohio. It is pretty certain that they will strike in this direction."[15]

Cincinnati was devoid of organized military forces, but a capable leader emerged to help the people man the ramparts. On the evening of September 1st, Major General Lew "Ben-Hur" Wallace arrived to take command of the defense of Cincinnati, as ordered by the Commander of the Department of the Ohio, Major General Horatio Wright. Wallace promptly declared martial law, suspended all business, ordered all citizens to report for duty, and assigned the police to act as provost guards until relieved by military units. His proclamation seemed all inclusive, insisting: "the labor . . . must be performed equally by all classes. . . . This labor ought to be that of love . . . Anyhow, it must be done. The willing shall be properly credited; the unwilling promptly visited. The principle adopted is, citizens for the labor, soldier for the battle."[16]

Wallace may have intended for all dwellers to aid in the city's defense, but local authorities, despite the Confederate menace, seemed bent on excluding the despised blacks. A significant change in the wording of the directions to report for duty hinted at this. Cincinnati's City Council, and also the mayors of Newport, Covington, and Cincinnati had met Wallace the evening of September 1st to coordinate action in the crisis. Wallace's Proclamation merely ordered citizens to "assemble in their convenient public places, ready for orders" by 11:00 A.M., Tuesday. September 2nd, an hour after the suspension of business took effect.[17] This order was to be carried out at each mayor's bidding. In its called meeting the evening of September 1st, the City Council approved the proclamation Mayor George Hatch would issue the following morning asking citizens to report for duty. As originally worded, and as approved by the Council, the Mayor's Proclamation stated all business would be suspended as of 10:00 A.M. Tuesday, "so that employers, and employed, may assemble, in their Respective Wards for the purpose of organizing themselves . . . for the defense . . . every man of every age, be he citizen, or be he alien, . . . are expected to be present. . . ." Later in the meeting, the Council approved a resolution offered by Councilman Stokes "That the Mayor in issuing his proclamation requesting the Citizens of the different Wards to meet to-morrow . . . , the usual places of voting be named as the places of meeting in each Ward. . . ."[18] Hence, when the Mayor's Proclamation appeared in the morning papers, it directed "all persons" to "assemble in their respective Wards at the usual place of voting. . . ."[19]

Designating the usual place of voting in each ward as the assemblage point may merely have been an innocent attempt to expedite by specifying a convenient site. Yet, as the Negroes were well aware, "The colored people had no places of voting"[20]; hence, this specification of the place to meet could take on sinister connotations. Since Mayor Hatch in 1861 had thwarted their attempts to organize for home defense, Negroes could easily doubt that he meant them even though he proclaimed that "Every man, of every age, be he citizen or alien, who lives under the protection of our laws is expected to take part. . . ."[21]

In view of their past experiences, the colored people might well have been justified in not responding to this new call. It was nothing new for them to be excluded. As one of the Black Brigade members, Marshall P. H. Jones, later pointed out: "Many calls for aid and assistance to suppress this gigantic rebellion . . . had been made, yet there was no demand for our services."[22] Nevertheless, patriotic sentiments overcame remembrance of past rebuffs, and the black man once more offered to serve. In fact, Ohio's great antiquarian, Henry Howe, insisted that the Negroes had "been the earliest to volunteer their services to our mayor, for the defense of our common homes."[23] Some Negroes, according to the chronicler of the Black Brigade, Peter H. Clark,[24] approached a policeman serving as a provost guard, with the following exchange taking place:

> To the question—humbly, almost trembling put—"Does the Mayor desire colored men to report for service in the city's defense" he replied "You know d—d well he doesn't mean you. Niggers ain't citizens." "But he calls on all—citizens and aliens. If he does not mean all, he should not say so." "The Mayor knows as well as you do what to write, and all he wants is for you niggers to keep quiet."[25]

It might have been better to have sought an official answer from mayor Hatch and General Wallace rather than a policeman on a beat.

Seemingly, the Mayor, Council, and police were not interested in enrolling the colored citizens. At the same time, General Wallace had decided to utilize them as laborers on the fortifications. If properly notified of Wallace's intentions, the Negroes would have flocked to serve.

Other elements of the population were allowed to volunteer first and only apprehended by provost guards for shirking. Obviously, "it would only have been fair to have given" the Negroes, a *Commercial* editorial declared later, "the opportunity that others had, of volunteering."[26]

Instead of fair treatment, there ensued a brutal and callous round up of the Negroes. Brigade member, M. P. H. Jones, recalled that "They were torn from their homes, from the street, from their shops, from everywhere, and driven to the mule pen on Plum street, at the point of the bayonet. . . ." An eyewitness, Henry Howe, recorded:

> The colored men were roughly handled by the Irish police. From hotels and barber shops, in the midst of their labors, these helpless people were pounced upon and often bareheaded and in shirtsleeves, just as seized, driven in squads, at the point of the bayonet, and gathered in vacant yards and guarded.

Constitutional guarantees of freedom from unreasonable search and seizure were flouted as the police "went from house to house, followed by a gang of rude, foul-mouthed boys. Closes, cellars, and garrets were searched; bayonets were thrust into beds and bedding; old and young, sick and well, were dragged out, and amidst shouts and jeers, marched like felons to the pen on Plum Street. . . ."[27]

No explanation was given the hapless victims. Inquiries met with curses, pleas for time were denied. Consequently, "dismay and terror spread among the colored women and children," not knowing where their husbands and fathers were taken and why.[28] Police ruffians, some drunk, were sent out with orders to "'bring all the niggers you can catch.'" The captain in charge of the conscript squads, William Honer, reacted bestially on finding some recruits, assembled in the pen across from the Cathedral, sitting in the shade while waiting several hours to go across the river; Clark reports that:

> Coming into the yard, he ordered them all to rise, marched them to another part, then issued the order, "D—n you, squat." Turning to the guard, he added, "Shoot the first one who rises." Reaching the other side of the river, the same squad were marched from the sidewalk into the middle of a dusty road, and again the order, "D—n you, squat," and the command to shoot the first one who should rise.[29]

Of Cincinnati's three major newspapers, the "copperhead" *Enquirer* kept silent, while the moderate *Commercial* and radical *Gazette* protested this outrageous round-up. The *Commercial* deplored the fact that: "The able-bodied colored men were impressed without warning, and marched off in the most summary style. . . . If they had been informed that their labor would be acceptable, there would have been little if any occasion for the harsh measures which were taken." The *Gazette* entreated: "Let our colored fellow-soldiers be treated civilly, and not exposed to . . . the insults of . . . poor-spirited whites. . . . It would have been decent to have invited the colored inhabitants to turn out in defense of the city. . . . since the services of men are required of our colored brethren, let them be treated like men."[30]

The mistreatment continued even after the Negro conscripts crossed the Ohio River on the marvelous pontoon bridge thrown up in a day to get troops, supplies, and laborers across into Kentucky. General Wallace had decided to construct formidable fortifications on the hills overlooking Newport and Covington and place his green troops behind the comforting breastworks to meet the Confederate onslaught. Negro and white noncombatants were to join the soldiers in the hasty building of these fortifications. But some of the troops "seemed to look upon the colored men as abandoned property, to be seized and appropriated by the first finder," commented Judge Dickson in the official report he made to the governor in 1864.[31] The regiments "detailed squads of soldiers," Dickson continued, "who appeared among the negroes at work, selected from them the number they wanted, and, at the point of bayonet, marched them off . . . to be employed as cooks, or in some menial capacity for the officers." This kidnapping alarmed the Negroes as "They justly apprehended that they might be carried off with the regiments, or abandoned in Kentucky, where their presence as freemen was one of the most grievous crimes known to that State's laws, punishable with . . . enslavement. . . ."[32] Here was the supreme irony: Cincinnati's Negroes had volunteered earliest, yet were forcibly dragged into service, and now faced danger of being carted into territory where these free men, eager to defend their city from conquest, might themselves wind up in bondage. No wonder Judge Dickson commented acidly in a letter to a friend later that month: "This disposition to outrage and oppress the negro current among all classes and parties in the U.S. makes all our sufferings just, indeed we deserve much more."[33]

Not all the people of Cincinnati were willing to see their colored fellow-citizens abused. The *Commercial* reported that the mistreatment "excited much indignation" among leading citizens who took up the matter with the commanding general. Whereupon, General Wallace "condemned" the injustice, according to Dickson, "and, for the purpose of protecting the colored men, and organizing them for their work requested me to take command of them. . . ." Wallace's order, dated September 4, 1864, proclaimed that "William Dickson is hereby assigned to the command of the negro forces from Cincinnati, working on the fortifications near Newport and Covington and will be obeyed accordingly."[34]

This order was the genesis of the "Black Brigade." Dickson organized a staff, recovered the Negroes kidnapped by the regiments, brought together the scattered units in which many were laboring, and formed his cohesive force. This brigade was organized into three "regiments" composed of seventeen "companies"; this terminology was merely for convenience and not related to formal military organization. Initially, this "brigade numbered about one thousand" men, but some three hundred were detailed to other duties before their names were secured so that the official muster roll appended to Dickson's report lists the names of only 706 of them. These 706 men were grouped into "companies" that ranged in size from 29 to 51, but averaged 42 men. Fourteen of the "captains" heading these "companies" were colored, three were whites. All five officers and seven aides on the "brigade" level were white. The Commandant, William Martin Dickson (1827–1889), was a native of Indiana, a graduate of Harvard Law School, and a former reporter, prosecuting attorney, and judge in Cincinnati. When detailed to form the Black Brigade, he was serving in one of Cincinnati's home guard regiments. Noted before the war for representing fugitive slaves in court and for fairness to the German element, Dickson continued championing of Negroes after the war, aiding them to gain the right to ride in the city's streetcars. Under Dickson's command, the Black Brigade stayed principally at Camp Lupton on the Licking River, which separates Covington and Newport. Not only Negroes from Cincinnati but also several hundred colored men from other parts of Ohio served in the Brigade.[35]

Colonel Dickson's fairness heartened the demoralized Negroes. He began by marching "them back to the city" and releasing them for the night so they could prepare for camp life and reassure their anxious families. He told them he was confident "that their sense of duty and honor would cause them to obey all orders given, and thus prevent the necessity of any compulsion. . . ." The men were overwhelmed by such manly appeals as seen in the words of their spokesman, M. P. H. Jones, who later told the judge that "the members of the Black Brigade . . . deeply thank you . . . for the kindness you have manifested to us in these trying times." So grateful were they that Jones soaringly proclaimed: "our mothers thank you, our sweethearts thank you, our children will rise up and thank you, and call you blessed."[36]

The troubles of the Negroes were not yet over. The police again pounced on the men as they headed home and dragged "numbers of

them, with blows and imprecations . . . to the nearest cells." Dickson had
to get "a peremptory order" from General Wallace to Mayor Hatch "prohibiting the arrest of any colored man, except for a crime" before the
jailors released the men. Several days later, when Wallace was transferred,
the police arrested in Cincinnati Negroes that Dickson had released from
duty for sickness or hardship. Another "peremptory order, this time from
General Wright to Mayor Hatch" secured the men's release. Thereafter,
Dickson noted, "no colored man has been arrested in the city of Cincinnati, merely because he was a colored man."[37]

Justifying Dickson's confidence in them, over 700 colored men vol
untarily reported for duty the morning of Friday, September 5, 1862. In
all their searching, the police had only been able to round up 400 of the
terrified Negroes. When the men assembled at Sixth and Broadway at
5:00 A.M., "glowing with enthusiasm," Captain James Lupton presented
them with a national flag inscribed "THE BLACK BRIGADE OF
CINCINNATI," and exhorted them, saying: "Members of the Black
Brigade, rally around it. Assert your *manhood,* be loyal . . . obedient,
hopeful, patient. Slavery will soon divide the slaveholders' rebellion . . .
will shortly and miserably perish." The colored patriots had already been
doing their share. On September 3rd and 4th, before becoming a separate unit, they had "proceeded cheerfully to the performance of the task
assigned them."[38] Now that they were a cohesive force, they marched
forth enthusiastically to remain in camp from September 5th to 20th. In
contrast to the jeering of a few days before, "They were cheered on their
way to work by the good words of the citizens who lined the streets and
by the waving handkerchiefs of patriotic ladies"; likewise, the regiments
of soldiers exchanged "mutual cheers and greetings" with them.[39]

Many white residents did not match the Black Brigade's dedication.
Initially, Wallace's call to serve was heeded so rigorously that grocers,
bakers, druggists, physicians, and morticians closed shop—even streetcars
ceased their clatter and schools shut their doors as street railway men and
school teachers enlisted for the duration of the siege. Wallace had to issue
orders restoring all these vital services. Such ardor soon waned and peri-
odic round-ups of shirkers became necessary. Modern pied pipers—a fifer
and drummer—were sent through the streets so that their "melodious
strains drew the able-bodied dodgers from their hiding places in large
numbers," whereupon they were arrested and "impressed into the shovel
brigade." Other cowardly shirkers "were found disguised in women's
clothing or hidden under beds. . . ."[40] The city had to resort to lures of
$1.00 a day for laboring on the fortifications in the second week, and
$1.50 a day the third week. Now many whites found the digging so much

more attractive than the drilling that it was reported "the offer of $1.50 per day for laborers in the trenches" had "depleted all the regiments"; one regiment had less than half its 1,000 men report.[41] By contrast, the members of the Black Brigade, sensing a chance to strike a blow for their outcast race, toiled devotedly. Thus, according to Goss, "it was the universal testimony of all who watched them that their conduct and their labors were such as to excite a new regard for their race." Likewise, a *Gazette* editorial held that "Most faithfully and cheerfully did they perform the services assigned to them."[42]

In their sector—along Three Mile Creek and Cemetery Ridge from the Alexandria Road to the Newport Turnpike and Licking River—the Black Brigade performed so spectacularly that they "did the most of the work upon the fortifications," surpassing the more numerous white civilians and troops erecting defenses elsewhere. In his farewell report, Dickson told the men "You have made miles of military roads, miles of rifle pits," cut down "hundreds of acres of the largest and loftiest forest trees, built magazines and forts." The supervising Engineer pronounced them "the most efficient laborers on the fortifications." At one time the blacks suggested an improvement in a military road they were building; the validity of their point was conceded, but prejudice was too strong for its acceptance.[43]

The Brigade's only casualty was Joseph Johns of "Company E" of the "2nd Regiment," killed instantly when a large tree he was chopping before Fort Shaler suddenly toppled crushing his skull and neck. Johns left a young widow and child in grief. The Brigade officers arranged for his burial.[44]

Working courageously far in advance of the Union lines, the Negroes were often in danger. Rebel sharpshooters got close enough to kill a soldier from Milton in Stark County. Not only did bullets from Confederate skirmishers whine overhead, the blacks also had to dodge missles from the Union lines. A shot carelessly fired by a soldier in Cincinnati's 4th Volunteer Regiment knocked the shovel out of the hand of John Williams of "Company D" of the Brigade's "1st Regiment"; though the bullet passed only a few inches above his head, Colonel Dickson reported that this "brave fellow never flinched" and continued his work. The entire Brigade was nearly annihilated when laboring on St. John's Hill above the Lickering River valley, nearly a mile in front of the Union line. Colonel Jonah R. Taylor of Ohio's 50th Volunteer Infantry, in charge of that section of the perimeter, ordered a battery to shell the Brigade thinking it was the enemy. Fortunately, "the officer in command of the battery . . . refused obedience, and when pressed fired blank cartridges, and then induced the sending of a flag of truce"; otherwise, the colored heroes might have perished.

Peter Clark caustically suggested that the jittery colonel should get "one of Gov. Tod's squirrel-hunting medals . . . and wear it, as a perpetual reminder that his prowess is terrible to squirrels only."[45]

Of what avail was the Black Brigade's labor? General Wallace considered the fortifications built by the city's white and colored defenders important to deterring the enemy. In a farewell public letter to the people of Cincinnati, Newport, and Covington, he asserted:

> "In coming there, strangers, viewing the works on the hills of Newport and Covington, will ask, 'Who built these intrenchments?' You can answer, 'We built them.' If they inquire the result, your answer will be 'The enemy came and looked at them, and stole away in the night.'"

Although he does not specifically acknowledge the herculean labors of the Black Brigade, Wallace must have included the unit with the general commendation in his open letter: "You have won much honor."[46]

Actually, Cincinnati was never in real danger. Smith held his army at Lexington to join Bragg in a decisive assault on Buell, but the now timid Bragg avoided the battle. One of Smith's divisions, led by Henry Heth, advanced to Covington, but did not attack the Queen City. This was not the objective; instead, Bragg and Smith sought to enroll Kentucky in the Confederacy, installing a rebel governor, Richard Hawes. With Unionist forces advancing, Smith pulled Heth's column back from the outskirts of Cincinnati, ending the threat of siege by mid-September. Meanwhile, Bragg let Buell reach supplies and reinforcements at Louisville and Buell now moved in, interrupting Hawes' inaugural party at Frankfort and colliding with part of Bragg's army at Perryville. After the indecisive battle of Perryville in early October, the armies of Bragg and Smith ignominiously returned to Tennessee.[47]

On Saturday, September 20, 1862, the Black Brigade, having completed its task returned to the city. In formation for the homeward march, the men presented a sword to their surprised commander, with their spokesman, Marshall P. H. Jones, stating that it was "a small expression of the high esteem the members of the Black Brigade entertain for you" confident "that whenever it is drawn, it will be drawn in favor of freedom." Colonel Dickson gratefully accepted the sword and then the Black Brigade "with music, and banners flying, their officers at their head on horseback" marched to the city, passing through Covington's dusty roads—where the police had forced them to squat cruelly three weeks before—on across the Ohio River on the pontoon bridge and then by Walnut, Fourth, Race, and Fifth streets to the corner of Fifth and Broadway where Judge Dickson dismissed them with a farewell address. The commander told the tired force: "You have labored faithfully. . . . The hills across yonder river will be a perpetual monument of your labors . . . you have . . . rendered a willing and cheerful service. Nor has your zeal been dampened by the cruel treatment you have received. . . . Go to your homes with the consciousness of . . . bearing with you the gratitude and respect of all honorable men." In their march back to the city the men were heartily cheered by soldier and civilian, men and women alike. As Colonel Dickson pointed out: "thus closed, in joy and happiness, a service that had been commenced with violence, in anxiety and gloom."[48]

The exemplary behavior of the Black Brigade won new admiration for the colored men from all observers except such "copperhead" organs as the *Enquirer.* Typical of unbiased sentiments was Goss's testimonial that "no other chapter in the history of the city is more to its credit than that which records the loyalty, the valor and the devotion of these black heroes. . . ." Colonel Dickson recounted that a German farmer, on learning the men were to labor in another area, requested that they remain since they neither stole nor trespassed—as troops so often did—but instead protected his property.[49] By their courage, patience, dedication, and honesty the men undoubtedly increased the stature of the Negro in Cincinnati.

The Black Brigade served humbly in only building fortifications, but the men were not unwilling to perform in a more valiant role. From Sumter's fall to the "siege" of Cincinnati, as Brigade member M. P. H. Jones pointed out, "the proferred aid" of the colored men of the city "for war purposes was coldly, we may add forcibly rejected." Notwithstanding, Jones pledged to Colonel Dickson when the Brigade was being disbanded that the men would eagerly "rally around your standard in the defense of our country."[50] Dickson's parting address acknowledged the Negro's anxiousness to enlist; his testimony is well worth recording:

> You have in no spirit of bravado, in no defiance of established prejudice, but in submission to it, intimated to me your willingness to defend with your lifes [*sic*] the fortifications that your hands have built. Organized companies of men of your own race, armed and equipped at their own expense, have tendered their services to act in the defense of our city. In obedience to the policy of the Government the authorities have denied you this privilege. In the department of labor permitted, you have, however, rendered a willing and cheerful service.[51]

Dickson's testimony helps rebut the popular misconception that Northern whites liberated the slaves while colored people, North and South, were passive onlookers. To the contrary, Negroes in Cincinnati and everywhere would have enlisted from the outset if permitted. It was the reluctance of the government, not the Negroes, that prevented the use of colored regiments until the war was one-third over.

The Black Brigade was one of the earliest organizations of colored men used for military purposes in the Civil War. Its service in the first three weeks of September, 1862, came as the long struggle to get Negro regiments accepted was finally succeeding. General David Hunter had begun recruiting a regiment of former slaves in South Carolina as early as April, 1862; lacking federal support, he had to disband the unpaid unit by mid-August. One company continued serving without pay and was enrolled in November as part of the First South Carolina Volunteer Regiment formed by Hunter's successor (Gen. Rufus Saxton) on the basis of the first federal authorization (dated August 25, 1862) to recruit Negroes. Led by Colonel Thomas W. Higginson, it ranks as the first Negro regiment although four other colored units were officially mustered into service earlier. Both Gen. Ben Butler in Louisiana and Gen. Jim Lane in Kansas began recruiting Negroes in August, 1862, without authorization. Confederate Louisiana had enlisted Negro regiments for home defense in 1861 but these men, at Butler's urging, now switched allegiance en masse. Three regiments of Louisiana Native Guards were mustered in during September, October, November, 1862, and the First Kansas Colored Volunteers, formed mostly of runaway slaves, was mustered in during mid-January, 1863, two weeks before the First South Carolina. The first regiments of free Northern Negroes, the 54th and 55th Massachusetts, were recruited by Gov. John Andrew after he received authorization in the New Year; the 54th was organized by April, 1863.[52]

Not only did the Black Brigade complete its service a week before the first colored regiment was officially mustered in (on September 27, 1862, in Louisiana), it antedated formation of nonwhite regiments in Ohio by more than a year. Ohio's Negroes flocked to join regiments in other northern states such as Massachusetts, which had less than 2,000 Negroes of military age and thus sought black recruits elsewhere. Former members of the Black Brigade fell with the noble Colonel Robert G. Shaw of the 54th Massachusetts in the assault on Fort Wagner. A Negro merchant in Oberlin, O. S. B. Wall, turned to Ohio's Governor Tod when the 55th Massachusetts was filled before one batch of 48 recruits he had raised for it was accepted. Tod secured federal authorization and a recruitment drive, aided by such Negro agents as Wall and John M. Langston, led to the formation of the 127th Ohio Volunteer Infantry, which was mustered in during early November, 1863, as the Fifth Regiment United States Colored Troops. This 127th Ohio or 5th U.S. Colored served with distinction during the Petersburg Campaign, bravely pressing the attack on Fort Gilmer on September 29, 1864, even though a white supporting brigade fled; led by Colonel Giles W. Shurtleff, the 127th had 333 casualties (85 dead and 248 wounded) that one day—over 60 percent of the 550 men in its ranks that morning. Men of the Black Brigade served in the outfit and also in another regiment of Ohio Negroes, the 27th Regiment of U.S. Colored Troops formed during the first half of 1864; like Ohio's 5th U.S. Colored, it served valiantly at Petersburg and at Wilmington.[53]

When given the chance, Negroes hastened to join the Union Army, some 178,895 black soldiers all told. They played an important role in the outcome with Negro troops at one stage totaling more than the entire effective forces in the Confederate armies. President Lincoln, in a letter to Isaac Schermerhorn on September 2, said: "We can not spare the hundred and forty . . . thousand [Negroes] now serving us. . . . This is . . . a question . . . of physical force. . . . Keep it and you can save the Union. Throw it away, and the Union goes with it."[54]

This then is the significance of the Black Brigade of Cincinnati. A war arising over slavery tried to ignore the Negro. To hold the border states and Northerners hostile to abolitionism, Lincoln initially defined it as a struggle to save the Union. There was no place for slaves or free Negroes in this "white man's war." Yet it became obvious that Union and slavery were incompatible. On September 22, 1862—two days after the Black Brigade disbanded—Lincoln issued the Preliminary Emancipation Proclamation. As the war now assumed the nature of an antislavery crusade, colored men could no longer be kept in the wings. The determination of black men to be free and to free their brethren provided the Negro soldiers and sailors who made the difference between a prolonged struggle a weary North might have terminated in disastrous compromise and the total victory won at Appomattox

The toil of the Black Brigade was a significant early step on the path of Lee's surrender. One of the few Northern cities to face attack, Cincinnati could not forget its prejudices even in time of peril to accept Negro volunteer laborers graciously. Hence colored residents were humiliatingly dragooned into service on fortifications they would have gladly erected and defended. But a service begun in disgrace ended in glory. Formed into the Black Brigade under the noble Colonel Dickson, they gave by their dedicated labor notice of the valiant service that was to be rendered by the 54th Massachusetts at Battery Wagner, by the 5th and 27th U.S. Colored regiments from Ohio in the Petersburg Campaign, and by the countless other Negro heroes. Colonel Dickson was conscious only "of having protected from outrageous slavery hundreds of poor helpless beings and of converting them into efficient workers and of having done good service for this country."[55] Little did the good judge realize that on the same day he penned these lines, September 27, 1862, the first Negro soldiers were being mustered into federal service, a trickle that became a torrent of black troops crucial to Union victory. The humble service of the Black Brigade in the Siege of Cincinnati displayed the tribulations of Northern Negroes in those perilous times, but also served as an early step on the long journey that ended with the Union victorious and slavery dead.

CHAPTER 14

※

Free Negroes and the Freedmen

Black Politics in New Orleans During the Civil War

Ted Tunnell

A T THE CLOSE OF the Civil War a young Radical Republican journal-ist—Whitelaw Reid—visited New Orleans in the retinue of Chief Justice Salmon P. Chase. A skillful reporter, Reid inspected Negro schools and churches, observed the brash behavior of defeated Rebels, and talked with local Union men about the political situation. One morning Thomas J. Durant, a prominent Unionist, arranged an inter-view between Chief Justice Chase and representatives of the "old Louisiana free-negro stock," the *gens de couleur,* in the residence where Reid was staying. Leaving his lunch, the journalist found Chase and a delegation of free blacks talking in the library. On first impression, Reid could hardly believe "that these quiet, well-bred gentlemen, scarcely one darker than Mr. Durant himself—many of them several shades whiter—were negroes." He even imagined that there was some mistake, "that some other party had got into the library by accident—some delegation of Rebel lawyers, perhaps, to remonstrate against the test oath." The free blacks asked the Chief Justice to explain to President Andrew John-son "that they paid heavy taxes" to maintain public schools which their children could not enter and that they contributed to the support of city and state government, "and were without voice in either." These facts, they believed, did not accord with the President's "well-known ideas of genuine democracy." What reply could men give who claimed to accept the Declaration of Independence? Reid asked.

Before the war, the journalist noted, the free Negroes "held themselves aloof from the slaves, and particularly from the plantation negroes." This attitude, he believed, no longer prevailed; as one free black candidly told him, "we see that our future is indissolubly bound up with that of the negro race in this country; and we have resolved to make common cause, and rise or fall with them. We have no rights which we can reckon safe while the same are denied to the field-hands on the sugar plantations." When he compiled his narrative for publication the following year, Reid failed to note that his informant's remarks and the tone and spirit of the interview between Chief Justice Chase and the "well-bred gentlemen" in the library were not entirely harmonious.[1]

The individuals described by Reid represented the elite of what had been the largest free black community in the deep South. In 1860, 18,647 free Negroes had lived in Louisiana, 10,689 of them in New Orleans. First as black Unionists, then as black Republicans, they played a critical role in Louisiana during the Civil War and Reconstruction. From their number came Oscar J. Dunn, P. B. S. Pinchback, James H. Ingraham, Caesar C. Antoine, Louis and J. B. Roudanez, Francis E. Dumas, and other black leaders. Though the slave population of New Orleans numbered 13,385 at the time of the Civil War, the city's black political leaders in the Reconstruction period, almost to a man, were former free men of color.[2]

From French colonial days down to the Civil War, the *gens de couleur* occupied a comparatively secure place in Louisiana society. True, they endured rigid social discrimination,[3] but it was also true, as the state Supreme Court ruled in 1856, that "in the eye of the Louisiana law, there is . . . all the difference between a free man of color and a slave, that there is between a white man and a slave." Moreover, "it has been settled doctrine here," the high court had held a decade earlier, that light-skinned "persons of color are presumed to be free."[4] Free Negroes owned real and personal property (including slaves), contracted legal marriages, testified against whites in courts of law,[5] learned trades and professions, and participated in music and the arts. Their achievements rested on a solid economic base. Federal census figures from 1850 list the occupations of 1,792 free Negro males in New Orleans. The enumeration includes 355 carpenters, 278 masons, 156 cigar makers, 92 shoemakers, 82 tailors, 64 merchants, 41 barbers, 18 butchers, 12 teachers, 11 overseers, 4 doctors, and 1 architect. Only 179 are classified as unskilled laborers.[6]

Throughout much of their history the people of color relied upon a unique institution to safeguard their rights in society: the free Negro militia. In 1729 a handful of black bondsmen, motivated by the promise of freedom, helped put down a savage uprising of the Natchez Indians. Thereafter free Negro militia fought in every battle against the foreign and domestic enemies of colonial Louisiana. From 1779 to 1781 they engaged the British as Spanish allies of the American revolution. After 1803 the Americans disbanded the black militia, but events soon led them to reconsider the decision. In 1811 free men of color volunteered to fight against rebellious slaves marching on New Orleans. Although white militia and American regulars put down the revolt, the territorial governor used a company of free Negroes to relieve the white units. The loyalty of the *gens de couleur* in that crisis led the government to revive "The Battalion of Free Men of Color," and in late 1814, with the British threatening New Orleans, it created a second battalion. Both units fought with distinction under Andrew Jackson in the Battle of New Orleans, winning the respect and approval of the hostile Americans. Their bravery in that last and greatest battle of the War of 1812, commemorated annually in antebellum New Orleans, helped secure the rights and privileges of free blacks down to the Civil War.[7]

Over the years the relationship between free Negroes and slaves was an uneasy one. Free Negroes too often, as in the slave revolt of 1811, achieved their gains at the expense of the slaves. In the colonial period the free black militia had constituted white society's strongest ally against servile revolt.[8] Nor did the origins of the free Negro population make for harmony with the slaves masses. In the wars and rebellions that ravaged Saint-Domingue in the 1790s and 1800s, light-skinned Negro freemen often fought as allies of the French, or after 1803 simply as enemies of the blacks. Free Negroes fled the island in ever increasing numbers and thousands eventually made their way to Louisiana. Mainly as a consequence of that immigration, the free Negro population of Louisiana grew from 1,300 in 1875 to nearly 8,000 in 1810. The second battalion of Negro militia formed during the Battle of New Orleans was comprised almost entirely of émigrés who had fought for the French in Saint-Domingue.[9] There also developed a class of black slaveowners. In 1830 some 750 free Negroes in New Orleans owned 2,351 slaves. Rural Louisiana evolved a larger class of slaveholding free blacks than any other Southern state. Whether it was true, as many slaves believed, that free Negroes made cruel masters or simply that psychologically it was more painful to serve a black master than a white one, the quip, "You be's as bad as a free nigger," was a common rebuke among bondsmen of antebellum New Orleans.[10]

Initially, free Negroes in Louisiana reacted to the outbreak of war between North and South in 1861 as if the British had once again landed on the Gulf Coast. In Pointe Coupee, Natchitoches, and Plaquemines

Parishes, slaveowning free blacks organized militia companies for protection against slave revolts and defense of the homeland. Well-to-do men of color in New Orleans contributed to the defense fund of the Committee on Public Safety, and the city's free Negro men offered their military services to the Confederacy. In response, Confederate Governor Thomas O. Moore authorized the formation of a regiment of free Negro militia, called Native Guards, for the defense of New Orleans. In subsequent months the Native Guards expanded until in early 1862, they numbered over 3,000.[11] At that time, a considerably larger proportion of the state's free Negroes were under arms for the Confederacy than white Louisianians.[12]

After New Orleans fell to the federals in May 1862, free Negroes maintained that they had sided with the Confederacy under duress. Little evidence exists to support that contention. The initiative for the Native Guards clearly came from the *gens de couleur*, and while the Confederates accepted their assistance, they remained suspicious of their Negro allies, limiting their military service to ceremonial duties. In the end, these suspicions proved thoroughly justified. When the Rebels abandoned New Orleans the free Negro regiments remained behind. General Ben Butler had not been in the city a month before the former Native Guardsmen asked him about fighting for the Union.[13]

Butler demurred, but that fall, desperate for troops, he recruited Native Guards for the Union Army. The following spring General Nathaniel P. Banks established the Corps d'Afrique and initiated the mass recruitment of Louisiana blacks. By the end of the war 24,052 Louisiana Negroes had served in the Union Army.[14] That is an impressive figure, and it becomes considerably more so when one recalls that most blacks in the state lived within Confederate lines throughout the war. Within Union territory, moreover, federal policy forced thousands of military-age Negro males to labor as field hands for "loyal" masters or government lessees. In fact, in proportion to the men available, the number of Louisiana blacks who carried arms for the Union was comparable with the estimated 56,000 Louisiana whites who served in the Confederate armies.[15]

Historians may quarrel about whether or not the Civil War was a revolution, but no Louisianian, white or black, ever doubted its reality from the first time he saw black men in dark blue uniforms marching in rank along the road or through the streets of New Orleans. To whites the sight aroused, as nothing else could, fears of race war and Negro domination as ancient as the South. But the scene was nonetheless revolutionary to blacks, raising up in reverse proportion to the fear and hatred of whites, hopes and dreams as old as slavery. "To Arms!" urged the Crescent City's black newspaper, *The Union*.

It is an honor understood by our fathers who fought on the plains of Chalmette [in 1815]. He who defends his fatherland is the real citizen, and this time we are fighting for the rights of our race . . . . We demand justice. And when an organized, numerous, and respectable body which has rendered many services to the nation demands justice—nothing more, but nothing less—the nation cannot refuse.

Some weeks later the newspaper declared:

From the day that bayonets were placed in the hands of the blacks . . . the Negro became a citizen of the United States . . . . This war has broken the chains of the slave, and it is written in the heavens that from this war shall grow the seeds of the political enfranchisement of the oppressed race.[16]

For the *gens de couleur,* as for other Southerners, the Civil War was the most important event in history. The enlistment of several thousand fathers and sons in the Union Army firmly tied the free Negro family as an institution to the Northern side of the war. That, in turn, profoundly affected other institutions: the fraternal orders and mutual assistance societies, and the Protestant churches. Probably no event of the war better illustrates this development than the funeral in July 1863 of Captain André Cailloux, the fallen black hero of the Port Hudson campaign. After a Catholic service in the Church of St. Rose of Lima, the march to the cemetery began, accompanied by the dirges of the 42nd Massachusetts regimental band. Beside the flag-draped hearse walked six Negro army officers and six members of the "Friends of the Order," Cailloux's fraternity which handled the funeral arrangements. Behind the hearse, the procession included a group of sick and wounded Negro soldiers, two companies of Native Guards, the carriages of the Cailloux family, and the fully liveried representatives of thirty-seven black societies:

> Friends of the Order
> Society of Economy and Mutual Assistance
> United Brethren
> Arts' and Mechanics' Association
> Free Friends
> Good Shepherd Conclave, No. 2
> Artisans' Brotherhood
> Good Shepherd Conclave, No. 1
> Union Sons' Relief
> Perseverance Society
> Ladies of Bon Secours

La Fleur de Marie
Saint Rose of Lima
Children of Mary Society
Saint Angela Society
Immaculate Conception Society
The Sacred Union Society
The Children of Jesus
Saint Veronica Society
Saint Alphonsus Society
Saint Joachim Society
Star of the Cross
Saint Eulalia Society
Saint Magdalen Society
God Protect Us Society
United Sisterhood
Angel Gabriel Society
Saint Louis Roi Society
Saint Benoit Society
Benevolence Society
Well Beloved Sisters' Society
Saint Peter Society
Saint Michael Archangel Society
Saint Louis de Gonzague Society
Saint Ann Society
The Children of Moses
Saint Theresa Society

Along the route the members of those societies lined Esplanade Street for over a mile.[17] On a lesser scale, such demonstrations became common in New Orleans during the war. In January 1865 a newspaper ad notified "all colored citizens and societies" to assemble at Lafayette Square "in full Regalia," to celebrate the emancipation of Missouri and Tennessee. The previous week a meeting had been called at the School of Liberty to read a letter from President Lincoln, acknowledging the gift of a special Bible from the colored people of New Orleans: "All citizens, pastors and officers of churches . . . all presidents, officers and members of different societies are respectfully invited to turn out in full Regalia. Our most distinguished colored speakers will be selected for the occasion."[18]

As the names of their societies would suggest, most free Negroes in New Orleans were probably Catholics. White Southerners controlled the positions of authority in the Catholic Church and, while some Negro Catholics abandoned their faith during and after the Civil War, the great majority did not.[19] An important reason, then, why Negro societies played vital political roles in the community was that, unlike black Protestants, black Catholics could not convert their churches into independent forums for social and political organization.

Negro Protestants, on the other hand, slave and free, did precisely that when the federal occupation freed them from white supervision. Several thousand blacks promptly deserted the Southern Methodist Episcopal Church and formed Negro congregations affiliated with the Methodist Episcopal Church North. The African Methodist Episcopal (AME) Church, the AME Zion Church, and the African Baptist Church also grew rapidly during the war. Protestant church buildings constituted the largest property holdings of the Negro community[20] and, quite logically, became the centers where most community business—social, charitable, political—was transacted. A religious writer complained in early 1865 that some churches had closed their doors against efforts at providing relief for Union soldiers: "As an excuse, we are told that churches are not the place to hold meetings in, except for religious purposes; granted. But what other places are we to assemble in?" The writer urged church officials to make their buildings available to the community.[21]

Under such conditions black ministers emerged as important political figures. In July 1864, for example, Negro leaders met at St. James AME Church to consider the expansion of the National Union Brotherhood Association, a black Unionist society. After the opening remarks, clergymen so dominated the discussion that an uninformed stranger coming in off the street would probably have mistaken the proceedings for a preachers' meeting. At length, the assembly approved a motion "to call a Ministerial Meeting and invite the ministers of all colored churches and denominations to meet in [St. Paul's] Wesleyan Chapel" and consider the question further.[22] Beginning in early 1865, two prominent AME ministers, William A. Dove and Robert McCary, edited a newspaper column called the "Religious Department"; they repeatedly stressed the vital importance of a "Religious and Political Union of Our People."[23]

The formation of the Louisiana Nation Equal Rights League revealed the full extent to which the war politicized the social and religious institutions of free Negro society. In October 1864 Negroes from eighteen states, including James H. Ingraham of Louisiana, met in a "National Convention of Colored Citizens of the United states" at Syracuse, New York, and established a National Equal Rights League. After Ingraham's return to New Orleans, black leaders formed a Louisiana NERL and made preparations for the state convention. They announced that any Negro society with 100 members was entitled to one representative in

the convention; societies with over 120 members received two representatives.[24] In January 1865 some 100 delegates met for a week in New
Orleans. At one session, the first order of business was a proposal to investigate the churches which had not contributed to the expenses of the convention. "The influence of ministers is very great," William A. Dove
asserted in support of the motion: "every minister of the Gospel has to
favor every thing tending to the elevation of his race . . . . If the elders or
deacons of the churches do not concur in this move let them be
removed." The delegates approved the investigation and later elected
Dove and Robert McCary to the NERL Executive Committee.[25]

Traditionally, French Catholics, so-called creole Negroes, comprised
the black elite in New Orleans and, indeed, exerted a major influence in
the community during the war. Paul Trevigne, for example, editor of *The
Union* (1862–1864) and an editor of the *New Orleans Tribune*
(1864–1869), had formerly taught at a Catholic school for free Negroes.
His father had fought in the Battle of New Orleans in 1815.[26] Dr. Louis
and J. B. (Jean Baptiste) Roudanez, the proprietors of the *Tribune,* were
the sons of a French merchant and a free Negro woman. A graduate of
the Medical Faculties of the University of Paris and Dartmouth College,
Louis practiced medicine in New Orleans throughout the Civil War and
Reconstruction. His brother J. B. was a skilled mechanic. In mid-1864
the brothers obtained control of the faltering *Union* and reorganized it
into the *Tribune.* From that time until the newspaper's demise in 1869,
they took part in every major racial controversy in the state.[27]

As the crisis of the Union deepened, though, leadership roles opened
up to new men—individuals like Oscar J. Dunn, James H. Ingraham, and
P. B. S. Pinchback, for example. By his own account, Dunn was born in
1826 and could never remember being anything but a free man. According to stories in the New Orleans press after his death, he was the son of a
free Negro woman, the owner of a rooming house for white actors, and a
mulatto stage carpenter. By those accounts, the future lieutenant governor learned elocution and rhetoric as a boy from the actors and singers in
the boarding house. It is certain that he was apprenticed to a plastering
firm as a youth and that such was his profession in antebellum New
Orleans. A small property owner of modest means, he ran an employment agency after the war, supplying servants and field hands to planters.
"I am a creole," he declared, and explained that anyone born in New
Orleans, regardless of color, was a creole.[28]

The literate freeman James H. Ingraham owed his prominence to a
good war record. In May 1863 two regiments of Native Guards attacked
a Rebel strongpoint at Port Hudson. Tactically, it was an ill-conceived

assault that led to pointless slaughter. Its significance lay in the revelation that Negro soldiers would suffer themselves to be slaughtered like whites. ("They fought splendidly!" General Banks informed his wife. "No troops could have been more determined or more daring.") The battle made a dead hero of Captain Cailloux and a live one of Captain Ingraham. He was introduced to the "National Convention of Colored Citizens" in Syracuse the following year as that bold young officer from Louisiana who had led his unit over the ramparts at Port Hudson. President of the NERL convention in 1865, Ingraham emerged as a forceful, intelligent, and articulate leader.[29]

P. B. S. (Pickney Benton Stewart) Pinchback represented a small but important class of free black leaders who migrated to Louisiana during the war. The eighth child of a white Mississippi planter and his manumitted mulatto mistress, Pinchback attended high school in Cincinnati, Ohio. His father died soon after his return to Mississippi, and Pinchback's mother fled to Cincinnati with her illegitimate children to escape their father's heirs. From that time until the Civil War, Pinchback worked on canal boats and riverboats, eventually becoming a steward.[30] He also learned to gamble. In *Forty Years a Gambler on the Mississippi*, George H. Devol recalled, "He was my boy. I raised him, and trained him. I took him out of a steamboat barber shop. I instructed him in the mysteries of card-playing, and he was an apt pupil." In particular, the gambler remembered the lucky streak that began the night "we sent Pinch to open a game of chuck-a-luck with the niggers on deck, while we opened the monte in the cabin." Less credibly, Devol has young Pinchback claiming, "Ise going to get into that good old Legislature; and I'll make Rome howl if I get there."[31] One concludes that Pinchback was more than a casual acquaintance of such card sharps as Devol.

In 1862 Pinchback jumped ship in Yazoo City, Mississippi, and made his way to occupied New Orleans. There he stabbed a free Negro, reputedly his brother-in-law, and served a month in jail. Light enough to pass for white, he joined the federal army after his release. When Ben Butler recruited Negro troops, Pinchback left his white unit and raised a company of Native Guards. In 1863 General Banks forced the resignations of black officers, including Captain Pinchback. Though Pinchback later recruited a company of Negro cavalrymen, Banks refused to recommission him. Following that disappointment, he left the army.[32]

Whatever their origins, the initial political goal of free Negroes during the war was to obtain the suffrage for the *gens de couleur*. But what started as the free Negro suffrage issue gradually became the Negro suffrage issue, and as it did the Crescent City's men of color confronted two of the most difficult questions of Reconstruction: to what extent would whites determine the interests of blacks? and to what degree would former "free" Negroes decide the interests of "freed" Negroes?[33]

In preparation for the wartime restoration of Louisiana to the Union, the registration of loyal white voters commenced in the early summer of 1863. The following November free men of color met at Economy Hall in New Orleans and adopted resolutions calling on Military Governor George F. Shepley to register free Negroes as voters. The petitioners described themselves as men of property who contributed to the commerce and industry of the state. Their forefathers had defended New Orleans in 1815, and under Butler and Banks they had taken up arms to defend the Union: "We are men, treat us as such."[34] Shepley—and Banks—ignored the petition, and the Free State government of Michael Hahn was elected in early 1864 without black participation.

Blocked in Louisiana, the *gens de couleur* appealed to President Lincoln and Congress, asking that black Louisianians, "born free before the rebellion," be registered as voters. Charles Sumner and other Radical Republicans received the petition favorably but were disturbed that it ignored the slave masses. They persuaded J. B. Roudanez and Arnold Bertonneau (a wine merchant and ex-captain of Native Guards), the bearers of the petition, to add a section asking the suffrage for all Louisiana Negroes, "whether born slave or free, especially those who have vindicated their right to vote by bearing arms."[35] Lincoln was also moved by the entreaty. The Louisiana constitutional convention of 1864 was scheduled to meet in April; the day after the president received the petition, he wrote Governor Michael Hahn suggesting privately that the convention enfranchise part of the colored population, "as, for instance, the very intelligent, and especially those who have fought gallantly in our ranks."[36]

Free Negroes probably did not expect much from the constitution-makers in New Orleans. If so, they were not disappointed. Left to themselves, the delegates showed a decided preference for the coarse fare of the proslavery argument, served up in generous portions. But they were not left to themselves. Aware of the expectations in Washington that the Louisiana constitution make some concessions to blacks, General Banks and Governor Hahn forced the convention, beyond abolishing slavery, to provide for Negro schools and to authorize the legislature to enfranchise blacks on the basis of military service, exceptional intelligence, or payment of taxes.[37]

Even the *New Orleans Tribune* conceded that the new constitution was an improvement over the Constitution of 1852.[38] That did not make it acceptable to the *Tribune* or to the *gens de couleur.* Free Negroes were already free, many of their children attended private schools, and a limited extension of the suffrage was merely authorized—not actually granted. As well as anyone else, they could see the means by which General Banks and Governor Hahn had wrung concessions from the convention majority, a perspective that did not inspire confidence in a legislature composed of similar men actually carrying out the educational and suffrage provisions of the constitution. Probably as important as anything else was the tone of the debates: the proslavery harangues, the endless talk about amalgamation, race war, Negro degeneracy and savagery, the enthusiastic response of the majority to proposals for excluding free Negroes from the state, denying them the suffrage, or barring them from learning trades or professions. Even the Negro's "friends" in the assembly compiled a record of gratuitous insults.[39] Under such leadership, Lincoln and Banks proposed to restore Louisiana to the Union. Black leaders were outraged.

Four days before the convention adjourned, and twelve days after the *Union* stopped publication, the first issue of the *New Orleans Tribune* appeared. In most respects, the *Union* had been a Radical and egalitarian newspaper. Taking its stand on the Declaration of Independence, and trusting in Christian reform, it had attacked the abuses of society from slavery to capital punishment. What it had not done was challenge the Reconstruction policies of Lincoln and Banks.[40] All that now changed. Had the South "desired a conservative President in 1860," the *Tribune* charged angrily,

> neither North nor South of the Potomac could they have found one who would have more zealously protected their rights of property in man; no one who would have lent the whole weight of the executive of the nation to the rigid enforcement of the Fugitive Slave Act; no one who would have preserved more inviolate the rights of the people of the Southern states under the Constitution than Abraham Lincoln.[41]

The record in Louisiana made plain what loyal men could expect from the president. The hidden goal of the Free State constitution was to secure Louisiana's electoral votes for Lincoln in the presidential election of 1864. That document was *"based on Executive usurpation"* and drafted by individuals "who had no higher principle of action than hatred of their fellows of African descent." Like the authors of the Wade-Davis Bill, the *Tribune* concluded that Reconstruction was a job for Congress, not the president.[42]

The second phase of the Negro suffrage controversy in Louisiana began when the Free State legislature met in the fall. Very probably at the instigation of federal officials, Charles Smith of St. Mary Parish introduced a bill in the senate which provided that "every person having not more than one-fou[r]th negro blood, shall be considered and recognized as white, in the State of Louisiana." Smith expressed concern that men who were three-fourths white were treated as Negroes, but it was not a concern shared by his fellow lawmakers. Most agreed with the senator who asked, "Does Mr. Smith wish the legislature to declare a colored man a white man? This bill is an absurdity." The senate disposed of the measure on November 14, but the very next day Smith returned with a new bill. He now proposed extending the suffrage to blacks who qualified by "intellectual fitness," a year in the army, or the payment of thirty dollars a year in property taxes. Since this merely carried out the explicit authorization of the new constitution, Smith perhaps expected a more sympathetic hearing. However, a big change had occurred in Louisiana since July; General Banks had returned to Washington to push for Congressional recognition of the Hahn regime. In his absence, Louisiana Unionists voted their prejudices unmolested; they rejected Smith's second bill on its first reading by a convincing vote of fifteen to five.[43]

Considering the finality of the vote in the senate, the whole question ought to have died down until after the war. It did not because the Negro suffrage question in Louisiana had become curiously adjoined to the national issue of Congressional recognition of Presidential Reconstruction in the state. Throughout 1863 the Louisiana Free State party had been dominated by the New Orleans Unionist Thomas J. Durant. In early 1864, General Banks undercut Durant and engineered the election of Michael Hahn as Free State Governor. By that action, Lincoln's general stirred up more trouble than he knew. Durant and his allies complained to Congress, persistently and articulately, that Banks had created a puppet regime in Louisiana. So effective was the charge, that Congressional support for the Hahn government was badly damaged.[44] At the time the Louisiana senate rejected the Smith bills, however, Congress was not in session, and the fate of Free State Louisiana was still undecided. When Congress met in December, Lincoln fought hard for the readmission of Louisiana to the Union. For weeks the administration and its supporters appeared on the verge of victory, but in late February 1865 a Radical filibuster, led by Charles Sumner, doomed the Louisiana resolution by preventing it from coming to vote.[45]

Throughout the controversy General Banks remained in Washington and lobbied for the Hahn government. Back in Louisiana the general's loyal lieutenants, the "Banks oligarchy"[46]—Major B. Rush Plumly, Thomas W. Conway, Anthony P. Dostie, and others—attempted to influence the readmission struggle in Congress: from December through February they urged the black community in New Orleans to petition the legislature for the franchise. In view of the state senate's action on Senator Smith's suffrage bill, that strategy requires an explanation. Perhaps they believed that the lawmakers might change their minds and receive such a petition favorably. But since the intelligence of Plumly, Conway, and Dostie is not in question, the answer must lie elsewhere. The only explanation that makes sense is that they expected Banks to return to New Orleans before the Louisiana question came to vote in Congress—return and force concessions from the recalcitrant Unionists in the legislature as he had forced concessions in the constitutional convention. In fact, Banks did return, but too late. The Radical filibuster in the United States Senate had ended, Governor Hahn had resigned, and the reactionary James Madison Wells was governor of Louisiana.

Ironically, for the *gens de couleur* the petition question turned into the most divisive issue of the war. While most black leaders opposed petitioning the legislature, a determined minority supported the move. The two factions closely resembled each other; both included prominent French Catholics, ex-soldiers, and Protestant ministers.[47] The major confrontation between the two occurred at the NERL convention when a special committee issued a divided report: a majority report in favor of petitioning the legislature and a minority report opposed. The supporters of the majority position argued that a petition was the logical step before appealing to Congress and that certainly nothing could be lost by trying. The opposition maintained that even if the legislature was inclined, which it plainly was not, it could only make a limited extension of the suffrage as authorized by the constitution of 1864. And beyond that, how could they appeal to a government which had systematically treated them with contempt? "If we have blood in our veins," James H. Ingraham asserted, "we will not seek to be once more rebuked." Under Ingraham's determined leadership, the convention overturned the majority report by a vote of fifty-one to twenty-two. Motions to reconsider the question were urged on subsequent days and voted down, but not so decisively. A proposal that the petition be held back until Congress readmitted Louisiana to the Union lost by the narrow margin of thirty-seven to thirty-two. In late January and throughout February, the issue continued to come up at public meetings and in the local chapters of the NERL.[48]

As the official organ of the NERL, the *Tribune* vigorously supported the anti-petition faction. The newspaper was now convinced that a Congressional extension of the suffrage to Southern Negroes was all but inevitable, because by themselves white Unionists would be overwhelmed after the war by the defeated Confederates. Should the conflict end in a month, it predicted, "the first general election . . . would place the government of the state in the hands of . . . the open foes of the Union." Hence, only by enfranchising Southern freedmen could the North prevent Rebel domination of the postwar South.[49] "Why then to be in such a hurry?" the journal asked the petitioners. "Can we not wait a little longer, in order to obtain the franchise for all, without distinction of classes?" Is any black man "bold enough and selfish enough to go to the ballot-box and exercise the right of voting, when thousands of his brethren, as good citizens as he, would be lookers on . . . declared unfit to be men?"[50] Despite the *Tribune*, the NERL, and charges of race treason, the petitioners persisted, and on February 17 a sympathetic senator introduced their petition, bearing some five thousand signatures, in the upper chamber. The senate consigned the memorial to a special committee, never to heard of again.[51]

Throughout the petition controversy, relations between the NERL and the *Tribune*, on the one hand, and the "Banks oligarchy," on the other, had steadily worsened. Nor was the petition the only cause of conflict. The Union Army, no less than generations of white Southerners, had practiced widespread discrimination against Louisiana Negroes throughout the occupation. In addition, many free blacks were outraged over the treatment of freedmen under the "free labor" program established by General Banks in 1863. But, whereas those issues united free Negroes, the petition question divided them. With some justice, the anti-petition leaders blamed Plumly, Conway, and Dostie for the split in the black community. By March the petition was history, but relations between black leaders and occupation officials did not improve; on the contrary, overnight the two antagonists found themselves locked in another bitter conflict. This time the cause was "free labor."

Since mid-1864 Negro leaders had grown increasingly critical of Banks's labor system. The *Tribune* repeatedly charged that "free labor," as defined in army regulations, was but a step removed from slave labor.[52] The NERL protested the program on similar grounds and called for major changes. To most black leaders the continuation of the system in the present form was unthinkable. Nonetheless, in March General Stephen A. Hurlbut renew the program in its entirety.[53] The NERL immediately condemned the decision and called on Hurlbut to reconsider. The *Tribune* argued that the renewal blasted the hope that the freedman would learn to take care of himself, because if nothing was done that year, he would be in the same condition in 1866, "and the same arguments will once more be used to keep him down . . . . When, then, will progress come? Is this apprenticeship to be perpetual?"[54] Incensed by the criticism, Hurlbut lashed out at the NERL, and Conway intrigued against the *Tribune*. Failing to deter their critics, the federals financed the old pro-petition faction in setting up a short-lived weekly newspaper, the *Black Republican,* as a rival to the *Tribune.*[55]

Over months of controversy in the winter and spring of 1865, the *Tribune* perceived a common patter: whether the issue was the petition or "free labor," white officials like Plumly, Conway, and Hurlbut acted as if they knew better than Negroes themselves what was in the best interests of black Louisianians. Negroes, those officials assumed, be they ex-slaves or freemen, ought to remain passive, letting whites decide policy and relying on their white friends and protectors to deal fairly with them. When blacks challenged those assumptions, the federals typically reacted as Conway did at a March meeting of the NERL Executive Committee: "gentlemen, I differ with you. I believe your present course to be ruinous, and you will find it out to your sorrow." Hurlbut at the same time urged Negroes to "wait and work" and "not call meetings and pass resolutions."[56] The *Tribune* called this pattern of federal paternalism tutelage:

> At the first step—not very material in itself—that we attempt to make, we find tutors around us, who take upon themselves to redress our conduct, and try to prescribe what we have to do. We have asserted our manhood, and we will do it again. We need friends . . . but we do not need tutors. The age of guardianship is past forever, and we shall act for ourselves.[57]

Of all the would-be tutors, none angered the *Tribune* more than Superintendent Conway of the Bureau of Free Labor. The NERL convention of January, the newspaper averred, had barely adjourned before Conway expressed disapproval of its decision on the petition question. "He seemed unwilling to understand that the Convention felt as colored men feel, while Mr. Conway could only feel as a white man feels."[58] Thus, as the war drew to a conclusion and the minds of public men turned increasingly to the tasks of Reconstruction, the *Tribune* repeatedly warned the federals that Negroes intended to run their own affairs. "There is no man in the world so perfectly identified with our interest as to understand it better than we do ourselves."[59]

Which Negroes would decide the interests of black Louisianians? Quick to see the paternalism of the "Banks oligarchy," free Negroes were much less perceptive about their own paternalism. To James H. Ingraham, as to most free blacks, the answer was self-evident: "Unless . . . [the] people of refinement and education act for the benighted ones, the ignorant will be trodden down."[60] The *Tribune* developed the idea more fully. "Louisiana is in a very peculiar situation," it said.

> Here, the colored population had a twofold origin. There is an old pop-
> ulation, with a history and mementos of their own, warmed by patrio-
> tism, partaking of the feelings and education of the white. The only
> social condition known to these men is that of freedom . . . . There is,
> on the other hand, a population of freedmen, but recently liberated
> from the shackles of bondage. All is to be done yet for them.

It was essential, the newspaper believed, that the two populations work
together. "The emancipated will find, in the old freemen, friends ready
to guide them, to spread upon them the light of knowledge, and teach
them their duties as well as their rights. But, at the same time, the
freemen will find in the recently liberated slaves a mass to uphold them;
and with this mass behind them they will command the respect always
bestowed to number and strength."[61] Put more bluntly, free Negroes
knew better than ex-slaves what were in the interests of black Louisianians. In the tasks ahead, the former bondsmen ought to remain passive,
letting the old freemen make policy and trusting in their more enlightened brethren to deal fairly with them.

A crucial aspect of free Negro paternalism was a concern for "elevation" of the freedmen—an ubiquitous subject in the minds of black leaders. Negro clergymen, for example, talked incessantly about "the great
work to be accomplished [in] the elevation of the African Race."[62] Similarly, the *Tribune* assured its readers that free Negro planters could offer
the ex-slaves inducements that white planters could not: "We can give
the freedmen, under the influenced of liberty, moral benefit and social
enjoyment, all that he estimates and contend[s] for. Let us go to work,
organize labor-colonies, and elevate our emancipated brethren, at the
same time that we take our legitimate share in the cultivation of the
country."[63] Did a General Hurlbut question the commitment of the old
freemen to the black masses? There then appeared a "Junius" to assure
him that "the old free colored people . . . have done and are doing all
that is in their power to morally and physically improve the condition of
the new freedmen."[64]

Religious uplift was a vital part of that program. The majority of our
people, asserted the *Tribune,*

> newly acquainted with the blessings of freedom, do not only need an
> intellectual education, but a religious guidance, too. On this point there
> must be no disputing. We have for some time contemplated to add to
> our paper a Religious Department, devoted to religious news and to the
> elucidation of religious points, in relation to moral education and
> improvement of the people.[65]

The "Religious Department" generally consisted of inspirational poetry or uplifting articles—"Earnestness in Prayer," "True Test of a Christian," "How to Become a Blessing"—reprinted from religious periodicals and reflecting the religious sensibilities of middle-class free blacks.[66] Not infrequently, however, the editors or other local people, "Light" or "M.B.A.," wrote pieces which revealed the immediate concerns of free Negro Protestants in New Orleans: articles emphasizing the vital importance of religious and political unity, of parents sending their children to school, of teaching the freedmen about the sanctity of marriage, of keeping young people out of the city's haunts of wickedness, and, most important, of churches being led by qualified pastors.[67] Without qualified ministers, none of those other goals could be met; the pulpit could not become "the great lever to inculcate a 'Union' of our people," nor could the great truths of scripture be properly taught. "Let us examine our pulpits," urged "Light," "and see if 'intelligence' is in them . . . . One ignorant man in the pulpit at this time is a mountain that retards our progress and development." On the other hand, "Every Church that passes into the hands of a worthy and competent minister is a lever of great moral power, that will exert a great influence in our behalf and be the means of *elevating our people* out of the present *chaos* of affairs." Competent ministers, he made plain, revealed themselves not only by their learning but also by "their correct deportment and gentlemanly conduct."[68]

Properly trained pastors were crucially important if the newly emancipated slaves were to learn the benefits of Christian marriage. To respectable free Negroes, as to other reformers—and no doubt the slaves themselves—among the worst features of the "Peculiar Institution" was that it had made marriage "a mere cohabitation among the slaves." With slavery gone, men of color looked for ways to undo the damage and make marriage an honored institution among the former bondsmen. If true progress was to be made, the marriage rites must be performed by real ministers of the Gospel and not the bogus kind. In this community, warned "Light," "there are [a] great many intruders who perform the marriage ceremony" in violation of religious law. No clergyman, he argued, "has any right to unite a man and woman in holy matrimony unless he has been regularly ordained to one of the following offices: Bishop, Elder, or Deacon. Among our colored Protestant churches there are but few men in this city now, that have the requisite qualifications to perform the duties." Negro men and women married "by incompetent authority," he cautioned, risked losing all the benefits and safeguards of lawful marriage, including the right to inherit one another's property and to have their children protected as legal heirs. He urged those "unlawfully united to immediately rectify their mistake . . . before it is too late."[69]

The concern over the qualifications of ministers is understandable. The great majority of freedmen, and many free Negroes as well, had very different concepts of Christianity than the "Religious Department" of the *Tribune*. Those differences were all the more apparent because of the numbers of runaway slaves that had crowded into New Orleans during the war. General Butler had put the figure at ten thousand in September 1862, and that number had doubled by February of the following year.[70] Under such conditions, crude makeshift churches appeared all over the city. George H. Hepworth, a federal chaplain, left an account of just how different those freedmen's churches were. In February 1863 Hepworth visited a "rude church" in a Negro camp outside New Orleans. Inside the low-build structure

> a full hundred blacks, of all shades . . . were gathered together; and, for a few moments, perfect silence prevailed . . . . At length, however, a single voice, coming from a dark corner of the room, began a low, mournful chant, in which the whole assemblage joined by degrees. It was a strange song, with seemingly very little rhythm . . . . It seemed more like a wail, a mournful, dirge-like expression of sorrow . . . . I was overcome by the real sadness and depression of soul which it seemed to symbolize.

After a half-hour of singing,

> an old man knelt down to pray. His voice was at first low and indistinct; the prayer was purely an emotional effort. He seemed to gain impulse as he went on, and pretty soon burst out with an "O good, dear Lord! we pray for de cullered people. Thou knows well 'nuff what we'se been through: do, do, oh! do gib us free!"

When the old man spoke these words,

> the whole audience swayed back and forward in their seats, and uttered in perfect harmony a sound like that caused by prolonging the letter "m" with the lips closed. One or two began this wild, mournful chorus; and in an instant all joined in, and the sound swelled upwards and downwards like waves of the sea.

The preaching represented the high point of the meeting. The first speaker whipped himself into a frenzy, "took flights of rhetoric which would have made Whately dizzy, and produced logic which brought tears—of laughter—to my eyes." When he resumed a seat, a hush fell over the room. After an interval, a tall figure stepped forward, a gifted individual who swayed "his rude audience with most perfect control; subdued them, excited them . . . did what he pleased with them." The man addressed himself to the plight of blacks in the camp working for the army without pay. Having labored thirty-six years for a master and never having received more than half a dollar, "surely I can work for Uncle Sam a little while,—just a little while,—until he can find a fitting place for me, for nothing." The spellbinder informed his listeners that he no longer cared about his own bondage: "'I have reached maturity, and can endure it: but' (and here his voice fell almost to a whisper) 'I have in yonder cabin a child, a boy . . . whom I love as I do my life; and I thank God, I thank God, that I am a freeman, *for his sake.*'"[71] The men and women who listened to this eloquent man were not such as to be concerned about ministerial credentials, or swayed by exhortations to "Earnestness in Prayer," or, even less, inspired by a free Negro version of the white man's burden.

In four years of war, free Negroes in New Orleans made a series of dramatic shifts: from Rebel militia to soldiers of the Union; from the suffrage for free blacks to the suffrage for all blacks; from acquiescence in slavery to criticism of federal "free labor"; from support of wartime Reconstruction to approval of the Wade-Davis bill; from unconcern with the slave masses to elevation of the freedmen. These changes reflected in part a genuine awakening of liberal conscience, but even more they resulted from a realistic perception of class interest, a perception that had remained remarkably in focus since 1729. So considered, the controversy over the petition in the last winter of the war reveals itself as a dispute over the best means of advancing that interest. The pro-petition leaders, in effect, pursued the old plan of asking the suffrage for the free Negro elite. Their opponents in the NERL and at the *Tribune,* decrying the selfishness and shortsightedness of that approach, championed the vote for all blacks, little doubting that once enfranchised, the freedmen would turn to the *gens de couleur* for political guidance. This belief was only partly illusory. Free Negroes would prove indispensable in the early organization of the Republican party, and they would dominate the constitutional convention of 1867–1868.[72] But before the final scenes of the revolutionary drama of war, emancipation, and Reconstruction were acted out, free Negroes would also learn that the ex-slaves had voices of their own.

Part 5

PREPARING FOR FREEDOM

CHAPTER 15

Union Chaplains and the Education of the Freedmen

Warren B. Armstrong

URING THE LAST SESSION of the 37th Congress (1862), Representative John Hickman of Pennsylvania urged that a bill for the raising of Negro regiments be amended so as to provide for the assignment to each company of "one teacher or chaplain's clerk." The purpose of his amendment, Hickman explained, was to offer the Negro soldiers in each regiment an opportunity to received a rudimentary education while they served in the army in order that they might be prepared for their new role as responsible citizens when their military service had ended.[1]

Although Representative Hickman's amendment failed to pass, the concern which he expressed for the education of the Negro soldier, and for the freedmen generally, was shared by many others in the North both in and out of Congress. This was particularly true in antislavery circles[2] and in the army, where commanders found it increasingly difficult to care adequately for the multitudes of destitute "contrabands"[3] who flooded Union lines whenever and wherever Federal forces penetrated new areas of the South. Many army chaplains were among those who voiced concern for the freedmen and who expressed the belief that education was absolutely essential if they were successfully to make the transition from their former status as slaves to that of responsible citizens. These men were convinced, furthermore, that national policy should include education of the Negro as an objective both during and following the war, for, they argued, without minimal educational achievement the former slave

223

would be the helpless victim of the unscrupulous and would be pitifully open to continued exploitation.[4]

Of the many chaplains who voiced such opinions, one of the most eloquent was Chaplain H. H. Moore, who wrote for the *Western Christian Advocate* an article which vividly portrayed the plight of the freedmen and indicated his hopes for their future. Arguing that the power and influenced which had effected the Negroes' emancipation should also assume the responsibility for making them a respectable and homogeneous element in the American social and political community, the chaplain declared his belief that such a project was not a task of visionaries. A full appreciation of the effect of slavery upon the mental and moral faculties of men was essential if one wished to avoid bitter disillusionment, for nothing in the institution of slavery prepared man for the responsibilities of freedom. He concluded with the optimistic prediction that "the elevation of the black men to citizenship, intelligence, virtue and prosperity, will be an addition of . . . worth, and honor, and power to the republic. . . . The Government proposes, not only emancipation, but paternal care and elevation."[5]

The chaplains who exhibited interest in education for the freedmen also expressed, in varying degrees, a commitment to the doctrine of racial equality. James B. Rogers, chaplain of the 14th Wisconsin Infantry, revealed his scorn for those who pointed to the degraded state of the Negro as evidence of innate inferiority. "At the present," Rogers acknowledged, "he is degraded, and why should he not be? He is not himself. He has never been permitted to express his manhood. He is forbidden to enjoy those rights which are claimed as so inalienable by the white race. These are the causes of his depressed condition." Yet despite the terrible handicap of enforced ignorance with which the Negroes were encumbered, Chaplain Rogers believed that they possessed both an aptitude and a thirst for learning. "Although some learn faster than others, yet all show that they are susceptible of instruction and mental improvement. I believe that their capacities for education are equal to those of white children, and their thirst for learning rather greater." Expressing his fear that racial prejudice might be an insurmountable barrier to the Negro in his quest for social acceptance in the future, Rogers urged education as the only means to that end. "Educate the negro, permit him to rise in the scale of being and assert his own personality," said the chaplain, "and he is a man."[6]

Chaplain George Pepper of the 80th Ohio Infantry was among those who shared the views expressed by Rogers. To point to the degradation of a race which had been held by force in perpetual bondage as evidence of inherent inferiority was grossly unfair, he argued. "Gifted with more than ordinary intellect, more exercised than cultivated, the Negroes have been kept in a fearful state of degradation which is too well known, and which ought to call forth the immediate attention of the General Government," Pepper asserted. "The aptness to learn and to acquire knowledge is attested to by thousands of instances of slaves who in an incredibly short period have mastered the usual branches of the common schools."[7]

Despite the pleas by chaplains, civilian churchmen, anti-slavery leaders, and Congressmen for governmental action to ensure the education of the freedmen, no consistent policy was adopted either by Congress or, through executive order, by the War Department, until the establishment of the Freedmen's Bureau in March of 1865. Yet earnest efforts to educate the former slaves continued throughout the war, and in many instances, despite their inconsistent and uncoordinated character, substantial progress was made. Church organizations, missionary societies, and a variety of philanthropic groups conducted organized programs in many areas of the South with the consent of the War Department. The chaplains, however, were in a unique position to engage in this type of activity and a large number of them grasped the opportunity to do so.

Many chaplains acted voluntarily, in an unofficial capacity, to assist the freedmen in his struggle to attain three basic goals—education, economic stability, and social equality and acceptance. While their approaches to the problems of the Negro varied, emphasis almost invariably was placed on the need for elevation through education. Chaplain Arthur B. Fuller of the 16th Massachusetts Infantry found it convenient to combine religious and secular instruction by organizing a Sunday school for "contrabands" and poor whites. Undertaking this project in the vicinity of Warrenton, Virginia, where his regiment was encamped during the autumn of 1862, Fuller was encouraged by the progress of his colored pupils, stating that there was good reason to believe that education could bridge the gulf between slavery and freedom.[8]

William K. Talbot, a hospital chaplain stationed at Beaufort, South Carolina, found time despite the multiplicity of his regular duties to teach Negro convalescents confined to his hospital. "I am able," he reported, "to spend two or three hours [daily] teaching the Colored convalesents [*sic*] to read, write, and the howes [*sic*] of figures, all of whom are learning to read." It was a fascinating and rewarding endeavor, he continued, as the avid thirst for knowledge which the Negro soldiers demonstrated was ample evidence of an ambition which had been denied fulfillment under slavery. Education was, in his opinion, the key to a successful transition from slavery to freedom.[9]

Chaplain William Eaton of the 12th United States Colored Troops maintained a school for the men of his regiment, despite the difficulties which arose from their assignment. The regimental duty, which involved guarding more than eleven miles of railroad near Kingston Springs, Tennessee, spread the men out over such an area that it was difficult to maintain regular classes. "Notwithstanding these peculiar circumstances," he reported, "we keep up a daily school with encouraging results." Books, paper, and other materials were supplied by the Christian Commission and the Pennsylvania Freedman's Aid Commission, and the classes were conducted in the tent of the sutler accompanying the regiment.[10]

The chaplain of the 3rd Rhode Island Heavy Artillery, the Reverend Frederic Denison, was involved in a cooperative education effort with the Reverend Solomon Peck, Secretary of the American Baptist Missionary Union. These men, hoping to aid the freedmen in the vicinity of Beaufort, South Carolina, left behind by masters who fled the Sea Islands in the face of imminent occupation by Union forces, used the large Baptist church in Beaufort as a schoolhouse during the week in order to provide the freedmen with an opportunity for a basic education. Both Peck and Denison reported excellent progress by the Negro students in their charge and were pleased at the growth in enrollment.[11]

Another enterprise, far more extensive, was that conducted in the Mississippi Valley by Chaplain John Eaton of the 27th Ohio Infantry. On November 11, 1862, Chaplain Eaton received an order from General U. S. Grant which placed him at the head of what was to become the most elaborate and extensive of all efforts on behalf of the freedmen.[12]

As Grant prepared during the autumn and winter months of 1862 for his push south against the Confederate fortress city of Vicksburg, Mississippi, he felt impelled to find some means to care properly for the Negroes who came into Union lines in increasing numbers. While his concern was military as well as humanitarian—he did not wish to have his army impeded in its pursuit of military objectives by the necessity of diverting its energies to the task of providing for the multitude of destitute Negroes—this in no way detracted from his accomplishments in behalf of the freedmen. Thus Grant, through Chaplain Eaton, launched the most systematic and continuous organized effort on behalf of the Negro undertaken throughout the war.

In explaining his instructions to Eaton (November 12, 1862), Grant stated his intention to turn a potential menace into a positive aid to the Union armies. The freedmen could perform many of the camp duties then being done by soldiers and could also lend assistance in roadbuilding, bridge repairs, the construction of fortifications, and the like. Women could be employed as laundresses, hospital aids, and cooks. He mentioned also the possibility of using the Negro as a soldier, eventually even making him a citizen and a voter. The appointment of Chaplain Eaton to the supervision of the project made him personally responsible for the administration of Negro affairs in the Department of the Tennessee (which later included all of Mississippi, Arkansas, Kentucky, Tennessee, and parts of Louisiana, as the Division of the Mississippi), from November, 1862, until the spring of 1865 when the Freedmen's Bureau assumed the task.[13]

Eaton believed that while the first responsibility in his new assignment was to provide material necessities, employment, and protection to the Negroes, this was first "in order only—not in importance." He believed that the mental and moral enlightenment of the freedmen was the truly great object to be secured through his labors, and that the achievement of at least a rudimentary school system for their education would produce ultimately the greatest benefits for the former slaves and the nation. "Accordingly from the very first, efforts were made to secure the assistance of army chaplains, and such other men as were likely to feel the importance of this matter." The aid of benevolent persons, either as individuals or in groups, was also welcomed by Eaton. Some of those he singled out for praise were the American Missionary Association, the Western Freedman's Aid Commission, and the Society of Friends.[14]

Progress was at first slow, uncoordinated, and very limited, due to the instability of the military situation in the valley and the fact that there was no real central authority over these efforts to educate the freedmen. Since Eaton's control was informal and hence minimal (as a chaplain he did not have rank with command), success depended upon cooperation among the many independent agencies and individuals working side by side to achieve the same ends but under different auspices. An increase in the number of volunteer workers followed the capture of Vicksburg and subsequent occupation of Natchez, which guaranteed Union control of the territory bordering the Mississippi, thus improving the security of those involved in this charitable work.[15]

To these volunteer teachers General Grant proffered welcome and, at first unauthorized, assistance in the form of transportation, quarters, rations and classroom facilities whenever military considerations made it possible for him to do so. This achieved a dual purpose, for in addition to facilitating and encouraging the work of those engaged in educating the freedmen, it also brought the agents of the societies into closer contact with Eaton, as it was through his Freedmen's Department that requests for such aid were channeled. In September of 1863, Secretary Stanton gave formal authorization to the aid program which Grant had under-taken on his own authority.[16]

Despite this aid and the increasing size of the volunteer teaching force there was much duplication of effort. A shortage of funds and facilities also hampered the work. Still further, there were difficulties arising from the jealousies and friction which are unavoidable when so many indepen-dent agencies are working on the same problems in the same area. This situation prevailed until September, 1864, when the need for a central-ized authority to control and systematize all efforts for the education of Negroes was recognized by the War Department. Eaton, in his capacity as General Superintendent of Freedmen,[17] was accordingly designated to serve as the coordinator of all educational efforts in the Department.[18]

On the basis of this order the chaplain, now Colonel Eaton,[19] appointed seven District Superintendents, four of whom were ministers and had been army chaplains.[20] He then called them to his headquarters in Memphis for a joint conference with the representatives of the freed-men's aid societies and church missions boards. At the conference there occurred an extended and frank discussion of the problems to be faced in the task of providing the Negroes with an opportunity for education. There resulted from this exchange of ideas, a general agreement concern-ing the need for a carefully regulated system, and a circular outlining the system agreed upon and the rules by which it would be operated was issued by Eaton's office on October 20, 1864.[21]

This circular, which went to all those engaged in educational work and to all commanding officers in the Department, instructed each school superintendent to report to the local superintendents of freedmen (Eaton's assistants) who were charged with the task of procuring and reg-ulating all school property. Clerical help for the district was to be furnished by Eaton when it was considered necessary in the judgment of the local superintendents of freedmen. Cities and towns were subdivided into school wards, and attendance in the school located in his district was required of each pupil except in cases of special permission from Eaton. The problem of deciding who would teach where was to be determined by consultation between local school superintendents and agency repre-sentatives. School hours, text books, organization, classification, and disci-pline were entirely the responsibility of the district school superintendents. A minimal tuition fee, in lieu of property taxes which were impossible to collect under wartime circumstances, helped to defray the cost of the pro-gram and had an added value, Eaton believed, in that it developed in the Negroes a sense of responsibility and dignity. The maximum fee was $1.25 per month per pupil to be paid by the parents or guardians of the pupil. The fee was flexible, however, and was based on the ability of the parent to pay. No child was denied education because of a parent's inability to pay and many attended these schools on a tuition-free basis. While Eaton did not support the fee system in theory but only out of necessity, he was convinced that it had a positive effect on the Negroes, for it gave them a feeling of having contributed to their own improvement. Night schools were also inaugurated under Eaton's aegis to provide adult freed men with an opportunity to obtain an education in the hours not given to labor.[22]

At the same time the circular was issued, Eaton, in his capacity as General Superintendent of Freedmen, wrote a lengthy report to Secretary Stanton in the form of an open letter, in which he detailed the work being done, the intent behind it, and prospects for the future. He concluded the letter with these words: "Sensible of the trying circumstances under which this action is taken, and the great responsibilities involved, we appeal under God to considerate judgment of every friend of universal education."[23]

Exact figures on the number of Negroes who benefited from the programs described above are not available, primarily because some agencies and individuals were unwilling to cooperate in complete friendliness with the Freedman's Department. The available statistics are reasonably accurate, however, and do indicate the size of the program inaugurated and supervised by the chaplain-colonel, John Eaton. For example, in one calendar year (from January 1, 1863, to January 1, 1864), Eaton's Freedman's Department cared specifically for 113,650 Negroes in a Department which according to the 1860 census had 770,000 blacks.[24] Multiply this by the increasing number of bondmen who were liberated by the deeper penetrations of the Union armies during 1864 and the spring of 1865, and an appreciation of the immensity of the task which devolved upon Eaton is possible.

These examples are by no means a complete record of the work of Union chaplains in educating the Negroes. They are sufficient, however, to indicate the general nature of their efforts, and to reveal their optimism regarding the beneficent effect of education upon the blacks. It is unfortunate, in a very real sense, that the United States Army was not better utilized as a training school for the freedmen. Perhaps a policy such as that suggested to his distinguished father by Charles Francis Adams Jr., who commanded a Negro regiment, might have warranted official consideration. "As soon as quieter times for soldiers shall come," he wrote, "I should hope to see Chaplains and schoolmasters attached to each regiment. . . . My hope is that for years to come our army will be made up of mainly blacks and number many thousand. I would have at least a four year term of enlistment and yearly send out of the Army from fifteen to twenty thousand black citizens, old soldiers and masters of some form of skilled labor. Such is my philanthropic plan for the race and I do not know that I can do better than to devote to it some few of the passing years of my life."[25] Earlier, Adams had doubted the wisdom of recruiting the Negro, but his service as an officer in the 5th Massachusetts Cavalry, a Negro regiment, had caused him to revise his estimate of the Negro soldier as a potential citizen.[26]

One cannot estimate with precision the value of the learning attained by freedmen from army chaplains and other concerned individuals. Certainly many Negroes were aided greatly in the traumatic transition from dependent bondage to independent and responsible citizenship by the education thus obtained. And education was an enduring contribution, a truth aptly expressed in the words of Chaplain Eaton: "Whatever education has been accomplished among the people cannot be taken from them."[27]

CHAPTER 16

Black Education in Louisiana,
1863—1865

William F. Messner

T HE HISTORY OF FREEDMEN'S education during the Civil War has
been a topic of considerable fascination for scholars interested in
the period of our national bloodletting. Much of this appeal is undoubtedly due to the fact that the establishment of educational facilities for the
former slaves was one of the few areas of freedmen's reform in which, to
paraphrase Willie Lee Rose, the revolution did not go entirely backwards.
Although substantial economic progress for black Americans did not
occur until well into the twentieth century and the political gains of the
1860s were largely nullified during the next several decades, the seeds of
educational advance planted during the war years were never completely
uprooted, despite the intense opposition which black education met
throughout the era of Jim Crow. In Louisiana especially, the federal military established a well organized system of black elementary education as
early as 1864, and by the end of the Civil War black youths gave evidence
of substantial educational progress. Despite the fact that Louisiana whites
did their best to limit black educational advance in the years following
Reconstruction, at least a limited effort continued nurtured by the
knowledge gained by a substantial segment of the black community
during the years of "Black Reconstruction."[1]

Although the story of the educational effort in the Gulf Department
has been told more than once, relatively little attention has been paid to
what motivated the normally frugal and conservative federal military to

embark upon a progressive and expensive educational program during the Civil War.[2] The reasons are not difficult to ascertain. A study of black education in Louisiana, while highlighting the altruistic motives of those northern teachers who traveled south to work with the freedmen, also brings into sharp relief the political dimensions of black schooling and clarifies the manner in which the philanthropic tendencies of liberal educators complemented the political goals of federal policymakers. In other words, black education served the interests of Union officials as well as those of the freedmen, for the federal military considered education to be not only a source of black enlightenment, but also a potent tool for black control. Federal officials in Louisiana believed, in fact, that control was the cornerstone of black enlightenment. Education would be a civilizing influence upon the freedmen, preparing them for the role they were to assume as contributing members of a free labor society, while simultaneously checking the blacks' unruly passions and insuring at least a minimum of black economic productivity. Education, viewed from this perspective, was one of the foundation blocks of the national administration's reconstruction efforts in Louisiana, for it promised to resolve the tension which existed between the hopes and fears of whites for the future of the black individual in American society.

Central to an understanding of the motivation which prompted the Union army to institute an educational program for blacks in the Gulf Department is a knowledge of the political goals of those federal officials who administered the Union occupation of southern Louisiana from 1863 to 1865.[3] By the end of the second year of the war the national government had been generally successful in its plan for seizing control of the lower end of the Mississippi Valley and was ready to begin the delicate task of restoring the area to the Union. President Lincoln based his selection of General Nathaniel Banks to command the department in late 1862 primarily upon this political consideration, and Banks' overarching goal during his tenure in the Southwest was to cultivate native white support for the Union in order to expedite the state's reconstruction. A former Republican governor of Massachusetts and Speaker of the House of Representatives, Banks believed that the revitalization of the area's staple economy, which had undergone serious deterioration in the early years of the war, was a necessary prerequisite for the development of Unionist support.[4] But the production of cotton and sugar was predicated upon a stable labor force, and the tumult engendered by the federal occupation of southern Louisiana had effected a significant derangement in labor relations on most plantations. Black workers, as a result of the war-induced turmoil, considered themselves free men in fact, if not in law, and many refused to assume any longer the role of servile plantation laborer. Consequently, a prime concern for department officials in early 1863 was the establishment of a plantation labor program which, while securing to blacks their rights as freedmen, maximized staple production by stabilizing labor relations.[5]

The course chosen by Banks for effecting a normalization of labor relations on Gulf Department plantations was the establishment of a compulsory system of free labor.[6] Through a judicious mix of economic inducement and compulsion Banks believed that his system would increase both Unionist sentiment and staple production while aiding the black man in his transition from slavery to freedom. The General's program required that the black worker return to the plantation and resume his role as a field hand while assuring him a minimum wage in return for his labor.[7] Furthermore, Banks stipulated that land owners who wished to work their estates under the provisions of the army's program were required to swear their loyalty to the federal government. Such a compulsory system, department officials hoped, would provide planters with a constant supply of labor while it inculcated the freedmen with the lessons of hard work and individual initiative. Loyal planters, as a result, would reap the profits to be gained from an inflated staples market while the black worker would be led, forcibly if need be, to a knowledge of the social and economic gains offered by the system of free labor.

Although Banks' plan had a pleasing symmetry to it in theory, military officials realized as early as the spring of 1863 that their plantation labor program had not succeeded in stabilizing labor relations. Rather, many black workers were disgruntled with being forced to labor once again as field hands for their former owners and most planters were, at best, skeptical regarding the likelihood of their former chattels functioning as industrious free laborers. The mutual suspicion and distrust evident on both sides was quickly manifested in a further degeneration of labor relations and a corresponding diminution in staple production. By the end of 1863 it was becoming painfully apparent that further alterations were needed in the army's free labor system in order to pacify plantation workers, promote staple production, and aid the reconstruction efforts of the Lincoln administration.

It is at this juncture that the story of black education in the Gulf Department comes to the fore. Before the 1863 growing season was even half completed General Banks was beginning to sense the connection between freedmen's education and reconstruction. In June, Thomas Conway, a northern clergyman who was serving as a chaplain in a regiment of black Louisiana troops, informed the commander that it was "a

fore-gone conclusion" that a department-wide system of freedmen's education would be a great aid to the government's reconstruction efforts.[8]
Later that summer Thomas Hooper, a Boston jurist, explained to Banks
that a federally sponsored program of black education would aid the General in gaining the support of northern reform groups for his reconstruction activities.[9] But the most persuasive testimony which Banks received
regarding the benefits to be derived from a system of freedmen's education came from a delegation of free blacks whom the General had
appointed during the summer to study the desires of plantation workers.
After visiting a portion of the plantations operating under the aegis of the
military's free labor program, the black representatives reported to Banks
that the freedmen would not labor effectively until their children were
assured of an education.[10] This report made clear to the commander that
the plantation workers of Louisiana considered the education of their
children to be a prime concomitant of emancipation. The freedmen's fervent desire for education was made amply evident in the following experience of a Presbyterian missionary sent to Louisiana in 1863:

> You have no idea of the state of things here. Go out in any direction
> and you meet negroes on horses, negroes on mules, negroes with oxen,
> negroes by wagon, car and buggy load, negroes on foot, men, women
> and children; . . . all hopeful, almost all cheerful, every one pleading to
> be taught, willing to do anything for learning. They are never out of our
> rooms, and their cry is for "Books! Books!" and "when will school
> begin?" . . . Every night hymns of praise to God and prayers for the
> Government that oppressed them so long, rise around us on every
> side—prayers for the white teachers that have already come—prayers
> that God would send more.[11]

As the military commenced its preparations for the 1864 growing
season Banks could no longer ignore the fact that the blacks' almost mes-
sianic belief in the efficacy of schooling as an agent of social change had
important implications for his efforts at stimulating the department's
staple economy. In a series of instructions to officials responsible for
administering freedmen's activities he made it known that he considered
the institution of schools for plantation workers to be an integral part of
his free labor program. "I want it understood that the negro children must
be educated," he informed one of his agents. "Planters should be
informed that it is impossible to continue the laborers in their employ,
unless provision is made for the education of their children."[12] The General was even more explicit in a circular sent to all parish provost marshals:
"I desire you to notify all persons interested, that it is indispensable to the

cultivation of the soil, that schools for colored children shall be maintained. The policy of the Government demands this, and nothing will be
allowed to interfere with its success. . . . Unless laborers are assured that
the education of their children will be provided for, they become discon-
tented, and will be allowed to remove to Parishes where such provisions
are made."[13]

As a preliminary to the institution of a department wide system of
black education the Union military during the fall of 1863 established an
elementary school program for black children in New Orleans. Banks delegated the authority for administering the city's black school system to
Lieutenant William Stickney of the Eighth Vermont. Considered a "practical teacher of the first rank" by northern abolitionists, Stickney was a
firm believer in the New England system of primary education and the
establishment of normal school for teacher drill and instruction.[14] By the
end of the third week of October the lieutenant had made considerable
progress with his educational program. Seven schools were already in
operation by that time, staffed by sixteen teachers and attended by 576
pupils. Stickney found facilities for four of his schools in churches, while
he housed the remainder in private residences.[15] By the end of the year
the number of black pupils attending the schools had doubled, and in
March of 1864, when Banks transferred the entire system to the newly
established Board of Education, the military was employing in its seven
schools twenty-three teachers who taught 1,422 pupils.[16]

The rapid growth of the New Orleans school system for blacks would
have been impossible without an adequate supply of both teachers and
money. Initially, the military had thought it would have to rely upon northern teachers to staff its schools. But even before the schools opened, applications from fifteen white women, all residents of New Orleans and recent
high school graduates, had been received for positions in the new schools.
Although most of these applicants lacked teaching experience, Stickney
chose to staff his schools with the young women. Both teachers and administrators benefited by this arrangement. The women received a liberal salary
for their efforts, general ranging from fifty to eighty dollars a month, while
the military was able to expedite the establishment of its schools and
avoided the risk of alienating native white sentiment by the importation of
northern "do-gooders."[17] In order to finance the system, the army had to
rely on its own resources and the money gained from the sale of confiscated
property. This operation proved to be an expensive undertaking for the
frugal military. Salaries alone totaled over one thousand dollars each month,
and the army furnished most schools with both supplies and furniture,
items which also cost a considerable amount of money.[18] The expense

involved in supporting a school system for freedmen presented government officials with a dilemma. By the beginning of the 1864 growing season the military was convinced that a department-wide system of freedmen's education was a necessary adjunct of a successful plantation program, but the army had no desire to fund such a costly innovation. In order, therefore, to expand the school system outside of New Orleans the army would first have to find a means for financing the operation.

By early February of 1864 Banks believed that he had found a solution to his financial problem. A general announcement of a comprehensive system of freedmen's schools was made in the commander's plantation labor order. Banks directed that "provision will be made for the establishment of a sufficient number of schools—one at least for each of the police and school districts—for the instruction of colored children under twelve years of age, . . ."[19] He followed this policy statement on March 22 by a general order for establishment of a three-man Board of Education. The Board was to establish school districts throughout the rural areas of the department, acquire tracts of land and build schools, employ teachers and purchase educational materials, regulate the course of study, and assess property taxes for the support of the schools. In addition, "for the purpose of giving greater care, industry and intelligence to the laboring classes of Freedmen, and inspiring them with a higher sense of their obligation to society, to their race and all rightful authority," the Board was also to establish Sunday schools for adult free laborers. The three men chosen for the new Board were Colonel H. N. Frisbie of the Twenty-Second Regiment, Corps d'Afrique, Lieutenant Edwin Wheelock of the Fourth Regiment, Corps d'Afrique, and Doctor Isaac Hubbs, a citizen of New Orleans and a local representative of the American Missionary Association. Shortly after his appointment, Colonel Frisbie was removed from the Board and replaced by Benjamin Plumly, a Philadelphia abolitionist who had previously served as a recruiter of black troops for the Union army and was now selected by Banks to chair the Board of Education.[20]

As was the case with most federal agencies in the Gulf Department, the administration of the Board of Education was marked by a mixture of dedication, corruption, and political maneuvering. Corruption was the province of Dr. Hubbs. Late in 1864 General Banks expelled the doctor from both the Board and the department for withholding money from the pay of teachers for his own use.[21] After Hubbs' departure, the school system was run by Plumly and Wheelock, both dedicated to their jobs and who worked untiringly to forward the education of the freedmen. Through their efforts 126 schools staffed by 222 teachers were established in the department by the end of the war. These schools served over fourteen thousand pupils, in addition to an estimated five thousand black adults who attended night and Sunday schools. For their service Wheelock received lieutenant's pay and Plumly served without remuneration.[22] But even these dedicated administrators did not escape the machinations of Louisiana politics. Plumly, especially, became involved in the battle for post-war supremacy within the Republican party. Arriving in the department a supporter of Treasury Secretary Chase, by 1863 he had switched his political allegiance to the more moderate Lincoln-Banks faction of the Republican party, thereby earning for himself the wrath of party radicals and various governmental positions from General Banks. Firmly convinced that the policies of the military were in the best interest of the freedmen, Plumly became an inveterate opponent of the radical Republican faction in Louisiana and its free black supporters and utilized his position to solidify the political power of Republican moderates.[23]

Not surprisingly, the most difficult problem which the Board of Education faced was financial. Opposed to the military funding of black education, Banks made provision in his general order for the levying of a tax upon all property, including crops, in each of the school districts. This tax effectively shifted the burden of financing black education from the military to the planter class. The sum to be raised by the property tax was considerable, for it cost approximately eighteen dollars each year to educate a single student. During the first year of the Board's operation an estimated $150,000 was spent for the education of freedmen, and by the summer of 1865 expenses reached almost a quarter of a million dollars.[24]

Both native whites and government officials resisted Banks' school tax. Planters, already hard pressed by the war, were especially resentful of this charge for the benefit of the black man. Many did their best to avoid payment, and most succeeded. As early as April, 1864, Edwin Wheelock reported to Banks that a substantial number of planters were falsifying their tax returns.[25] White antipathy toward black education never abated during the war, and well into the post-war period the military found it difficult to collect even a small percentage of the sum owed by planters for school taxes.[26] Faced with a determined planter resistance to paying school taxes and reluctant to drain the army's coffers, several government officials favored placing at least part of the financial burden for black schools on the freedmen themselves. Wheelock suggested to the commanding general that a tax be imposed on all black males for the support of their schools. Not only would this device secure badly needed funds, but it would also "silence the murmur that white men are being taxed for the benefit of the black, and it is believed that the Freedmen themselves would feel a more living and personal interest in the success of this most benign plan, should they contribute of their own means toward It."[27] Banks, however, opposed this plan, just as he opposed the attempts of the Freedmen's Bureau during the spring of 1865 to place a school tax on freedmen, for he believed that the blacks would be unable to bear the financial burden and would thereby be deprived of a school system. Unable to collect sufficient funds from property owners and unwilling to tax the freedmen, Banks was forced to rely upon the military's treasury for financing most of his educational program.[28]

A potential source of aid for the Gulf Department's black schools was the various freedmen's aid societies established in the North during the war. Several of these northern societies did send varying amounts of aid to Louisiana. The National Freedmen's Relief Association and the United States Christian Commission supplied books and other educational materials to the freedmen, and the Boston-based American Baptist Home Missionary Society sent several teachers to New Orleans.[29] But the society most active in aiding the education of Louisiana freedmen was the American Missionary Association. During 1864 twenty-seven teachers and missionaries from this association were working in the Gulf Department. The most notable of the schools established by these northern teachers was located in the School of Medicine in New Orleans. Association teachers, aided by army officers and New Orleans' matrons, instituted a Sunday school in this building in which they taught 950 students. Another large school was established by association teachers at Baton Rouge, while two of the society's representatives worked among the black soldiers stationed at Port Hudson.[30]

Although the military did exploit the aid of northern philanthropic societies, the army never utilized the support of these organizations in southern Louisiana as fully as it did in other areas of the South. Most of the freedmen's aid societies concentrated their work in Virginia and South Carolina or in the upper Mississippi Valley. Of the three freedmen's organizations established specifically to aid the blacks of the Southwest, only the Northwestern Freedmen's Aid Commission did an appreciable amount of work in the Gulf Department.[31] This was in marked contrast to other areas of the South in which freedmen's education was carried on almost exclusively by northern teachers supplied by northern freedmen's aid societies. In the Gulf Department, however, while books and other supplies were received from the North, except for the teachers of the American Missionary Association, very few northerners taught among the freedmen.[32]

The scarcity of northerners among teachers of Louisiana freedmen is attributable to a disinclination on the part of Gulf Department officials to utilize northern teachers and a corresponding reluctance by philanthropic organizations to send their teachers into the Louisiana climate. In presenting to General Banks the outline of a district school system, Superintendent of Negro Labor George Hanks had suggested that the commander continue the practice begun in 1863 of giving preference to loyal Louisianans as teachers.[33] Banks agreed with Hanks' suggestion and in his education order directed that the Board of Education select teachers "as far as practicable, from the loyal inhabitants of Louisiana."[34] These teachers, Banks believed, had a superior knowledge of southern blacks and would also be more effective in counteracting white prejudice against black education.[35]

The relatively small part played by northern philanthropic organizations in educating Louisiana blacks is also an indication of the military's desire to retain control over all programs instituted for the freedmen in the Gulf Department. General Banks believed that the control of freedmen's affairs was a potentially powerful political tool which could aid both himself and the state's moderate Republicans, whom he led, in expediting the return of Louisiana to the Union. Throughout his tenure in the Gulf Department, therefore, he waged an effective campaign to maintain authority over all aspects of freedmen's affairs. In 1863 he defeated an attempt by the War Department to consolidate under an independent command the recruitment of Louisiana blacks into the federal army and a year later he successfully resisted the efforts of Treasury agents to take control of his free labor program.[36] In a similar fashion he limited the intrusion of northern missionaries into the educational program established for the freedmen, for these teachers would have operated outside the army's control. Banks and other school administrators especially viewed the teachers of the American Missionary Association as a threat to their free labor program, for the missionaries' perception of black emancipation was generally more expansive than that which prevailed among army officials. These northern teachers were particularly critical of the period of "tutelage" imposed upon blacks by the army's compulsory free labor program and advocated that the freedmen be placed on a par with white laborers.[37] In an attempt to stifle this criticism, the Board of Education limited the numbers and influence of northern teachers in the Gulf Department and also attempted to assume control of the few schools which the missionaries had successfully established in New Orleans.[38]

By the early summer of 1864 General Banks had advanced a considerable distance in the establishment of a comprehensive school system for black youths. In late May Edwin Wheelock reported that forty-nine schools staffed by ninety teachers were in operation. Particularly encouraging was the fact that fifty-two of these teachers, all of whom were native

Louisiana females, were serving outside of New Orleans in the rural parishes. "The Country Schools are rapidly multiplying," the Commissioner proudly proclaimed, "and their success has already placed beyond reasonable dispute the capacity of the African to receive our civilization. The more intelligent of the Planters are comprehending that whatever contents and dignifies their labor, is a reciprocal benefit to themselves."[39] Parish provost marshals had laid out school districts of three miles square and required all black children under twelve years of age to attend school. Blacks above the age of twelve who desired to attend classes could, with the permission of their employer, attend the day schools, or else attend the night and Sunday schools operated by the military.[40]

Despite the success which the army experienced in establishing schools in the rural parishes, a continuing source of difficulty for the military was obtaining funds to finance its educational program. One of the prime inducements which Banks had used to secure an adequate supply of teachers for his black school was a liberal salary scale ranging from sixty to ninety dollars per month.[41] By the beginning of 1865, however, many teachers were complaining bitterly that due to the Board of Education's inability to collect the school tax, they were not being paid promptly.[42] This development worked a special hardship on the teachers, for most were young women without funds of their own and who could not obtain credit in the parishes in which they taught.[43] Compounding the teachers' difficulties was their inability to secure adequate boarding facilities. In Saint James Parish the military constructed nine schools but could not obtain housing for any of the teachers sent to staff them. Throughout the department similar incidents of white hostility to boarding teachers occurred, and most of the women were forced to rely upon their own meager financial resources to provide accommodations for themselves.[44] The teachers' plight was troublesome to the military, not only as it worked a hardship on the women, but also because, in the words of one official, it was "a great drawback to the success of Free-Labor."[45] Faced with a breakdown in his school system due to the financial concerns of his teacher corps, Banks ordered that all teachers were to be provided with "proper accommodations as to Board and Residence." If the people of the individual school districts refused to provide these items at their own expense, the provost marshals were to "assess the cost of the people upon the property and collect the sum without delay." Freedmen's education was considered central to the reconstruction of Louisiana, and Banks was intent upon insuring the continued existence of this vital program.[46]

The opposition of many whites to a comprehensive system of black education was made evident at the convention called by the commanding general in the spring of 1864 to restructure the state's constitution. Prompted by the President to work for an early reconstruction of the state government, Banks hoped that along with abolishing slavery the convention would provide for the public education of freedmen.[47] But although the delegates were generally attuned to the wishes of the commanding general, they balked at the public financing of black education.[48] Soon after the convention began the members received the report of the Committee on Public Education which called for the establishment of free public schools for all children supported by a general property tax. Although black children were included in this proviso, the committee specifically designated that the races would be educated separately.[49] Soon afterwards, the convention bogged down in a debate over public support of black education, segregated or otherwise. If the convention incorporated the Education Committee's report into the new constitution, these delegates contended that the slaveholders of the state would be placed in double jeopardy. Not only would they lose millions of dollars by the emancipation of their slaves, but they also would be forced to spend additional funds to educate the freedmen.[50] Other delegates, however, argued that black education would benefit the entire state population despite the financial burden, for schooling would transform the freedmen into "a blessing instead of a curse to the white race." Black education was also essential, declared a supporter of the committee's report, for "it is a matter of preservation for all of us to do them justice, because a race that has for ages and generations suffered injustice, may at last revolt against it."[51] The convention's debate was clear evidence of the split in native white thinking regarding the advisability of black education. The more "enlightened" among white Louisianans appreciated the fact that education could be an effective tool for controlling a potentially subversive population. But such speculative theorizing was not appreciated by the majority of whites who were burdened with the high cost of a lost rebellion. For these individuals black education was simply an added financial cost to be borne in the interests of a free black population, whose mere presence was considered to be enough of a hardship for whites to bear.

The issue of public financing of black education came to a head more than two months after the convention received the report of the Education Committee. On June 27, 1864, the convention approved the committee's recommendation for a comprehensive public school system by a 49–29 vote. A few days later it defeated by a 66–15 margin a proposal calling for the integrated schooling of the races.[52] With these two votes the convention gave its approval to a system of state-supported public instruction on a segregated basis. But overnight the membership seemingly had a change of

heart, for on July 1 the delegates adopted without a recorded vote an article providing for segregated schools financed separately by the races which
they served.[53] This article, if sustained, would have effectively precluded any
possibility for a system of black public education, for within the black community funds were not available for financing a school system. Realizing
full well the implications of this vote, the supporters of black education,
aided no doubt by the persuasive patronage powers of General Banks,
reached a compromise with their opponents and placed into the new constitution a provision for the public instruction of all children, leaving it to
the state legislature to decide upon the method of financing.[54]

At the time most participants in the convention's maneuverings considered the final outcome a victory for the proponents of black public education. Banks transmitted the convention's decision to the President and
informed him that the compromise "requires the Legislature to provide
means for the education of *all* children without restriction of color." Both
Lincoln and Banks considered this clause adequate.[55] The opponents of
black education concurred in Banks' estimation that the convention's final
decision aided the General's cause. The delegates branded the convention's end product "disgraceful" and labeled those who had changed their
votes "hirelings" of the army.[56] But the declarations of victory by the proponents of black education were premature, for before a state-supported
system of black schooling could be established the state legislature was
required to provide funds to finance the program. Unfortunately for the
military, the legislature was no more anxious than the convention had
been to go on record in support of public taxation for black schooling.
During the first weeks of the 1864 legislative session the State Superintendent of Public Education called upon the legislators to "provide for the
systematic and free education of the people but recently . . . delivered
from the lash of the taskmaster."[57] But the rhetoric of the Superintendent
did not move the legislators. Instead, the lawmakers defeated by a 16–30
vote a resolution for the establishment of a committee to "inquire into the
condition and resources of the schools for colored children, now in existence."[58] During the entire legislative session the only bill passed which
made mention of the delicate matter of black education forbade integrated
schooling.[59] The legislature's refusal to vote funds for freedmen's education was one more sign that the white opposition would ultimately prove
fatal to the military's program of black schools.[60]

Although the military failed to provide an adequate financial base for
its educational program, Banks was at least partially successful in establishing a comprehensive system of black schooling for the freedmen of
the Gulf Department. In numerical terms the educational system was a

success. By early 1865, of the estimated 20,000 black children within Union lines, 11,000 were attending school. Added to this number were the many freedmen who attended the sixty Sunday schools and twenty night schools operating in southern Louisiana.[61] But the success of the military's educational program cannot be gauged by attendance figures alone, for they give only a vague impression of the educational strides made by many black students. The Board of Education's report of 1864 stressed the rapid advance on the part of "children who eight weeks ago were beginning the alphabet, [and] are now reading the First Readers, and solving with facility problems in the primary rules of arithmetic." Even more impressive gains had been made by the "advanced classes which were working in the Fourth Readers and doing problems in long division, fractions, and multiplication."[62] While a certain amount of exaggeration undoubtedly crept into the reports of educational administrators, this exaggeration was based upon an enthusiasm created by the academic progress of a people who only a few years before had been considered virtually uneducable by most Americans.

The educational accomplishments of black children had a double meaning for those individuals involved in freedmen's education. Most significantly for the blacks themselves, their educational success was tangible evidence of their potential for contributing to the establishment of a free labor society in Louisiana. Blacks could, and would, learn, and thereby gain the skills necessary for functioning successfully as freedmen. After only a few months of instruction the Board of Education proclaimed that the freedmen were "rapidly demonstrating the capacity of the African to receive our civilization."[63] Other educators concurred in this assessment. Two missionary teachers at Baton Rouge, after a year's work with the freedmen, were "now fully convinced that the colored children can learn."[64] An agent of the American Bible Society was equally optimistic in his assessment that the blacks "possess more mind than has usually been credited to them: . . . [and] the embarrassments which they now meet with, though great, are such as may eventually be removed by a proper education on their part."[65] The most fulsome praise for black scholars came from the irrepressible Benjamin Plumly. "The aptitude of these color'd children to learn, is equal to that of the men of color for the art of war," he maintained. "Neither of them is excelled in their respective places, by any race on record."[66]

A second facet of the freedmen's educational program was the influence which schooling had upon black plantation labor. General Banks had instituted his educational program for freedmen with the hope that schooling would not only act as an instrument of social uplift, but also of social control. Education, in other words, would result in a willing and efficient labor force. Measured against this standard military officials also felt that the school system had been a success. Late in 1864 Banks told a northern audience that "the greater interest they [freedmen] have in their crops and families and schools, the more they earn, and the better they labor for their employers."[67] More straightforward in their judgment were various soldiers and administrators on the local scene. A provost marshal wrote: "In those districts where schools are in operation the negroes are more contented and work better than where schooling is denied their children. . . . Educate the children, let their influence be felt at home and free labor will prove an entire success."[68] A soldier serving in New Orleans attributed the decline in "vagabondage" among blacks to their education.[69] These themes were emphasized by Superintendent of Negro Labor George Hanks in a report to the commanding general. "The fact that these children are receiving an education, is a remarkable incentive to industry in the parents, and results in their being much more contented and happy," Hanks concluded. "Many of them have spoken of it to me: some say they would sooner work for nothing, than have their children deprived of learning to read."[70]

As a result of the military's educational program a substantial number of freedmen, perhaps as many as fifty thousand, were brought into contact with at least the rudiments of an elementary education. Although the effect of this education on Louisiana's black population is difficult to pinpoint, the success of the freedmen at grasping the basics of an education did have an effect on white observers and their opinion of the potential of the black man to function in a free labor society. A more sanguine attitude on the part of administrators and military officials in the Gulf Department existed at the end of the war in regard to the feasibility of blacks succeeding as freedmen, because of the educational program. A precise statement of this attitude was made in late 1864 by General Banks: "The whole of this population is in the rapid process of evaluation and education. The report made of the advance both of young and old, is surprising as well as gratifying, and leaves no doubt that the negro population will not only answer the requisitions for voluntary labor, and the just expectation of the Government, but will justify by their great improvement, the extension of the right of suffrage."[71] The linkage between education and black voting was also sensed by Benjamin Plumly, who was usually attuned to the political dimensions of reformism. As early as the summer of 1863 Plumly proposed that education rather than property holding should be the criterion for black voting, and late the following year the erstwhile school administrator promised that as a result of his school program he would have 300,000 black Republican voters ready at the next presidential election.[72] A more general assessment of the effect of black education was made by Plumly's colleague on the Board of Education, Edwin Wheelock. "Three years ago," he declared, "it was a crime to teach their race. Now they read the Testament and the news paper. They are learning the geography of the world. They are gaining the knowledge of figures, with which to do the business of labor and life. They are singing the songs of the Union and freedom. They show a healthy mentality, and have made it appear to reasonable minds that they are very much like the rest of mankind, and are thus entitled to a fair chance in the world."[73]

The military's educational program provided, then, the bedrock for the restructuring of Louisiana's political economy. As a result of this program, the black population of the state, the backbone of the area's labor force and potentially the most volatile element in southern society, was inculcated, in Wheelock's words, with northern "instruction, counsel, [and] culture."[74] Educated in this manner, the freedmen would elevate themselves in social status, provide a bulwark for southern Unionism, and supply a stable labor force for the revivification of the section's plantation economy. Black schooling, therefore, provided an answer to what one historian has termed "the central ambiguity of the free labor attitude toward the Negro."[75] On the one hand northern whites talked of providing opportunities for black advancement, while at the same time serious doubts existed as to the capabilities of blacks to advance themselves in a white society. Education, a process which inculcated the black man with the central tenets of free labor ideology, provided the best, and perhaps the only, means of enabling blacks to free themselves from their base passions and contribute to American society. The contention of Wheelock that under General Banks' administration "the school-house takes the place of the whipping-post and scourge," and the belief of a northern missionary who worked with Louisiana freedmen that "if we do not teach them, they will be a terrible power," are understandable when placed within this framework.[76] Just as plantation discipline had been viewed by southerners as the only means for both controlling and civilizing black slaves, so in the northern context education assumed these complementary functions. Education, in the military's estimation, both enabled blacks to compete in a free labor society, and insured that they did so in terms that were socially acceptable to middle class Americans.

CHAPTER 17

Notes on the Education of Negroes at Norfolk and Portsmouth, Virginia, During the Civil War

Sing-Nan Fen

ACCORDING TO PROFESSORS Jackson and Russell, in 1860, free Negroes constituted 24 percent of the total Negro population in Norfolk.[1] Because of the state laws after 1830 forbidding teaching letters to Negroes in groups, free Negroes were about as illiterate as the slaves.[2] In the process of emancipation during the Civil War, these laws were nullified. Legally speaking, emancipation consisted no more and no less in the nullification of the laws which governed free Negroes as well as those which governed slaves in slave territory. But the spirit of the law survived the letter of the law. This extra-legal survival has been generally attributed to social customs and mores. Frequently it was the result of a more intentional and collective action, namely, political action. In connection with the education of the freedmen during the War, there were many instances in which they were deprived of the educational help of the missionary society not because of mores or customs, but simply because of political actions of certain individuals or groups of individuals. By the same token, there were also instances in which the education of the freedmen prospered, not because of the change of mores or customs overnight, but simply because of the politics of the parties concerned. The contrast between the education of the freedmen north of the Hampton Roads, Fortress Monroe and Hampton, and the education of the freedmen south of it, Norfolk and Portsmouth, is a case in point.

247

One essential difference between the two sides of Hampton Roads with regard to the education of the freedmen at the beginning of the War was this: On the northern side, the serious problem was the lack of buildings. In contrast, buildings were available on the southern side. Missionary and education work did not start until 1863, although the territory comprising Norfolk and Portsmouth was occupied by the Union forces early in May, 1862, under General Wool.

C. L. Lockwood, the first missionary sent to Virginia by the American Missionary Association in September, 1861, lost no time in exploring the field on May 19, 1862, after the Union forces occupied Norfolk on the heel of the planned retreat of the Confederate Army. He spent a Sabbath there, but was barred from speaking at a colored church. According to Lockwood, the secessionistic tendency of the minister was the reason.[3] Thus, the mission and schooling was delayed about a year. Unlike Fortress Monroe and Hampton, Norfolk and Portsmouth were "surrendered," not conquered. Those who surrendered the city, Mayor Lamb for example, remained Confederate in spirit with the connivance of military authority such as General Viele. General Viele, according to Professor Wertenbaker, was "benevolent" in comparison with General Butler, who closed white schools because teachers rejected the oath of allegiance.[4]

On the other hand, not until General Butler resumed full command on both sides of the Hampton Roads in 1863, did the educational work on behalf of the freedmen on the southern side of Hampton Roads begin to prosper.[5] It was he who appointed Orlando Brown to superintend Negro affairs south of the James River, which was under general supervision of Lieutenant Colonel Kisman.[6] With Brown in this position, the educational work of the AMA was greatly expedited. Missionary teachers received rations from the military authorities. They were also assigned public buildings as their classrooms and residences, only to have them taken away to accommodate white children immediately after the War.[7] To this day, Negro education in the South sinks and swims with politics; one essential ingredient of Southern politics, by the same token, has been Negro education.

For evident reasons, Negroes themselves, during the War, played no significant and conspicuous part in the politics of their own education. They had had no experience in political organization. On the other hand, the Southern whites were full of political power and sagacity. They were omnipotent and omniscient in spite of military defeat. The first AMA missionary at Norfolk, the Reverend G. Greene, wrote on May 13, 1863, that the secessionists demonstrated against the education of Negroes, and the boarding of their teachers was a serious problem.[8] Thus, Norfolk set the pattern of hostile attitude toward Negro education of the unreconstructed South.

Despite the unfavorable local political climate, however, the first two schools sponsored by the AMA were held at the Negro Baptist and Methodist churches with 550 day scholars and 500 night scholars. There were four teachers and fifteen monitors engaged in teaching in both schools.[9] This arrangement was possible at Norfolk simply because stronger power in favor of Negro education existed. Due to the presence of Negro troops, order and the law favoring Negro education were maintained.[10]

In contrast, Newport News was given up as a missionary field by John Oliver, a Boston Negro, because of the prejudice of the local white population. For fear of retaliation even the colored church there could not be used.[11] Oliver found Portsmouth, a city not far from Norfolk, a better place. There he established the first Sabbath school on January 5, 1863.[12] In 1865 this school became an institution for advanced students from the most prosperous families in Portsmouth; these persons aspired to be teachers. Soldiers with sabers were regularly stationed in the building to prevent rebels from molesting.[13]

IT WAS evident that Negroes would have a very difficult time as freedmen. To survive the difficulty, they resorted to the "opiate" of the masses, religion.

Before the War, Negroes in Virginia did not follow the dominant religious denominations of white people, Episcopal and Presbyterian. At Norfolk and Portsmouth free Negroes, mostly Baptists and Methodists, had their own churches and managed their own church affairs, including the appointment of white ministers.[14] One immediate consequence of this fact was that, unlike Hampton and Fortress Monroe across Hampton Roads, there was no lack of buildings ready for use in the schooling of the freedmen. The two earliest and most prosperous schools at Norfolk were housed in Bute Street Baptist Church and Fenchurch Street Methodist Church, respectively.[15]

The experience of religious autonomy served the Negroes in the Tidewater area of Virginia before the War just as Trevelyan described it as serving the working class in Britain in his *British History in the Nineteenth Century*:

> Many of the more self-respecting of the new proletariat found in the Baptist or Wesleyn Chapel the opportunity for the development of talents and the gratification of instincts that were denied expression elsewhere. The close and enthusiastic study of the Bible educated the imagination. . . . And in chapel life working men first learnt to speak and to organize, to persuade and to trust their fellows. Much effort that

soon afterwards went into political, trade union and co-operative activities, was then devoted to the chapel community. It was in Little Bethel
that many of the working class leaders were trained. In a world made
almost intolerable by avarice and oppression, here was a refuge where
men and things were taken up aloft and judged by spiritual and moral
standards that forbade either rage or despair.[16]

That religious congregation has been a training ground of Negro
leadership is a familiar story now. Its place in the scheme of life of the Negro
people in general, particularly during the War, deserves some further understanding. It was improbable that, during the War, there was a clear distinction in the minds of most Negroes between learning secular lessons from
teachers in schools and worshiping God with preachers in churches. Possibly the majority of them were after neither knowledge nor salvation, but
simply congregation, simply living together, and experiencing fellowship in
churches as well as in schools. With this understanding, it is clear why freedmen, old and young, liked schools and their teachers so much that they
seized every opportunity to enroll themselves in schools, day and night.

To associate freedmen's schools during the War with congregation
has historical precedent. Words like *colleges* and *schola* in Roman times
referred to associations of the plebeian class, the great object of which
had been the "cheerfulness of intercourse, the promotion of fellowship,
and goodwill, the relief of the dullness of humdrum lives."[17] Like Roman
plebeians, many of whom had happened to be recently emancipated
freedmen, too, Negro freedmen during the War "did not need much
ingenuity to multiply occasions for reunion."[18]

The existence of a variety of schools—day schools, Sabbath schools,
evening schools, sewing schools, industrial schools—not only delineated
the various functions of education, but also multiplied the various occasions for gatherings among which the regular church attendance on Sun-
days would hardly be missed.

The letters of teachers were full of testimonies of good feelings and
fellowship. The free flow of sentimentality, or even the unreserved expression of ecstasy, in the correspondence of certain teachers might very well
arouse a tough-minded historian's strong suspicions.[19] Reading with the
understanding that these letters were written amidst a human situation in
which "scorched creatures moisten with each other's saliver," as an
ancient Chinese philosopher, Chung-tze expressed it, makes clear the
genuineness of the feelings expressed.

More prosaic facts, such as the proliferation of educational organizations such as the Human Aid Society, the Temperance Society, and the
Anglo-African Educational Society, may also be interpreted from the point

of view of congregation. These organizations, as a rule, consisted of President, Vice-President, Secretary, Treasurer, and Board of Visitors, leaving a much smaller number of common members than officers.[20] The featherbedding might be a subject for satire. To this day, Negro society is notorious for its meretricious formality. Once more, Dill helps in understanding the congregational significance.

> Individually weak and despised, they might by union, gain a sense of collective dignity and strength. To our eyes, as perhaps to the eyes of the Roman aristocrat, the dignity might seem far from imposing. But these things are greatly a matter of imagination, and depend on the breadth of the mental horizon. When the brotherhood, many of them of servile grade, met in full conclave, in the temple of their patron deity, to pass a formal degree of thanks to a benefactor, and regal themselves with a modest repast, or when they passed through the streets and the forum with banner flying, and all the emblems of their guild, the meanest member felt himself lifted, for the moment, above the dim, hopeless obscurity of plebeian life.[21]

In view of the physical and spiritual poverty of Negroes during the War, schools served a more general function than that of intellectual learning. It was another occasion for assembly. If there were white people around to participate on equal footing, all the better for the morale. Amidst the bloodiest struggle, rooted on a soil soaked with their own sweat without any certainty of the morrow's bread and next of kin, these freedmen were thirsty for a little human warmth, physical and spiritual, generated by gathering together. By accenting congregation, even such details as how and why Negro children were at their best in their choral singing and why freedmen liked to "shout" in their prayer meeting are understandable. On the other hand, if they did not always find what they wanted, i.e., emotional satisfaction, in schools, they simply quit school, just as they were uninterested in a cold and stern sermon from a Northern puritan. In the last analysis, for the freedmen, schools met urgent and fundamental needs, human fellowship and association. From the letters of a number of teachers it is apparent that human fellowship and association were also what these Northerners needed and secured.

The school is a cultural institution. Schooling develops in stages corresponding to those of cultural development. Microscopically, the different school routines are also hinged on cultural development. Lecturing was more prevalent in the Middle Ages than now. Discussions could not be considered education in an authoritarian culture. The school routine which the missionary teachers attempted in the South for the benefit of the freedmen during the War was itself a comparatively new institution. It had taken root in the New England states only one generation before the War.

What characterized the common school most distinctly was its management, which had been simply nonexistent in the district school. First of all, in the common school, students were no longer taught individually. They were graded and taught as classes. Secondly, lessons were given according to grade placement. For example, the learning of mental arithmetic preceded the learning of written arithmetic. The learning of geography was generally considered the crowning achievement. Above all, discipline was no longer maintained by the teacher's brutal force, but rather by the status of the teacher backed by a recognizable organization of which the principal was the head. Thus, from the point of view of social organization, common schools were much better organized and thus much better managed than district schools. In terms of children's experience, going to school, after Horace Mann's reformation, was to follow a common routine or go through a common mill. Naturally, nothing would please the missionary teachers more than to have their Negro students go through this common routine with ease, thereby serving to prove that they were equal to their white brethren. Leaders such as General Butler explicitly and consistently attempted to transplant this New England common school system to the Southern soil for the benefit of freedmen.

This study has examined the political obstacles to this transplantation. It has also studied the uncanny use by Negroes of this transplanted institution, common schools, as occasions for their much needed socializing. It shall show also that doubt was raised in the minds of certain field workers about the transplantation of the common school routine. H. S. Beals was such a field worker.

When Beals applied to the AMA for work in the South, he was between forty and fifty years old. Behind him, he had seventeen years of teaching experience in Massachusetts. As the principal of a school, he was earning five hundred dollars per annum. He was an elder and deacon in the local Presbyterian church. He also had owned a manufacturing business which had been destroyed by fire. One of his hands was crippled. He asked four hundred dollars to support his wife and children. His first choice of location was Washington, D.C.[22] According to the Reverend William Niles, who wrote a letter of recommendation for him, Beals had worked also for the American Tract Society, which he had repudiated when it had become pro-slavery.[23] In his letter accepting the AMA appointment of March 5, 1863, he mentioned his mother's influence during his early childhood on his attitudes toward Negroes.

Thus, Beals came to Portsmouth with age, experience, and a definite racial outlook.

By all measure he was a good schoolman, like Coan at Norfolk and Day at Hampton. Under his leadership the day schools at Portsmouth prospered. Unlike Norfolk and Hampton, Portsmouth was relatively peaceful for missionary workers, fewer petty personal quarrels were recorded in the correspondence of teachers. Nevertheless, his own letters were full of torments deeply affected by the abject poverty of the freedmen. He wavered between his role as a school teacher and that of a relief worker. In his letter of March 26, 1864,[24] Beals reported that there were three hundred of the "most needy, helpless portion of the people" from Maryland, most of whom were Catholics. Evidently for this portion of freedmen, from his point of view as an outsider, earning a living should take precedence over getting an education. Consequently, the best help need not be formal education. After much soul searching, Beals finally decided to give up his teaching position at Portsmouth and went to work on the nearby Taylor Farm. What motivated Beal's decision was naturally opaque. What unsettled him and his fellow workers was understandable. Where should Negroes go from here? What kind of education would be most pertinent to Negroes given the existing condition?

Under the condition existing during the War, the quest for the aims and objectives of Negro education was not armchair philosophizing. The problem was thrust on all parties concerned. To the conservative Southerners, schooling for Negroes was basically undesirable, unnecessary and impossible. To Negroes themselves, it was desired, not for intellectual and moral discipline, but for congregation. To the sensitive missionary workers, it was becoming more and more a problem, rather than an answer. Some of them began to find that Negroes were perhaps not quite ready for common schools and that perhaps other kinds of schooling would be more relevant to their lives. Woodbury, one of the architects of the Negro school system, for example, maintained that for freedmen instruction in sewing was more important than book learning. Other teachers also speculated on the same problem.

Miss Daffin, for example, a Negro teacher from Philadelphia, sincerely doubted the wisdom of book learning for the newly emancipated Negroes.[25] Miss Burdich, on the other hand, thought what freedmen needed was not necessarily formal education but festivity, which freedmen themselves would certainly embrace. She also strongly resented the cruelty of the discipline used in schools.[26] Thus, the proper and pertinent education for Negroes emerged as a problem long before Washington and Du Bois came to the American scene.

DESPITE THE obstacles, misunderstandings and misgivings, Negro education as a "system" took root at Norfolk and Portsmouth. For this,
William L. Coan and the Reverend W. S. Bell were responsible.

William L. Coan arrived at Fortress Monroe on December 26, 1861.
His wife worked as the housekeeper of the teachers' residence at Hampton, the Tyler House, provoking the unanimous hostility of the residents.
Coan himself was interested originally in being the Superintendent of
Contraband at Fortress Monroe, but the post went to C. B. Wilder
instead. When the freedman, Davis, was selected by Lockwood to present
the freedmen's cause in the North, Coan accompanied him, sharing his
trial and triumph. Finally, Coan, followed by his wife, settled in Norfolk in
April, 1863, and remained there until the end of the War. Apparently, he
then had charge of a graded primary school at the Negro Methodist
Church with a number of female teachers under his thumb. By virtue of
the formal organization, his school served as a model for other scattered
small schools.

Norfolk was a showplace for Negro education. At the peak of his
work, Coan had 564 scholars enrolled in his day primary school, with a
daily average attendance of 375, and 681 evening scholars, whose ages
ranged from four to sixty-one.[27] Edward Pierce of Boston, C. L. Lockwood of Hampton, and Chaplain C. Raymond of the Butler School visited his school and were impressed with his achievement. Captain
O. Brown, the Superintendent of Contraband Affairs south of the James
River, was encouraged by the enrollment. The highest studies in Coan's
school included geography, history, and written arithmetic. Sander's
Series was adopted as readers.

Coan was particularly proud of his new measures of discipline, which
were supposed to be milder than whipping, and which consisted of tying
one ear with a thread, tying the faces of two boys together so they could
smell each other, requiring standing on one foot, and using "rebel" as a
nickname for the misbehaver.[28] He was uneasy about the soliciting of
students by neighboring schools and proceeded to grade schools on the
basis of student achievement.[29] He was also jealous of his own power of
assigning teachers. As a matter of fact, this was his quarrel with Woodbury, his superintendent.

During his tenure at Norfolk, Coan also worked hard to resolve the
racial conflict between teachers. On this issue, he seemed to have had the
cooperation of Woodbury. From the very beginning, local Negroes were
used as monitors. A little later, qualified Negro teachers came from the
North to teach in Norfolk. On March 11, 1864, Coan wrote that he was
planning to have Negro teachers "break in."[30] Woodbury, while praising

the Negro teachers as helpful and successful, maintained that they should take full and separate charge of one school.[31]

According to Miss Darrin, she, Miss Harris, and Miss Smithe did have full and separate charge of a school.[32] Daffin seemed to be satisfied with her school, but she was not at all satisfied with her living conditions. Her letter of September, 1864, complained that as a Negro teacher she felt uncomfortable in the mission house and asked Woodbury to improve the situation.[33] A white teacher, Mary Reed, in an earlier letter of July 18, 1864, expressed her unwillingness to live with the Negro teachers, thinking that they had overstepped their bounds; she wished to live separately from them.[34] Addressing himself to this difficulty, Coan wrote his "position paper" after he had left the Norfolk school:

1. There should be no discrimination in employment and remuneration of service on account of color.
2. Persons, including the superintendent, with color prejudice should be dismissed.
3. No low seat should be assigned to people because of color when boarding together.
4. Social relationships between males and females of different colors should be discouraged.
5. Separate boarding is preferable.[35]

This document is significant in that it is about a century old. It could be used as a good measure of the progress of our present day thinking and practice, especially as it came from the pen of an ordinary schoolman.

At the end of the War, both Coan and Woodbury worked in Richmond, Coan taking charge of a large school and Woodbury becoming an assistant superintendent of the Freedmen's Bureau. The Negro school system at Norfolk, built by both within one year and a half under the sponsorship of the AMA, was taken over by H. C. Percy. Percy inherited six thousand children, half of whom had had some instruction.[36] He inherited also an established practice of governmental help, specifically teachers' rations, transportation and shelter, as well as school buildings.[37] Percy proposed to grade schools according to student ability in reading. Each teacher was to take two grades only.[38] Thus, teachers would have a relatively homogeneous group to teach. According to his report, there was an industrial school in operation, in addition to day schools.[39]

The Negro school system at Norfolk under the regime of Coan, Woodbury, and Percy was a distinctive achievement. In 1867, the local prominent citizens visited "Percy's Schools," were genuinely impressed and urged the local whites to emulate and to imitate.[40] Emulate and imitate they did to the extent that they drove away the Negro students and converted the buildings into white schools. But there was a better and earlier story of emulation, that of schools at Portsmouth under the Reverend Bell.

When Beals left Portsmouth to work on the Taylor Farm, he took away hundreds of children by order and several teachers by need. His departure caused chaos for a while. A. M. Eastman, his successor, for one reason or another, could not fit in the situation. Teachers such as Drummond felt uncertain about the schools.[41] The Reverend W. S. Bell of the nearby Wise Farm ruthlessly exposed Eastman's incompetency. The uncertainty lasted about three months until Bell and Eastman changed places. Bell was aggressive, and Eastman retreated gracefully.

When Bell took over the Portsmouth schools, there were five teachers for four hundred scholars. After four months' time, Bell planned to maintain the teacher-pupil ration at one to fifty. He apparently carried on with a style all his own.[42]

His regime was earmarked by a number of things. (1) Through the help of Captain Brown, a new mission house was secured. At the beginning, teachers had to board with Negro families. In November, 1863, a house was assigned as teachers' residence by the government. The new house big enough to accommodate six teachers was one of Bell's prizes. (2) More buildings for schools were also secured. (3) Benches were made for five hundred pupils. (4) The city was districted and schools were graded. The highest grade contained girls who had studied for more than a year and aspired to be teachers. Bell declared that no effort would be spared to give them good training in English. (5) In addition to day schools, Bell and his teachers were also engaged in night schools and Sabbath schools which were typical and as rewarding at Portsmouth as anywhere else.[43]

Compared with Norfolk schools, Bell unashamedly announced, Portsmouth schools were better. This could have been a boast in his moment of elation when eight new teachers arrived to meet the urgent needs. Unmistakable, however, was the spirit of emulation and competition. Bell's ambition was also exhibited in his intent to secure a melodeon costing a hundred dollars, this luxury to be paid for in six months through students' offerings. Somehow, he got his melodeon, too. He was also serious about establishing a singing school.[44]

Bell also had opinions about teaching methods. He confidently concluded that "word recognition" or "contextual cue" was not a good method of learning language. He insisted that spelling should come before reading. Most of his ideas were carried out. Letters from teachers working with him indicate that the ratio of fifty students to one teacher became an established fact. Monitors were trained by the Reverend J. L. Mars during vacation time. Bell's achievements were praised in 1865 by Mars when Portsmouth became an education model for cities farther west, such as Petersburg. Thus, the common school tradition not only took root in Portsmouth, but also set an example for other western cities.

The single-mindedness of schoolmen like Coan and Bell in their determination to transplant the new social institution, the common school, to Southern soil for the benefit of the newly emancipated freedmen was at once sincere and naïve. They honestly believed in the equality of men. They believed that freedmen's children could go through the common school routine with ease equal to that of white children. Their naivity lay in their belief in the power of individual salvation. Education was supposed to be an effective way, to bring out this power. As events followed, this belief in individual salvation, whether through religious or lay education, proved to be a myth. Freedmen in Virginia were to be suppressed under the collective strength of tradition and institutions against which the common school routine did not equip them to deal. Only today, a sizeable portion of Southern Negroes begin to realize again, as their forebears did during the ill-fated Reconstruction period, that the life of Negroes in general and their education in particular depend more than anything else on organized and sustained political action on their own part.

CHAPTER 18

The American Missionary Association and Black Education in Civil War Missouri

Joe M. Richardson

T HE CIVIL WAR RESULTED in emancipation for approximately 115,000 Missouri slaves. Many former bondsmen were poorly prepared for their new status. Slavery had provided little opportunity for formal education which seemed essential for the newly liberated freedmen's successful adjustment to freedom. Fortunately a majority of blacks eagerly sought knowledge. One of the earliest sources of instruction for Missouri freedmen was the American Missionary Association (AMA) which had a representative in Saint Louis as early as 1862.[1]

Missouri as a mission field was not new to the American Missionary Association. Organized September 3, 1846, as a protest against the silence of Northern churches on the question of slavery, the association attempted to convince slaveholders of the evils of the peculiar institution. Though it was unsafe to send missionaries to the deep South, representatives went to the border states to organize churches on an "avowed anti-slavery basis" and to give "testimony against slavery and the sin of caste."[2]

The association's pre-Civil War activity in Missouri was limited. A visitor to Missouri in 1856 encouraged the AMA to send missionaries by writing that he had talked with slave owners who believed slavery to be wrong and dying in the state. However the association did not send a permanent representative until 1858.[3] Early in that year Reverend W. Kendrick occupied a mission field in northern Missouri. He reported soon after his arrival that he had held "protracted meetings" at Lancaster

259

and "hopefully converted" forty persons.[4] Kendrick believed that Missouri experienced slavery in its mildest form. "I was credibly informed by the best class of citizens, both slaveholders and non-slaveholders," Kendrick wrote, "that they expect Missouri will be a free state in less than five years." Apparently "thousands from the free States have come in and are changing the whole aspect of things."[5]

Kendrick's experience resulted in the AMA sending Reverend G. H. Pool to Saint Charles County in early 1859. Pool held a revival at Saint Charles which slaves and masters attended together. He thought many of the owners opposed slavery. Pool soon learned, however, that the local people were "very suspicious of a stranger coming into their midst these exciting times. They watch him well. . . ." A Presbyterian minister warned Pool that it was the wrong time "to work for freedom, there is too much excitement now." The minister refused to permit Pool to preach in his church even if he promised to say nothing of slavery. Simply the knowledge that Pool represented the AMA would wreck his church, the minister claimed.[6]

Pool also preached at Glasgow, Fayette and other small towns. He decided that Missourians were "*bitterly opposed*" to abolitionist principles. A free church could not exist, he believed.[7] Shortly after Pool's arrival in Missouri, AMA Executive Secretary S. S. Jocelyn chided him for doing too little against slavery. Pool responded that he opposed slavery though perhaps not in the same manner Jocelyn would. Pool believed the slaveholder should be treated kindly and convinced that the AMA labored for "*his highest present* and eternal good." Otherwise the association would be considered an enemy and its agents could be of no value in the antislavery struggle. Pool dryly added that he doubted being mobbed was "indispensable evidence" of his preaching the Gospel to slaveholders."[8]

Other antislavery emissaries sent to Missouri were Amos B. Hills, a missionary to Jamaica before going to Saint Francois County,[9] and Stephen Blanchard who went to Holt County from Oberlin College. Blanchard, the most active missionary in Missouri, settled in Oregon, Holt County, in September 1859. His travels had persuaded him that many antislavery people resided in the area. Though a few local slaveholders still lived there, a resident told Blanchard that the day of mob violence against abolitionists had passed in Oregon. However, both Blanchard and Hills found that the reaction to John Brown's raid in Virginia in October 1859, increased hostility toward them.[10] In late 1859, an Oregon grand jury indicted Blanchard as an incendiary, in part, for selling Hinton Helper's vigorous attack on slavery, *The Impending Crisis*. The indictment was dropped on advice of a judge who said it could not be sustained.[11] The grand jury made a further investigation of Blanchard in early 1860. His landlady, when called to testify, was asked if Blanchard had tried to sell Frederick Douglass's *Life* to her. She said he had not. She failed to mention that Blanchard had loaned her a copy of the book. Again the jury dropped charges after the judge warned that prosecuting Blanchard would be the most effective method of producing antislavery Republicans.[12]

Despite increased hostility toward abolitionists on the eve of the Civil War, Blanchard apparently found as many Holt County sympathizers as enemies. Even slaveholders sometimes respected his right to circulate his views. A Dr. Reynolds had asked the grand jury to investigate Blanchard. In a later confrontation Reynolds charged the missionary with publicly accusing him of selling a slave woman. Blanchard claimed he had not mentioned Reynolds by name, but considered it his right on all suitable occasions to speak against slavery. Reynold's "heartily assented" to Blanchard's right to do so.[13]

A few churches closed their doors to Blanchard, but most permitted him to speak. The Saint Joseph *Free Democrat* published articles written by Blanchard in which he tried to show that the Bible opposed rather than supported slavery. He constantly circulated antislavery literature which, he said, seemingly was "received with pleasure." After the 1860 election the Holt County newspaper permitted Blanchard to write a weekly column discussing slavery. Opponents threatened to tar and feather Blanchard and drive him from the county. On at least one occasion those who advocated violence against him received threats of counter violence by men whom Blanchard did not even know.[14] By January 1861, however, with the war about to begin and with tempers rising, Blanchard received threats of indictment and hanging. After several warnings from local friends, he found it expedient to take his family to Iowa. After the war broke out, all AMA missionaries left Missouri for several months. Blanchard courageously returned to Holt County in May 1862, to continue his preaching against slavery.[15] In the meantime, the AMA thrust had changed from converting slaveholders to educating former slaves.

Though not created for freedmen's aid, the American Missionary Association had funds which enabled it to answer the call of destitute blacks on the outbreak of the Civil War. With the freeing of the first slaves, the AMA led the way in systematic relief and education. It sent missionaries to Fortress Monroe, Virginia, as early as September 1861. Teachers and missionaries followed Union troops and by 1866 the association employed more than 350 persons in schools and churches for former slaves. The AMA proved the most important of many educational associations spawned by emancipation.

The first AMA educational representative to go to Missouri, Reverend George Candee, arrived in Saint Louis in early 1862. Candee probably was a poor choice. He quickly determined that there were a number of blacks in the city, including about 1,500 fugitives from farther South, but he concluded that it was impossible to get fugitives together for teaching. They did not want to be known as fugitives, Candee said, and anyway they could not be protected from mob violence except by a guard of soldiers. Furthermore, many were just transients. From a reading of his numerous letters it appears that Candee did little. He wanted to avoid the "poisonous" air in the freedmen's hospital and barracks because it made him ill. He was reluctant to preach in black churches for fear black ministers would disapprove. Though sick most of the time, Candee did some Sabbath school work and preached across the river in Illinois and wrote many letters to the AMA complaining about his circumstances.[16]

Serious educational work began when J. L. Richardson arrived in Saint Louis in March 1863. He immediately went to the Missouri Hotel, contraband headquarters,[17] and asked for a place to teach. Richardson placed alphabet charts on the kitchen wall and began teaching anyone who would attend. After about two weeks women of the Contraband Relief Society fitted up a room in the hotel as a classroom. Richardson was much impressed with his black students. They were, he said, "the most earnest scholars to learn that I ever met. Young men especially seem to feel the new relation they sustain to society and are determined to learn." Young and old attended his classes, and all made "commendable progress."[18] In April, Lydia A. Hess, a "thorough, practical teacher," arrived to assist Richardson.

The increasing number of students soon outgrew the available hotel space. Richardson secured the Ebenezer Church on Washington Avenue, a building that would accommodate up to 400 students. A local merchant, who had funds from the Switzerland Penny Society for black education, paid the rent on the building. School opened, May 18, with fifty students. The next day sixty pupils attended, but unfortunately on the third day the building was burned by a "few low wicked boys most likely backed by Secesh men."[19] The guilty were never known for certain, but obviously the AMA philosophy had irritated many white Missourians. AMA officials considered themselves "Christian abolitionists," and to them emancipation meant more than striking off the slaves' fetters. It included divesting freedmen of the shackles of ignorance, superstition and sin. The association purposed to free the bodies, souls and minds of black people. Its representatives believed that the Civil War was a God-sent punishment for the sin of slavery. Only when blacks were recognized as equal to whites would God's anger be appeased. As Richardson wrote from Saint Louis, we wish to "demonstrate to the world that colored people with equal advantages are equal to whites."[20]

The AMA advocated full citizenship for blacks. Lewis Tappan, the association's guiding spirit until his death in 1873, wrote in 1865 that blacks would never have their rights until they had "a musket in one hand and a ballot in the other." This advocacy of full equality for blacks disturbed even some otherwise sympathetic Union men in Missouri.[21]

After the Ebenezer Church burned, Richardson moved his students back to the Missouri Hotel without missing a day of classes. By June 5, he had secured another schoolroom, and within three weeks the school averaged more than 100 in daily attendance. In addition to the day schools, Richardson, Hess and Reverend Candee operated Sunday schools with more than 800 scholars.[22] Most observers agreed that black students in Saint Louis were eager and able. Chaplain Samuel Sawyer, the area Superintendent of Contrabands, wrote: "Mr. Richardson gathers as many as he can each day in the school room, and with tact and energy he devotes himself to their improvement. It is surprising how they take hold." The student's quickness in learning to read and write amazed Sawyer. Richardson reported that blacks as a class exhibited "a desire to improve which is truly commendable." Miss Hess found her students "generally quick to learn, the secret is perhaps, their great anxiety to know how to read."[23]

When the 1863 fall school term began, the AMA still limited its educational work in Missouri to Saint Louis. Richardson, ably assisted by Lydia Hess, opened the American Free School in a building on Seventh Street.[24] Fortunately the American Free School was not the only one for black children in Saint Louis. Even though education for blacks had been forbidden in Missouri since 1847, free blacks had operated a few schools in defiance of the law for almost a decade before the Civil War. In 1856 Hiram R. Revels, later a black senator from Mississippi, began to teach black children in Saint Louis. Apparently Revels's school had lasted only through the winter. The Sisters of Sacred Heart also provided some education for black youth in Saint Charles and Florissant. These schools received new impetus with the war. Unfortunately all the black schools combined in Saint Louis served only about 10 percent of the eligible children. For example, in December 1863, Richardson advised that only 350 blacks attended these schools.[25]

In early 1864, Richardson turned the American Free School over to Miss Hess and her mother, Mrs. L. A. Montague, and opened a new school. He quickly had around forty students, thirteen of whom were white. Richard urged the white youth to attend the free city public schools and all but two eventually left. In April, Miss Hess reported an enrollment of 104 pupils with 99 reading and spelling, 54 studying arithmetic and 10 working with geography. Most of the students at the American Free School were former slaves who had been freed farther south and had migrated to Saint Louis. Blacks in Saint Louis with a tradition of freedom, according to Mrs. Montague, "spurn the idea of sending their children to the same school with these poor children. . . ."[26] The addition of Richardson's new school unfortunately had limited impact on the educational needs of the black community.

Blacks themselves took action in 1864 to provide education for their youth. On February 4, 1864, ten black men, chosen at an earlier mass meeting to comprise the school board, carried out the wishes of their constituency by appointing four white members to the board. Included in the foursome was Reverend George Candee. He became the corresponding secretary, a member of the prudential committee and general superintendent. The board appointed two black men, M. M. Clark and William N. Evans, as president and recording secretary.[27]

Since the new board of education depended upon voluntary funds, its organization did little to solve the need for more schools. AMA teachers, though still paid by the association, became a part of the new system, but the total number of schools remained the same. All the schools were now free, however, where only AMA institutions had been before. The new organization also provided for better coordination among teachers.

In June 1864, Candee reported that the "free system" was not working well. Part of the problem proved to be a lack of funds, but, more important, in Candee's view, blacks disliked whites. A proud and able community, the Saint Louis free blacks had capable leaders and wanted a black superintendent. On the other hand, Candee found it difficult to cooperate with blacks as equals. He apparently had no objections to social relations with blacks but believed whites should hold leadership positions. Candee claimed that blacks on the board could not be persuaded to accept first class teachers regardless of race. They were more concerned with "getting positions for poorly qualified teachers of their own color. . . ." Parents found white teachers less acceptable than black ones. Candee believed this emphasis on race would gradually cause Saint Louis blacks to fall behind the freedmen coming from the South, whom they now considered their inferiors.[28] Candee recommended that the AMA withdraw from Saint Louis since its teachers would be unable to work with the black board of education. Candee claimed that blacks were "exceedingly jealous of the whites—they hate them."

Fortunately AMA officials failed to heed Candee's advice. Other white teachers worked successfully with Saint Louis blacks, and, in deference to black desire for black teachers, the AMA sent George C. Booth to Saint Louis in the fall of 1864. By October, Booth had a class of 240 students. Board president M. M. Clark expressed local pleasure with Booth and asked the AMA if still another black teacher could be sent. In January 1865, Green Wilkerson arrived to assist Booth.[29]

Up to 1864, most AMA work in Missouri centered in Saint Louis, but during that year the association sent representatives to other towns. By 1865, there were eight representatives in Saint Louis,[30] one in Warrensburg, Blanchard was still in Holt County, three teachers and one missionary were in Kansas City and there were two teachers each in Carondelet and Jefferson City. Though Richardson's school had been burned, reputedly by incendiaries, AMA teachers in Saint Louis generally had been treated with polite indifference by most whites. In other areas teachers frequently encountered greater hostility. Mrs. C. A. Briggs from Saint Anthony, Minnesota, wrote from Warrensburg in January 1864, that she had arrived in "Dixie Land which I have found by sad experience is not yet the land of the Free or the Home of the Brave." Aided by the local military post, she believed herself in no danger "unless it be from the citizens who are mostly Secesh and oh, so ignorant." A Warrensburg resident reported in May that Mrs. Briggs had been "persecuted and treated with utmost contempt, because she toils for these unfortunate ones." Local whites, the writer added, "each and all are greatly opposed" to educating blacks. Mrs. Briggs explained her problems to Governor Thomas C. Fletcher who ordered the military to protect her at bayonet point if necessary.[31]

Opposition to Mrs. Briggs's school continued into 1865. Some of her students were beaten—one so badly that he was out of school several days. There also were attempts to intimidate Mrs. Briggs into leaving. When she appealed to the military, the local commander said he though her enemies would do her no harm. They were only trying to scare her away and she needed "only to go ahead with a brave and determined spirit." Local whites claimed to favor black education but opposed Mrs. Briggs's methods. A white editor, William Baker, wrote that Mrs. Briggs had "negro on the brain" and put blacks "*above the whites.*" Blacks had been respectful before her arrival, he continued, but now daily insulted whites. The editor further contended that white prejudice had increased since Mrs. Briggs descended upon the town. "An ill-judged influence has been brought to bear which is calculated to increase the troubles of the poor negro," he added.

Baker accused Mrs. Briggs of "picking quarrels" with whites, threatening violence against "little boys upon the streets" for every little insult offered and applying to civil and military authorities for punishment of those who "commit a fault against the school." Mrs. Briggs further scandalized the entire community by asking the governor for unnecessary protection. Certainly not always tactful, Mrs. Briggs found considerable anti-black prejudice in Warrensburg. Many white residents were bitterly opposed to black education and black equality. A sign in editor Baker's office window—"No place for niggers and rowdies"—reflected the view of many locals.[32]

Other teachers met with problems similar to those of Mrs. Briggs. Laura M. Pinney, who had previously worked in the Contraband Hospital in Saint Louis, went to Carondelet in June 1864, to start a school. After nine weeks the family with whom she boarded left the town and Miss Pinney closed the school. She claimed that white opposition to black education was so great that she could not secure a boarding place. Alma Baker soon reopened the school. No whites would board her so she stayed with a black family. Other blacks in the neighborhood, at great personal sacrifice, collected enough money to pay her board bill of sixteen dollars per month.[33]

Miss Baker frequently failed to understand both blacks and whites in Carondelet, but she stayed for two years teaching at her school and working in the black church. She found blacks with whom she worked addicted to the normal vices, but she thought "laboring whites" were even more wicked, and "much lower than the blacks in morals." Though whites seldom talked with her, she sometimes dropped "a word of warning," hoping that God would "trouble them" until some repented. Miss Baker believed that black religion was more emotion than substance and at times wondered if local whites had any religion at all. "The hardest thing I bear," she wrote, "is the entire exclusion from Christian society."[34]

Opposed to black education, whites refused to give assistance to Miss Baker. Upon hearing that the wife of Henry Blow was a benevolent woman, Miss Baker went to see her. Mrs. Blow informed the teacher that she had lowered herself by living with a black family, that talk of equality was nonsense, and that trying to elevate blacks was useless since it could not be done. Eventually Mrs. Blow relented and agreed to give at least verbal support to the school which, Miss Baker hoped, would encourage others to do the same. Still as late as 1866, Miss Baker wrote, "a white woman seldom notices me."[35] Despite discouragement she stayed in Carondelet primarily because of black dedication to education and the willingness of parents to sacrifice for their children.

AMA teachers also confronted hostility in Jefferson City. Mrs. L. A. Montague left Saint Louis in June 1864, to open a school at the capital. A friend wrote in October that the population ridiculed Mrs. Montague, referring to her as the "nigger teacher" and both houses where she taught had been stoned on several occasions. Soon after her arrival in the "den of Copperheads" some "white boys" went through the windows, destroying books and wrecking furniture. Mrs. Montague's biggest problem was trying to protect her students from being stoned on their way to and from class.[36] Despite some opposition she found considerable white support and her school grew rapidly. Within two weeks of the school's opening, attendance averaged eighty students, some of whom were still slaves. Their masters permitted them to attend classes when they completed their work for the day. When the mayor threatened to close the school other whites advised Mrs. Montague to "hold our ground." One local white urged Mrs. Montague to keep the school open "at all hazards." If hostile whites tried to drive her away, he added, "stone them, or take any course" necessary to protect the school. If they offered violence, "shoot them."[37]

While whites sometimes opposed black schools, black Missourians strongly supported them. Teachers were often startled at the privations poverty-stricken parents would undergo to send their children to school. The small black community in Carondelet paid the rent on the school building, which also doubled as a church, and helped pay Miss Baker's board. Before fall classes started in 1865, they had accumulated a school fund of more than $100. Such a sum was raised only by severe self-denial. Indeed, Carondelet blacks were reluctant to accept money from whites for their schools. When Miss Baker suggested that an attempt be made to get white subscriptions, blacks demurred. "They had been niggers long enough," Miss Baker was told. We "now want to be me."[38] Blacks also helped pay rent on the school building in Warrensburg and Jefferson City. In 1865, blacks paid seven dollars a week board for the Jefferson City teacher. Though the black Board of Education in Saint Louis had serious problems it paid some teachers and helped pay the board of others.

By the end of the Civil War, the AMA had established black schools in six Missouri towns.[39] After the war the association continued partial support of several Missouri schools,[40] including Lincoln University, but concentrated its educational efforts in states farther south. Support of black schools fell largely to blacks themselves, the state and other benevolent societies. Still the Civil War educational activities of the AMA played a small role in laying the groundwork for a system of black education in Missouri.

Part 6

THE QUEST
FOR
SELF-DETERMINATION

CHAPTER 19

Black Churches and the Civil War

Theological and Ecclesiastical Significance of Black
Methodist Involvement, 1861–1865

Sandy Dwayne Martin

THE ADVENT, DURATION, AND impact of the American Civil War
marked an ecclesiastical and theological turning point for independent black Christianity. One might argue that the civil conflict occasioned
a kind of rebirth for independent black denominations. Theologically,
black Christians, especially as the war progressed, interpreted the event as
an intervention of God in human history. Finally, God, acting through
and in spite of the activities of mortals, had heard the cries of an enslaved
people, and as God had done in the past, the Divine One was liberating
them from a hard-hearted Pharaoh. But the faithful must not remain
simply quiescent and passive; they must join in partnership with God to
carry out the divine work in the world. Hence, black church leaders urged
their communities to respond by becoming soldiers in their physical battle
and missionaries, chaplains, and teachers in the spiritual and educational
struggle. During this period and because of it, the independent black
Methodists and Baptists did more than drastically augment their memberships to the extent that the numerical bases of the churches shifted south.
In addition, they rejected merger with white groups and reaffirmed their
identity and sense of mission as *black* churches through whom God would
act to uplift their race spiritually and temporally throughout the world.[1]

The purpose of this article is to examine *in a limited manner* the ecclesiastical and theological impact of the Civil War upon the black churches. I
have selected for treatment three developments and activities relating to

black churches and occasioned by the advent of the Civil War: (1) the role of the black churches in the recruitment of black soldiers, focusing on the Reverent Henry M. Turner and the African Methodist Episcopal Church (AME); (2) the missionary activities sponsored and supported by the churches during the conflict, concentrating on the efforts of the Reverend James Walker Hood and the African Methodist Episcopal Zion Church (AMEZ or Zion); and (3) the movement to form organic unions involving the AME and AMEZ.

Some background information concerning the principal players might be useful. The AME and AMEZ[2] are both independent black groups that began separating from the original multiracial, but white-controlled, Methodist Episcopal Church (ME) in the late 18th century. The AME was established as a separate denomination in 1816, the AMEZ, or Zion, in 1821 or 1822. Though they both seceded from the Methodist Episcopal Church, politics of personalities and leadership styles prevented a consolidation of their forces. Later in 1844, the ME under pressure of the black and white abolitionist-minded members on one hand and the pro-slavery white members on the other, finally separated over the issue of slavery, roughly along geographical lines. The resulting Methodist Episcopal Church, South (ME, S) and the ME both retained significant numbers of black members.

Henry M. Turner was born in South Carolina in 1831. He was licensed to preach in the ME-South, and he affiliated with the AME in 1858. He was designated elder in 1862, and elected the 12th bishop of the AME in 1880. He journeyed south as an officially commissioned Chaplain of black U.S. troops during the war and served in various positions of the Georgia state reconstruction government. Writer, race spokesperson, newspaper founder, and devoted church worker, Turner died in Canada in 1915.[3] James Walker Hood's life paralleled that of Turner's in many ways, although the roots of the former lay in the North. Hood was born and spent most of his early years in Pennsylvania. He was licensed to preach in the AMEZ in the late 1850s and spent time as a pastor in Nova Scotia. Ordained as elder in 1862, Hood in early 1864 journeyed to North Carolina as a missionary and church organizer and participated in Reconstruction era politics after the war. He was elevated to the bishopric in 1872 and served actively until 1916. A promoter of education, newspaper founder, and writer, Hood died in 1918 in Fayetteville, North Carolina.[4]

Henry M. Turner, the AME, and Military Involvement

LET US first turn to the AME and the recruitment of black soldiers. During the earliest days of the Civil War black churchpeople felt that they had no vested interest in its ultimate outcome. Indeed, many of them tended to exhibit a rather hostile attitude toward President Abraham Lincoln because he did not originally pursue the war on the premise of Americans as full members of the nation. With continued defeats, small victories, and stalemates, the government realized that the war would not be of short duration and that drastic measures were required to break the stubborn will of the Confederacy. Ever mindful of the resentment among many white northerners about fighting a war to liberate black slaves, Lincoln, nonetheless, felt compelled to draft in 1862 an Emancipation Proclamation, which became effective January 1, 1863, and granted freedom to all slaves held by those persons in active rebellion against the United States. In addition, the American government became much more receptive to the idea of using black soldiers in its campaign to defeat the South.

By May 1863 the recruitment and organization of black troops were well underway. One area in which black troops were recruited and trained was Washington, D.C., and Virginia, and the Reverend Henry M. Turner, AME minister, was among those in the forefront in recruiting the regiment. There were genuine concerns expressed by the black religious leaders as well as the general black populace regarding questions of equity for black soldiers. These soldiers faced discrimination in terms of pay, harsher treatment by the Confederates on the battlefields and in prison camps, and being required to serve under only white officers.

Black soldiers obviously felt more comfortable when white officers who commanded them had histories of abolitionist sympathies and activities rather than those whose commitments and sympathies were unknown. But there remained resentment among some ebony soldiers over the fact that only whites were permitted to assume command. But the black community endured the insult for three reasons. (1) Despite the discomfort and insult of the situation, the organization of black soldiers by the government to fight southern but *white* Confederates represented a huge step forward in the country in racial matters, especially given the fact that many secular and religious black leaders had been calling for such a step for sometime. (2) The indignities of the moment could be subordinated to the glory of fighting on the battle field for the liberation of their racial siblings. (3) By proving their courage and manhood on the fields of battle black soldiers would pave the way for all blacks to enjoy equal treatment before the law in post–Civil War America.[5]

In the final analysis, Turner and other members of the religious community provided active support for military measures to support the Union cause. For example, Turner joined other prominent members of the black community in a mass meeting at the black Ebenezer Church on July 6, 1863, to examine the advisability of organizing a home guard of patriotic black men to fend off the very real possibility of an invasion from southern forces in the capital city. Turner heartily endorsed the idea that was crystallized in a series of resolutions and adopted unanimously by those assembled. The document offers insights into the motives of those urging their racial counterparts to become militarily involved, including the idea that black men by the willingness to shed blood for the Union cause would demonstrate that, "the colored American will deserve the citizenship which he now holds in common with the white man." The resolutions called for blacks in obedience to the President to rise above their minor concerns and unite as husbands and fathers to secure the safety of the Capitol as well as their wives, children, and homes against any possible aggressors. Thirty-six men enrolled as members of the home guard.[6]

Turner and others discovered, however, that while support from the community was generally good, there were strong pockets of resistance to both the military regiment and the home or domestic guard. The opposition came from two constituencies: (1) many freed people or "contrabands of war," who had been liberated in battle or had escaped as opportunities presented themselves and (2) residents of the city. Those who had been enslaved probably felt that since whites inaugurated slavery, they should be the ones paying the price of abolishing it. Perhaps they too feared, and correctly so, that capture in battle would bode a much worse set of circumstances for them than for their white compatriots.[7]

Sometimes this opposition within the black Washington community manifested itself in very pointed and heated criticisms of those who struggled to organize the black militia. An article in the AME *Christian Recorder*, September 26, 1863, captured the vociferous response of the pro-militia AME leaders to the accusations of those termed "Colored Copperheads and Dead Heads." Some of these opponents argued that the activities of Henry M. Turner and others had led to the action of Congress in March 1863 to impose the military draft. The writer of the article disputed this contention by pointing out that Congress had acted before any black man had actually enlisted.[8] Furthermore, the writer reiterated the classic argument that Turner and others used for raising a black militia: the presence of the black soldier in the U.S. Army had done wonders in illustrating clearly that black men were both capable and willing to demonstrate their right to equality under the law. The black community needed to understand that the present conflict involved the destinies of both blacks and whites. This was a battle for both "God and liberty," for noble ends, a pure cause, and universal results.

The opponents to black military involvement were portrayed as unshakeable in their hardened, absolute opposition to the supporters of the war efforts. The black Copperheads were too ignorant or unmotivated to demonstrate their manhood by fighting for the very rights and opportunities they claimed to value. In addition to opposing black involvement in the regular military, some very influential people in the Washington community had little use for the idea of a "home guard." For example, a meeting of those concerned with the formation of the home guard had to abandon plans for their July 10, 1863, meeting because the trustees of a local church refused them the right to use its facilities.[9]

Black Methodists not only answered the charges leveled against them by these black Christian critics but also responded to the white Copperheads who abhorred the idea of risking their lives to bring freedom to black people. A *Christian Recorder* commentator noted the anti-black, proslavery riots in New York City in 1863. This writer resented the fact that though blacks had been among the first to settle in the country every group which came thereafter had joined in the oppression of the race. The article reflected on-going tensions and conflicts between Irish immigrants and indigenous black Americans that resulted in some black-style nativist sentiments of corresponding intensity to that of native-born whites. "Even the 'Irish,' who were kept down and oppressed in their country, . . . and . . . in a certain sense of the word, were servants, are allowed to come over in all their grease and dirt, and are put above the most refined colored persons in the country. . . ." Originally the Irish had been unaccustomed to regarding themselves as superior to any race or group of people. The new immigrants initially had little difficulty in their impoverished state with moving into the same neighborhoods with blacks. But soon they learned that customs and laws would permit them to ride roughshod over the rights of blacks. They were encouraged by "a class [of people] here who buy them rum and [whiskey] to get them to vote and swear men's lives away." But despite all of this mistreatment, African Americans still remained loyal to their government, unlike many of the pro-southern, Copperhead Irish.[10]

Opposition notwithstanding, many black Christians proceeded to involve themselves ministerially as well as militarily in the conflict. In May 1863 the first AME missionaries for work below the Mason Dixon line sailed from New York City, James D. S. Hall of the New York Conference and James Lynch of the Baltimore Conference. In November 1863, Henry M. Turner left for the southern missionary field as the official Chaplain of the First District Regiment of U.S. Colored Troops. Turner's commission as Chaplain was the first awarded an African American in history.

Many laudatory but also some critical comments were attached to the pastor of Israel Bethel AME Church in Washingon.[11] One thing is clear, however: the *Christian Recorder* during the Civil War years attests that Turner played a major role in the war effort and in debates within the AME Church. The Chaplain among other things (1) kept the denomination informed about the military bravery, heroism, activities, and conditions of black troops; (2) served as an advocate for their concerns, including their complaints about unequal treatment and pay in the army; (3) distributed copies of the denominational newspaper (*Christian Recorder*); (4) kept the general black populace informed on the progression of the war; and (5) passed along his viewpoints concerning theology and church politics as well as national politics. After the war, he remained in the South as a pastor and served in political offices during the Reconstruction.

James W. Hood, the AMEZ, and Black Church Expansion

AS INDICATED earlier in this paper, representatives of independent black denominations—Methodists and Baptists—ventured south as designated missionaries to the newly freed people behind advancing government forces. This phenomenon also reveals black church involvement in the conflict and the impact that that involvement had upon the black church. We now turn to the AMEZ and its participation in this arena. During the years 1863–1864 Bishop Joseph Jackson Clinton of the AMEZ Church dispatched four individuals to the southern mission fields, David Hill, W. G. Strong, W. F. Butler, and J. W. Hood. By practically all accounts J. W. Hood emerged as the most successful of these missionaries in terms of organizing churches and expanding the Zion denomination. By the time he was elected bishop in 1872 the majority membership of Zion had clearly shifted south. Various accounts credit him as establishing approximately 600 churches and supervising the erection of five hundred buildings in the South. The crucial role of Hood and other southern missionaries manifests itself in the establishment in North Carolina of the denominational newspaper *The Star of Zion* and Livingstone College in Salisbury, North Carolina (founded by J. C. Price with the active support of Hood). Of course there were other significant players in the missionary expansion. But clearly, Hood stands out as the most successful and the state of North Carolina, heavily influenced by him, emerged as the mother state of Zionism, a reality still supported by the fact that Charlotte, North Carolina, remains the headquarters for the group.[12]

Hood arrived in New Bern, North Carolina, in January 1864 following the Union forces. He came with the intention of spreading the gospel and improving the conditions of the black race. He must have come to the new field of duty with both a keen sense of opportunity and a degree of trepidation. In his person is symbolized the fact that northern and southern black Christians were uniting and reuniting and that the northern black church in a spiritual sense was returning home. For example, Hood was surely aware of the fact that one of the earliest superintendents of the AMEZ, Christopher Rush, was born and spent some of his early life in New Bern, North Carolina, the site of Hood's first missionary activities. And, now he was returning as a denominational agent to the same area. To be sure, the missionary spent a substantial portion of his early days serving as a non-commissioned, but *de facto,* Chaplain for African American soldiers. Indeed, the New Bern area was still a battleground, both religiously and militarily, in 1864. Two major military battles were fought in the vicinity during the time following his arrival. Undoubtedly, the situation posed some physical danger for Hood.[13]

But the greater area of conflict for Hood and the AMEZ lay in the ecclesiastical domain. Andrews Chapel proved to be the center of Hood's first contest. Three other denominations were fighting for the allegiance of this congregation—the northern Methodist Episcopal Church represented by a Reverend J. E. Round, the Congregational Church represented by a white minister named Fitz, and finally the northern AME group. Hood masterfully pulled off a coup for the Zionites. First, he already enjoyed the advantage of having credentials of approval from the War Department. When the Secretary of War ruled that the members of Andrews Chapel themselves must be permitted to choose their affiliation, Hood moved quickly. On Easter Sunday he preached a very spiritual message after which he informed the people of the ruling. Perhaps given the powerful service led by Hood and the knowledge of some type of connection between them and the Zionites through the person of Christopher Rush, the congregation voted to join the Zion Family. This historic Andrews Chapel would later be renamed Saint Peter's Church and become the "Mother Church of Zion Methodism in the South" and the mother of several churches in the immediate area. Within the first four months Hood had secured his first and historically significant victory on the mission field.[14]

The above description of the Andrews Chapel episode demonstrates the reality of evangelism in the South during the Civil War and post-war era. We normally associate "missions" with the conversion of people from one or no religion to another given religion. Actually, much of the theological rhetoric of the northern churches, black and white, Methodists and non-Methodists, during this time generally supported the idea that they were traveling south to save the poor, unfortunate, degraded, non-Christian slaves or former-slaves from barbarianism and non-religion to the Christian faith. In reality, as Wheeler and other historians illustrate, much of the increased memberships in the missionary denominations in the South derived less from converts in this particular understanding of conversion than by persuading and encouraging black southern church people to transfer their memberships from white-controlled southern groups to the missionary groups. Most of the new members in the AME, AMEZ, and the Christian Methodist Episcopal Church (CME), founded in 1870, came at the expense of declining black membership within the Methodist Episcopal Church, South. In 1861, the southern ME church included in its membership 207,000 black communicants. By 1866 that number had been reduced to 78,000 with the largest percentage of this number having defected to black Baptists and to Methodists, white and black.[15] It should be noted, however, that many if not most southern black Christians placed their true religious allegiance not in the outward, visible structure of the churches supervised by the white southern Methodists but in the unobserved, secret "invisible institution" of slave religion which convened during the night, behind cabin doors, or in other secluded spaces.[16]

We must grant the presence of northern denominational rivalries. But we must not suppose that southern black Christians were mere unthinking pawns in the hands of outside forces. To be sure, these northern denominations provided valuable services to the southerners in terms of humanitarian ministries and by providing *institutions* whereby they could practice their faith and enjoy a degree of public, ecclesiastical freedom largely unknown during the era of slavery. Not surprisingly, northern black denominations secured the largest share of southern blacks' allegiance because of the attractiveness of organizations controlled at all levels by black Christians and offering, in general, clearer possibilities for the greatest display of racial dignity and leadership. But the affiliations were made *by thinking, southern black Christians* based upon their perceptions of their interest and viewpoints.

Hood extended his organizational skills and enthusiasm to other areas of the South, especially in the North Carolina cities of Wilmington, Fayetteville, and Charlotte. Because of Hood's labors and those of other ministers and missions, Bishop J. J. Clinton, the supervisory bishop, was able to organize the North Carolina Annual Conference composed of a dozen ministers and 400 congregants on December 17, 1864. From this conference others developed in later years. In Wilmington, Hood extended the hegemony of the Zionites at the expense of the Allenites. The AME had followed the Union forces into the port city and acquired the allegiance of two black congregations, Saint Stephens and Saint Luke. Later, however, Hood was successful in persuading the congregation of Saint Luke to transfer its allegiance to Zion. According to the Zion historian, Bishop Walls, Hood was "an adroit maneuverer and experienced missionary" who "worked ardently and manipulated matters so that the St. Luke Church withdrew from its compact with Bethel."[17]

The AMEZ changed the title of its supervisory officers from "superintendent" to "bishop" in 1868. Perhaps part of the motivation was to demonstrate the authenticity of the group's Methodism by emphasizing the compatible structural make-up with the AME and the northern ME, with whom the Zionites were contemplating merger. Also, it is possible that the title "bishop" carried more prestige and apparent authority than "superintendent" and thus made Zion more equal in its ecclesiastical contests with other Methodist bodies for the allegiance of southern churchpeople. At any rate, we observe the impact of the war upon this black church, even in a matter so minor (or major) as the renaming of an ecclesiastical office.

Hood's organization skills and successes undoubtedly played a key role in elevating him to the office of bishop in 1872 and, in conjunction with the efforts of others, securing for North Carolina a central place in Zion Methodism. The General Conference of 1872, convening in Charlotte, struggled with a number of significant issues. One was the election of bishops. Hood seemed to have been the only *new* bishop elected in 1872. With the death of Bishop J. J. Moore in 1894 after 25½ years of service, Hood became the *senior* bishop of the Church.[18] Upon Hood's removal from active service in 1916 he had served as bishop for a total of 44 years.

The Civil War and Black Methodist Ecumenicity

THE THIRD and final area of concern in this article is the significance of the war for intraracial movements toward the union of Methodist bodies. During the Civil War years and the immediate period thereafter a number of individuals in the black Methodist Churches and the white ME Church and ME Church, South, turned their attention toward organic union. From the perspectives of the black Methodists, efforts toward union were in two directions: (1) the creation of one pan-black Methodist body, and (2) union with the ME Church and in one instance an interest in some type of affiliation or union with the ME Church, South.

Though there were sincere efforts on the part of both blacks and whites, union of the ME and the black denominations failed for a number of reasons: the abiding sense among black Methodists that they had a special, providential mission as *black* churches; the freedom, authority, and power of black religious leadership that could not be enjoyed in white contexts; lingering racial prejudice among many white Methodists; and the ME's subordination of black interests to that of reuniting with white southerns.[19]

The most serious possibility for ecumenical union involving black Methodists, which in part was created by the conditions of the Civil War and emancipation, was that between the AME and AMEZ. There were some minor differences in the disciplines and practices of these two black organizations. For example, the Zionites permitted a greater role in governance for the laity and until 1868 referred to its episcopal leaders as "superintendents" rather than "bishops." But these relatively minor obstacles were surmountable and as early as 1864 the two groups worked out an agreement on union under the name "The United African Methodist Episcopal Church in America." The Articles of Confederation extolled union as consistent with Christian tradition and worldwide evangelism and the document addressed the specific condition occasioned by the Civil War, the need to unite black forces for "the instruction and elevation of the millions of freedmen in the South."[20]

The anticipated union of black denominations, however, did not materialize in 1868 as planned. Both AME and AMEZ General Conferences approved the plan, but there appears to have been more opposition among the quarterly and Annual conferences of the AME. Surrendering positions of power and influence, reducing their impact, and forsaking certain aspects of denominational traditions seem to proved the obstacles black church people could not surmount. Bishop Walls in Chapter 20 of his massive work gives an account of the Zionites' ecumenical efforts during this period. As the merger between the AME and the AMEZ was appearing to falter by 1868, the latter turned its attention to union with the ME. But by 1872 the Zion bishops had stated their opposition to any union with the white group and from 1880 onward chances for union of Zion and Me became increasingly remote. When the ME, S supported the formation of the black Christian Methodist Episcopal (CME) Church from its membership in 1870, this action eventually encouraged the AME and Zion to begin merger negotiations afresh in 1884. But by 1896 it was clear that no pan-African Methodist union was within reach and each group resorted to blaming the other for the failure.[21]

Perhaps the greatest regret within the ranks of the independent black Methodists came not over the failure to unite with each other or with the white-controlled Methodist group. Rather, it was the creation of the Colored (later, Christian) Methodist Episcopal Church in 1870. As indicated above, this group came into existence with the support of the ME, South.

The predominantly white group assisted its black membership of approximately 80,000 members to establish their own independent church free of both white and northern black control. The AME and Zion groups both interpreted the inauguration of this denomination as a sinister plot on the part of ME, S to prevent the further consolidation of black Methodist forces. Bishop Walls and other Zion as well as AME historians have tended to portray CME leaders such as bishop William H. Miles and Richard H. Vanderhorst at best as pawns in the hands of whites and at worst as "Uncle Toms." To support this analysis they point to the fact that during the post–Civil War era the CME denomination tended to remain aloof, officially speaking, from political activities that were understood as detrimental to the desire of many southern whites to exercise political and economic domination over blacks.

CME historians, such as Bishop Othal Lakey, conversely emphasize the active role of CME leaders in the formation of the denominations. These leaders in creative, diplomatic, and self-sacrificing ways did the best that could be expected in a relatively sensitive and difficult situation. Though as an official policy the denomination did not encourage partisan politics, neither did it prohibit individual ministers and laypersons from exercising their civil rights. Lakey points out the fact that the church properties that CME occupied were legal possessions of the ME, S and that some compromise had to be drafted to secure full control of these by the CME.[22] It is also instructive that the AMEs and AMEZs did not operate from unmixed motives. One might argue that the independent black groups saw the southern blacks as pawns to buttress their own organizations' power and influence. At some point, the CME historians seem to posit, the southern black Methodists made it clear that they were not pawns or "spoils" of battle, but free people who would decide their own destiny. There is abundant evidence that northern black and white Christians coming south had distorted and incomplete impressions of the enslaved and formerly enslaved. Northerners often undervalued the significant role that southern black Christians had played in the interpretation and dissemination of the gospel among themselves. Conversely, they overrated the influence of the white proslavery ministers and the inhibiting socioeconomic factors of American chattel slavery as they related to southern black interpretations of the faith.

Both the critics and the CME historians have some truth on their side. It is very reasonable to suspect that the many white southern Methodists had no intention of permitting independent black Methodists to consolidate their ecclesiastical power in the South if it endangered white political domination. They would surely prefer to place their legally owned church properties into the hands of those who would not use them in overt political, Republican causes. On the other hand, it is too simplistic and probably unfair to credit the organization of the CME solely to the political machinations of southern white Methodists. Rather, it must be judged possible that Miles and Vanderhorst left the AME because they saw greater opportunities for service, influence, and recognition in a newly created CME. In addition, we must not forget the average layperson. In many instances he or she preferred the church surroundings, ministers, and styles of worship with which he or she was accustomed. These took precedence over disputes and opinions about more distant bishops and quarterly, annual, and general conferences.

Conclusion

WE MAY conclude that factors relating to and arising from the Civil War had a profound impact upon both the theology and structure of the independent black denominations: the campaign to enlist black soldiers; the fervent conviction that God was liberating an enslaved people and creating a racially inclusive Christian democracy; black sponsorship of missionaries and church organizers for work in the South; greatly increased memberships and ecclesiastical hegemonies of independent black denominations; union of southern and northern black Christians in the AME and AMEZ; and the organization of a new body, the CME.

Black Methodist denominations did not succeed in forming ecumenical union, but the fact that so many black Christians actively and earnestly pursued this goal so consistently was such that it reminded them that in some real, significant way they were nevertheless racially and spiritually united as one people and had some collective, providential destiny and responsibility.

Finally, the Civil War meant emancipation for thousands of black Christians who for the first time in American history knew the substantial meaning of open, freely expressed worship. These ex-enslaved people's love for religious and political liberties, nurtured by the history of a chattel bondage that had sought to stamp out or vastly curtail both, reinvigorated the originally northern-based churches and greatly strengthened the new CME. In sum, the Civil War for nineteenth century black Christians and their white sympathizers was not simply a military conflict; it was a new Exodus.

CHAPTER 20

———————

Sherman Marched—and
Proclaimed "Land for the Landless"

Howard C. Westwood

W HEN GENERAL WILLIAM TECUMSEH SHERMAN undertook to march from Atlanta to the sea we may be sure that it never occurred to him that he would create a heated controversy over whether black men or white men would own thousands of acres of rich plantation lands along the South Atlantic coast. But that happened.

Not long after Sherman occupied Atlanta in early September 1864, he decided that he ought to strike out for salt water. But not until the second of November did his general in chief, Grant, after some hesitation, tell him to "go as you propose."[1] The move seemed risky, for Confederate forces, including considerable cavalry under General Joseph Wheeler, if coordinated and divining Sherman's course, could seriously cripple him by persistent harassment far from any base. Nor was it possible to send him help, for it could not be known where he would march; at his outset he himself was not sure whether his destination would turn out to be Savannah or Pensacola or Mobile.[2]

The march began on November 15. While the army was large—about 60,000 infantry, with cavalry of some 5,500 led by General H. Judson Kilpatrick—it was spread wide. There were two wings, each of two corps, each corps in a separate column strung out for miles on different routes, each separated from any of the others by as much as twenty miles. But, though Wheeler's cavalry on occasion kept Kilpatrick busy, deception of the Confederates so succeeded that by December 10, after some three hundred circuitous miles, Sherman had reached the outer defenses of Savannah.[3] Three days later Confederate Fort McAllister, below Savannah guarding a waterway to the sea, fell to his assault and at last he could communicate with the outside world. At once he met with General John G. Foster, heading a small Union army that since November 1861 had been based at Port Royal occupying portions of the sea islands. Sherman intended to have Foster move a force to the north of Savannah to complete an investment.[4]

Within Savannah Confederate General William J. Hardee commanded some 10,000 troops. Sherman thought there were more. They were well fortified and watery land would allow attack only over five narrow causeways. Sherman took time to get set. To his surprise and chagrin, on the night of December 20 Hardee slipped away to the north before that route could be blocked. Early the next morning Union troops were entering the city unopposed.[5]

When Sherman had confronted Savannah's defenses his army was in superb condition, its morale high.[6] Though at the beginning of his march he did not know what he would propose on reaching the sea, by the time he got there he had so gained confidence in his army that his conclusion was clear: he wanted to drive on northward and, with Grant, quash the rebellion after administering bitter medicine to the South Carolinians who had started it. Indeed, as he had marched through Georgia some Georgians had urged him to give those Carolinians a good taste of the war they had begun.[7] While Grant had held very different ideas, after he and Sherman exchanged messages Grant agreed to Sherman's wish, and Sherman began to ready a northward drive.[8]

The time from December 21, when he entered Savannah, to the end of January was one of the busiest in Sherman's career. Savannah was to be left in General Foster's hands, for whom Sherman had to get reinforcements from Grant. The fortifications around Savannah had to be adjusted to the Unionists' posture. Supplies had to be gathered for a trip that would be longer and much more contested than the journey from Atlanta. Provision had to be made for the 20,000 or so of Savannah's civilians whose money had become worthless overnight and whose link with friends had been severed. And, not least of all, something had to be done about thousands of refugee blacks.[9]

Before Sherman left Atlanta, Grant had suggested that he "move . . . the negroes" from the country he would traverse, adding: "As far as arms can be supplied, either from surplus or by capture, I would put them in the hands of the negro men. Give them such organization as you can. They will be of some use."[10] Though Sherman had some blacks among his pioneer corps when he started, and as he marched on welcomed able-bodied black men as laborers in a variety of functions, he did not arm them as soldiers. That is understandable. Combatant blacks in the Union armies were in units separate from the whites. The last thing Sherman needed for the success of his seemingly dangerous march was untrained, undisciplined units.[11] Also, while he doubtless fully understood Grant's point that he "move . . . the negroes" to mean that he should deprive the Confederates of their labor force, he cautioned his commanders that refugee blacks should not "be encouraged to encumber us on the march."[12] That, too, is understandable. Women, children and the infirm would clutter and slow the march and would consume food that might be critically needed by the troops. Unquestionably, early in the march effort was made to minimized the refugees, masses of whom did run to the blue coats, hailing the Day of Jubilee. Unquestionably, too, the efforts to minimize met with some success. But as the march proceeded efforts to keep refugees away became lax. There are no reliable figures as to the number who flocked into Savannah with Sherman. There were at least six or seven thousand. But it is quite possible that there were thousands more then or soon thereafter; Sherman once said that one of his wings "reports 17,000 negroes."[13] In any case, the problem of their care cried for Sherman's attention before he moved onward.

Initially, before he entered Savannah, he had assumed that there was a simple solution to the problem—that all he had to do was to order all the refugee blacks, along with his surplus and broken down horses and mules, sent to General Rufus Saxton who had headquartered at Beaufort, South Carolina, in Foster's department. When the Union landing at Port Royal had occurred in November 1861 the whites had fled the area but their slaves had stayed. In March 1862 the Treasury Department, given responsibility for abandoned property, had launched there what history has called the Port Royal Experiment. Northern businessmen, missionaries, and teachers came to put the blacks to work on the plantations, to teach them, and to introduce them to the way of self-sufficiency as free people. In June 1862 Saxton had been sent there, by special order of Secretary of War Stanton, as the military governor of affairs on the occupied coastal islands. While the experiment had undergone considerable vicissitude and change during the ensuing two and a half years, by December 1864 there were some 15,000 former slaves busy in their new life, with Saxton the governor and policeman. Sherman thought it quite appropriate that Saxton take on his refugees, and on December 16 ordered that they be sent to Port Royal "where they can be more easily supplied."[14]

But very shortly Sherman had word from Saxton that the problem was not simple. Saxton told him that "every cabin and house" in the area around Port Royal was already "filled to overflowing." Saxton pointed out, however, that St. Simon's Island (below Savannah on the Georgia coast) and Edisto Island (on the Carolina coast between Port Royal and Charleston), once occupied by the Union forces but since vacated, probably were free of Rebels—a sort of no man's land—and had a large number of vacant houses. Saxton thought that those islands could be reoccupied readily by a small force and suggested that the refugees be sent there. It was apparent the Sherman would have to consider the refugee problem more thoroughly.[15]

Then, in early January, Sherman received a personal letter from General Henry W. Halleck, chief of staff in Washington, that certainly made him think twice about black refugees. Halleck wrote that, though Sherman was receiving praise from most people, there were some leading men very critical of his treatment of the blacks, that they thought Sherman rejected the blacks "with contempt." "They say," wrote Halleck, "you might have brought with you to Savannah more than 50,000, thus stripping Georgia of that number of laborers and opening a road by which as many more could have escaped from their masters; but that instead of this you drove them from your ranks, prevented them from following you by cutting the bridges in your rear, and thus caused the massacre of large numbers by Wheeler's cavalry." Halleck knew, of course, that Sherman probably had to discourage refugees because of limited supplies on his march, but, he suggested, perhaps Sherman now could open avenues for the escape of slaves from their masters by arrangement for their subsistence on the coastal plantations. Halleck said that were Sherman thus to foster slaves' escape his critics would be silenced.[16]

If Sherman, on reading Halleck's letter, did not know what was referred to by the charge that he had left refugees to the tender mercy of Wheeler's cavalry, he was quickly to find that the reference was to an incident at Ebenezer Creek about twenty miles from Savannah that had occurred on December 8 and 9 in the march of one of the corps of the left wing. On January 10 Secretary Stanton arrived at Savannah to see what was going on; his visit may have been prompted in part by reports of the Ebenezer Creek incident.[17]

The corps involved had been commanded by General Jefferson C. Davis. Not altogether because of his name, Davis was reputed not to love blacks. Nor had he the reputation of a cool head; in the fall of 1862 he had had a quarrel with his former commanding officer and had killed him.[18] Thus any report of Davis' brutal treatment of blacks would be read by Republican politicians with a believing eye. Even today the Ebenezer Creek incident is recalled as "an inhuman barbarous proceeding." But despite testimony seeming to warrant that label the incident may not have been quite that bad.[19]

Within a week after Sherman's march had started, Davis had warned his corps, "Useless negroes are being accumulated to an extent which would be suicide to a column which much be constantly stripped for battle and prepared for the utmost celerity of movement." Wagons, he said, were too overloaded to allow them to carry also women and children, and he cautioned that "every additional mouth consumes food, which it requires risk to obtain." While, as we have noted, it seems that restraint on numbers of refugees became lax as the march proceeded, this may not have been quite true of Davis' column, especially by December 8 when, being on the extreme left of Sherman's swath, it faced the task of keeping up in the convergence on Savannah. Thus, among the final reports of Davis' units, one regimental report says of refugee negroes: "Large numbers of both sexes and all ages were prohibited from following the command, in obedience to stringent orders issued on that subject from superior headquarters."[20]

In any event on the night of December 7 the column had reached Ebenezer Creek after a hard march on timber-obstructed roads, with Confederate attacks from the rear on Kilpatrick's cavalry and other firing heard in the distance. The creek was wide; the column was entering watery country. Pontoon bridging was required. The bridge was completed at mid-morning of December 8. The corps' crossing was not completed until daylight of December 9, with demonstrations from a Confederate gunboat and troop skirmishing all of the preceding day. After the crossing heavy cannonading was heard from ahead. Sherman's success in deception had fostered an idea that he might be headed for Charleston, accounting, perhaps, for attempted Confederate activity over on the Union left.[21]

In the long crossing of the stream an effort had been made to keep all refugees in the rear, presumably to facilitate the troops' move. When the troops' crossing was completed the bridge was immediately pulled across, leaving a mass of blacks, including many women and children, stranded on the far bank with Wheeler's cavalry soon to come at them. It is said that the refugees panicked, not a few attempting to swim across or to get there clinging to logs, with some assistance from sympathetic solders on the other side. Not many made it. Some drowned. Most eventually were picked up by the Confederates. Rumor was to spread that the Confederates shot them down. Of that there is not good evidence and it is most unlikely; much more likely is it that they were simply returned to slave life.[22]

In assessing this incident it must be kept in mind that Davis' position at the creek was ticklish, that in watery country he sometimes was confined to narrow passages that could be blasted by a single opposing cannon, and that he was under great pressure to maintain coordination with the rest of the army on the final approach to Savannah's outer defenses, just then being reached. Indeed over on the Union right wing an officer had managed, on the evening of the day Davis completed his crossing of the stream, to go on ahead of the army and soon got all the way to the coast and reached Foster with word of Sherman's coming.[23] One should be hesitant about condemnation of Davis for having the pontoon bridge pulled quickly with Confederates hovering at his rear. Sherman's own judgment, expressed in a January 12 letter to Halleck during Stanton's visit and after Sherman had queried Davis about the creek incident, was that the story of "turning back negroes that Wheeler might kill them is all humbug." At the watercourse, wrote Sherman, Davis did "forbid certain plantation slaves— old men, women, and children—to follow his column; but they would come along and he took up his pontoon bridge, not because he wanted to leave them, but because he wanted his bridge."[24]

Whatever the pro or con concerning the Ebenezer Creek incident, it did make clear that when the Union army was on a swift move black refugees could not be handled adequately by the mere edict that they should not be allowed to "encumber us." Some program was essential for the ultimate disposition that unit commanders could take into account in meeting the exigencies of invasion and that would promise the blacks a haven more secure than the wake of a marching column. Halleck's letter and Stanton's visit made Sherman focus sharply on such a program. On the evening of January 12, at Sherman's headquarters, he and Stanton had a meeting with twenty black churchmen, all but one Savannah residents, including leaders in the black community; the one was a Maryland free black who had been a missionary for the past two years in connection with the Port Royal Experiment. Nine of them had been slaves until Sherman's coming; one of those nine had been a slave of a leading Confederate, Robert Toombs. At the meeting when asked how the blacks could best take care of themselves and assist the government, their response was that it would be best that they have land to cultivate and so to maintain themselves, with their young men in the meantime enlisting in the army. Then, when asked whether they would rather live in colonies by themselves or be scattered among whites, all but the Marylander said that because of the prejudice in the South they would prefer to live by themselves.[25]

After this meeting, as Sherman explained in a letter to the President a year later, Stanton "was satisfied the Negros could with some little aid from us by means of the abandoned Plantations on the Sea Islands and along the Navigable Waters take care of themselves. He requested me to draw up a plan that would be uniform and practicable. I made the rough draft and we went over it very carefully, Mr. Stanton making many changes."[26] The result was that, on January 16 immediately after Stanton's departure, Sherman issued Special Field Orders, No. 15. Foster's command was the Department of the South, embracing South Carolina, Georgia, and into Florida, but the department now had been made subject to Sherman's orders.[27] Thus his Order 15 was the law for that department. It was among the most notable, if not the most notable, of the several military provisions for refugee blacks made during the war.

It provided as follows:

"The islands from Charleston south, the abandoned rice-fields along the rivers for thirty miles back from the sea, and the country bordering the Saint John's River, Fla., are reserved and set apart for the settlement of the negroes now made free by the acts of war and the proclamation of the President of the United States."

The order was to be administered by General Saxton, given the title of Inspector of Settlements and Plantations, with police and general management power over the area.

Whenever "three respectable negroes, heads of families," selected a locality within the specified area for settlement, Saxton was to give them a license, and, under Saxton's supervision, they would subdivide the land in the locality among themselves and others choosing to join them so that each family would have "a plot of not more than forty acres of tillable ground." Saxton was to provide each family head, "subject to the approval of the President of the United States, a possessory title in writing, giving as near as possible the description of boundaries"; such titles would be treated "as possessory." Their possession would be protected by the military "until such time as they can protect themselves or until Congress shall regulate their title."

On the islands and in such settlements "no white person whatever, unless military officers and soldiers detailed for duty, will be permitted to reside; and the sole and exclusive management of affairs will be left to the freed people themselves, subject only to the United States military authority and the acts of Congress." However, the order would not change the existing settlements "on Beaufort Island" or affect "any rights to property heretofore acquired"—referring, presumably, to the whites engaged in the Port Royal Experiment and to property that had been acquired, mainly by Northern whites, under tax sales by the Treasury Department during the war when the old owners were dutiful to the Confederacy instead of to the United States tax collectors.

Finally, young black men were encouraged to enlist in the Union army. Saxton was given charge of such recruiting and the organization of black military units.[28]

Sherman's January 12 letter to Halleck had said, "I do and will do the best I can for negroes, and feel sure that the problem is solving itself slowly and naturally. It needs nothing more than our fostering care." Nor, indeed, had Sherman ever been blind to the need to make some provision for the blacks. Even before leaving Atlanta, when he had ordered that refugees should not be encouraged to "encumber us," he had added that "at some future time" he would be able to provide for those "who seek to escape the bondage under which they are now suffering."[29] Surely his Order 15 provided the basis for the fostering care for all the refugees who had followed him to Savannah and who would flock to him when at last he marched on northward through the Carolinas. The fact is that on March 14, after Sherman had emerged at Fayetteville, again to make contact with the outside world via a Union force by then at Wilmington, he ordered that the black refugees "that have clung to us during our march through South Carolina" could be sent to General Saxton back at Beaufort.[30]

If the fighting had gone on for another year or so it is very likely that the kind of self-sufficient black communities envisaged in Sherman's order would have become firmly established and that the social and economic development of the blacks in the South Atlantic coastal region would have been very different. The Port Royal Experiment already had shown considerable success but it was limited to the Port Royal-Beaufort vicinity, and, to Saxton's special distress, allowed for but little land ownership by the blacks. Indeed in Saxton's annual 1864 report to Stanton there was a note of his unhappiness on that score.[31] But now Sherman's order gave Saxton what seemed plenary authority, based on the nearly untrammelled war power of the military, to provide land for the landless over a stretch of hundreds of miles of rich plantation lands. With the imprimatur of Sherman, at that time regarded in much of the North as the nation's greatest hero, Saxton was fired with enthusiasm and hope.

Saxton's hope seemed well grounded. He had visited Sherman at the end of December but apparently had not been encouraged about what might happen to the blacks. However, on Stanton's coming the outlook changed. Saxton had gone at once to Savannah to meet with the Secretary, telling of his recent annual report that Stanton had not yet received in which he had objected to the failure to provide for black land ownership; the interview had been "agreeable" and Stanton had promised Saxton "to put him all right," and had sent him back to Beaufort to return with a copy of the report. Saxton had brought it to Stanton just prior to the Secretary's meeting with the black churchmen. Then on January 14 Stanton, on leaving Savannah, came to Beaufort for an overnight stay that proved most congenial, highlighted by disclosing to Saxton an advance copy of Order 15. As though to seal Saxton's authority, there was delivered to him, just after Stanton's departure, his promotion from brigadier general to major general of volunteers.[32]

But the fighting did not last. In only a few weeks it ended. And as it was ending President Lincoln's assassination brought to the presidency a man who did not share Saxton's vision of land for the black man.

During those few weeks Saxton faced a huge task of administration with a limited staff. By early June he was to report an estimate that he had settled 40,000 blacks under Sherman's order. Later he was to reiterate that estimate. But there is no evidence that Saxton was able consistently to follow the method prescribed in the Sherman order—that is, having three black heads of families mark out a settlement and then, under his supervision, subdivide tracts for self-governing communities, with Saxton issuing precisely defined possessory titles to the settlers. That he could have done so in such a short time seems impossible in view of the chaotic conditions in the vast territory, the limited means of transport, the ignorance of the settlers, the shortage of facilities, and the extent and variety of his responsibilities which included, it will be recalled, recruiting of soldiers. The likelihood is that, working under great pressure, Saxton's procedure was makeshift.[33]

As the fighting dwindled—Charleston itself was evacuated in mid-February as Sherman drove northward and isolated it—some of the former white owners began drifting back to the area, seeming to think that somehow they could resume control of the plantations. On April 22 Saxton issued a circular, publishing the key provisions of the Sherman order and giving "unauthorized persons" thirty days' notice to vacate the area; thereafter trespassers would be arrested, to be punished by sentence of a military commission.[34] But hardly had that thirty-day period lapsed than two things happened that signaled impending change from what Saxton otherwise might have established, that foreshadowed that the nearly all-black enclave from Charleston along the coast into Florida, provided by Sherman's order, would never be realized.

One of these was the implementation of the Freedmen's Bureau Act of March 3, 1865.[35] The Act provided that during the war and for one year thereafter a bureau in the War Department, headed by a Commissioner, would have charge of the affairs of the freed blacks in the Confederate States. It also provided that the Bureau, from land within those states that was abandoned or owned by the United States by confiscation or otherwise, could rent to a male freedman on favorable terms up to forty acres for three years with the freedmen's privilege of purchasing "such title thereto as the United States can convey." But the Act did not mention Sherman's order nor did it provide for the exclusion of whites from any area or even hint at the creaction of self-governing black communities. On May 12 there took office, as the Bureau's Commissioner, General Oliver O. Howard. He had been Sherman's right wing commander. During the time that Sherman was getting ready for the drive northward from Savannah, Howard had been posted for a considerable time at Beaufort where he had been most favorably impressed with Saxton. On May 22, on the very day that Saxton's April 22 circular had provided that unauthorized whites would be arrested if they had not vacated the area defined in Sherman's order, Howard wrote Saxton of his appointment as the Bureau's Assistant Commissioner in charge of South Carolina and Georgia and, temporarily, Florida. Thus did Saxton lose his autonomy even as the special status of the Sherman lands was clouded.[36]

The second event occurred on May 29, one week after General Howard wrote Saxton of his altered office. The new President Johnson issued a sweeping Amnesty Proclamation for all those who now would take a loyalty oath.[37] While the proclamation excluded various limited classes who had "voluntarily participated" in the rebellion, they were assured that on special application for pardon "clemency will be liberally extended." It was soon to become clear that such assurance was very real. Needless to say, under a Constitution giving the President sweeping power to pardon, amnesty to an old owner seemed to destroy all basis for denying him a return of his abandoned land. The loyalty oath takers were plentiful, and in hardly more time than it takes to tell were clamoring for the lands' return. Nowhere was the clamor to be more persistent than in the area embraced in Sherman's order, and especially in South Carolina where Saxton's work was most concentrated. And it was abandoned lands that were the principal supply for carrying out that order, or, indeed, the land provision of the more general Freedmen's Bureau Act.[38]

On the face of things it would seem that these two events would have ended abruptly further administration of the Sherman order. In fact there is no indication that Saxton attempted to carry out the bar against white residents in the Sherman area after expiration of the thirty-day notice in his April circular, and in early June General Howard wrote him that whites should be no more excluded there than in other areas where the Freedmen's Bureau operated.[39] Otherwise, however, Saxton proceeded as though the Sherman order were fully in effect. He had become a crusader for the newly freed blacks. On June 4, in his initial report to Howard as one of the new Assistant Commissioners of the Bureau, he said that his "colonists" under the Sherman order had "many thousands of acres" in cultivation, whence "ample crops will be raised to support the present population, and a large amount of sea island cotton for market will be provided." The crops, he said with pride, "completely astound the former masters who have visited the plantations, while the friends are delighted and encouraged." And in the months following, Saxton continued settling black "colonists" under the Sherman order.[40]

Meanwhile, the clamor of the amnestied whites for a return of their lands mounted, with a sympathetic ear in the White House. It would seem that the President could have eliminated any claim to the lands by the blacks, and cleared the way for the clamoring whites, by simply disapproving any "titles" that had been issued under the Sherman order. For the order itself, it will be recalled, provided that the "titles" were "subject to the approval of the President." But the President did not resort to that provision. If he focused on it, perhaps he hesitated to resort to it lest that imply that he regarded the Sherman order as still in force. Or perhaps— and this is more likely—the President hesitated lest he alienate some members of Congress whose support he wanted on many other issues when Congress came into session in the following December. Congress had not met since the Presidency had descended on Johnson; at the coming session his whole program for the nation's reunion would be at stake.

In any event, though the President made it clear that he agreed with the clamoring whites that they should have their lands, he stopped just short of peremptorily insisting to General Howard that all the Sherman lands be restored at once. Instead, he told Howard to try to work out, between the white claimants and the black "title" holders, some accommodation—such as agreement by the black to the white ownership in exchange for employment of the black and some tenancy for him and his family.[41] In the meantime Saxton, though by the end of the summer his authority over Georgia and Florida had been transferred to others, leaving him only South Carolina, had been fighting as hard as ever for his "colonists." He urged, to Howard, that when Congress met it would decide that the Sherman order had "all the binding effect of a Statute."[42] While some lands were restored to the whites, many blacks resisted and Howard vacillated, stalled with support from Stanton, and finally, when Congress met, began working with a leading Senator, Lyman Trumbull of Illinois, on proposed legislation that he hoped would be a final solution.[43] At length, in February, Congress did act. It adopted a measure extending indefinitely the life of the Freedmen's Bureau and providing variously for the welfare of the freedmen, including a provision that the holders of Sherman "titles" would be confirmed in their possession for three years.[44] While that at least strongly implied that the white man would have the land restored in three years, that doubtless seemed a long time for the old planters to wait before beginning their recovery from the economic chaos left by the war.

During this time the interest of the white planters had been ably represented in Washington by a lobbyist, William Henry Trescot, the "Executive Agent" of the State of South Carolina. Trescot had come to Washington in the fall of 1865 with authority conferred by the South Carolina Convention, and had been busy at the Executive Mansion, on the Hill, and in the War Department. On January 31 as Congress neared its action, Trescot, with associates, met with the President, telling him that General Sherman was in the city and that they understood he would be willing to state what he had meant by his Order 15. The President suggested that they see Sherman. They immediately went to General Grant's headquarters. It happened that Grant was in conference with Sherman and Generals George H. Thomas and George G. Meade. But Grant invited them in, and "they all participated in the discussion of the real meaning of Gen. Sherman's order." The result was that before the end of the day Trescot delivered a note to the President saying that Sherman had said that his order "was meant to be temporary" and that he would "make such a statement . . . upon a reference from you." On the next day the President wrote Sherman asking for a statement of the "purposes" of his order. On the day following, February 2, Sherman replied, "I knew of course we could not convey title to land and merely provided 'possessory' titles, to be good as long as War and our Military Power lasted. I merely aimed to make provision for the Negros who were absolutely dependent on us, leaving the value of their possessions to be determined by after events or legislation."[45] When, a few days later in February, Congress' act reached the President he vetoed it. Among his many objection to the whole measure he stated that the provision for the Sherman "title" holders violated the white owners' Constitutional rights to their property. The veto came to the Senate where the measure had originated. Thirty Senators voted to override but eighteen voted to sustain, falling short of the two-thirds required to override.[46]

Surely now all the Sherman lands would go back to the white owners with no further controversy. One problem for the whites—that is, the activity of General Saxton, the aggressive crusader for the blacks—had been solved. From about the time when lobbyist Trescot had begun his work in Washington there had been rumor that President Johnson wanted to be rid of Saxton and hoped he would ask to be relieved. But Saxton was stubborn; he refused to quit. Finally, however, in January the axe fell. Saxton was removed. Though offered a Bureau position elsewhere he declined and wound up in Army quartermaster duty far from

Carolina.[47] With Saxton out of the way and with the President's veto sustained, Trescot called on General Howard on February 21 and thought he had secured agreement on the issuance of an order for the immediate restoration of the Sherman lands. But Howard worried after their meeting until one o'clock at night; the next day he informed Trescot that he would issue no such order without further instruction from the President. The next day Howard wrote the President that his existing instructions concerning the Sherman lands were that he was to attempt "to make an arrangement mutually satisfactory between the land owners and the resident freedmen." Under those instructions, he noted, many lands had been restored to the whites. But, said he, "In order not to break faith with these freedmen, who had received possessory titles, or who occupied lands under General Sherman's order, I had hoped to render them some *equivalent or indemnity;* possibly this may yet be afforded them by some future action of Congress." He concluded that he still felt "unwilling to make any sweeping restoration of the lands above named to their former owners without more definite instructions than I have yet received either from yourself or the Secretary of War."[48]

Executive Agent Trescot was very much on the job. General Howard wrote his letter in duplicate, one to go through War Department channels and one to be delivered by Trescot himself to the Executive Mansion. Trescot delivered his copy with a covering letter to the President urging that the regular Army authorities in South Carolina (not Howard) should determine whether a white owner was willing to make some fair arrangement with any tenants under the Sherman order, and that Howard should be told to get on at once with all the lands' restoration.[49] While no peremptory order for such restoration was issued, it seems that Trescot's suggestion for having the regular Army authorities handle the matter was—or perhaps already had been—substantially adopted, at least for the area in South Carolina. Howard's view was that there should be restoration only if the white owner and the black "title" holder reached a "mutually satisfactory" arrangement. But the regular Army authorities would restore if only the white owner tendered a deal that they deemed "fair"—whether or not the black "title" holder was satisfied—and even that condition would be imposed only if they found that Sherman "title" held by the tenant was technically quite correct in its specification of the land he occupied. Howard protested this interference with his administration. Indeed when by early March he had received no new instructions from the President he ordered Saxton's successor in South Carolina to maintain the possession of the "title" holders "until some definite action is had by the Government." As he had intimated in his February 22 letter to the President, he was hoping for some further action by Congress to provide "some equivalent or indemnity" to the "title" holders if the lands were to be restored to the whites. It is not clear how the conflict between the regular military and the Bureau stood when the whole matter finally became academic in July 1866.[50]

At that time Congress again acted. Again it adopted an amendment to the Freedmen's Bureau Act, this time to extend the life of the Bureau for a limited period, with various provisions for the freedmen's welfare, and again it addressed the question of the Sherman "title" holders. But this time it gave in to the white owners. It did provide that any Sherman "title" holders still on the lands could not be ousted until they had harvested current crops and had been fairly compensated for any betterments they had made. Otherwise a Sherman "title" holder, whether or not he had yet been dispossessed, was given no relief except the privilege of buying at $1.50 an acre a twenty-acre plot to be provided from several thousand acres in the Port Royal area that the United States had acquired from tax sales during the war. Again there was a veto by a President who seemed to take a dim view of even limited Government aid to the blacks. But this time the veto was overriden. So at last the way was cleared for all the abandoned lands to be restored to the white owners, and finally resolved was the long controversy having roots reaching as far back as Ebenezer Creek.[51]

But when at length the dust of controversy had settled there was something pathetic in the outcome. In the haste, tension, and confusion of Saxton's administration of the Sherman order, settlers' "titles" were not always written with required specificity, many settlers never received any "title" papers at all, and others settled elsewhere than on the locations their papers provided for. Still others, through ignorance or discouragement, had simply given up and wandered away. Furthermore, any "title" holder at a point far from the Port Royal area, even if he heard of the opportunity afforded by the July 1866 statute, probably was reluctant to move there to see what might be available to him.[52] The result is that the books of the United States tax authorities, who issued the allotments from the tax lands, show a total of only 1,398 purchases by blacks pursuant to the 1866 statute. Moreover, while the statute provided quite definitely that the plots were to be for twenty acres, any for that amount are almost indiscernible; most were for but ten acres, and not a few for smaller plots, as little as two acres.[53]

How far short that was from the great black enclave that General Saxton thought General Sherman had created.

Part 7

African Americans and the Lincoln Legacy

CHAPTER 21

Lincoln and Black Freedom

La Wanda Cox

A CENTRAL CHALLENGE OF RECONSTRUCTION history can be defined by two questions: first, how did it happen that a racist, white North freed black slaves and made all blacks the equal of whites before the law and at the ballot box? Second, what went wrong? *Lincoln and Black Freedom* focuses on pieces of the puzzle: the actual and potential roles of the presidency, specifically of Lincoln as president; and then, on the limits of the possible—the opportunity, if any, for Republican leaders in the 1860s to have established firmly in practice the equality that they made the law of the land. The focus required a re-examination of Lincoln's presidential record in respect to the status of Southern blacks. Lincoln emerged as a consistent, determined friend of black freedom, but a friend whose style of leadership obscured the strength of his commitment—and still does.[1]

In the popular mind the image of Lincoln as Emancipator may endure. Scholarship, though divided on the issue, has cast serious doubt upon its historical validity. More than that of any other historian the work of J. G. Randall, for two decades the leading academic authority on Lincoln, in stripping emancipation of its "crust of misconception" (Randall's phrase) discredited the Emancipation Proclamation and Lincoln as Emancipator. His Lincoln acted against slavery without enthusiasm, forced by political and military necessity to issue a paper pronouncement that set no slave free. Though recognizing Lincoln's strong moral judgment against slavery, Randall portrayed Lincoln as more deeply committed to gradualism, compensation, and colonization than to emancipation itself. Randall's views reverberated across college campuses in the arresting prose of two distinguished historians, Richard Hofstadter and Kenneth M. Stampp. According to Hofstadter, the proclamation "had all the moral grandeur of a bill of lading." In Stampp's words, "If it was Lincoln's destiny to go down in history as the Great Emancipator, rarely has a man embraced his destiny with greater reluctance than he." Richard N. Current, who completed Randall's *Lincoln the President* after Randall's death and became a leading authority in his own right, found justification for the title of Emancipator in Lincoln's support for the Thirteenth Amendment, but he let stand Randall's view that expediency had pushed Lincoln the president into an actively antislavery policy. As more recent historical writing increasingly, and validly, presents blacks as active participants in achieving emancipation, Randall's interpretation is implicitly accepted, Lincoln's role diminished, and the popular image of the Emancipator overtly attached as robbing blacks of credit "for setting themselves free."[2]

The term *freedom* as I have used it encompasses more than the absence of property rights in men. It includes as well release from the bondage of discrimination imposed by white prejudice through law. More than the reassertion of Lincoln's claim to the title of Emancipator, the conclusion that Lincoln was a friend of black civil and political rights is controversial. Here again the persistence of Randall's influence has been significant. Hostile to abolitionists and Radicals, Randall found and commended contrasting qualities in Lincoln: pro-Southern empathy, generosity toward the vanquished, an unqualified priority for speedy restoration of the Union, respect for state rights, willingness to let the Southern people (i.e., white Southerners) "solve their own race problem."[3]

Historians writing in the spirit of the civil rights revolution of our time repudiated Randall's pro-Southern, anti-Radical bias but generally accepted his characterization of Lincoln's policy. One wrote regretfully that it was difficult to reconcile Lincoln's role "with our own consciences."[4] Current found a way. He enlisted Lincoln on the side of civil rights by holding him up as an example of "man's ability to outgrow his prejudices," citing as evidence the respect with which Lincoln as president treated blacks, notably Frederick Douglass.[5] This was limited reassurance. Other historians discovered a bond between Lincoln and the Radicals, in goal if not in method. A few went so far as to hold that at the time of his death Lincoln was about to align himself with the Radical policy of a broad enfranchisement of Southern blacks. That view has not been generally accepted. Indeed, Lincoln's racial attitudes have attracted closer scrutiny than his racial policy.

For a time in the 1960s and 1970s, particularly after Lerone Bennett's charge in *Ebony* that Lincoln was a white supremacist, the Lincoln image seemed in danger of being transformed into a symbol of white America's injustice to black America. Even sympathetic scholarly replies left Lincoln sadly wanting in moral indignation at the racial discrimination that permeated American society, North and South. He was also faulted for lack of thoughtful concern for the future of the freed slaves. By the 1970s another development compromised the Emancipator. Writings on Reconstruction had become sharply critical of federal policy toward Southern blacks and traced back to the war years what were seen as its fatal flaws in the postwar era. Lincoln was not the focus of these studies but by implication, and at times by direct accusation, he was held responsible.

The vulnerability of Lincoln's reputation as friend of black freedom in his day, and in the historiography of ours, derives in considerable part from his style of presidential leadership. In dealing with matters affecting the status of blacks it left his purpose and his resolve open to understandable doubt. On occasion he acted boldly. More often, however, Lincoln was cautious, advancing one step at a time, and indirect, exerting influence behind the scenes. He could give a directive without appearing to do so, or even while disavowing it as such. Seeking to persuade, he would fashion an argument to fit the listener. Some statements were disingenuous, evasive, or deliberately ambiguous.

Examples of Lincoln's less than forthright style are familiar, though not always recognized as such. Best known is his response to those urging emancipation during the weeks when he had decided to issue the proclamation but was awaiting a propitious moment. He gave no public indication of his intent, he questioned the efficacy of an executive order, and he wrote the famous reply to Horace Greeley. That letter was skillfully fashioned to deflect criticism from both Radicals and their opponents, but principally the latter. Lincoln stated that what he did, or did not do, about slavery and "the colored race" was determined by what he believed would help save the Union. Later he acknowledged that even as he issued the proclamation he had been uncertain whether it would do more good than harm. The same action might not have been taken by another president, equally committed to saving the Union but of lesser moral conviction that all men everywhere should be free.

Lincoln's decision on the proclamation was not his first decision as president to move against slavery. His earlier offensive also is illustrative of his presidential style. It was behind the scenes in late 1861 that he pressed Delaware to enact a plan of emancipation, drafting alternative bills to guide the state legislature. More open was the initiative that followed in

March 1862 when he sent Congress a special message asking passage of a joint resolution promising financial aid to any state that would adopt gradual abolishment of slavery. More open, but not altogether open. He had worked three months on the message—"all by himself, no conference with his cabinet." Shortly thereafter he confided to Wendell Phillips that he meant slavery "should die," that the message, like the drink slyly requested by the Irishman in legally dry Maine, contained, "a drop of the crathur . . . *unbeknown to myself*"; that is, the message was stronger than it appeared to be.[6] A passage therein characterizing the resolution requested of Congress as "merely initiatory" and expressing hope that it "would soon lead to important practical results" had suggested as much but ambiguously.[7] Seeking implementation of the proposal, Lincoln attempted to persuade border-state representatives with assurances and arguments that strain credulity. His basic argument, though fervent, was unrealistic: compensated emancipation by Union slave states would discourage the enemy and shorten the war. If such action were taken, Lincoln told their congressmen, he would countenance no coercive measure against slavery by the federal government. This assurance must not be made public lest it force a quarrel with the Greeley Radicals.

Lincoln followed his initial request with two additional ones to Congress. A special message in July presented the draft of a bill to compensate any state that abolished slavery "either immediately or gradually." In December his annual message included the text of a constitutional amendment to the same end—giving the states until 1900 to act. Ostensibly conservative and deferential to the rights of the states, the proposed amendment held more than a single "drop of the crathur." One provision stated that all slaves "who shall enjoy actual freedom by the chances of war" would be "forever free." Note that for a not inconsiderable number (many slaves were already fleeing to Union lines), freedom would be legalized not by state action but by constitutional amendment. Only loyal owners would be compensated. Although Lincoln expressed, and would continue to express, the judgment that gradual rather than sudden emancipation would be better for all, the amendment he drafted would have sanctioned immediate emancipation. Here was antislavery medicine of stronger proof than its label. A comparable stratagem was embodied in the preliminary Emancipation Proclamation. It offered, or seemed to offer, protective immunity to slavery in the Confederate states if they returned to the Union. The likelihood that any would do so within the 100–day grace period between the two proclamations was practically nil. This was not the only product of Lincoln's pen that appeared to offer more protection to slavery than he was prepared to give.

With the final Emancipation Proclamation issued, Lincoln in early 1863 turned his antislavery effort to occupied Louisiana, again acting indirectly and discreetly. An earlier effort at restoration had led to the election of two Unionists as congressmen, and they were briefly seated during the last days of the Thirty Seventh Congress. Lincoln made it a point to cultivate them. As Benjamin F. Flanders, one of the two, later reminded Lincoln: "You took me by the hand and said there was a strong effort to break down your administration and asked me to support you. . . . I did it then to the extent of my influence and have ever since."[8] Lincoln used Flanders and his colleague Michael Hahn as conduits to encourage local Union leaders to take an antislavery stance. He dispensed patronage as Flanders, Hahn, and the local Free State leader, Thomas J. Durant, considered necessary in order to carry the state for freedom. Through Secretary Salmon P. Chase, Lincoln not only dispensed such patronage but sought to neutralize the influence of proslavery Unionists. One of their number was appointed to the important post of collector of the New Orleans customhouse with the understanding that his brother-in-law, the owner and editor of an influential proslavery newspaper, would change its editorial policy to one of support for emancipation.

All this, and more, Lincoln did in such a way as to keep an appearance of neutrality and of respect for the right of Louisianians (white) to decide freely the slavery issue. He so adroitly rejected an overture from proslavery Unionists to return Louisiana to the Union with the old slave constitution that their first reaction was disbelief—surely, Lincoln would not refuse readmission to a state because of slavery! They continued to expect that he would make proslavery concessions; so did some Free State leaders. Even to Gen. Nathaniel P. Banks, who had taken over command from Benjamin F. Butler, Lincoln expressed his objective—i.e., to end slavery by state action before readmission—as only a wish, something he would be "glad" for Louisiana to do. He admonished, however, that reorganization as a free state be "pushed forward," completed by the time Congress met in December 1863.[9]

Lincoln acted directly to obtain his goal only when the leader of the Free State movement, and registrar, wrote him in the fall of 1863 that it would not be possible to complete the work of reorganization before Congress met, that public sentiment in occupied Louisiana could not by then be brought to support emancipation. Durant gratuitously added that no harm would come of delay, a conclusion incompatible with Lincoln's fear of political defeat in 1864 with incalculable consequences for the advancement of emancipation. Thereupon Lincoln turned to Banks as commanding general, making him "master of all."

Lincoln's Proclamation of Amnesty and Reconstruction was similarly precipitated by the situation in Louisiana. Its purpose was to hasten the return of Louisiana and other occupied territory as *free* states by removing the condition Lincoln had been understood as desiring, namely a broad geographic and electoral base for reorganization. Now, in order to obtain emancipation, he would accept reconstruction by a small minority, a mere one-tenth of prewar voters. Yet the requirement that slavery be abolished, instead of being explicitly stated in the proclamation, was so worded that Richard Current has recently concluded that "it did no such thing."[10] Lincoln had obfuscated his purpose even while pushing it forward. Yet there is no question but that he was determined to insist on the destruction of the institution of slavery as a prerequisite to readmission. His approval of General Banks's plan to destroy slavery by using military authority to set aside the slavery provisions of the old state constitution and *then* obtaining the consent of voters for the fait accompli—a policy of "consent *and* force"—makes Lincoln's purpose unmistakable.

There is even evidence strongly suggesting that General Banks, with the president's approval, was prepared to set aside the confirming election if won by candidates identified as proslavery. Lincoln's appoval of high-handed military action to obtain state sanction of slavery's demise was not limited to Louisiana. He directed Gen. Frederick Steele to follow a similarly manipulative procedure in Arkansas, but there the plan was overtaken by the course of local events.

My favorite example of Lincoln's elusive style is the note he wrote that ensured passage of the Thirteenth Amendment through the House of Representatives on January 31, 1865. The Democratic opposition had been assiduously and secretly undermined by Lincoln's promises of patronage and by Secretary of State William H. Seward's mobilization of an extraordinary lobby, but opposition to the amendment gained last-minute strength from rumors that Southern commissioners were on their way to Washington for peace talks. When James Ashley, in charge of the measure on the floor of the House, feared the vote would be lost without a denial of the rumor direct from the president, Lincoln sent a one-sentence response: "So far as I know, there are no peace commissioners in the city, or likely to be in it."[11] Peace commissioners, as he well knew, were on their way—not to "the city" but to Fortress Monroe.

The style of presidential leadership that characterized Lincoln's effort on behalf of freedom is only partially explained by his skill as pragmatic politician. It derived as well from the nature of the man, the goal he sought, and the obstacles to its attainment. The goal and the man were integrally related. Holding to the principle that all men are created equal and entitled to certain inalienable rights, Lincoln's goal was to realize that principle, to use his own words, "as nearly . . . as we can." The qualification is as critical to an understanding of Lincoln's role as is the objective: "So I say in relation to the principle that all men are created equal, let it be as nearly reached as we can."[12] The words carry no expectation for perfection, no demand for immediate fulfillment. By temperament Lincoln was neither an optimist nor a crusader. Human fallibility, of which he was keenly aware, did not lessen his conviction that in a self-governing society a generally held feeling, though unjust, "can not be safely disregarded."[13] Lincoln would accept what he saw as "necessity," i.e., a limitation imposed by realities. He did not, however, submit to necessity with complacency. Characteristic was his query: "Can we all do better?"[14] He stood ready to do more when more could be accomplished.

As Lincoln advanced the nation toward freedom for all, the direction he set was steady; the pace was determined by his political judgment, his sense of timing, and his acute awareness of the constraints under which he labored. Those constraints were formidable. There was the need to preserve the Union and the duty to uphold the Constitution, a constitution that recognized and protected slavery. Both obligations were those of solemn oath and of deep conviction. There was the practical imperative of keeping power out of the hands of an opposition party that would sustain slavery and the political hazard of any step toward equality for blacks in view of the intractable racism pervasive among whites. Fully alert to the force of racial prejudice, Lincoln met it by maneuver and sapping rather than by frontal attack.

War, and the participation of blacks as soldiers, made it possible to "do better." And Lincoln did. Keeping political support intact, he moved from his prewar advocacy of restricting slavery's spread to a foremost responsibility for slavery's total, immediate, uncompensated destruction by constitutional amendment. To borrow the terms used by George Mac-Gregor Burns, Lincoln's presidential leadership was both "transactional" (i.e., a matter of exchange, compromise, deference to majority sentiment) and "transforming" (i.e., a moral leadership that helps achieve needed social change). The title of Emancipator is validated by the consistency of direction evident throughout his presidency, not alone by the Emancipation Proclamation and/or the Thirteenth Amendment, and validated by his skill in seizing the opportunities war opened. Lincoln was not pushed into antislavery action by military and political expediency. He was no reluctant emancipator.

To recognize Lincoln's role as "transforming" leader in no way diminishes that of others—of the forthright abolitionist, the outspoken Radical in

Congress, the slave fleeing to precarious freedom, the black soldier fighting with spade and arms (with arms less often than he wished). All were essential participants in the process that led to slavery's destruction. To credit Lincoln is a reminder, however, that presidential leadership can be critically important in effecting social change. It also constitutes recognition of "transactional" skill added to moral purpose as an essential of effective presidential statesmanship. The demise of an entrenched, evil social institution, even after it has become an anachronism, does not automatically follow upon an appeal to conscience; nor did death for the South's peculiar institution follow with inevitability the outbreak of civil conflict.

There is less evidence of Lincoln as friend of black rights than of Lincoln as Emancipator. That evidence, however, conforms to the pattern of Lincoln's style and purpose in dealing with emancipation, and thereby carries weight. Its significance is further enhanced by recognition that Lincoln's first priority was the destruction of slavery, an objective that could be jeopardized by open support for the rights of free blacks. From the distant perspective of a century, victory over slavery may appear to have been inevitable and Lincoln's priority misplaced. To contemporary antislavery spokesmen the outcome as late as mid-1864 was frighteningly uncertain, contingent upon the success of Union forces on the battlefield and of the Republican party in the political arena. Frederick Douglass held that a victory for the Democratic party in 1864 would have been "a fatal calamity," leaving slavery "only wounded and crippled not disabled and killed."[15] Lincoln's concern that slavery be "killed" continued even after passage of the abolition amendment through Congress. His apprehension that the amendment might not be ratified is evident in his very last public address.

Once Lincoln's style and the priority he gave emancipation are recognized, there is no mistaking the fact that he considered the unequal treatment of free blacks an injustice. "Not a single man of your race is made the equal of a single man of ours," he bluntly stated to a group of black leaders upon whom he was urging colonization. He added: "It is a fact, about which we all think and feel alike, I and you."[16] The interpolation has been generally overlooked, for which Lincoln may have been as responsible as the historians who have deleted it. Whether or not he had arranged the interview in order to use colonization as a means of diffusing opposition to emancipation, as many historians now believe, Lincoln's purpose certainly was not the disclosure of his racial attitude. Yet as he indicated to his black audience, Lincoln's emotions as well as his sense of justice were stirred by the inequality to which white prejudice subjected blacks. His feelings are evident in the sardonic response he ordered sent to the man who wrote him that "white men is in class number one and black men is in class number two and must be governed by white men forever." The reply asked whether the writer was a white man or a black one "because in either case you can not be regarded as an entirely impartial judge. It may be that you belong to a third or fourth class of yellow or red men, in which case the impartiality of your judgment would be more apparent."[17] Similarly, Lincoln responded with indignation on learning of the exploitation of freed slaves by lessees of abandoned plantations in the Mississippi Valley. Only matters of utmost import loosened the tight rein Lincoln kept on a display of emotional reaction.

Although the uncertainty of slavery's destruction, the political hazard posed by white racism, and the multitude of wartime demands necessarily left decisive action to the future, Lincoln took steps toward equal status for blacks where he felt it possible to do so. His initiative brought the official diplomatic recognition of two black nations, Haiti and Liberia. In urging colonization upon black Americans, and in directing efforts to find suitable places, he sought assurance from governments that black colonists would be made citizens, legal "equals of the best." Through an official opinion of the attorney general, the Lincoln administration quietly repudiated the Dred Scott dictum that blacks were not citizens and had no rights as such under the Constitution. That opinion was made available to the military governor of Louisiana in August 1863 when, on the president's instruction, he was authorized to register all loyal citizens, an encouragement, though not a directive, to enroll as voters the free blacks of New Orleans. With issuance of the Reconstruction Proclamation in December 1863 Lincoln appeared to rule out black voting in the reorganization of seceded states; in fact, he did not. Publicly he indicated only in general terms that variants from the procedure outlined would be accepted; privately through Secretary Chase he again gave approval for the registration of blacks. Lincoln's actions were generally unknown, discreet, and indirect. Until a free state was established, he left to others the initiative in respect to black enfranchisement.

Louisiana was the one state that provided Lincoln relative freedom to push for more than emancipation. The plan General Banks put into effect was highly irregular and rested upon the military to an extent Lincoln had hoped to avoid, but it gave Louisiana a reorganized, elected government that Lincoln could and did recognize as a free state—i.e., one with slavery abolished—*before* a state convention met to rewrite the prewar constitution. This was not the case in Arkansas or Tennessee. Nine days after the inaugural of Michael Hahn as free state governor, Lincoln sent him a mere "suggestion"—that the upcoming Louisiana constitutional convention admit some blacks to the franchise, mentioning specifically "the very intelligent," and "those who fought gallantly in our ranks." Marked "private," the letter was not made generally public, though Governor Hahn used it behind the scenes. Both he and General Banks recognized Lincoln's "mild and graceful" suggestion (Hahn's phrase) for what it was, a directive.[18] Neither man had previously looked with favor on black enfranchisement, at least so soon, yet they pressured members of the convention. Their effort did not succeed in fulfilling Lincoln's wish, but by changing at least twenty votes it reversed a majority decision to forbid ever giving the vote to blacks and in its place obtained a constitutional provision authorizing black enfranchisement on the basis of military service, taxation, or intellectual fitness (the latter an extremely elastic qualification) by simple act of the Louisiana legislature. This limited but not insignificant advance unmistakably was due to Lincoln. Governor Hahn after Lincoln's death (and B. Gratz Brown while Lincoln still lived) attributed the provision to the president. Hahn also credited to Lincoln's influence other constitutional provisions favorable to blacks, the education of all children without distinction of color and the enrollment of all men, black and white, in the state militia. Lincoln's desire that blacks share public education is well documented.

The framing of the Louisiana constitution did not mark the end of Lincoln's interest and influence. He helped mobilize support for ratification of the document by letting "the civil officers in Louisiana, holding under me, know this is my wish," and implied discipline for those who did not "openly declare for the constitution."[19] When Louisiana's representatives came knocking at the doors of Congress, Lincoln privately assured Radicals reluctant to seat them that the administration's influence was being exerted for enfranchisement. William D. Kelley, the Pennsylvania Radical, was among those convinced. Extension of suffrage to blacks "was not a mere sentiment with Mr. Lincoln. He regarded it as an act of justice to the citizens, and a measure of sound policy for the States."[20] Working with Lincoln for Louisiana's admission in the fall and winter of 1864, Banks too gave private assurances. And in his public speeches in New England, the general interpreted the authorization in the Louisiana constitution as "under the circumstances . . . a command."[21] Back in New Orleans, Republican leaders of the Lincoln-Banks faction, both white and black, openly supported black enfranchisement.

Of utmost significance was Lincoln's insistence that Banks return to New Orleans for the express purpose of "advancing the new State government." His return was with "plenary power," to use Secretary of War Edwin M. Stanton's phrase. Lincoln further strengthened Banks's hand by stating publicly in his last address his own desire for qualified suffrage, and did so in such a way as to leave open the possibility of a broad enfranchisement. By the time Banks reached New Orleans Lincoln had been assassinated. At a memorial mass meeting Banks directly assured blacks in the audience that "Abraham Lincoln gave his word that you will be free, and enjoy all the rights invested to all citizens," and that the last day of fulfillment "was not far distant."[22] Listeners recognized that the general was promising enfranchisement. Apparently he expected to succeed by ruthless removals of Conservatives from office (which he began) and by influencing the next elections. He informed Lincoln's successor, Andrew Johnson, that "we can carry an election triumphantly at any time if we are not disturbed [i.e., not disturbed in ousting hostile officeholders]." Even the question of Negro suffrage, he stated, would then be settled "without involving the Administration in any trouble, and satisfactorily to the country."[23] President Johnson did not leave General Banks undisturbed. Instead of sustaining the general, Johnson dismissed him from command.

Lincoln's support for black suffrage is sometimes minimized as limited to suffrage for only the black elite. This was not the case. Lincoln recognized, and used, military service as the most persuasive argument for extending the franchise. Most black privates could not sign their names. Nor did Lincoln restrict his encouragement for black suffrage to Louisiana. Chase did not understand as limited to that state the presidential approval for black voting during the process of reorganization. Banks believed Lincoln meant enfranchisement in Louisiana to be a model for other states. B. Gratz Brown cited Lincoln's pressure on Louisiana as an argument for extending suffrage to blacks in Missouri. Moreover, we now know that in December 1864 Lincoln was ready to accept Reconstruction legislation that would admit Louisiana with its 1864 constitution but require other returning states to include black suffrage in theirs. Although the extent of enfranchisement Lincoln desired is a matter of some uncertainty, my conclusion is that he was ready to go at least as far as the majority in Congress. With the Radicals unable to obtain any such legislation by the time Congress adjourned in March 1865, Banks's mission indicates Lincoln's intent to use executive power to obtain whatever was possible at the state level. In short, Lincoln was still looking to realize the principle of equality "as nearly . . . as we can."

No student of history can with confidence fault Lincoln's political judgment of what was attainable in the 1860s, or how best he could achieve the maximum possible. The distance between the dominant racial sentiment of Lincoln's day and that of our own is too great. As late as October 1864 the electorate of Maryland, except for the soldier vote, would have rejected emancipation and celebrated not the end of slavery but the "Death Knell of Abolitionism."[24] The best that could be obtained from Unionist Missouri in 1863 was emancipation as of July 4, 1870, with continuing servitude for those over forty during their entire lifetime and for those over twelve until they reached twenty-three. Immediate and unconditional emancipation was established in Missouri only after Lincoln's death, in June 1865. In the free North white opposition to equal status for blacks suffered erosion during the course of the war, but remained tenacious. In August 1862 Illinois voters rejected a new constitution as a whole but overwhelmingly approved provisions that would have enshrined in the state's constitution prohibitions against any Negro migrating into the state and against any resident Negro voting or holding office. Before the war only four states, all in New England, provided equal suffrage. No others extended this right to blacks during the war years. In the fall of 1865 Republican attempts to do so in Connecticut, Wisconsin, and Minnesota failed in referendum voting.

The time has come to disengage Lincoln from the present and let the historic record speak for itself. To do so will diminish neither the man nor the tasks that remain before us to attain racial justice. Without hazard we can relinquish Lincoln as a mirror of the present and beacon to the future, whether of guidance or of warning. Grant that his circumspect style of presidential leadership as an instrument to reach equality irrespective of race offers no acceptable model for the present, since forthright advocacy from the oval office can now mobilize a national consensus to this end. Grant that the achievements beyond abolition that Lincoln nurtured, though essential, are insufficient for the 1980s. But let us take care to recognize that Lincoln's record as friend of freedom is impressive—that it was no reluctant concession to the pressures of a grim war, or the expediency of politics.

To summarize: Lincoln let war come rather than retreat on the expansion of servitude. Within a year of the war's beginning he determined that slavery "should die." Nine months later he boldly proclaimed as a war measure emancipation for the slaves of loyal and disloyal alike in areas of rebellion. He did so though uncertain whether the Emancipation Proclamation would strengthen, or weaken, the Union war effort. By mid-1863 he was ready to deny readmission to any state unwilling to abolish the institution. In order to force state action in occupied territory he boldly employed the power of patronage plus that of military authority—the latter without the covering justification of military necessity. Refusing to let freedom rest solely upon the precarious authority of presidential proclamation and congressional legislation, or upon the uncertainty of state action, Lincoln succeeded in obtaining passage of the abolition amendment. Meanwhile he had officially recognized blacks as citizens and used the weight of his high office in an effort to set former slaves on the road to equality through access to the ballot box.

On the most divisive issue this nation has ever faced, the status of black Americans, Lincoln's presidential record stands without need of myth, apology, or transformation into symbolism. The preeminent meaning of Lincoln the president lies in the historic substance of his role as friend of black freedom. It is a meaning sufficient for all time.

During the years immediately following Lincoln's death his party established an impressive record on black rights. Republicans passed the first civil rights legislation in the nation's history, and passed it over President Andrew Johnson's veto. In the face of unrelenting opposition from Democratic opponents, the party also succeeded in making the Fourteenth and Fifteenth Amendments the supreme law of the land. They followed the amendments with federal enforcement acts of broad scope. Yet the Republican record has suffered harsh censure from historians of our day, criticism prompted in large measure by the failure to realize equal citizenship in practice. That the promise of legislation and constitutional amendment was fulfilled in the South only briefly and partially is a fact beyond dispute. Subjected to white violence and soon deprived of the potential for political power granted in 1867, the vast majority of freed slaves remained for decades an impoverished agrarian underclass, economically dependent upon white landowners and merchant creditors, socially subordinated as a caste to whites of all ranks. It does not necessarily follow, however, that Northern Republicans were responsible for what went wrong. The last section of *Lincoln and Black Freedom* examines an assumption and a related accusation often accepted as fact: namely, the assumption that the political leaders of the 1860s had the power to insure a democratic, racially equalitarian outcome and the accusation that they promised racial equality, then wantonly betrayed the promise.

To examine the indictment it is necessary first of all to make clear what it was Republicans in the immediate post-Civil War years sought to realize through the courts and the ballot box. It was not racial equality. What they sought for the freed slaves was equality of citizenship. Strictly speaking, racial equality is a biological condition rather than a consequence of political or societal action. In our day race itself is a challenged concept. That no inferiority or superiority is biologically inherent in a people because of color or ethnicity is now generally accepted. Discrimination or enforced segregation based upon either is regarded as morally insupportable. These perceptions were not commonly held in the mid-nineteenth century, at least not among white Americans. Republican leaders sought and obtained equal citizenship in law while lacking scientific assurance or personal conviction of racial equality. It might be argued that this should enhance rather than diminish their achievement. However that may be, what was sought through public policy in the 1860s was more limited than the goals of the 1960s but as fundamental to the broader objectives of the Second Reconstruction as the destruction of slavery had been essential to the establishment of nationwide equality of legal status. To indict Republicans for betraying a promise of racial equality comports neither with logic nor with historic reality.

To recognize the indictment as faulty does not dispose of the charge that the seed of failure lay in the racial prejudice of Northern Republicans, a view widely held. Although it was their Democratic opponents who flagrantly exploited racial prejudice in the interest of party there is no gainsaying the fact that racism in one degree or another permeated the ranks of Republicans. Racial prejudice did not, however, prevent the growth of a majority consensus within the Republican party first for the recognition of black citizenship, that is of basic human rights and equality before the law, and more tardily for equality at the ballot box. If the commitments were not effectively enforced in the South during the 1870s and 1880s, the explanation does not lie primarily in Republican racism. It is true that opposition to what was viewed as an attempt to legislate social equality helped weaken Republican political power in the election of 1874 and that racist assumptions made some political equalitarians susceptible to Southern white propaganda that attributed political corruption and chaos to the enfranchisement of blacks. However, Republican racism was only one of the many factors in the Northern retreat from enforcement of black civil and political rights in the South. No historian has established its effect as more than incidental.

Another explanation of Reconstruction's failure, so widely held as to have been identified in 1973 as the "New Orthodoxy in Reconstruction Historiography," is that Republicans had too tender a regard for property rights to confiscate plantation lands and redistribute them to the freedmen. The assumption behind the contention is that a land program would have provided the former slaves with power to safeguard their freedom and with insurance against poverty. The difficulty with this counterfactual projection is that small land-ownership in the South during the postwar decades could not protect blacks against either white violence or poverty, though it would have lightened their economic burden and immensely heightened their sense of personal freedom from white dominance. White terror struck black landowner and tenant alike. The cotton economy perpetuated poverty for both, alternative agrarian markets were scarce, and a non-market homestead offered little beyond subsistence. The escape hatch of industrial or commercial employment for blacks was narrow. Mid-nineteenth-century America with it optimistic assumption of economic opportunity for the individual and of prosperity for a transformed free labor South lacked awareness of impending economic realities as well as the skills requisite to meet them. A formerly dependent and deprived agrarian population is not readily lifted out of poverty. Indeed, as the present difficulties in third world nations (and the recent work of Jane Jacobs and others) remind us, no certain remedy has yet been found to assure escape from poverty. A prosperous New South, for whites as well as blacks, proved elusive; historians and cliometricians continue to pursue the reasons why.

A third major explanation for what had gone wrong was offered by constitutional historians in the 1960s: the constitutional conservatism of Republican lawmakers. A revolutionary destruction of state authority, it was argued, had been necessary. Deference to the traditional federal structure of the Union denied the national government sufficient power to protect the rights of blacks. Interestingly, this view has been substantially modified, if not abandoned, by some of the very authorities who set it forth. Others have made a strong case that the Supreme Court could have developed an expansive construction of national power to protect blacks under the Reconstruction amendments and laws.

The indictment against Republican leaders of the 1860s rests upon a counterfactual assumption that is invalid. Republicans did not possess unlimited power and opportunity. Respect for Constitution and constitutionalism, the intractable nature of postwar poverty in the South, and racial prejudice in the North placed boundaries on the possible. In the postwar years, however, the most decisive barrier to realization of the limited but essential equalitarian goals established in law was not one of these but rather the pervasiveness of Southern white resistance. That the white South resisted Republican policy is no recent discovery, but historians who reexamined Reconstruction free of the racial bias of an older generation have only belatedly recognized the full force and significance of that opposition. It is now clear that Southern whites continued the North-South conflict by determined, persistent, guerrilla-type warfare that enjoyed the overwhelming support or acquiescence of their fellows. The objective was defeat of the Northern-imposed status for Southern blacks as equal citizens and as free laborers. Recent historical writings increasingly look to internal conditions in the South for explanation rather than to Northern policy, yet more often than not, the primary role of Southern white resistance in defeating the Republican attempt to reconstruct the South is muted.

Those who attribute the failure of Reconstruction to a lack of Northern will, and influential historians still do, assume that the North could force the white South to accept blacks as equal citizens. To the contrary, without a substantial degree of consent not only from Southern white political leaders but from their white constituencies, no amount of coercion could have achieved that goal. And once Southern armies had surrendered, it was not possible for the North as a society committed to government by consent and the rule of law to sustain the prolonged use of military force and military authority necessary even to make the attempt. A very considerable amount of force and hundreds of criminal prosecutions were in fact used, far more than during the civil rights revolution of the twentieth century. Despite the limits on the possible, presidential leadership might have made a significant difference. The historic challenge of the immediate postwar years was to induce white Southerners to accept a substantial measure of freedom and equality for blacks and to institutionalize their acceptance in an effective, biracial political party. Captive to his heritage of section, class, and party, Lincoln's successor was incapable of perceiving, let alone meeting, that challenge.

Andrew Johnson identified himself as a man of the South. Until the pressures of war and politics forced him to embrace emancipation, loyalty to slavery was for Johnson a basic component of loyalty to section. As late as the spring of 1862 he assured fellow Tennesseans that he believed "slaves should be in subordination and will live and die so believing." He also assured them that Lincoln and his party had no intention of waging war to free slaves. Apparently Johnson never doubted but that, in his words, the Negro "is an inferior type of man," "not created equal in the very beginning." Unlike Lincoln, Johnson had no purpose to realize as nearly as possible the principle that all men are created equal. He held that Jefferson in writing the Declaration of Independence had meant "the white race, and not the African race." In his veto of the civil rights bill of March 1866, Johnson objected to conferring citizenship upon "the entire race designated as blacks, people of color, negroes, mulattoes, and persons of African blood."[25]

The direction indicated by Andrew Johnson's racial attitude was reinforced by his concern for state rights, his lack of loyalty to the Republican party with which he was aligned only as a Union Democrat, his desire for Southern approbation, and his ambition to be elected president in his own right. Johnson had no reason to use presidential power and persuasion, as Lincoln surely would have done, to build a Republican or predominantly Republican Union party in the South. Johnson looked with favor upon a reorganization of parties that would be a major realignment, with former Democrats at least equal partners. His break with the congressional majority in 1866 was followed by an unsuccessful attempt to create a new political party of conservative Republicans and cooperative Democrats, the former a distinct minority in their own party but the latter a powerful, perhaps predominant, influence in the Northern Democracy. For such a party, a substantial measure of equality for blacks was a condition to be avoided rather than a goal to be attained.

At war's end, party loyalties in the North were too intense to permit a major realignment, but in the South the situation was fluid. Elements existed for a broad coalition in opposition to the old planter-dominated secessionist Democracy: Unionists of varying degrees, opponents of secession, critics of the Confederate leadership, old Whigs, urban dwellers including laborers, men with origins abroad or in the North, those whose class or intrasectional interests created hostility to planter domination— plus blacks to the extent that they might be enfranchised. Such a coalition at best would be an uneasy one. Conflicting economic interests and personal ambitions would require reconciliation. There would be the ever-present hazard of deeply embedded mores of black-white relations. These were exploitable by the opposition and within a biracial party would trigger division on issues viewed by whites as social. Despite the difficulties, in the spring of 1865 the task of building a stable Union-Republican party in the South was not beyond the limits of the possible. But it would require careful nurture and, if it were to function as an instrument of social change, a purposeful direction.

Presidential nurture and direction were precluded by Lincoln's assassination and Johnson's succession. When congressional leaders attempted the task, they were faced not only with its inherent difficulties but with added obstacles. Johnson's policies had encouraged the hope among white Southerners that they would be able to maintain control over race relations, thereby strengthening resistance to change. And warfare between president and Congress had created chaos in the process of Southern political reorganization. Some elements that would otherwise have entered a Union-Republican party remained attached to Johnson's political fortunes.

Since Republicans wished to avoid a break with the president, Johnson's policies had dammed up for a time the growing sentiment for black legal equality, citizenship, and enfranchisement. When the dam broke, the accompanying flood created its own havoc. Renewed military control, immediate universal enfranchisement of black men, and the disfranchisement of some whites, intensified the bitterness of defeat and the resolve to resist. Except within limited geographical areas, the Republican party in the South was viewed as an alien intruder. It could obtain neither the loyalty of a substantial number of white Southerners nor their acknowledgment of its legitimacy. The power that it briefly held could not be consolidated without both.

A stable two-party system in the South was not assured had Lincoln lived out his second term of office, but its successful establishment would have been much less unlikely. Bonds between Lincoln and his party were strong, too strong to allow differences to escalate into open warfare. Moreover, unlike Johnson, Lincoln had the will to nurture an essentially Republican party in the South. And he possessed the skill to build one. He was experienced in consolidating a political coalition by dispensing "justice to all [factions]." He had demonstrated ability to retain the political loyalty of Southern proslavery Unionists who disliked his policy. Politically he deftly used others but did not allow others to use him. His compassion, his Southern ties, and his style of leadership admirably fitted the postwar need to minimize bitterness and undermine resistance to change. They appeared to set him apart from the hated Radical of "Black Republicanism." Yet it was Lincoln rather than the Radicals who had inaugurated a Southern policy that used "consent and force" to attain a political end. His insistence that General Banks return to Louisiana signaled that Lincoln would when necessary continue to supplement persuasion with coercion.

Lincoln would also bind up the nation's wounds. Too often the eloquent closing paragraph of his Second Inaugural has been read as concern only for white America. His words need not be so narrowly construed. He enjoined the nation "to finish the work we are in" "with firmness in the right, as God gives us to see the right." "The right" as God gave him to "see it" was for Lincoln color-blind. There is no reason to believe that he ever abandoned the goal of realizing "as nearly . . . as we can" the principle that all men (not whites alone) are created equal. The performance of blacks during the war and the outpouring of trust and gratitude from those freed of their bondage could only have deepened his commitment to that goal. How nearly it could have been reached in the lifetime of this generation Lincoln did not know, nor can we. To achieve a moral objective not universally held, it is necessary to make change "acceptable to those who must support it, tolerable to those who must put up with it."[26] If any man could have met that challenge in respect to the rights of blacks in freedom, the man was Lincoln. His untimely death changed the course, and perhaps the outcome, of the Republican effort to reconstruct Southern society in the interest of free labor and racial justice.

CHAPTER 22

Lincoln and Race Relations

Hans L. Trefousse

IN RECENT YEARS, THE problem of race relations in the United States has become steadily more important. Not that it was not crucial before, but in an ever more competitive world, in which the United States has achieved a leading position, the essential flaw in America's vaunted democracy—the persistence of racial prejudice and its resulting difficulties—is now even more significant than previously. In view of this fact, the failure of post-Civil War Reconstruction, America's first attempt at racial justice, would seem to be more ominous than ever, and this failure might have been prevented had President Abraham Lincoln not been assassinated at the very hour of Northern victory.

John Wilkes Booth, it now appears, shot much better than he knew. Having long plotted to kidnap the president, he made up his mind to go ahead with his alternate plan of assassination when he was present at the White House when Lincoln delivered his last speech. Hearing the president advocate limited black suffrage for Louisiana, he asked Lewis Payne, one of his henchmen who was with him, to shoot the speaker right away. Failing to get the wanted reaction, he turned to his other companion, David Herold, and said, "That means nigger citizenship. Now, by God, I'll put him through." Vowing that it would be the last speech Lincoln ever made, three days later the actor killed the president at Ford's Theater.[1]

The immediate consequence of the crime was the accession of Andrew Johnson, the only Senator from a seceding state to remain loyal to the

Union. Born a poor white in North Carolina, Johnson was apprenticed to a tailor at the age of ten, ran away from his master a few years later, and eventually migrated to Eastern Tennessee, where he married, set up his own tailor shop, and ultimately acquired wealth and prominence. Elected repeatedly to the state legislature and to Congress as a Democrat, he became governor in 1853, was reelected in 1855, and in 1857 sent to the United States Senate. Reflecting the sentiments of his East Tennessee neighbors who voted against secession, he refused to go with his state in 1861 and became a hero in the North. In 1862 Lincoln appointed him military governor of Tennessee, and in 1864 he won the vice presidency as Lincoln's running mate.[2]

His loyalty, however, did not mean that he failed to share his constituents' pronounced racism. He had been a slaveholder himself and was convinced that the blacks were inherently inferior to the whites, a prejudice he had made abundantly clear in 1844 in the House of Representatives, when he said, "If one portion of the community were to be masters [and] another menials . . . , he had no hesitancy in bringing his mind to a conclusion on the subject, believing, as he did, that the black race of Africa were inferior to the white man in point of intellect—better calculated in physical structure to undergo drudgery and hardship—standing as they do, many degrees lower in the scale of gradation that expresses the relative relation between God and all that He has created than the white man." If the laws did not distinguish between white and black, they would "place ever splay-footed, bandy-shanked, hump-backed, thick-lipped, flat-nosed, woolly headed, ebon-colored negro in the country upon an equality with the poor white man."[3] And although during the 1864 campaign he told the blacks he might be their Moses to lead them out of bondage,[4] he never abandoned his prejudices and as late as 1868 still complained to his private secretary, Colonel W. G. Moore, that blacks and not whites were employed on the grounds of the White House. He was determined to keep the South a white man's country, and it might well be argued that he fully achieved that aim.[5]

Now it so happened, as Professor Thomas Turner has so well shown, that the period following the assassination was one not only of deep mourning but also of greatly aggravated feelings toward the defeated South, held responsible for the atrocious deed.[6] Not knowing what was in store for them, Southerners, stunned by events, were ready to accept almost any conditions, including even black suffrage, to restore peace and quiet.[7] Had Lincoln been alive, he might well have used this feeling to set a new course for the defeated section, and there is little doubt that it would have been different from Johnson's plan of Reconstruction, or rather, restoration, as he preferred to call it, which was so mild that Southerners immediately began to oppose concessions to the freedmen, particularly the franchise.

The reasons for assuming this pronounced difference between the two executives are clear. Lincoln's attitude toward the race question was the exact opposite of that of his successor. In the first place, unlike Johnson, who had been a defender of slavery until wartime necessities caused him to espouse emancipation, Lincoln had always abhorred slavery. As early as 1837, he was one of two members of the Illinois legislature to condemn the "peculiar Institution" as "founded on injustice and bad policy."[8] In 1849, he prepared a bill for the emancipation of the slaves in the District of Columbia, and in 1854 in his famous Peoria Address he again denounced the institution in no uncertain terms.[9] His subsequent campaigns and speeches in Illinois and elsewhere rarely omitted a castigation of bondage, culminating in his antislavery campaign against Stephen A. Douglas in 1865. Finally in 1860 he was elected president on a platform pledging an end to the extension of slavery.

It is true that Lincoln never, prior to 1862, advocated federal action to end slavery in the states where it existed. Constitutional obligations were important to him, and he hoped that putting an end to the expansion of the institution would in the end cause its demise in the South. As he said in his famous House Divided Against Itself Speech at Springfield in June 1858, "I believe this government cannot endure, permanently half slave and half free. I do not expect the Union to be dissolved; I do not expect the house to fall, but I do expect it will cease to be divided. It will become all one thing or all the other. Either the opponents of slavery will arrest the further spread of it, and place it where the public mind shall rest in the belief that it is in course of ultimate extinction, or its advocates will push it forward, till it shall become alike lawful in all the States, old as well as new—North as well as South." He then deplored the apparent tendency to the "latter condition," and in the winter of 1860 refused to entertain any compromise involving the further spread of slavery.[10]

While president, Lincoln, for reasons of political necessity, emphasized that the war was fought, not for the abolition of slavery, but for the preservation of the Union; he never wavered from his conviction that slavery was wrong. In view of the fact that he had been elected by a minority of some 39 percent of the voters, most of whom had no sympathy with abolitionism, and that he had to retain their loyalty, he could not emphasize his antislavery convictions. This was especially true because he was anxious to retain the border slave states—he is reputed to have said that he hoped God was on his side but he must have Kentucky—and any antislavery move would have heightened the danger of further secessions.[11] Nevertheless, there were various instances in which he could still show that he had hardly abandoned his long held views, and he rarely hesitated to do so. Even though he had stated in his first inaugural that he had no intention of interfering with slavery in the states where it existed, in his first address to Congress on 4 July 1861, while repeating this purpose, he added that after the suppression of the rebellion he "probably" would have no different understanding of his powers.[12] Little more than a month later, he signed the first Confiscation Bill freeing bondsmen used by the Confederates against the United States;[13] then, in December 1861 he asked the lone representative from Delaware to inaugurate a scheme of compensated emancipation in that border state, and in March 1862 made this suggestion publicly to apply to all the border states.[14] And while none of these saw fit to accept his suggestion, in April he signed a bill freeing the slaves in the District of Columbia, followed in June by one abolishing the institution in the territories. And although he hesitated to sign the second Confiscation Act, freeing the slaves of all insurgents, after insisting on certain modifications, he approved of it also.[15]

It is true that during this entire period Lincoln did not hesitate to revoke orders of individual generals seeking to effect emancipation on their own. In September 1861 he annulled John C. Frémont's edict for this purpose in Missouri, and in May 1862 a similar order by David Hunter in the Department of the South.[16] These steps, however, were merely taken for political reasons, and by June 1862 he had decided that the time was ripe to go further. Preparing his Emancipation Proclamation freeing slaves in areas still in rebellion within a given time, he submitted it to the cabinet in July. Advised to postpone it until the federal army had achieved some victory, he issued it on 22 September in his capacity as commander in chief of the army and navy to go into effect within one hundred days.[17] If shortly before the publication of the Preliminary Proclamation he still gave his well known reply to Horace Greeley's "The Prayer of Twenty Millions" in which he stated that his primary purpose was to save the Union, and that he would do so if it meant freeing all slaves, some of the slaves, or none of the slaves, he nevertheless added that he had merely given his opinion of public duty and that he intended no edification of his "oft-expressed personal wish that all men everywhere could be free."[18]

The final proclamation followed on 1 January 1863, and having already told a delegation of Kentuckians that he would rather die than to take back a word of it, he made it known that he would never repeal it. He affirmed its validity to James C. Conkling in August 1863, and in April of the next year wrote to A. G. Hodges, "If slavery is not wrong, nothing is wrong."[19] He exerted pressure on the governors of the states exempt from the proclamation to take steps to abolish the institution in their own jurisdictions, while making the acceptance of the proclamation a condition for his offer of amnesty to insurgents.[20] In 1864 he assented to his renomination on a platform endorsing a constitutional amendment for the abolition of slavery, signed the bill repealing the Fugitive Slave Law, and after his reelection, he used the full powers of his office to secure the adoption of the amendment in the House of Representatives which had failed to secure the necessary two-thirds vote in the previous session. Thus there is little doubt about his detestation of the "peculiar institution."[21]

Lincoln's views on race are less unequivocal. Born in a slave state and raised in deeply racist southern Indiana, he could hardly have escaped the all-present notions of racial inequality which in the nineteenth century prevailed not only in the United States but throughout the world. Considering the fact that modern anthropological findings about the equality of human races did not appear until after the turn of the century, it is not surprising that hardly anybody espoused them previously. To be sure, there were a few abolitionists and foes of slavery who preached the doctrine of human equality—Charles Sumner, Wendell Phillips, Thaddeus Stevens, and Gerrit Smith, for example—but they were an exception and even many opponents of human bondage were not free from prejudice.[22] Consequently, Lincoln too was affected by his surroundings and prior to the Civil War never advocated full racial equality.

But in spite of this failure, he never made a point of racism, as so many of his opponents were wont to do.[23] Whether equal to the whites or not, he always considered the African Americans human beings, and not a separate species. In 1841 while returning from a trip to Kentucky, he observed some slaves who were being taken down to the river. As he described the incident to the sister of his friend Joshua Speed, a fine example was presented on board the boat for contemplating the effect of *condition* upon human happiness. A gentleman had purchased twelve Negroes in different parts of Kentucky and was taking them to a farm in the South. They were chained six and six together. A small iron clevis was around the left wrist of each, and this fastened to the main chain by a shorter one at a convenient distance from the others; so that the Negroes were strung together precisely like so many fish on a trot-line. In this condition they were being separated forever from the scenes of their childhood, their friends, their fathers and mothers, and brothers and sisters, and many of them, from their wives and children, and going into perpetual slavery where the lash of the master is proverbially more ruthless and unrelenting than any other where; and yet amid all these distressing circumstances, as we would think of them, they were the most cheerful and apparently happy creatures on board. One, whose offense for which he had been sold was an over-fondness for his wife, played the fiddle almost continually; and the others danced, sang, cracked jokes, and played various games with cards from day to day: "How true it is that 'God tempers the wind to the shorn lamb,' or in other words, that He renders the worst of human conditions tolerable, while He permits the best, to be nothing better than tolerable."

Even though in later years, he recalled the incident as an affront to him because of its cruelty, at the time he was more interested in its illustration of human psychology and obviously considered the subject of race a fit example for such observation.[24]

His unusually liberal racial views can again be illustrated by a fragment on slavery which he probably wrote in 1854. Asking if "A" could prove that by right he might enslave "B," why then was not the same thing true the other way around? If the answer were color, then the first man with skin fairer than "A's" might be justified in enslaving him. If the answer were not color, but the assumption that whites were intellectually superior to the blacks, then "A" would be a slave to the first person he met with an intellect superior to his. Lincoln's racial feelings were obviously very malleable.[25]

In 1855 he again gave an example of his tolerance. He said he was not a Know Nothing, for how could anyone who abhorred the oppression of Negroes be in favor of degrading classes of white people. "As a nation," he continued, "we began by declaring that 'all men are created equal.' We now practically read it 'all men are created equal, except negroes.' When the Know Nothings get control, it will read 'all men are created equal, except negroes, and foreigners, and Catholics.' When it comes to this, I should prefer emigrating to some country where they make no pretence of loving liberty—to Russia, for instance, where despotism can be taken pure, and without the base alloy of hypocracy."

The future Great Emancipator again clarified his notions of equality by stating in 1857 that because he did not want a black woman for a slave he must necessarily want her for a wife. "I need not have her for either," he continued. "I can just leave her alone. In some respects she is certainly not my equal; but in her natural right to eat the bread she earns with her own hands without asking leave of anyone else, she is my equal and equal of all others." He repeated this sentiment several times, unusual though it was for the age. In addition, in 1858 he pleaded, "let us discard all this quibbling . . . about this race and the other race being inferior, and therefore must be placed in an inferior position—discarding our standard that we have left us. Let us discard all these things, and unite as one people throughout this land, until we shall once more stand up declaring that all men are created equal."[26]

Advanced as these sentiments were, not even Lincoln could, in a political campaign, advocate the social equality of the blacks. This political reality was especially true during his debates with Senator Douglas, when, at Charleston, answering questions about his view, he replied, "I will say then, that I am not, nor ever have been in favor of bringing about the equality of the white and black races—that I am not nor ever have been in favor of making voters or jurors of negroes, nor of qualifying them to hold office, not to intermarry with white people; and I will say in addition to this that there is a physical difference between the white and black races which I believe will forever forbid the two races living together on terms of social and political equality. And inasmuch as they cannot so live, while they do remain together there must be the position of superior and inferior, and I as much as every other man am in favor of having the superior position assigned to the white race." These remarks have often been quoted to prove that Lincoln was a thorough racist, but they must be compared with Douglas's incessant harping on black inferiority, his insistence that a Negro could never be a citizen because of belonging to a race incapable of self government. As he said to make his point clear, "Why, they brought Fred Douglass to Freeport when I was addressing a meeting there in a carriage driven by the white owner, the negro sitting inside with the white lady and her daughter." His remarks had the desired effect. They elicited cries of "Shame" from the racist audience.[27]

During the 1860 presidential campaign and its secession aftermath, the race question was somewhat muted, but after the outbreak of Civil War, it could not long be disregarded. The question of what to do with the blacks who entered Union lines, or, following the Emancipation Proclamation, who were freed, had to be met. As early as August 1862 Lincoln sought to meet this problem by suggesting colonization of blacks outside of the United States, a solution which had long been advocated by Whigs such as Henry Clay, whom he admired. Whether the president really believed in the feasibility of this course of action or whether he utilized it to assuage the conservatives is not quite clear, but he did invite a number of black leaders to the White House to ask them to initiate the process. The very fact that he invited blacks to the executive mansion showed his lack of pronounced racial prejudice, and the way he presented the problem to his guests reinforced this point. "You and we are different races," he told them. "We have between us a broader difference than exists between almost any other two races. Whether it is right or wrong, I need not discuss, but this physical difference is a great disadvantage to us both, as I think your race suffer very greatly, many of them by living among us, while ours suffers from your presence." He then continued by deploring the wrong inflicted upon the blacks and pointing out that even when free they were not treated as equals. Thus separation might be the answer.[28] Nothing came of this particular interview, but some time later, Lincoln did initiate the colonization of Île la Vâche off Haiti, an experiment that ended in utter failure and his sending vessels to bring back the survivors.[29]

In 1863 he had the opportunity of meeting the famous black abolitionist Frederick Douglass, who had come to the White House to seek better treatment for black troops. Not knowing how he would be received, he was uneasy, but Lincoln quickly put him at ease. Arising from his chair, he offered Douglass his hand and bade him welcome. He then listened to his visitor's complaints and promised to do what he could. Douglass was deeply impressed and even more so when on another occasion Lincoln, discussing matters with the black leader, made Governor William A. Buckingham of Connecticut wait in spite of Douglass's pleading that he should see the other visitor first. Whatever racial prejudices Lincoln may have had were rapidly becoming less pronounced than ever, as he showed during his second inaugural when Douglass, attempting to be admitted to the evening's festivities, was rudely rejected by the guards on duty. Lincoln, on being informed of the African American's presence, interfered and said, "Here comes my friend Douglass. I am glad to see you." Ushering him in, he asked him what Douglass thought of the inaugural address. Telling him there was no man in the country whose opinion he valued more. As Douglass wrote, "In his company, I was never reminded of my humble origin, or of my unpopular color."[30]

There were other indications that Lincoln's ideas on race were rapidly becoming more flexible than ever. One of the most radical propositions in 1864 was the proposal to enfranchise the freedmen. In spite of his political caution, the president gradually came to the conclusion that he ought to further the idea. As he wrote to James Wadsworth, probably in January, "I cannot see, if universal amnesty is granted, how, under the circumstances, I can avoid exacting the return universal suffrage, or at least, suffrage on the basis of intelligence and military service." And in March of the same year, he admonished Governor Michael Hahn of the new Free State Government of Louisiana to see if the suffrage could not be extended to the more intelligent blacks and to those who fought for the Union. At the time, it was still too early to make his views public, but in his last speech, he referred to them and publicly announce his convictions about the desirability of suffrage for some of the freedmen.[31]

It is of course impossible to know what would have happened had Lincoln lived. In a brilliant chapter in her book *Lincoln and Black Freedom,* LaWanda Cox has tried to speculate about this problem and came to the conclusion that not even the president might have been successful.[32] Yet, it is equally clear that, despite many assertions to the contrary, he would not have committed Johnson's faults. As Carl Schurz summed it up so well,

> Had he [Lincoln] lived, he would have as ardently wished to stop bloodshed and to reunite all the states, as he ever did. But is it to be supposed for a moment that, seeing the late master class in the South, still under the influence of their old traditional notions and prejudices and at the same time sorely pressed by the distressing necessities of their situation, intent upon subjecting the freedmen again to a system very much akin to slavery, Lincoln would have consented to abandon these freedmen to the mercies of that master class? Can it be imagined that he would have been deaf to the sinister reports coming from the South, as Johnson was? Would he have sacrificed the rights of the emancipated slaves and the security of the Union men to a metaphysical abstraction as to the indestructibility of states? Did he not repeatedly warn against the mere discussion of just such abstractions as something useless and misleading? To assert in the face of all this that the Johnson Reconstruction policy was only Lincoln's policy continued, is little less than a perversion of historic truth.[33]

Thus Lincoln's death was indeed a disaster. It removed the one statesman who, because of his political genius, might have succeeded in effecting some sort of solution of the problem posed by some four million freedmen. His successor was not primarily interested in this question, and the result was a calamity for the United States, for race relations, and the integration of the freedmen into the American society.

Notes

Chapter 1: *"Beckoning Them to the Dreamed of Promise of Freedom"*

1. Quoted in Benjamin Quarles, *Frederick Douglass* (New York, 1968), p. 277.
2. On self-emancipation, see Barbara J. Fields, "Who Freed the Slaves?" in Geoffrey C. Ward, Ric Burns, and Ken Burns, *The Civil War: An Illustrated History* (New York, 1990), pp. 178–81.
3. On the African-American response to Lincoln's wartime measures, see Benjamin Quarles, *Lincoln and the Negro* (New York, 1962); James McPherson, *The Negro's Civil War: How American Negroes Felt and Acted during the War for the Union* (Urbana, 1982). See also Edna Green Medford, "'Something More Than the Mere "Union" to Fight For': African-Americans Respond to Lincoln's Wartime Policies," in *Lincoln and His Contemporaries*, Charles M. Hubbard, ed. (Macon, Ga., 1999).
4. January First, 1863," *Douglass' Monthly* (January 1863).
5. Ibid.
6. "The Great Emancipation Demonstration," *The Anglo-African* (January 10, 1863). *The Anglo-African*, published in New York throughout most of the war, was the premier newspaper devoted to African-American concerns at the time. In addition to reporting on the progress of the war and on the effort to push the nation toward emancipation, the newspaper featured the observations of the most prominent men in the black community. Its editorials and news coverage were always pro-emancipation and often vehemently opposed Lincoln's wartime policies.
7. "Remarks of O. P. Anderson," *The Angol-African* (January 10, 1863).
8. William C. Nell was a free born Bostonian who had served at one time as a journalist on the papers of both William Lloyd Garrison and Frederick Douglass. Before the war, he had gained some degree of fame from publication of *Colored Patriots of the American Revolution*. Charles Lenox Remond, a free born black man from Salem, Massachusetts, was a professional lecturer on the anti-slavery circuit. He joined men like William Wells Brown, who had been born into slavery in Lexington, Kentucky. After making his escape as a young man, Brown became an anti-slavery lecturer and a writer of some note. His book *The Black Man, His Antecedents, His Genius, and His Achievements* was published during the Civil War. John S. Rock was a bit of a renaissance man, having engaged at one time or another in the professions of medicine, dentistry, education, and the law. He was one of the most outspoken critics of Lincoln's colonization proposal and the president's handling of the slavery question in the early stages of the war.
9. James Mellon, ed., *Bullwhip Days: The Slaves Remember* (New York, 1990), p. 337; John Blassingame, ed., *Slave Testimony: Two Centuries of Letters, Speeches, Interviews, and Autobiographies* (Baton Rouge, 1977), pp. 616 and 618; James McPherson, *The Negro's Civil War*, p. 65.

10. On the changing relationship between master and slave, see "The Destruction of Slavery, 1861–1865" in Ira Berlin et al., *Slaves No More: Three Essays on Emancipation and the Civil War* (New York, 1992).

11. John Hope Franklin, *The Emancipation Proclamation* (Garden City, N.Y., 1963), pp. 92–93.

12. Benjamin Quarles, *The Negro in the Civil War* (New York, 1989), p. 165.

13. "The Great Event," *The Anglo-African* (January 3, 1863).

14. For discussion of the use of African-American laborers in the Confederacy, see Bell Wiley, *Southern Negroes: 1861–1865* (New York, 1953); and James Brewer, *The Confederate Negro: Virginia's Craftsmen and Military Laborers, 1861–1865* (Durham, 1969).

15. Ibid. The Tredeger Iron Works in Virginia, for example, employed more than 1,200 enslaved and free blacks during the war. See also Ervin L. Jordan Jr., *Black Confederates and Afro-Yankees in Civil War Virginia* (Charlottesville, 1995).

16. Quarles, *Lincoln and the Negro*, pp. 136–39; Franklin, *Emancipation Proclamation*.

17. "Remarks of O. P. Anderson," *The Anglo-African* (January 10, 1863).

18. "The Proclamation and a Negro Army, speech delivered at Cooper Institute, New York City, February, 1863," in Philip S. Foner, *The Life and Writings of Frederick Douglass*, 4 vols. (New York, 1950–55), vol. 3, pp. 321–27.

19. "The Great Event," *The Anglo-African* (January 3, 1863).

20. Ibid.

21. "The Great Emancipation Demonstration," *The Anglo-African* (January 10, 1863).

22. "The Present—and Its Duties," *The Anglo-African* (January 17, 1863).

23. Foner, *Life and Writings*, p. 335.

24. Ibid.

25. "Michigan State Convention," *The Anglo-African* (March 7, 1863).

26. "Speech of T. Morris Chester, Esq. of Liberia, In the Cooper Institute, New York, January 20, 1863," in *The Anglo-African* (February 7, 1863).

27. For discussion of the role of African-Americans in the war effort and in the demise of slavery, see Ira Berlin, *Slaves No More*. The issue of numbers escaping to the Union lines is mentioned in McPherson, *The Negro's Civil War*, p. 56.

28. B. A. Botkin, *Lay My Burden Down; A Folk History of Slavery* (Chicago, 1945), p. 240.

29. Quoted in Ira Berlin et al., *Free at Last: A Documentary History of Slavery, Freedom, and the Civil War* (New York, 1992), p. 349.

30. Ibid., p. 450.

31. Ibid., pp. 450–51.

32. Ibid.

33. "The Great Event," *The Anglo-African* (January 3, 1863).

Chapter 2: The Civil War in Kentucky

1. William E. Woodward, *Meet General Grant* (New York: H. Liverright, 1928), 237. Source cited by James M. McPherson, *The Negro's Civil War* (New York: Pantheon Book, 1965), viii.

2. Steven A. Channing, *Kentucky: A Bicentennial History* (New York: W. W. Norton and Co., 1977), cited by James M. McPherson, *The Negro's Civil War* (New York:

Pantheon Books, 1965), viii, 128. *New York Tribune,* May 3, 11, 1861. *Cincinnati Daily Commercial,* May 11, 1861.

3. Harry Smith, *Fifty Years of Slavery in the United States* (Grand Rapids, Michigan: West Michigan Publishing Co., 1891), 116–17. Chauncey H. Cook to Mother, May 23, 1863, "Letters From a Badger Boy in Blue," *Wisconsin Magazine of History,* 4 (1920–1921), 438.

4. Elijah P. Marrs, *The Life and History of the Reverend Elijah P. Marrs* (Louisville: Bradley and Gilbert, 1885), 16–17.

5. Allan Pinkerton, *Spy of the Rebellion, Being a True History of the Spy System of the United States Army* (New York: G. W. Carleton and Co., 1883), 187. Letitia P. Wallace, Nelson Furnace, Kentucky, April 1, 1861, Edmund T. Halsey Collection, Filson Club Historical Society.

6. "Waukegan," Chaplain, Ninth Illinois Regiment, Paducah, Ky., to T. M. Eddy, *Northwestern Christian Advocate* (Chicago), September 25, 1861. "W," Camp White, Paducah, Ky., to Mother, September 15, 1861, *The Kenosha Telegraph* (Kenosha, Wisconsin), September 26, 1861.

7. *Cincinnati Daily Gazette,* March 24, 1862.

8. William W. Blair to Children, December 24, 1861, Bardstown, Civil War Letters of Dr. W. W. Blair, Indiana Historical Society. "W" to Editor, Camp near Lexington, Ky., August 27, 1862, *Ashtabula Sentinel,* Jefferson, Ohio, September 3, 1862. Letter from a Soldier, 22nd Wisconsin Regiment, Camp Wells, Ky., October 14, 1862, *Beloit Journal and Courier,* October 30, 1862. "Bogandus" to Editor, 23rd Wisconsin Regiment, Paris, Ky., October 27, 1862, *Wisconsin State Journal,* Madison, Wisconsin, November 5, 1862.

9. William W. Blair to Children, December 24, 1861, Bardstown, Ky., Civil War Letters of Dr. William W. Blair, Indiana Historical Society. "Beta," Camp Haycraft, November 18, 1861, *Cincinnati Gazette,* November 23, 1861, "Justitia," to Editor, March 12, 1862, Twenty-Eighth Illinois Regiment, *The Schuyler Citizen,* Rushville, Illinois, March 26, 1862. T. J. Wright, *History of the Eighth Regiment Kentucky Volunteer Infantry* (St. Joseph, Missouri, 1880), 42. Chauncy Cook to Mother, April 10, 1863, "Letters of a Badger Boy in Blue," *Wisconsin Magazine of History,* 4 (1920–21), 332. B. F. Crary, Chaplain, 3rd. Minnesota Regiment, Fort Heiman, Ky., to Editor, May 6, 1863, *Northwestern Christian Advocate,* May 27, 1863.

10. "W.J.G.," Newport, Ky., to Editor, October 7, 1862, *The Portage County Democrat,* October 22, 1862. "Dode," Camp Clay, Ky., to Editor, November 2, 1862, *Cleveland Daily Plain Dealer,* November 7, 1862. For additional evidence that the Kentucky blacks understood the meaning and the course of the war as well as the whites, see "M.N.H.S.," Co. B., Fifth Indiana Cavalry, April 1863, to Isaac H. Julian, *The Indiana True Republican* (Centreville, Indiana), May 7, 1863, and "Carleton" to Editor, *Boston Journal,* cited by *Waukesha Freeman,* December 2, 1862.

11. "T" to Editor, Camp Wickliffe, Ky., January 12, 1862, *The Jeffersonian Democrat* (Chardon, Ohio), January 24, 1862. "Otheo" to Editor, Camp Nicholas, Ky., October 10, 1861, *The Religious Telegraph* (Dayton, Ohio), October 23, 1861. A soldier stationed at Newport, Ky., told of a conversation he had with three Kentucky slaves who told him that the blacks were on the point of raising a force to fight for their freedom, but more conservative minds advised them to wait a little because the army would grant them freedom. See "W.J.G.," October 7, 1862, *The Portage County Democrat,* October 22, 1862.

12. "Senor," Owensboro, Ky., November 13, 1861, *Louisville Daily Democrat,* November 17, 1861. *Frankfort Yeoman,* January 17, 1862, cited by *Cincinnati Daily Commercial,* January 18, 1862. See *The Louisville Daily Journal,* July 17, 1862, citing *Madison* (Indiana) *Courier* for a similar stampede from Ghent, Kentucky.

13. *Cincinnati Daily Commercial,* January 18, 1862, cited by *Frankfort Yeoman,* January 17, 1862.

14. Alfred Pirtle, "My Early Soldiering Days," pp. 6–7, Alfred Pirtle Manuscripts, Filson Club Historical Society. P. S. Fall to Betty Fall, February 26, 1862, Philip Slater Fall Manuscripts, Kentucky Historical Society, (Microfilm Copy). Colonel John Cook, Fort Holt, Ky., claimed that "almost if not all the officers employed free blacks from Illinois as servants." See John Cook to John A. Rawlins, Fort Holt, Ky., December 25, 1861, *War of the Rebellion: Official Records of the Union and Confederate Armies* (Washington: Government Printing Office, 1894), ser. 2, vol. 1, p. 795. Hereafter OR.

15. Agate," Nolin, Ky., Camp Haycraft, November 7, 1861; "Vale," November 20, 1861; "Xenophan," Paducah, Ky., December 17, 1861, *Cincinnati Daily Gazette,* November 9, 17, 23, 1861. "Invisible," Mumfordsville, Ky., January 10, 1862, *Daily Times* (Cincinnati), January 18, 1862.

16. "Ed. T. P." to Editor, Lebanon, Ky., September 2, 1862, *Cleveland Morning Leader,* September 8, 1862.

17. "Christian," Hopkinsville, Ky., to Editor, August 18, 1862, *Cincinnati Daily Times,* August 26, 1862. "Knox" to James Dumas, Editor, November 12, 1862, *Mahoning (Ohio) Register,* November 27, 1862. E. H. Bush, Chaplain, 49th. Ohio Regiment, Camp Wood, Greenbrier, Ky., January 17, 1862, *Cleveland Morning Leader,* January 22, 1862. Correspondence, Camp Mumsfordville, Ky., *Cincinnati Times,* cited by *Daily Zanesville Courier,* January 22, 1862.

18. N. B. Hull to Daughter, Kentucky River, Kentucky, 96th. Illinois Regiment, November 14, 1862. "Carleton" to Editor, *Boston Journal,* cited by *Waukesha Freeman* (Wisconsin), December 2, 1862. Peter Bruner, *A Slave's Adventures Toward Freedom: Not Fiction, But the True Story of a Struggle* (Oxford, Ohio: Peter Bruner), pp. 41, 42.

19. Narrative of Mrs. Mary Crane, Indiana Narratives. Slave Narratives: A Folk History of Slavery in the United States, 6, p. 10 (*The American Slave: A Composite Biography,* Westport, Conn., Greenwood Publishing Company, 1972.)

20. B. F. Crary to Editor Columbus, Ky., June 1863, *Northwestern Christian Advocate,* July 1, 1863.

21. *New York Daily Tribune,* April 4, 11, 23; May 6, 1863, citing *Frankfort Commonwealth. National Anti-Slavery Standard,* April 23, May 9, June 11, 1863. *Louisville Daily Journal,* May 7, 1863. Journal of the Senate of the General Assembly of Kentucky (1863), 849. Journal of the House (1863), 1009. Acts of the Commonwealth of Kentucky (1863), 362–64. J. T. Boyle to Selby Harney, December 9, 1862, Provost Marshall, Field Organization, Louisville, Letters Received, 1862–1865, Box No. 1, Record Group 393, National Archives.

22. Joseph Holt to E. M. Stanton, April 24, 1863; Stanton to A. E. Burnside, April 29, 1863, Record Group 94, Office of the Advocate General, Generals' Papers, National Archives.

23. Nashville Union, cited by *Grant County Witness* (Platteville, Wisconsin), November 19, 1863.

24. *Louisville Daily Journal,* August 3, 1863; February 23, March 1, 1864. *Congressional Globe,* 38th Cong., 1st Sess., 1863–1864, pt. 1, 333–334, 338, 516, 598, 599, 768, 836; pt. 4, Appendix 102.

25. George Parker to Commander, Dept. of Ky., November 20, 1864, Letters Received, Abstracts, Dept. of Ky., pt. 1, vol. 109, p. 356, Record Group, 393. W. H. Sidell to S. G. Burbridge, December 15, 1864, Provost Marshal, General, Ky., Letters sent, November, 1864 to September, 1866, vol. 23, pp. 117–18, Record Group 110, National Archives. "Humanitas," *New York Tribune,* correspondent, November 28, 1864, cited by *Louisville Daily Democrat,* December 6, 1864. Senate Executive Documents, 38th Congress, 2nd Session, No. 28, pp. 10–11.

26. "Humanitas," November 28, 1864, *New York Tribune,* cited by *Louisville Daily Democrat,* December 9, 1864. Affidavit of Joseph C. Miller, November 26, 1864, "A Colored Soldier," Camp Nelson, in *Louisville Daily Democrat,* December 9, 1864. *The Liberator,* December 9, 1864. T. E. Hall to Eluathan Davis, December 14, 1864, AMA Correspondence.

27. "Report of Kentucky, Commissioners of Investigation of Colored Refugees," Senate Executive Document, No. 28, 38th Cong., 2nd Sess., p. 21. John Fee to George Whipple, January 2, 1865, American Missionary Correspondence, Dillard University, "Affidavit of a Colored Soldier," Camp Nelson, Ky., November 26, 1864, Joseph Clark Miller, "Humanities" to Editor, *New York Tribune,* Camp Nelson, November 28, 1864, *Louisville Democrat,* December 9, 1864. *The Liberator,* December 9, 1864. John G. Fee to Editor, *Louisville Daily Press,* March 27, 1865; John Fee to Editor, *Louisville Daily Journal,* May 27, 1865.

28. T. E. Hall to Eluathan Davis, December 14, 1864, American Missionary Correspondence.

29. Letter from Anonymous Correspondent to Henry Wilson, in *The Liberator,* June 24, 1864, Henry Wilson, *History of the Rise and Fall of the Slave Power* (Boston: James R. Osgood and Co., 1877), 3:403.

30. J. S. Brisbin to T. E. Bramlette, April 20, 1865, *New York Daily Tribune,* May 1, 1865, General Orders, No. 6, May 1, 1865, Lorenzo Thomas, "The Negro in the Military Service of the U.S., 1865–1867," 6:3636, 3643–3644, National Archives (Microfilm Copy). James B. Fry to W. H. Sidell, May 8, 1865, Provost Marshal General, Bureau Record Group 110, National Archives.

31. *Ottawa Republican* (Illinois), June 6, 1863.

32. *Grant County Witness* (Platteville, Wisconsin), June 11, 1863.

33. J. S. Wheeler to Mattie Wheeler, January 13, 1865, Captain and Mrs. Leland Hathaway Papers, University of Kentucky. "Pontiac," Louisville, August 3, 1865, *National Anti-Slavery Standard,* August 12, 1865.

34. General Orders, No. 43, June 18, 1865, General John Palmer, in *Semi-Weekly Lexington Observer and Reporter,* June 28, 1865. *Louisville Daily Journal,* September 13, 1865.

35. *New York Times,* June 4, 1865. John Palmer, *Personal Recollections of John Palmer, The Story of an Earnest Life* (Cincinnati: Clarke Press, 1901), pp 240–42; 254. *Cincinnati Daily Gazette,* June 9, 1865. T. S. Bell to Joseph Holt, June 2, 1865, Joseph Holt Papers, John Palmer to Andrew Johnson, July 29, 1865, Letters Sent, February to December, 1865, vol. 1, p. 190, Dept. of Ky., Record Group 393, National Archives, John Palmer to Dave M. Payne, August 7, 1865, Letter Book of J. M. Palmer, p. 52. John J. Palmer Papers, Illinois Historical Society. *Cincinnati Daily Enquire,* August 3, 1865, *The Colored Tennessean* (Nashville) August 12, 1865.

36. Daily Frankfort Commonwealth, June 8, 1865. *Chicago Daily Tribune,* June 2, 8, 1865. U.S. Statutes, At Large, 13, 200. *Collected Works of Abraham Lincoln,* edited

by Roy P. Baster (New Brunswick, New Jersey: Rutgers University Press, 1953–55), 6:358.

37. See Victor B. Howard, "The Kentucky Press and the Black Suffrage Controversy, 1865–1872," *The Filson Club Historical Quarterly,* 47, No. 3 (July 1973). "The Kentucky Press and the Negro Testimony Controversy, 1866–1872," 71, No. 1, (January 1973).

38. Victor B. Howard, "Negro Politics and the Suffrage Question in Kentucky, 1866–1872," *The Register of the Kentucky Historical Society,* vol. 72, No. 2, April, 1974. "The Black Testimony Controversy in Kentucky, 1866–1872," *Journal of Negro History,* 58, No. 2 (April 1973). "The Struggle for Equal Education in Kentucky, 1866–1884," *Journal of Negro Education,* 46, No. 3 (Summer 1977).

Chapter 3. "Uncle Billy" Sherman Comes to Town

1. Mrs. Henry Taylor Journal, December 25, 1864, MS vol. 7, Phillips-Myers Papers, Southern Historical Collection, University of North Carolina, Chapel Hill, N.C.; James M. Simms, *The First Colored Baptist Church in North America* (1888; reprint ed., New York, 1969), 137. The Taylor journal has been published as Spencer B. King Jr., ed., "Fanny Cohen's Journal of Sherman's Occupation of Savannah," *Georgia Historical Quarterly* 41 (December 1957): 407–416.

2. Oliver O. Howard, *Autobiography of Oliver Otis Howard,* 2 vols. (New York, 1907), 2:189; December 23, 1864 , in *The War of the Rebellion: A Compilation of the Official Records of the Union and Confederate Armies,* 130 vols. (Washington, D.C., 1880–1901), ser. 1, vol. 44, p. 793 (hereinafter cited as *OR*).

3. E. P. Burton, *Diary of E. P. Burton, Surgeon,* December 11, 1864 (Des Moines, 1939), 47. See also Berrien M. Zettler, *War Stories and School-Day Incidents for the Children* (New York, 1912), 132–33; David P. Conyngham, *Sherman's March Through the South* (New York, 1865), 290; *New York Tribune,* December 30, 1864.

4. John M. Gould, *History of the First- Tenth- Twenty-ninth Maine Regiment* (Portland, Maine, 1871), 580; Charles C. Coffin, *Four Years of Fighting* (Boston, 1866), 416; Mrs. Jane Wallace Howard Diary, February 15, 1865, in Frances T. Howard, *In and Out of the Lines* (New York, 1905), 204–206.

5. Arnold to Mrs. Thomas D. Miller, March 18, 1865, in Richard H. Shyrock, ed., *Letters of Richard D. Arnold M.D.: 1808–1876* (Durham, N.C., 1929), 118; Mrs. William H. Stiles to William Stiles, March 2, 1865, Mackay-Stiles Papers, Series A, Southern Historical Collection; Charles Seton Henry Hardee, *Reminiscences of Old Savannah* (n.p., n.d.), 11–12. See also Thomas C. Clay to his mother, January 20, 1865, Clay Papers, Georgia Historical Society, Savannah Georgia: Mrs. H. J. Wayne to her mother, December 23, 1864, quoted in Clarence L. Mohr, *On the Threshold of Freedom: Masters and Slaves in Civil War Georgia* (Athens, Ga., 1986), 111.

6. Caroline A. N. Lamar to Charles A. L. Lamar, December 23–28, 1864, Charles Augustus Lafayette Lamar Family Papers, Georgia Department of Archives and History, Atlanta, Georgia.

7. Mrs. Henry Taylor Journal, December 30, 1864, MS vol. 7; George W. Nichols, *The Story of the Great March* (New York, 1866), 107.

8. Coffin, *Four Years in Fighting,* 431; Rebecca Mimms to Mrs. Barnsley, July 27, 1865, quoted in Alan Conway, *The Reconstruction of Georgia* (Minneapolis, Minn., 1966), 30; Maria M. B. Postell to son, February 28, 1865, in Mrs. Homer H.

Berger, contributor, "Sherman's Occupation of Savannah: Two Letters," *Georgia Historical Quarterly* 50 (March 1966): 112; George A. Mercer Diary, June 24, 1865, Southern Historical Collection; Mrs. G. J. Kollock to George J. Kollock Jr., June 25, 1865, in Susan M. Kollock, ed., "Letters of the Kollock and Allied Families, 1826–1884," *Georgia Historical Quarterly* 34 (December 1950): 318.

9. Arnold to Mrs. Thomas D. Miller, March 18, 1865, Arnold to Dr. George C. Shattuck, May 23, 1865, in Shyrock, *Letters of Richard D. Arnold*, 118, 121.

10. Mrs. Jane Wallace Howard Diary, February 15, 1865, in Howard, *In and Out of the Lines*, 205.

11. Quoted in Leon F. Litwack, *Been in the Storm So Long: The Aftermath of Slavery* (New York, 1979), 122; *OR*, January 6, 1865, ser. 1, 44:280; John T. Trowbridge, *The South: A Tour of Its Battlefields and Ruined Cities* (Hartford, Conn., 1866), 508; Lafayette McLaws to wife, December 24, 27, 1864, Lafayette McLaws Papers, Southern Historical Collection; *New York Times*, January 13, 1865.

12. Coffin, *Four Years of Fighting*, 417; Nichols, *Story of the Great March*, 103. See also Simms, *First Colored Baptist Church*, 137.

13. Coffin, *Four Years of Fighting*, 426, 428.

14. *OR*, February 2, 1865, ser. 1, vol. 47, pt. 2, p. 210; Mrs. Sarah A. Gordon to Nellie Gordon, February 3, [1865], Gordon Family Papers, Mrs. W. W. Gordon Series, Southern Historical Collection: Mrs. William H. Stiles to William Stiles, March 2, 1865, Mackay-Stiles Papers, Series A.

15. Middleton to George Lyman Appleton, June 7, 1865, Arnold-Appleton Papers, Southern Historical Collection: A. Porter to A. L. Alexander, August 17, 1865, Alexander-Hillhouse Papers, Southern Historical Collection: William Gordon to Nellie Gordon, May 30, 1865, Gordon Family Papers, Mrs. W. W. Gordon Series, Southern Historical Collection: William Gordon to Sarah A. Gordon, June 21, 1865, Gordon Family Papers, Georgia Historical Society, Savannah.

16. Rev. Wesley J. Gaines, *African Methodism in the South; or Twenty-Five Years of Freedom* (Atlanta, 1890), 5–6; Rev. A. W. Wayman, *My Recollections of African M.E. Ministers* (Philadelphia, 1881), 105–106; George A. Singleton, *The Romance of African Methodism* (New York, 1952), 102; Litwack, *Been in the Storm So Long*, 467.

17. Simms, *First Colored Baptist Church*, 141–42; *Savannah Daily Herald*, July 27, 1865.

18. Report of W. J. Richardson, January 2, 1865, enclosure to I.[?] P. W. to Brother Strieby, January 25, 1865, in American Missionary Association Manuscripts, Amistad Research Center, Dillard University, Tallahassee, Florida (hereinafter cited as AMA MSS); *Savannah Daily Herald*, March 20, 1865; Wayman, *Recollections*, 106. The slave mart interested a number of observers. See Trowbridge, *The South*, 510; James A. Padgett, ed., "With Sherman Through Georgia and the Carolinas: Letters of a Federal Soldier," *Georgia Historical Quarterly* 33 (March 1949); 64: Coffin, *Four Years of Fighting*, 435.

19. Whitelaw Reid, *After the War: A Southern Tour* (Cincinnati, Oh., 1966), 152; Magill to Secretaries A.M.A., February 6, June 10, 1965, AMA MSS; *OR*, May 6, 1865, ser. 1, vol. 47, pt. 3, p. 418. See also Haygood S. Bowden, *Two Hundred Years of Education* (Richmond, Va., 1932), 242–44.

20. *Savannah Daily Herald*, June 9, 1865; undated petition, [September 1865?], Andrew Johnson Papers, Duke University.

21. Magill to Secretaries A.M.A., February 3, 1865, AMA MSS; Reid, *After the War*, 142, 147.

22. *OR*, December 26, 24, 1864, ser. 1, 44:812, 802; *Savannah Daily Herald*, February 1, 1865; *New York Times*, January 15, 1865.

23. Mrs. Jane Wallace Howard Diary, December 27, 1864, March 12, 1865, in Howard, *In and Out of the Lines*, 186, 208–209; Ira Pettibone to William E. Whiting, February 22, 1865, AMA MSS; Mrs. G. J. Kollock to George J. Kollock Jr., June 25, 1865, in Kollock, "Letters of the Kollock and Allied Families," 34:318.

24. January 10, 1865, in Mary S. Jones and Mary J. Mallard, *Yankees A'Coming: One Months' Experiences During the Invasion of Liberty County, Georgia, 1864–1865*, ed. Haskell Monroe (Tuscaloosa, Ala., 1959), 75; Allen to parents, December 23, 1864, Edward S. Allen Papers, Southern Historical Collection: January 6, 1865, in John J. Hight, *History of the Fifty-Eighth Regiment of Indiana Volunteer Infantry* (Princeton, Ind., 1895), 452; testimony of Charles Jess, March 12, 1873, in Ira Berlin, ed., *Freedom: A Documentary History of Emancipation, 1861–1867*, 2 vols. (Cambridge, Mass. 1985), 1:143–46. See also W. B. Hazen, *A Narrative of Military Service* (Boston, 1885), 334–35.

25. William T. Sherman, *Memoirs of General W. T. Sherman*, 2 vols. (New York, 1875), 2:249; Nichols, *Story of the Great March*, 103; January 15, 1865, in M. A. DeWolfe Howe, ed., *Home Letters of General Sherman* (New York, 1909), 328.

26. *OR*, December 31, 1864, ser. 1, 44:841. For more of Sherman's views, see January 15, 1865, in Howe, *Home Letters*, 328; *OR*, January 12, 1865, ser. 1, vol. 47, pt. 2, pp. 36–37; ibid., December 30, 1864, 44:836.

27. Sherman, *Memoirs*, 2:249; Henry Hitchcock, *Marching with Sherman*, ed. M. A. DeWolfe Howe (New Haven, Conn., 1927), 202; December 25, 1864, in Howe, *Home Letters*, 319. See also Nichols, *Story of the Great March*, 101; *Savannah Daily Loyal Georgian*, December 26, 1864.

28. Reid, *After the War*, 143–45.

29. *OR*, January 12, 1865, ser. 1, vol. 47, pt. 2, pp. 37–41: L. E. Chittenden, *Personal Reminiscences* (New York, 1893), 268. See also Sherman, *Memoirs* 2:245–57; Howard, *Autobiography* 2:189–91; Simms, *First Colored Baptist Church*, 138, 261–62; Josef C. James, "Sherman at Savannah," *Journal of Negro History* 39 (April 1954): 127–37.

30. Luis F. Emilio, *A Brave Black Regiment: History of the Fifty-Fourth Regiment of the Massachusetts Volunteer Infantry, 1863–1865*, 2nd ed. (Boston, 1894), 286–87; Thomas Wentworth Higginson, *Army Life in a Black Regiment* (1869; reprint ed., Boston, 1926), 264–65. Sixty-seven black Savannahians joined the 33rd U.S.C.T. in the first few months of 1865. Mohr, *On the Threshold of Freedom*, 87.

31. John Middleton to George Lymen Appleton, June 7, 1865, Arnold-Appleton Papers; Gordon to Nellie Gordon, June 5, 1865, Gordon Family Papers, Mrs. W. W. Gordon Series, Southern Historical Collection; *Savannah Republican*, March 19, 1865.

32. For exceptions to this rule, see Mrs. Jane Wallace Howard Diary, March 13, 1865, in Howard, *In and Out of the Lines*, 211; *Savannah Daily Herald*, April 3, 4, 11, 1865. For an example of white southern exasperation at a black soldier's lack of obsequiousness, see Mrs. Georgia Conrad, *Reminiscences of a Southern Woman* (Hampton, Va., 1901), 25.

33. *Savannah Republican*, March 19, 1865; *Savannah Daily Herald*, April 11, 1865; Mrs. Jane Wallace Howard Diary, May 13, 1865, in Howard, *In and Out of the Lines*, 222; Lafayette McLaws to wife, December 27, 1864, Lafayette McLaws Papers.

34. James A. Connolly, *Three Years in the Army of the Cumberland*, ed. Paul M. Angle (Bloomington, Ind., 1959), 362; *New York Times*, January 15, 1865; Chittenden,

Personal Reminiscences, 261. See also Reid, *After the War,* 150; T. Conn Bryan, *Confederate Georgia* (Athens, Ga., 1953), 128.

35. Sidney Andrews, *The South Since the War* (Boston, 1866), 368; *New York Times,* January 14, 1865. On deaths among blacks in 1865 generally, see W. Duncan, *Tabulated Mortuary Record of the City of Savannah* (Savannah, Ga., 1870), 33. His figures for much of 1865 are very incomplete. See also Mrs. Wm. H. Stiles, March 2, 1865, Mackay-Stiles Papers, Series A; William W. Gordon to Nellie Gordon, June 5, 1865, Gordon Family Papers, Mrs W W Gordon Series, Southern Historical Collection; George A. Mercer Diary, June 11, 1865; Bryan, *Confederate Georgia,* 18. On hunger in and around the city, see Hight, *History of the Fifty-Eighth Regiment,* 452; Connolly, *Three Years in the Army of the Cumberland,* 360; *Savannah and Boston: Account of the Supplies Sent to Savannah* (Boston, 1865), 22: Edward Rhodes Paper, Georgia Historical Society.

36. For details on the relief expedition, see *New York Tribune,* January 7, 11, 13, 30, 1865; *New York Times,* January 15, 1865; Coffin, *Four Years of Fighting,* 406. An interesting thing happened when the ships, laden with provisions, arrived in Savannah. According to L. F. Chittenden, a delegation of local whites called on Colonel Amos Beckwith, Sherman's commissary officer, and asked that he send troops and wagons to unload and transport the cargo. Beckwith was enraged. "No! A hundred times no!" he replied. "What lazy, miserable curs slavery made of men! A few years more of it and you would have had a nigger to open your eyes in the morning and to work your jaws at breakfast. No. I'll see you damned first." The whites did, in fact, unload the steamer themselves—fittingly, wrote Chittenden, "to the song and chorus of a darkey." Chittenden, *Personal Reminiscences,* 256–58.

37. Coffin, *Four Years of Fighting,* 417; January 9, 1865, quoted in William S. McFeely, *Yankee Stepfather: General O. O. Howard and the Freedmen* (New York, 1968), 54.

38. Connolly, *Three Years in the Army of the Cumberland,* 367–68; *OR,* December 22, 1864, ser. 1, 44:787; *New York Times,* January 15, 1865. See also Willie Lee Rose, *Rehearsal for Reconstruction: The Port Royal Experiment* (New York, 1964), 320–22.

39. *OR,* January 12, 1865, ser. 1, vol. 47, pt. 2, pp. 39–40. The one exception was not from the local area. James Lynch, free-born in Baltimore, was in Savannah as a missionary. He would soon leave and go to Mississippi, where he would become secretary of state.

40. John Hope Franklin, ed., *The Civil War Diary of James T. Ayers* (Springfield, Ill., 1947), 78; *OR,* January 16, 1865, ser. 1, vol. 47, pt. 2, pp. 60–62. See also *Sherman Memoirs* 2:249–52; Howard, *Autobiography* 2:191–92.

41. *New York Tribune,* January 30, 1865.

42. Coffin, *Four Years of Fighting,* 419–23; *Savannah Daily Herald,* February 3, 1865; S. W. Magill to Secretaries A.M.A., February 3, 1865, AMA MSS: George W. Pepper, *Personal Recollections of Sherman's Campaigns* (Zanesville, Ohio, 1866), 290–91.

43. Coffin, *Four Years of Fighting,* 433–34.

44. Claude F. Oubre, *Forty Acres and a Mule: The Freedmen's Bureau and Black Land Ownership* (Baton Rouge, La., 1978), 47; Edward Magdol, *A Right to the Land: Essays on the Freedmen's Community* (Westport, Conn., 1977), 104–105; Coffin, *Four Years of Fighting,* 425. See also Russell Duncan, *Freedom's Shore: Tunis Campbell and the Georgia Freedmen* (Athens, Ga., 1986), 20.

45. For details on the government's repudiation of its promises, see Oubre, *Forty Acres and a Mule,* 18–71; Duncan, *Freedom's Shore,* 16–36; Rose, *Rehearsal for Reconstruction,*

328–77, esp. 330–32, 337–39, 349–52, 356–57, 374; McFeely, *Yankee Stepfather,* esp. pp. 93–106; Foner, *Reconstruction,* 159–64; Litwack, *Been in the Storm So Long,* 400–407; Dorothy Sterling, ed., *The Trouble They Seen: Black People Tell the Story of Reconstruction* (Garden City, N.Y., 1976), 29–77; Edwin D. Hoffman, "From Slavery to Self-Reliance," *Journal of Negro History* 41 (January 1956): 20–35; Manuel Gottlieb, "The Land Question in Georgia During Reconstruction," *Science and Society* 3 (Summer 1939): 364–77; La Wanda Cox, "The Promise of Land for the Freedmen," *Missouri Historical Review* 45 (December 1958): 413, 429–31.

46. Oubre, *Forty Acres and a Mule,* 69–70, 55, 42–43; Leases between various freedmen and J. F. Waring, January 1866, Joseph F. Waring Papers, Georgia Historical Society; Duncan, *Freedom's Shore,* 34; Sterling, *The Trouble They Seen,* 39–40.

47. Mrs. G. J. Kollock to G. J. Kollock Jr., June 25, 1865, in "Letters of the Kollock and Allied Families," 34:317–18; petition quoted in Oubre, *Forty Acres and a Mule,* 53–54 (brackets eliminated). See also Mary Ames, *From a New England Woman's Diary in Dixie in 1865* (Norwood, Mass., 1906) 95–103, 119–25.

48. *Savannah Daily Herald,* November 11, 1865; Register of Land Titles Issued to Freedmen, April-September 1865, in Records of the Assistant Commissioner for the State of Georgia, Bureau of Refugees, Freedmen, and Abandoned Lands, 1865–1869, Roll 36, microfilmed copy at Emory University, originals in Record Group 105, Records of the Bureau of Refugees, Freedmen, and Abandoned Lands, National Archives, Washington, D.C.; Oubre, *Forty Acres and a Mule,* 37.

Chapter 4: "We'll Hang Jeff Davis on the Sour Apple Tree"

1. Roger B. Taney to J. Mason Campbell, October 19, 1860, Benjamin C. Howard Papers, Maryland State Historical Society, Baltimore, Md.; Don E. Febrenbacher, "Roger B. Taney and the Sectional Crisis," *Journal of Southern History* 43 (November 1977): 556–57.

2. H. B. Jolly to Father, October 28, 1860, George H. S. Jordan Papers, Louisiana State Archives, Baton Rouge, La.

3. Arthur M. Schlesinger Jr., ed., *The Almanac of American History* (New York, 1983), 277–78.

4. James D. Richardson, ed., *A Compilation of the Messages and Papers of the Presidents* (New York, 1897), 3158.

5. James G. Blaine, *Twenty Years of Congress: From Lincoln to Garfield* (Norwich, Conn., 1884), 253.

6. Jefferson Davis, *Jefferson Davis Constitutionalist: His Letters, Papers and Speeches,* ed. Dunbar Rowland (Jackson, Miss., 1923), 5:30.

7. C. J. Mitchell to Jefferson Davis, April 27, 1861, Jefferson Davis Papers, Rice University, Houston, Tex.; Armstead L. Robinson, "In the Shadow of Old John Brown: Insurrection Anxiety and Confederate Mobilization, 1861–1863," *Journal of Negro History* 65 (Fall 1980): 279.

8. *Daily Picayune* (New Orleans), August 18, 1860; William W. White, "The Texas Slave Insurrection of 1860," *Southwestern Historical Quarterly* 52 (January 1949): 279–80.

9. *Daily Picayune,* May 8, 1861.

10. Herbert Aptheker, "Maroons within the Present Limits of the United States," *Maroon Societies: Rebel Slave Communities in the Americas,* ed. Richard Price (Baltimore, 1979), 164.

11. *Daily Picayune,* May 30, 1861; and Roger A, Fischer, "Racial Segregation in Ante Bellum New Orleans," *American Historical Review* 74 (February 1969): 936.

12. *Attakapas Register* (Franklin, La.), May 30, 1861.

13. Ibid., June 13 and 20, 1861.

14. State Auditor Journal G, 1 January 1860–31, December 1861, Louisiana State Archives, Baton Rouge, La.; I. Lynn Smith and Homer Hitt, "The Composition of the Population of Louisiana State Penitentiary, 1859, 1860, and 1861." *Southwestern Social Science Quarterly,* 20 (March 1940): 372.

15. Howard Hines to John Pettus, May 14, 1861; J. D. Davenport to John Pettus, May 14, 1861, Governor John J. Pettus Papers, Mississippi State Archives, Jackson, Miss.; Bell Irvin Wiley, *Southern Negroes 1861–1865* (London, 1965), 82.

16. 1861 Grand Jury Reports MSS, Clerk of Court's Office, Tensas Parish Courthouse, St. Joseph, La.; United States Bureau of the Census, *Population of the United States in 1860; Compiled from the Original Returns of the Eighth Census, Under the Direction of the Secretary of the Interior* (1864; Reprint, New York, 1990), 1:188–97.

17. For a complete investigation of these incidents see Winthrop D. Jordan's *Tumult and Silence at Second Creek: An Inquiry into a Civil War Slave Conspiracy* (Baton Rouge, 1993).

18. Testimony from a vigilante trial is a rather suspect form of documentation. The testimony is included here because of supporting accounts by two eyewitnesses, but the information should still receive critical consideration.

19. Lemuel P. Conner and Family Papers, 1861; William Minor Diary MS, September 25, 1861, Louisiana and Lower Mississippi Valley Collections, Louisiana State University Libraries, Baton Rouge, La.; Clement Eaton, *Freedom of Thought in the Old South* (Durham, N.C., 1940), 106–7.

20. Ibid., Conner Papers.

21. William Minor Diary MS, September 25, 1861.

22. Robinson, "In the Shadow," 286.

23. E. L. Roberts to Wife, December 18, 1861, Harrison-Roberts Family Papers, University of Virginia Libraries, Charlottesville, VA.

24. Charles Godfrey Leland, "Servile Insurrection," *The Knickerbocker* 58 (November 1861): 377–83.

25. William N. R. Beall to Earl Van Dorn, July 31, 1862, Earl Van Dorn Papers, Library of Congress, Washington, D.C.

26. *Herald* (New York), September 9, 1862; and William F. Messner, "Black Violence and White Response: Louisiana, 1862," *Journal of Southern History* 41(February 1975): 21.

27. Messner, "Black Violence," 22; J. Carlyle Sitterson, *The Cane Sugar Industry in the South, 1753–1950* (Lexington, KY, 1953), 209–10; and "A Louisiana Rebel" MS, August 4, 1862, New York Historical Society Library, New York, NY.

28. Benjamin F. Butler to Salmon P. Chase, July 10, 1862, Salmon P. Chase Papers, Pennsylvania Historical Society, Philadelphia, Pa.

29. Joseph Cephas Carroll, *Slave Insurrections in the United States, 1800–1865* (New York, 1968), 207.

30. Messner, "Black Violence," 24; James Parton, *General Butler in New Orleans: History of the Administration of the Department of the Gulf in the Year 1862* (New York, 1864), 518–19.

31. Messner, "Black Violence," 26–29; Mark M. Boatner III, *The Civil War Dictionary* (New York, 1988), 109–10, 650; Jefferson Davis to CSA Congress, August 18,

1862, *The War of the Rebellion: A Compilation of the Official Records of the Union and Confederate Armies,* ser. 4, vol. 2, (Washington, 1900), 53.

32. Stephen B. Oates, *With Malic Toward None: The Life of Abraham Lincoln* (New York, 1977), 317–23.

33. Robinson, "Shadow of Old John Brown," 293; Daniel Ruggles to Samuel Cooper, October 8, 1862, *War of the Rebellion,* ser. 1, vol. 15, 83.

34. *Journal of the Congress of the Confederate States of America* (Washington, 1904), 2:268; Everette B. Long and Barbara Long, *The Civil War Day by Day: An Almanac 1861–1865* (New York, 1971), 277–78.

35. *Times* (London), September 19, 1862.

36. Dunbar, *Jefferson Davis,* 5:352.

37. Count Mejan to Godfrey Weitzel, August 12, 1862, *War of the Rebellion,* ser. 1, vol. 15, 618–19.

38. Daniel Ruggles to Benjamin F. Butler, July 15, 1862, Confederate Imprints.

39. Robert R. Barrow, October 7, 1861, "Remarks on the Present War, the Objects of the Abolition Party," Confederate Imprints.

40. Kate Mason Rowland and Mrs. Morris L. Croxall, eds., *The Journal of Julia LeGrand: New Orleans, 1862–1863* (Richmond, VA, 1911), 58–59; Harvey Wish, "Slave Disloyalty Under the Confederacy," *Journal of Negro History* 23 (October 1938): 438–39; Eaton, *Freedom of Thought,* 106.

41. Dan T. Carter, "The Anatomy of Fear: The Christmas Day Insurrection Scare of 1865," *Journal of Southern History* 42 (August 1976): 359.

42. George H. Hepworth, *The Whip, Hoe and Sword or, The Gulf-Department in '63,* ed. Joe Gray Taylor (Baton Rouge, La., 1979), 158–59.

43. C. Peter Ripley, *Slaves and Freedmen in Civil War Louisiana* (Baton Rouge, La., 1976), 18–19.

44. Ripley, *Slaves and Freedmen,* 98–99; David C. Edmonds, *The Conduct of Federal Troops in Louisiana During the Invasions of 1863 and 1864* (Lafayette, La., 1988), 201.

45. *An Ordinance Organizing and Establishing Patrols for the Police of Slaves in the Parish of St. Landry* (Opelousas, La., 1863), 2–29.

46. James A. Seddon to Thomas O. Moore, July 18, 1863, Lyon G. Tyler and S. A. Ashe, "Secession, Insurrection of the Negroes, and Northern Incendiarism," *Tyler's Quarterly Historical and Genealogical Magazine* (July 1933): 12–13; and G. P. Whittington, "Concerning the Loyalty of Slaves in Northern Louisana in 1863: Letters from John H. Ransdell to Governor Thomas O. Moore, dated 1863." *Louisiana Historical Quarterly* 14 (October 1931), 491.

47. Walter Lord, ed., *The Fremantle Diary—Being the Journal of Lieutenant Colonel James Arthur Lyon Fremantle, Coldstream Guards, on his Three Months in the Southern States* (Boston, 1954), 72.

48. Nannie E. Case to Pet, April 1864, Albert A. Batchelor Papers, Louisiana and Lower Mississippi Valley Collections, Louisiana State University Libraries, Baton Rouge, La.; Wish, "Slave Disloyalty," 441, 444–45; and C. L. R. James, *A History of Negro Revolt* (New York, 1938), 30–31.

49. George P. Rawick, ed. *From Sunup to Sundown: The Making of the Black Community,* vol. 1 of *The American Slave: A Composite Autobiography* (Westport, Conn., 1972), 95; and Frantz Fanon, *The Wretched of the Earth: The Handbook for the Black Revolution that is Changing the Shape of the World* (New York, 1968), 52–53.

Chapter 5: Emancipation in Missouri

1. Three modern studies of reconstruction which emphasize black participation are Kenneth M. Stampp, *The Era of Reconstruction* (New York: Alfred A. Knopf, 1965); Leon Litwack, *Been in the Storm So Long: The Aftermath of Slavery* (New York: Alfred A. Knopf, 1979); and Eric Foner, *Nothing But Freedom: Emancipation and Its Legacy* (Baton Rouge: Louisiana State University Press, 1983.)

2. The most complete general studies of blacks in the Civil War are Benjamin Quarles, *The Negro in the Civil War* (Boston: Little Brown, 1953); Dudley T. Cornish, *The Sable Arm: Negro Troops in the Union Army, 1861–1865,* 2nd ed. (New York: W. W. Norton, 1966); James M. McPherson, *The Negro's Civil War* (New York: Pantheon, 1965); McPherson, *The Struggle for Equality: Abolitionists and the Negro in the Civil War and Reconstruction* (Princeton: Princeton University Press, 1964), 192–220; and Ira Berlin et al., eds., *Freedom: A Documentary History of Emancipation, Series 2, The Black Military Experience* (Cambridge, England: Cambridge University Press, 1982).

3. Walter H. Ryle, *Missouri: Union or Secession* (Nashville: George Peabody College for Teachers, 1931), 3. Ryle's study is the most comprehensive political, social and economic analysis of Missouri in the period leading up to the Civil War. Also see William E. Parrish, *A History of Missouri, Volume 3: 1860–1875* (Columbia: University of Missouri Press, 1971); Parrish, *Turbulent Partnership: Missouri and the Union, 1861–1865* (Columbia: University of Missouri Press, 1963; Arthur R. Kirkpatrick, "Missouri on the Eve of the Civil War," *Missouri Historical Review* 55 (January 1961): 99–108; and Robert E. Shalhope, "Eugene Genovese, the Missouri Elite, and Civil War Historiography," *Bulletin of the Missouri Historical Society* 26 (July 1970): 271–282.

4. *Eighth Census of the United States, 1860: Population* (Washington, D.C.: Government Printing Office, 1864), 3:301.

5. See James F. Hopkins, *A History of the Hemp Industry in Kentucky* (Lexington: University of Kentucky Press, 1951); Miles W. Eaton, "The Development and Later Decline of the Hemp Industry in Missouri," *Missouri Historical Review* 43 (July 1949): 346–367.

6. *Eighth Census of the United States, 1860: Agriculture* (Washington D.C.: Government Printing Office, 1864), 2:234. Slavery in Missouri is analyzed in Robert W. Duffner, "Slavery in Missouri River Counties, 1810–1865" (Ph.D. dissertation, University of Missouri-Columbia, 1974); Harrison A. Trexler, *Slavery in Missouri, 1804–1865* (Baltimore: John Hopkins University Press, 1914); Philip V. Scarpino, "Slavery in Callaway County, Missouri: 1845–1855," *Missouri Historical Review* 71 (October 1976, April 1977): 22–43, 266–283; George R. Lee, "Slavery and Emancipation in Lewis County, Missouri," ibid., 65 (April 1971): 294–317; and James William McGettingan Jr., "Boone County Slaves: Sales, Estate Divisions and Families, 1820–1865," ibid., 72 (January and April 1978): 176–197, 271–295.

7. J. H. Ellis to Colonel ?, Chillicothe, 24 February 1863, Odon Guitar Papers, Joint Collection, University of Missouri Western Historical Manuscript Collection, Columbia and State Historical Society of Missouri Manuscripts.

8. See Abraham Lincoln to John C. Frémont, 2, 11, September 1861, in Roy P. Basler, ed., *The Collected Works of Abraham Lincoln* (New Brunswick: Rutgers University Press, 1953), 4:506–507, 517–518; and Andrew Rolle, *He Must Blaze a Nation: The Controversial John Charles Frémont* (Forthcoming), chap. 15.

9. Dan Holmes to his Parents, Kansas City, 15 November 1861, Daniel R. Holmes Collection, Chicago Historical Society; Quarles, *The Negro in the Civil War,* 20. Daniel Holmes did not approve of such independent abolitionism by army units if it were not official Union policy. "I don't fight under any other banner than the stars and stripes; if Col. Jennison pursues a course the government will not sanction I don't fight with him."

10. A. J. McRoberts to Molie, Saline County, 19 April 1863, A. J. McRoberts Papers, 1859–1876, Joint Collection, WHMC-SHS, Columbia.

11. Lt. Colonel A. Krekel to General John M. Schofield, St. Charles, 10 March 1862, U.S. War Department, *The War of the Rebellion: A Compilation of the Official Records of the Union and Confederate Armies,* 4 ser. 128 vols. (Washington, D.C: Government Printing Office, 1880–1902), ser. 1, vol. 8, 333.

12. Ephram J. Wilson to General Odon Guitar, near Palmyra, 27 July 1863, Odon Guitar Papers.

13. Stanley E. Lanthrop to his Parents, Wittsburg, Arkansas, 18 July 1862, Stanley E. Lanthrop Correspondence, State Historical Society of Wisconsin, Madison.

14. Charles E. Cunningham to Governor H. R. Gamble, Sedalia, 13 August 1862, Missouri Militia Papers, Manuscript Department, William R. Perkins Library, Duke University, Durham, North Carolina.

15. Court Martial of James Johnson, Jefferson City, 18 May 1863, Case MM 1021, Judge Advocate General—General Court Martial Records, Record Group 153, National Archives, Washington, D.C.

16. Mrs. J. R. Roberts to General James B. Long, Quincy, Illinois, 7 April 1864, Provost Marshal File, Letters Received 2786, Department of the Missouri Record Group 393, National Archives.

17. Entry for 25 February 1863, Forsyth, Missouri, Timothy Phillips Diary, State Historical Society of Wisconsin, Madison.

18. Entry for 22 May 1862, Dr. Joseph H. Trego Diary, Kansas State Historical Society, Topeka. On the deep-rooted Kansas-Missouri hatred see Michael Fellman, "Rehearsal for the Civil War: Antislavery and Proslavery at the Fighting Point in Kansas, 1854–1856," in Lewis Perry and Michael Fellman, eds., *Antislavery Reconsidered: New Perspectives on the Abolitionists* (Baton Rouge: Louisiana State University Press, 1979), 287–307.

19. Brigadier General James A. Pile to Major General William S. Rosecrans, St. Louis, 23 February 1864, Letters Received File 2593, Department of the Missouri Record Group 393.

20. Captain Louis F. Green to Alexander Calhoun, Independence, 14 February 1864, Odon Guitar Papers.

21. Entry for 6 March 1863, Timothy Phillips Diary.

22. James L. Morgan to James M. Nash, Glasgow, 30 July 1863, James Lorenzo Morgan Papers, The Southern Historical Collection, University of North Carolina Library. Chapel Hill, North Carolina.

23. Margaret J. Hayes to her Mother, Westport, 12 November 1861, Upton Hayes Papers, Kansas State Historical Society, Topeka.

24. J. B. Henderson to J. O. Broadhead, Louisiana, Missouri, 23 October 1862; R. C. Vaughan to Broadhead, Lexington, 3 May 1863, James O. Broadhead Papers, Missouri Historical Society, St. Louis.

25. "In the Matter of John Lemmel," Osage County, 28 January 1864, Provost Marshal File, Letters Received 2786, Department of the Missouri Record Group 393.

Subsequent events became complicated. The Osage County constable arrested John Lemmel, a white colleague of Jim, for shooting at Reynolds. The provost marshal of the county arrested Reynolds in return, claiming that Reynolds's sons, supporters, and the constable were a pack of Copperheads and returned rebels. The military disallowed a civil trial of Reynolds in part because they were sure Lemmel would be shot if he were to testify. It is not clear from the record if Reynolds ever was tried by a military tribunal. Civilian justice in this case supported the violent suppression of those ex-slaves whom the Union military supported because they were, after all, Colored Union soldiers.

26. Included in the letter to A. H. Lancaster to the Provost Marshal at Hannibal, New London, 16 March 1865, Letter Received File 2593, Department of the Missouri Record Group 393.

27. S. F. Aglar to General William S. Rosecrans, St. Louis, 17 November 1864, in ibid.

28. Deposition of Paris Bass, Callaway County, Two or More Name Citizen File 2637, Department of the Missouri Record Group 393.

29. Spottswood Rice to Kettey Diggs, St. Louis, 3 September 1864, enclosed in F. W. Diggs to General W. S. Rosecrans, 10 September 1864, Letters Received File 2593, Department of the Missouri Record Group 393, quoted in Berlin, *Freedom*, 690.

30. Dan Smith to his Parents, Boonville, 17 September 1861, Daniel R. Smith Papers, Illinois State Historical Library, Springfield.

31. Court martial of Fanny Houx, Warrensburg, 19 July 1864, Case NN 2733, Record Group 153.

Chapter 6: Being Free

1. Carter G. Woodson, *A Century of Negro Migration*, Washington, D.C., 1918.

2. Daniel M. Johnson and Rex R. Campbell, *Black Migration in America: A Social Demographic History*, Durham, N.C., 1981.

3. Johnson and Campbell, *Black Migration*, Ch. 4; Woodson, *Century of Migration*; Bell Irvin Wiley, *Southern Negroes, 1861–1865*, New Haven, 1938; Peter Kolchin, *First Freedom: The Responses of Alabama's Blacks to Emancipation and Reconstruction*, Westport, Conn., 1972; Nell Irwin Painter, *Exodusters: Black Migration to Kansas After Reconstruction*, New York, 1977.

4. Daniel Patrick Moynihan (now a U.S. Senator) was Assistant Secretary of Labor under Presidents Kennedy and Johnson and author of a report on the black family, U.S. Department of Labor, Office of Policy Planning and Research, *The Negro Family: The Case for National Action*, Washington, 1965. His argument that the deterioration of family structure, traceable to the slave experience, was largely responsible for the social pathology of the black community is also set out in his article "Employment, Income and the Ordeal of the Negro Family," *Daedalus*, 94, Fall, 1965, pp. 745–70. The controversy surrounding the publication of Moynihan's report is set out in Lee Rainwater and William L. Yancey, *The Moynihan Report and the Politics of Controversy*, Cambridge, Mass., 1967.

5. See, for example, John W. Blassingame, *The Slave Community: Plantation Life in the Antebellum South*, New York, 1972, George P. Rawick, *From Sundown to Sunup: The Making of the Black Community*, Westport, Conn., 1972; Eugene D. Genovese, *Roll, Jordan, Roll: The World the Slaves Made*, New York, 1974; and Leslie Howard Owens, *This Species of Property: Slave Life and Culture in the Old South*, New York, 1976.

6. David M. Katzman, *Before the Ghetto: Black Detroit in the Nineteenth Century,* Urbana, Ill., 1973; Kenneth L. Kusmer, *A Ghetto Takes Shape: Black Cleveland, 1870–1930,* Urbana, Ill., 1976; Elizabeth Hafkin Pleck, *Black Migration and Poverty: Boston 1865–1900,* New York, 1979.

7. Herbert G. Gutman, *The Black Family in Slavery and Freedom, 1750–1925,* New York, 1976; *Slavery to Freedom,* New York, 1977; Leon F. Litwack, *Been in the Storm So Long: The Aftermath of Slavery,* New York, 1979.

8. Litwack, *Been in the Storm,* p. xii.

9. Woodson, *Century of Migration,* pp. 117–20; Peter Kolchin, *First Freedom,* pp. xix, 4.

10. Richard L. Morrill and O. Fred Donaldson, "Geographical Perspectives on the History of Black America," *Economic Geography,* 48, January, 1972; pp. 1–23. On a regional basis Morrill and Donaldson estimated the following slave shift between 1820 and 1860:

Virginia, Maryland, Delaware	-230,000
North Carolina & South Carolina	-160,000
Georgia, Florida, Tennessee, & Kentucky	no change
Alabama, Louisiana & Mississippi	+180,000
Arkansas, Texas & Oklahoma	+150,000

   See also John Fraser Hart, "The Changing Distribution of the American Negro," *Annals of the Association of American Geographers,* 50, September, 1960, pp. 242–3. Several aspects of the northward migration are discussed in Woodson, *Century of Migration,* New York, 1970 ed., pp. 1–100.

11. Morrill and Donaldson, "Geographical Perspectives," pp. 5, 11. The black shift from 1860 to 1910 is estimated as follows:

Virginia, Maryland & Delaware	-200,000
North Carolina & South Carolina	-131,000
Georgia, Florida, Tennessee & Kentucky	-100,000
Alabama, Louisiana & Mississippi	-108,000
Arkansas, Texas & Oklahoma	+210,000.

12. Ibid., p. 11

13. Ibid.

14. Hart, "Changing Distribution," pp. 234–4.

15. Although there is some evidence that the normal positive relationship that exists between distance of migration and income level of migrants is less of a barrier to the movement of disadvantaged minority groups, like blacks, in the mid-twentieth century United States, the resources available to former slaves after the war and black migrants today cannot be compared. Arnold M. Rose, "Distance Migration and Socio-Economic Status of Migrants," *American Sociological Review,* 23, August, 1958, 420–3; Philip Nelson, "Migration, Real Income and Information," *Journal of Regional Science,* 1, Spring, 1959, 43–78, p. 58.

16. Everett S. Lee, "A Theory of Migration," *Demography,* 3, 1966, pp. 47–57.

17. Nelson, "Migration . . . and Information," pp. 49, 57; Leonard Blumberg and Robert R. Bell, "Urban Migration and Kinship Ties," *Social Problems,* 6, Spring, 1959; 328–33, p. 330; Clyde V. Kiser, *Sea Island to City: A Study of St. Helena Islanders in Harlem and Other Urban Centres,* New York, 1952, p. 194; Morton Rubin, "Migration Patterns of Negroes from a Rural Northeastern Mississippi Community," *Social Forces,* 39, October, 1960, 59–66, p. 65.

18. *The Freedmen's Record,* 1, October, 1865, p. 161: Col. Fullerton. Supt. Washington, to Brt. Brig. Gen. C. H. Howard, Asst. Commissioner, D.C., February 6, 1866, Bureau of Refugees Freedmen and Abandoned Lands, Assistant Commissioner for the District of Columbia, National Archives, Washington, D.C., Record Group 105, Letters Sent, vol. 6, p. 209, No. 44; Mrs Griffing, Visiting Agent, Report on Activities of the National Freedmen's Relief Assn., D.C., October 20, 1866, BRFAL, D.C., Letters Received, Box 3, vol. 2, No. 44.

19. The largest growth rates were found in the states of the old Northwest—Wisconsin, Michigan, Iowa, Illinois, Indiana and Ohio. While the rate of increase in those states is exaggerated by the relatively small number of persons involved, it does suggest a changing distribution of the black population. In 1860 areas north of the Ohio River contained 982,444 blacks (22.1 percent of the national total). In ten years that number grew by 26.5 percent to 1,242,456 and more than a quarter of the national total. All figures computed from information in U.S. Secretary of the Interior, *Ninth Census of the United States,* Washington, D.C., 1872–1874, vol. 1, *The Statistics of the Population of the United States,* Washington, D.C., 1872, p. 5.

20. Lee, "Theory of Migration," p. 47.

21. The western counties of Virginia, not shown in Map 2, mostly experienced an increase in the number of blacks between 1860 and 1870.

22. The counties and their respective cities were:

Counties	Cities
Norfolk, Princess Anne & Elizabeth City	Norfolk, Portsmouth
Henrico	Richmond
Baltimore, Baltimore City	Baltimore
Alexandria, Fairfax & D.C	Washington, Georgetown & Alexandria

23. The population of the area declined from 734,354 in 1860 to 731,636 in 1870. Secretary of the Interior, *Ninth Census, Statistics of the Population,* pp. 97, 163, 278–81.

24. The largest of these collections is the multi volume work edited by George P. Rawick under the title *The American Slave: A Composite Biography,* Westport, Conn., 1972. Virginian narratives not included in Rawick's collection have been published as Charles L. Perdue Jr., Thomas E. Barden and Robert K. Phillips, eds., *Weevils in the Flour: Interviews with Virginia Ex-Slaves,* Charlottesville, Va., 1976.

25. Litwack, *Been in the Storm,* esp. chap. 6; Paul D. Escott, *Slavery Remembered: A Record of Twentieth-Century Slave Narratives,* Chapel Hill, N.C., 1979. The reliability and limitations of slave sources have been the subject of considerable discussion. Among the better guides to the effective use of slave narratives and interviews conducted with former slaves in the 1930s are Eugene Genovese, "Getting to Know the Slaves," *New York Review of Books,* September 21, 1972; John Blassingame, "Using the Testimony of Ex-Slaves: Approaches and Problems," *Journal of Southern History,* 41, 4, November, 1975, pp. 473–92; C. Vann Woodward, "History from Slave Sources," *American Historical Review,* 79, 2 April, 1974, pp. 470–92; David Thomas Bailey, "A Divided Prism: Two Sources of Black Testimony on Slavery," *Journal of Southern History,* 46:3, August, 1980, pp. 381–404; and Escott, *Slavery Remembered,* pp. 3–17.

26. Ibid., p. 297.

27. The determination to reunite families split by slavery or war was a particularly strong motive as evidenced by the amount of time expended by Freedmen's Bureau officials

In trying to trace family members, particularly in the first year of existence. The *Freed-men's Record,* 1 October, 1865, p. 161; S. J. Bowen, President National Freedmen's Relief Association, "Report, January 30, 1866," Bureau of Refugees, Freedmen and Abandoned Lands, National Archives, Washington, D.C., Record Group 105, Letters Received, Box 1, vol. 1, No. 641. See also Table 1 below.

28. Litwack, *Been in the Storm,* p. 311.
29. Ibid.
30. Purdue et al., *Weevils in the Flour,* p. 268.
31. Escott, *Slavery Remembered.*
32. Escott, *Slavery Remembered,* p. 138.
33. Litwack, *Been in the Storm,* p. 226.
34. Ibid., p. 273.
35. Unfortunately there are limitations in any case study. For example, the migration to Washington, while rich in statistical evidence, is not so well represented in the sources used by Escott and Litwack.
36. The data in Figure 1 is presented on a semi-log scale to enable comparison of the rates of increase for the different components of the city's population. Populations with the same rate of growth, despite differences in the size of the populations concerned, will have parallel gradients on the graph.
37. "Census Returns of the Black Population of the District of Columbia, Alexandria, Freedmen's Village and Loudon and Fairfax Counties, Virginia," Bureau of Refugees, Freedmen and Abandoned Lands, Assistant Commissioner for the District of Columbia, National Archives, Washington, D.C., Record group 105, Miscellaneous Box 16, Item 494. An estimate of the number of freedmen in the District of Columbia in the care of the Bureau put that figure at 25,748, Washington *Evening Star,* September 2, 1865.
38. "Census of the District of Columbia, November 11, 1867," U.S. Congress, House, Special Report of the Commissioner of Education on the Condition and Improvement of Public Schools in the District of Columbia, H. Exec. Doc. 315, 41st Cong., 2nd sess., 1871; *Statistics of the Population,* 1870, p. 97.
39. "Census of the District of Columbia, 1867."
40. In all there are records for more than eleven thousand black refugees who passed through camps in the Washington area. Each new arrival was registered by the officer on duty who recorded information on his or her age, sex, marital status and place of origin. Unfortunately, some officers were less diligent than others in recording information and so the evidence available varies from time to time and from camp to camp. The camp registers do, however, provide a valuable record, particularly for the period between January 1863 and September 1864. The history of the camps is set out in Gladys Marie Fry, The Activities of the Freedmen's Aid Societies in the District of Columbia, 1860–1870, M.A. Thesis, Howard University, 1954 and Felix James, Freedmen's Village, Arlington, Virginia: A History, M.A. Thesis, Howard University, 1967. See also the author's Surviving Freedom: The Black Community of Washington, D.C., 1860–1880, Ph.D. Thesis, Duke University, 1980, pp. 187–7. The term "contraband" was applied to the refugees by General Benjamin F. Butler, commander of Fort Monroe in southern Virginia, who, faced with an influx of slaves from the surrounding countryside into his camp and lacking official guidance, hit on the idea of treating slaves as he would any other property of rebel Southerners—contraband of war. Benjamin F. Butler to Lt. Gen. Winfield Scott, May 24, 1861, U.S. Depart-

ment of War, *The War of the Rebellion: A Compilation of the Official Records of the Union and Confederate Armies,* ser. 2, vol. 1, p. 752.

41. "Register of Freedmen at Camp Barker, D.C." (Cover title: "Lists of Contrabands, Contraband Camp, Va.") Bureau of Refugees, Freedmen and Abandoned Lands, Assistant Commissioner for the District of Columbia, National Archives, Washington, D.C., Record Group 105, vol. 101, Item 570, p. 184.

42. It seems most likely that the arrivals from La Vache were returning from one of the failed Haitian immigration schemes set up to attract free black emigrants from the United States. Those schemes are analyzed in some detail in Christopher Dixon, Antebellum Schemes of Black Emigration from the United States with Particular Reference to Haiti, MA Thesis, University of Western Australia, 1986.

43. A detailed analysis of the evolution of these policies is contained in the authors "Surviving Freedom," chap. 4.

44. Everett S. Lee, "A Theory of Migration," *Demography,* 3, February, 1966, p. 50.

45. For a fuller discussion of this point see Johnston, Surviving Freedom, chap. 4.

46. Information on age and gender was only recorded in camp records spasmodically. The analysis here is based on the records of Camp Barker for the period from June 1862 to December 1863. For that period the register contains information on the "condition of life" of the arrivals. Individuals were listed either as married men or women, single men or women, widows or widowers, or children. "Register of Freedmen at Camp Barker, D.C."

Chapter 7: Nashville's Fort Negley

1. Stanley F. Horn, "Nashville During the Civil War," *Tennessee Historical Quarterly,* 4 (1945), 3–22.

2. J. F. Gilmer to Lt. Colonel W. W. Mackall, Bowling Green, Kentucky, December 7, 1861, *The War of the Rebellion: A Compilation of the Official Records of the Union and Confederate Armies,* ser. 1, vol. 52, pt. 2 (Washington, 1898), 233.

3. H. W. Crew, ed., *History of Nashville* (Nashville, 1890), 101–02.

4. Doug King, ed., *Nashville City Directory,* 1865 (Nashville, 1865), 1–10.

5. Stanley F. Horn, *The Army of Tennessee: A Military History* (Indianapolis, Indiana, 1941, 1952), 394–411.

6. *War of the Rebellion,* ser. 1, vol. 27, pt. 2, 268; Mark M. Boatner, *The Civil War Dictionary* (New York, 1959), 571; Morton authored several books on fortifications; Paul M. Angle, ed., *Three Years in the Army of the Cumberland: The Letters and Diary of Major James A. Connolly* (Bloomington, Indiana, 1959), 37–39; Thomas Jordan and J. P. Pryor, *The Campaigns of Lieut.-Gen. N. B. Forrest* (Dayton, Ohio, 1973), 179.

7. *Annals of the Army of the Cumberland* (Philadelphia, 1864), 181–91: Mead Holmes, *A Soldier of the Cumberland: Memoirs of Mead Holmes Jr., Sergeant for Company K, 21st Regiment, Wisconsin Volunteers* (Boston, 1952); Fred A. Shannon, *The Organization and Administration of the Union Army, 1861–1865,* 2 vols. (Cleveland, Ohio, 1928); Thomas Van Horne, *History of the Army of the Cumberland: Its Organization, Campaigns, and Battles* (Cincinnati, Ohio, 1875). Note: the Corps of Engineers and the Corps of Topographical Engineers merged as the Corps of Engineers. The Engineering Department and the Pioneer Corps made heavy use of hired and impressed black labor.

8. Buell to Morton, Kentucky, August 6, 1862, and Morton to Col. J. B. Fry, Nashville, August 13, 1862, *War of the Rebellion,* ser. 1, vol. 26, pt. 2, 326–27.

9. Jordan, *The Campaigns of Lieut.-Gen. N. B. Forrest;* Frederick A. Dyer, ed., *A Compendium of the War of the Rebellion: Numbers and Organization of the Armies of the United States,* 3 vols. (New York, 1959).

10. Nashville *Dispatch,* and Nashville *Daily Union,* August 13, 1862.

11. Nashville *Daily Union,* October 18, 1862.

12. Buell to Morton, Kentucky, August 20, 29, 1862, *War of the Rebellion,* ser. 1, vol. 26, pt. 2, 408.

13. "Yanks in Nashville," in the Chattanooga *Rebel,* October 12, 1862, quoted by the *Daily Union,* October 18, 1862. The Union Army recognized the claims of area citizens for properties destroyed by the Federal Army—see Report on Nashville Defenses, *War of the Rebellion,* ser. 1, vol. 49, pt. 3, 197.

14. *Annals of the Army of the Cumberland,* 194, includes a sketch of the Negroes leaping from the church windows; *The Official Atlas of the Civil War* (New York, 1958), plate 134, contains an illustration of blacks working on Fort Negley, as reported in the *War of the Rebellion,* ser. 1, vol. 49, pt. 3, October 15, 1862.

15. Slave testimony, George P. Radwick, ed., *The American Slave: A Composite Autobiography, God Struck Me Dead: Religious Conversion Experiences of Ex-Slaves,* vol. 18 by Fisk University's Social Sciences Division (Westport, Ct., 1941, 1975), 121–25; Mechal Sobel, "'They Can Never Both Prosper Together': Black and White Baptists in Antebellum Nashville, Tennessee," *Tennessee Historical Quarterly,* 38 (1979), 296–307; Federal Writers Project, Works Progress Administration, Tennessee Slave Narratives in Radwick, ed., *The American Slave,* vol. 16, pp. 3, 68.

16. *War of the Rebellion,* ser. 1, vol. 49, pt. 3, 196–98. The October 15, 1862, report by Chief Inspector of Fortifications, General Z. B. Tower, does not mention a secret tunnel; however, local rumor has it that Fort Negley had a secret tunnel that permitted Union soldiers to emerge from the Old City Cemetery just east of the fort. A recent (1980) engineering report did not confirm the existence of a tunnel but did not rule it out; archaeologists will have to have the final word.

17. *The Photographic History of the Civil War,* 10 vols. (New York, 1957), vol. 3, 266–70 and 248–58 contain illustrations and actual photos of Fort Negley in 1864 and just prior to the Battle of Nashville.

18. Louise Davis, "Box Seat on the Civil War: Rachel Carter's Diary," *The Tennessean Magazine,* Nashville, April 1979, 6–11.

19. "Box Seat on the Civil War," 6–11; Nashville *Banner,* December 16, 1961; Juanita Gaston and Samuel Shannon, *Cameron-Trimble Neighborhood Project: A Pictorial Guide* (Nashville, 1979), 1–10.

20. Nashville *Daily Union,* August 10, 1862.

21. Nashville *Dispatch,* February 27, 1863.

22. This camp was between Church and Demonbreum streets. Benjamin "Pap" Singleton held his organizational meetings for the Black Exodus to Kansas in the former Edgefield contraband camp between 1877 and 1879. A housing project and interstate highways occupy the Edgefield site. Urban renewal also cleaned the blacks out of "Black Bottom," the Crawford Street area and the Church/Demonbreum area. Some moved into the Napier and Taylor housing projects.

23. Slave testimony, Radwick, ed., *The American Slave,* vol. 19, *Unwritten History of Slavery,* by Fisk University pp. 128–29.

24. Peter Maslowski, *Treason Made Odious: Military Occupation and Wartime Reconstruction in Nashville, 1861–1865* (Milwood, Illinois, 1978), 100–12; Porter Nimrod Diary and Notebook, 1861–1898, Southern Historical Collection, University of North Carolina, Tennessee State Library and Archives, Manuscripts Division, Nashville.

25. *Banner,* December 16, 1862.

26. *Annals of the Army of the Cumberland,* 620–33.

27. Metro Historical Commission, Application to the National Historic Register, February 21, 1975, Nashville; *Fort Negley: A Study for the Metropolitan Historical Commission* (Nashville, 1980), A-1.

28. *Three Years in the Army of the Cumberland,* 37–39; Frank L. Byrne, ed., *The View From Headquarters: Civil War Letters of Harvey Reid* (Madison, Wisconsin, 1965), 121–26; *Photographic History of the Civil War,* 248, has a photo of a battery manning the fort; *Southern Battlefields: On and Near the Lines of the Nashville, Chattanooga and St. Louis Railroad* (Nashville, 1956); Federal Writers' Project, WPA, *Tennessee Forts and Fortresses,* Della Yoe, "Fort Negley," (Nashville, 1940), TSLA, MD; Bruce Grant, *American Forts Yesterday and Today* (New York, 1965), 58; Federal Writers Project, WPA, *Tennessee, A Guide to the State* (New York, 1939); Harold L. Peterson, *Forts in America* (New York, 1964), 1–25.

29. *The View From Headquarters,* 121–26; Susan K. Parman, "The Battle of Nashville," M.A. thesis, George Peabody College for Teachers, 1932.

30. Slave testimony, *God Struck Me Dead,* 116. It is likely that nearly 2,000 blacks served in the Confederate Army of Tennessee as laborers and personal servants to officers. Some of the black Confederates received state pensions as a result of the 1906 Confederate Pension Act being amended in 1921 to include former black servants. Nearly 300 Colored Men's Pension Applications are filed at the TSLA, Nashville. However, Thomas' Union Army of the Cumberland used thousands of black laborers as part of his Quartermaster Corps, Engineering Corps, Pioneer Corps, Medical Department, and Subsistence Department. For this reason, Thomas was able to place a huge number of soldiers in the battle itself. It is likely that Union blacks and Confederate blacks made some abrasive contact during the Battle of Nashville.

31. The Negro in the Military Service of the U.S., 1630–1866, NARS, Washington; Compiled Service Records of Military Units in Union Organizations: U.S. Colored Troops, Tennessee, part of Record Group 94, NARS; Bobby L. Lovett, "The Negro's Civil War in Tennessee, 1861–1865," *Journal of Negro History,* 59 (1976), 31–50; Dudley T. Cornish, *The Sable Arm: The Negro in the Union Army, 1861–1865* (New York, 1956), 248–49; George Washington Williams, *A History of the Negro Troops in the War of the Rebellion, 1861–65* (New York, 1888, 1968), 273–90.

32. *Special Orders No. 301,* Department of the Cumberland, Nashville, November 10, 1863, Adjutant General's Office, RG 21, TSLA; *War of the Rebellion,* ser. 1, vol. 31, pt. 3 (Washington, 1890).

33. *General Orders No. 43,* Department of the Cumberland, Nashville, November 1, 1864, Adjutant General's Office, RG 21; "The Negro's Civil War in Tennessee," 31–50.

34. Tower to Thomas, Nashville, November 1, 1864, *War of the Rebellion,* ser. 1, vol. 49, pt. 3, 755–81; William Waller, *Nashville in the 1890s* (Nashville, 1970) contains a map showing the approximate positions of the old forts; Thomas to Gen.

Rousseau, Chattanooga, January 31, 1864, *War of the Rebellion,* ser. 1, vol. 33, pt. 3 (Washington, 1891), 203.

35. Tower's 1865 Report, *War of the Rebellion,* vol. 49.

36. Samuel R. Watkins, *Maury County Grays: First Tennessee Regiment, C.S.A.* (Nashville, 1882), 225; J. F. C. Fuller, *Decisive Battles of the U.S.A.* (New York, 1942), 292–323; *The Army of Tennessee,* 394–411; S. F. Horn, *The Decisive Battle of Nashville* (Baton Rouge, 1966); William J. McMurray, *History of the Twentieth Tennessee Regiment Volunteer Infantry, C.S.A.* (Nashville, 1904), 329; *History of Nashville,* 198–201.

37. Slave testimony, *God Struck Me Dead,* 116.

38. Slave testimony, Unwritten History of Slavery, 121; Battles of the Civil War: A Pictorial Presentation, 1861–1865 (New York, 1960), includes a color illustration of Thomas' black troops attacking the Confederate positions on Overton Hill (Peach Orchard Hill), December 16, 1864, where the blacks suffered greatly; however, the Negro troops took the hill. A Metro Historical Commission marker designates the site near the corner of Harding Place and Franklin Road.

39. "Fort Negley," 1–2, by Yoe is brief but informative.

40. "Fort Negley," 1–2; see also: Directory of WPA Manuscripts, TSLA.

41. Photos of Fort Negley Restoration, Department of Conservation Photographs, TSLA.

42. Application, Metro Historical Commission.

43. *Fort Negley: A Study,* Metro Historical Commission, 1980.

Chapter 8: Black Violence and White Response

1. See George M. Fredrickson, *The Black Image in the White Mind: The Debate on Afro-American Character and Destiny, 1817–1914* (New York and other cities, 1971) for a discussion of racial imagery in nineteenth-century America.

2. Extended discussions of contraband programs in Louisiana can be found in Louis S. Gerteis, "From Contraband to Freedmen: Federal Policy Toward Southern Blacks, 1861–1865" (unpublished Ph.D. dissertation, University of Wisconsin, 1969); J. Thomas May, "Continuity and Change in the Labor Program of the Union Army and the Freedmen's Bureau," *Civil War History,* 17 (September, 1971), 245–54; and William F. Messner, "The Federal Army and Blacks in the Gulf Department, 1862–1865" (unpublished Ph.D. dissertation, University of Wisconsin, 1972). For a general treatment of black behavior during the war see Bell I. Wiley, *Southern Negroes, 1861–1865* (New Haven and London, 1938).

3. George H. Hepworth, *The Whip, Hoe, and Sword; or, The Gulf-Department in '63* (Boston, 1864), 151; Eliza McHatton-Ripley, *From Flag to Flag: A Woman's Adventures and Experiences in the South During the War, in Mexico, and in Cuba* (New York, 1889), 20–21.

4. Neal Dow, *The Reminiscences of Neal Dow* (Portland, Maine, 1898), 668–69.

5. Harrison Soule to his parents, May 8, 15, 1862. Harrison Soule Papers (Michigan Historical Collections, University of Michigan, Ann Arbor, Mich.); Frank D. Harding to his father, May 3, 1862, Eddy Harding Correspondence (State Historical Society of Wisconsin, Madison, Wis.); John W. DeForest, *A Volunteer's Adventures: A Union Captain's Record of the Civil War,* edited by James H. Croushore (New Haven and London, 1946), 17, 39–40; Dow, *Reminiscences,* 673–74.

6. O. W. Lull to Benjamin Butler, May 11, 1862, Benjamin F. Butler Papers (Manuscript Division, Library of Congress, Washington, D.C.).

7. *New York Times,* June 23, 1862.

8. John M. Stanyan, *A History of the Eighth Regiment of New Hampshire Volunteers* (Concord, N.H., 1892), 105–107.

9. De Have Norton to his parents, June 9, 1862, De Have Norton Correspondence (State Historical Society of Wisconsin).

10. *New York Times,* August 1, 1862.

11. Ibid., August 26, 1862.

12. *New York Herald,* September 9, 1862.

13. Quoted in J. Carlyle Sitterson, *Sugar Country: The Cane Sugar Industry in the South, 1753–1950* ([Lexington, Ky.], 1953), 209–10.

14. Ibid.; *New Orleans Daily Picayune,* October 11, 1862.

15. Throughout the summer of 1862 military headquarters in New Orleans received a constant stream of requests from planters for aid in controlling their slaves. *New York Times,* August 26, 1862; W. Mitthoff to Benjamin Butler, May 29, 1862, Benjamin F. Butler, *Private and Official Correspondence of Gen. Benjamin F. Butler During the Period of the Civil War* (5 vols., Norwood, Mass., 1917), 1:525–27, Polycarpe Fortier to Butler, June 4, 1862, ibid, 553–54.

16. *New Orleans Daily Picayune,* July 22, August 14, 1862.

17. MS diary of "A Louisiana Rebel" entry for August 4, 1862 (New York Historical Society; New York City).

18. Day and Night Police Reports, Third District, New Orleans Police Department (New Orleans Public Library, New Orleans, La.).

19. *New Orleans Daily Picayune,* August 22, 1862.

20. Ibid., July 22, 1862.

21. Although the boundaries of the Gulf Department shifted during the war with the fortunes of the Union army, for the purposes of this study the Gulf Department is defined to include those parishes in southern Louisiana which President Lincoln excluded from the operation of the Emancipation Proclamation. These parishes are St. Bernard, Plaquemines, Jefferson, St. John, St. Charles, St. James, Ascension, Assumption, Terrebonne, Lafourche, St. Mary, St. Martin, and Orleans.

22. Butler's contraband policy at Fort Monroe is discussed in Gerteis, "From Contraband to Freedmen," 14–31.

23. Butler to Edwin Stanton, June 29, 1862, Butler, *Private and Official Correspondence,* 2:13–16 (quotation on page 14).

24. Butler to Stanton, May 25, 1862, Butler Papers.

25. Butler to Chase, July 10, 1862, Salmon Portland Chase Papers (Historical Society of Pennsylvania, Philadelphia, Pa.).

26. Proclamation, May 1, 1862, Butler, *Private and Official Correspondence,* 1:433–36.

27. General Order No. 32, May 27, 1862; Special Order No. 45, May 27, 1862; General Order No. 44, June 21, 1862, *The War of the Rebellion: A Compilation of the Official Records of the Union and Confederate Armies* (70 vols. in 128, Washington, 1880–1901), ser. 1, vol. 15, 445–46, 492; cited hereafter as *OR.*

28. *New York Tribune,* August 13, 1862; *New Orleans Daily Picayune,* June 4, August 2, 1862; Police Reports, Third District, New Orleans Police Department. During the summer over one hundred slaves were arrested as "runaways" in the Third District of New Orleans alone. In addition, city police jailed slaves for "safekeeping" on the

request of their owners. Military authorities also permitted city jailers to whip insubordinate slaves and city newspapers to print notices of fugitive slaves. *New York Tribune,* August 5, 1862; *New Orleans Daily Picayune,* June 6, October 1, 1862; J.P.M. to Butler, July 18, 1862, Butler, *Private and Official Correspondence,* 2:84–86.

29. *New Orleans Daily Picayune,* May 13, 24, 29, 1862; *New York Times,* August 18, 1862; New York *National Anti-Slavery Standard,* August 30, 1862; R. Smith to Butler, May 21, 1862, Butler Papers; Harrison Soule to his parents, May 8, 1862, Soule Papers.

30. *New York Times,* August 6, 14, 1862; *New York Tribune,* August 2, 1862; New York *National Anti-Slavery Standard,* August 16, September 27, 1862; David D. Porter to Thomas T. Crave, June 24, 1862, *Official Records of the Union and Confederate Navies in the War of the Rebellion* (30 vols., Washington, 1894–1922), ser. 1., vol. 18, 571–72; Selim F. Woodworth to Porter, July 1, 1862, ibid., 664–66.

31. Phelps's ideas must be pieced together from his correspondence, essays, and diaries, John Wolcott Phelps Papers (New York Public Library, New York City). His first recorded public statement on slavery was made in December 1861 shortly after his arrival at Ship Island. James Parton, *General Butler in New Orleans* (New York, 1864), 198–200.

32. Phelps to R. S. Davis, June 16, 1862, *OR,* ser. 1, vol. 15, 486–90 (quotation on page 487). For a complete discussion of the Phelps-Butler controversy see Messner, "The Federal Army and Blacks in the Gulf Department," 30–38.

33. Phelps to R. S. Davis, July 30, 1862, *OR,* ser. 1, vol. 15, 534–35.

34. Butler to his wife, August 5, 1862, Butler *Private and Official Correspondence,* 2:154.

35. R. S. Davis to Phelps, July 31, 1862, Parton, *General Butler,* 506; Phelps to Davis, July 31, 1862, *OR,* ser. 1, vol. 15, 535; Phelps to Lorenzo Thomas, August 2, 1862, Butler, *Private and Official Correspondence,* 2:146–47.

36. To the end of his stay in the Gulf Department Phelps continued to stress the need for constructing new mechanisms for controlling the slaves. In August he informed Butler that Louisiana society was "on the verge of dissolution, and it is the true policy of the Government to seize upon the chief elements of disorder and anarchy, and employ them in favor of law and order." According to Phelps the black man threatened "to be a fearful element of ruin and disaster, and the best way to prevent it is to arm and organize him on the side of the Government." Phelps to Butler, August [6], 1862, Butler, *Private and Official Correspondence,* 2:155–57 (quotations on page 157).

37. Butler to his wife, July 28, 25, 1862, ibid., 115, 117, 109.

38. Chase to Butler, July 31, 1862, Chase Papers; Stanton to Butler, August 7, 1862, *OR,* ser. 1, vol. 15, 543.

39. Butler was informed of the passage of the Second Confiscation Act in early August by Secretary Stanton. Stanton to Butler, August 7, 1862, *OR,* ser. 1., vol. 15, 543. See James M. McPherson, *The Struggle For Equality: Abolitionists and the Negro in the Civil War and Reconstruction* (Princeton, 1964), 106–18, for a discussion of the growth of antislavery sentiment in the North during the summer of 1862.

40. Mrs. Butler to her husband, August 8, 1862, Butler, *Private and Official Correspondence,* 2:164. See also Mrs. Butler's letter of September 28, 1862, to her husband regarding the political gains which could be made by arming the slaves. Ibid., 335–36.

41. Butler to Stanton, August 14, 1862, *OR*, ser. 1, vol. 15, 549.

42. Butler to Halleck, August 27, 1862, ibid., 55–56. A discussion of the Rebel origins of the Native Guards can be found in Mary F. Berry, "Negro Troops in Blue and Gray: The Louisiana Native Guards, 1861–1863," *Louisiana History*, 8 (Spring 1967), 167–70.

43. Berry, "Negro Troops," 174–76; *New York Times*, September 29, 1862.

44. Joseph T. Wilson, *The Black Phalanx. A History of the Negro Soldiers of the United States in the Wars of 1775–1812, 1861–'65* (Hartford, 1888), 195, see also George Denison to Salmon Chase, September 24, 1862, Salmon P. Chase Correspondence (Manuscript Division, Library of Congress).

45. Denison to Chase, October 8, 1862, Chase Correspondence.

46. Berry, "Negro Troops," 174–176; Wilson, *Black Phalanx*, 169–170.

47. Butler to Godfrey Weitzel, October 30, 1862, *OR*, ser. 1, vol. 15, 587–88; Berry, "Negro Troops," 176–79; *Senate Reports*, 37 Cong., 3 Sess., No. 108: *Report of the Joint Committee on the Conduct of the War* (Serial 1154, Washington, 1863), Pt. 3, pp. 358–59.

48. Even during the one major battle in which blacks assumed a combat role in the Gulf Department, the Battle of Port Hudson, the most important contribution of the Native Guards to the Union effort was the completion of extensive labor details. Messner, "The Federal Army and Blacks in the Gulf Department," 301–36; Dudley T. Cornish, *The Sable Arm: Negro Troops in the Union Army, 1861–1865* (New York, 1956), 142–44.

49. Butler to Halleck, September 1, 1862, Butler Papers; *New York Times* December 21, 1862.

50. Chase to Butler, July 31, 1862, Butler, *Private and Official Correspondence*, 2:131–35; Pierce to Butler, August 20, 1862, Butler Papers; see also annual report of Secretary of War Stanton, December 1, 1862, *OR*, ser. 3 vol. 2, 910–12, for a similar opinion concerning the institution of wage labor in the South.

51. *New York Times*, November 3, 1862.

52. Parton, *General Butler*, 523–24; G. Strong to G. Weitzel, November 2, 1862, *OR*, ser. 1, vol. 15, 162–63.

53. General Order No. 91, November 9, 1862, ibid., 592–94.

54. F. S. Nickerson to William Hoffman, December 23, 1862, Records of United States Continental Army Commands, 1821–1920, Department of the Gulf, Box 5, Record Group 393 (National Archives, Washington, D.C.); cited hereinafter as RG 393, NA.

55. Report of the Star Plantation, July 22, 1863, Records of Civil War Special Agencies of the Treasury Department, Third Special Agency of the Treasury Department, vol. 71, Record Group 366 (National Archives).

56. Benjamin Smith to Nathaniel Banks, March 7, 1863, Department of the Gulf, Box 3, RG 393, NA.

57. Emory to William Hoffman, January 27, 1863, ibid.; see also John Clark to Richard B. Irwin, January 30, 1863, ibid.; *Second Annual Report of the New England Freedmen's Aid Society (Educational Commission)* (Boston, 1864), 46.

58 Hanks to Banks, March 5, 1863; B. F. Smith to Banks, March 7, 1863, Department of the Gulf, Box 3, RG 393 NA, De Forest, *A Volunteer's Adventures*, 76; Edwin B. Lufkin, *History of the Thirteenth Main Regiment* (Bridgeton, Manie, 1898), 42–43.

59. *De Bow's Review*, ser. 2 vol. 3 (January 1867), 100–101.

60. General Order No. 23, February 3, 1864, *OR,* ser. 1, vol. 34, pt. 2, 227–31. See Messner, "The Federal Army and Blacks in the Gulf Department," 106–200 for a description of Banks's free labor program.

61. *New York Times,* January 16, 1863.

62. Shaffer to Lincoln, December (?), 1862, Robert Todd Lincoln Collection, Abraham Lincoln Papers (Manuscript Division, Library of Congress); see also George Denison to Chase, November 14, 1862, Chase Correspondence.

63. Butler to Lincoln, November 28, 1862, Butler, *Private and Official Correspondence,* 2:447–50; quotations on page 450.

64. Butler was removed from the command of the Gulf Department for political reasons. His controversial activities in Louisiana had alienated a good portion of the New Orleans diplomatic community, and his Democratic background and volatile behavior were considered detrimental to the delicate process of restoring Louisiana to the Union. Charles Sumner, to Butler, January 8, 1863, *OR,* ser. 1, vol. 53, 546. Banks, on the other hand, was a moderate Republican politician who had shown a genius for placing himself in the mainstream of national political movements. Fred H. Harrington, *Fighting Politicians: Major General N. P. Banks* (Philadelphia and London, 1948).

65. Messner, "The Federal Army and Blacks in the Gulf Department," chaps. 3–7.

66. Although Banks gave lip service to the ideal of black proprietorship of farm land, during his administration the military made neither land nor credit available to aspiring black farmers. Rather, under both Butler and Banks the army placed sole emphasis upon compelling blacks to work on plantations as field laborers under white direction and control. Ibid., 242–57.

67. Banks's inspectors were George Hughes Hepworth and Edwin Wheelock, both of whom were Unitarian ministers from Massachusetts and active members of the anti-slavery movement.

68. Wheelock and Hepworth to Banks, April 9, 10, June 15, 28, 1863, Nathaniel P. Banks Papers (Manuscript Division, Library of Congress).

69. George Hanks to James McKaye, March 28, 1864, quoted in J. McKaye, *The Mastership and Its Fruits: The Emancipated Slave Face to Face with His Old Master* (New York, 1864), 17.

70. Quoted in Henry T. Johns, *Life with the Forty-ninth Massachusetts Volunteers* (Washington, 1890), 166–70; quotation on page 167.

71. Ullmann to Henry Wilson, December 4, 1863, *OR,* ser. 3 vol. 3, 1126–28; quotation on page 1126.

72. Testimony of Benjamin Butler before the American Freedmen's Inquiry Commission, General Correspondence and Related Records, Records of the Adjutant General's Office, Record Group 94, National Archives Microfilm Series M-256, roll 200, frames 79–84. See Fredrickson, *The Black Image in the White Mind,* 168–71, for a discussion of the relationship between black Union soldiers and the Sambo image.

Chapter 9: From Slavery in Missouri to Freedom in Kansas

1. James A. Rawley, *Race and Politics: "Bleeding Kansas" and the Coming of he Civil War* (Philadelphia: J. B. Lippincott Co., 1969), vii–xi, 1–99; Roy F. Nichols and Eugene H. Berwanger, *The Stakes of Eighteen Forty-five—Eighteen Seventy-seven,* rev.

ed. (New York: Hill and Wang, 1982), 47–59, 66–69; David M. Potter; *The Impending Crisis, 1848–1861* (New York: Harper and Row, 1976), 199–224, 297–327; Eugene H. Berwanger, *The Frontier Against Slavery: Western Anti-Negro Prejudice and the Slavery Extension Controversy* (Urbana: University of Illinois Press, 1967), 97–118; Benjamin Quarles, *The Negro in the Civil War* (Boston: Little, Brown, and Co., 1953), 113–15, 120, 126–7; William E. Parrish, *Turbulent Partnership: Missouri and the Union, 1861–1865* (Columbia. University of Missouri Press, 1963); Albert Castel, *A Frontier State at War: Kansas, 1861–1865* (Ithaca, N.Y.: Corner University Press, 1958); James C. Malin, "The Proslavery Background of the Kansas Struggle," *Mississippi Valley Historical Review* 10 (December 1923): 285–305; James C. Malin, *John Brown and the Legend of Fifty-Six* (Philadelphia: American Philosophical Society, 1942); G. Raymond Gaeddert, *The Birth of Kansas* (Lawrence: University of Kansas, 1940).

2. John G. Haskell, "The Passing of Slavery in Western Missouri," *Kansas Historical Collection, 1901–1902* 7 (Topeka: State Printer, 1902), 28–39.

3. Ibid., 32–33; Harrison Anthony Trexler, "Slavery in Missouri, 1804–1865," *Johns Hopkins University Studies in Historical and Political Science*, ser. 32, no. 2 (1914), 9–56.

4. Trexler, "Slavery in Missouri," 10–13.

5. Ibid., 178–79, 203–4.

6. Ibid., 202–4.

7. George M. Beebe, Acting Governor, to President James Buchanan, dated Lecompton, Kansas Territory, November 26, 1860, "Governor Medary's Administration," *Kansas Historical Collections, 1889–1896* 5 (Topeka: Kansas State Printing Co., 1896), 632.

8. Richard Cordley, *A History of Lawrence, Kansas: From the First Settlement to the Close of the Rebellion* (Lawrence: E. F. Caldwell, 1895), 162–64, 183; Richard Cordley, *Pioneer Days in Kansas* (New York: Pilgrim Press, 1903), 122–36.

9. James B. Abbott, "The Rescue of Dr. John W. Doy," *Kansas Historical Collections 1886–1888* 4 (Topeka: Kansas Publishing House, 1890), 312–13.

10. This letter is printed in Wilbur H. Siebert, *The Underground Railroad: From Slavery to Freedom* (New York: Macmillan Co., 1898), 348; it is undocumented.

11. Ibid., 358. For a critical essay on the Underground Railroad legend, see Larry Gara, *The Liberty Line: The Legend of the Underground Railroad* (Lexington: University of Kentucky Press, 1961), 190–94.

12. Louis S. Gerteis, *From Contraband to Freedmen: Federal Policy Toward Southern Blacks, 1861–1865* (Westport, Conn.: Greenwood Press, 1973), 3–7, 11–26, 31–40, 120–25.

13. Parrish, *Turbulent Partnership,* 1–47.

14. Leverett W. Spring, *Kansas: The Prelude to the War for the Union,* rev. ed. (Boston: Houghton, Miffin, and Co., 1913), 257–67.

15. James Henry Lane's chief biographer is Wendell Holmes Stephenson, *Kansas Historical Publications: The Political Career of General James H. Lane* 3 (Topeka: Kansas State Printing Plant, 1930). Other biographies are: John Speer, *Life of Gen. James H. Lane, "The Liberator of Kansas"* (Garden City, Kan.: John Speer, 1897); William Elsey Connelley, *James Henry Lane, The "Grim Chieftain" of Kansas* (Topeka: Crane and Co., 1899); Albert Castel, "Jim Lane of Kansas," *Civil War Times Illustrated* 12 (April 1973); 22–29.

16. Stephenson, *Political Career of General James H. Lane,* 105–10; Thomas A. Beler Jr., "Military Operations in Missouri and Arkansas, 1861–1865," 2 vols. (Ph.D. diss., Vanderbilt University, 1958), 1:177–79.

17. H. D. Fisher, *The Gun and the Gospel: Early Kansas and Chaplain Fisher* (Chicago: Kenwood Press, 1896), 42–43, 155–56; Stephenson, *Political Career of General James H. Lane,* 126.

18. Fisher, *Gun and Gospel,* 155–57.

19. *Lawrence Republican,* November 21, 1861.

20. *Congressional Globe,* 37th Cong., 2d sess. Pt. 3, May 15, 1862, p. 2149, pt. 4, July 10, 1862, p. 3235; *Official Records of the War of the Rebellion,* ser. 1 (Washington: Government Printing Office, 1881), 3:742–43; for Lane's New York speech, see *Leavenworth Daily Conservative,* June 12, 1862; Stepheson, *Political Career of General James H. Lane,* 127.

21. Fisher, *Guns and Gospel,* 164–69; *Freedom's Champion,* Atchison, April 4, 1863.

22. J. B. McAfee, *Official Military History of Kansas Regiment During the War for the Suppression of the Great Rebellion* (Leavenworth: W. S. Burke, 1870), 61–63.

23. *Freedom's Champion,* February 8, 1862.

24. W. M. Paxton, *Annals of Platte County, Missouri* (Kansas City: Hudson-Kimberly Publishing Co., 1897), 337–38.

25. Pearl W. Morgan, ed., *History of Wyandotte County, Kansas and Its People,* 2 vols. (Chicago: Lewis Publishing Co., 1911), 1:232.

26. Records of the Governor's Office, Correspondence Files, Administration of Gov. Thomas Carney, 1863–64, box 2.1, folder 14, Archives Department, Kansas State Historical Society [hereafter cited as KSHS]; Trexler, "Slavery in Missouri," 206–7.

27. Recent excavation by archeological consultant Larry Schmits and his firm, Environmental Systems Analysis, Inc., has revealed artifacts from Quindaro, an abolitionist river port on the Missouri River in Wyandotte County, Kansas. Founded in 1857 with help from the New England Emigrant Aid Society, the town served as a major port of entry for freed and escaped slaves and free-soil settlers. The town grew rapidly to a population of about two thousand, but by 1862 was a ghost town. John Reynolds, assistant state archeologist with the Kansas State Historical Society, who toured the site, said that the findings were much more extensive and significant than most expected. *Kansas City Times,* July 16, 1987, p. 10A.

28. *Kansas 1865 MS, Census,* vol. 10, Compendium of Statistics reported to the Legislature, Archives Department, KSHS. In a Report of the Committee on Freedmen to the General Association of the Congregational Churches of Kansas in June 1865, two ministers wrote, "that there are not less than fifteen thousand freedmen in Kansas. Most of them have become free since the commencement of the war. They are most numerous in the eastern part of the State, especially in and near the larger cities and villages." *The Congregational Record,* 7 (June 1865):13.

29. *Osawatomie Herald,* reprinted in the *Conservative* (daily), Leavenworth, January 25, 1862; *The Fort Scott Bulletin,* November 29, 1862.

30. *Leavenworth Daily Conservative,* May 27, 1863; Stephenson, *Political Career of General James H. Lane,* 132–33.

31. John B. Wood to George L. Stearns, November 19, 1861, Papers of George Luther Stearns and Mary Elizabeth Stearns, Manuscripts Department, KSHS; Cordley, *Pioneer Days in Kansas,* 137–38.

32. Agnes Emery, *Reminiscences of Early Lawrence* (Lawrence: 1954), 20–21.

33. *Lawrence Republican,* January 2, 1862; Cordley, *Pioneer Days in Kansas,* 138–44; Cordley, *History of Lawrence,* 182–85.

34. *Lawrence Republican,* October 9, 1862; Cordley, *Pioneer Days in Kansas,* 144–49.

35. Emery, *Reminiscences,* 20; Cordley, *Pioneer Days in Kansas,* 145; *Lawrence Republican,* July 20, August 7, 1862; *Kansas Daily Tribune,* Lawrence, December 25, 1863; Kathe Schick, "Lawrence Black Community" (unpublished manuscript, Watkins Community Museum, Lawrence), chaps. 1 and 12, cited by Marilyn Dell Brady, "Kansas Federation of Colored Women's Clubs, 1900–1930," *Kansas History* 9 (Spring 1986):19–30.

36. *Kansas 1865 MS. Census,* vol. 3, Douglas County.

37. Ibld.

38. *Leavenworth Daily Conservative,* February 7, 1862.

39. Ibid., July 8, 1862. For his autobiography of Henry Clay Bruce, a slave who escaped from his master in Brunswick, Missouri, and, together with his intended wife, came to Leavenworth, Kansas, and lived there for some years, see H. C. Bruce, *The New Man: Twenty-Nine Years a Slave, Twenty Nine Years a Free Man* (York, Pa.: P. Anstadt and Sons, 1895; reprinted New York, 1969); The author is indebted to William Lewin for calling his attention to this book.

40. *Leavenworth Daily Conservative,* February 8, 1862; Richard Warch and Jonathan F. Fanton, eds., *Great Lives Observed: John Brown* (Englewood Cliffs, N. J.: Prentice-Hall, 1973), 41, 53–56; Quarles, *The Negro in the Civil War,* 126–28.

41. *Leavenworth Daily Conservative,* February 12, 1862.

42. Ibid., February 13, 15, March 15, 1862.

43. Ibid., March 15, 1862; [Richard J. Hinton], *Kansas Emancipation League; To the Friends of Impartial Freedom* (Leavenworth: 1862).

44. *Conservative* (daily). January 29, 1862.

45. Ira Berlin, ed., *Freedom: A Documentary History of Emancipation 1861–1867; Series 2, The Black Military Experience* (Cambridge: Cambridge University Press, 1982), 6, 9, 37, 67–71; Stephenson, *Political Career of General James H. Lane,* 127–32.

46. *Leavenworth Daily Conservative,* August 6, 1862; *Freedom's Champion,* August 16, 1830.

47. *Leavenworth Daily Conservative,* August 28, 1862; *Freedom's Champion,* September 13, 1862; Stephenson, *Political Career of General James H. Lane,* 129; Daniel W. Wilder, *The Annals of Kansas* (Topeka: Kansas Publishing House, 1875), 325.

48. Edward H. Samuel to President Lincoln, dated Liberty, Missouri, September 8, 1862, quoted in *Official Records of the War of the Rebellion,* ser.1 (1885), 13:619; also quoted in Stephenson, *Political Career of General James H. Lane,* 130; *White Cloud Kansas Chief,* August 21, 1862, quoted in Grant W. Harrington, *Annals of Brown County, Kansas* (Hiawatha: Harrington Printing Co., 1903), 32.

49. *Leavenworth Daily Conservative,* quoted in *Lawrence Republicans,* November 6, 1862; *Leavenworth Daily Conservative,* November 9, 1862, August 6, 1863; Stephenson, *Political Career of General James H. Lane,* 132; Dudley Taylor Cornish, "Kansas Negro Regiments in the Civil War," *Kansas Historical Quarterly* 20 (May 1953): 426. Dudley Taylor Cornish, *The Sable Army: Black Troops in the Union Army, 1861–1865.* Foreward by Herman Hattaway Lawrence: University Press of Kansas, 1987), 69–78.

50. Cornish, "Kansas Negro Regiment in the Civil War," 426–27; Wilder, *Annals of Kansas,* 422–23.

51. *Fort Scott Bulletin,* July 26, 1862; *Leavenworth Daily Conservative,* May 19, June 7, 1863; Berlin, *Freedom,* 37, 44, 68–73; Stepheson, *Political Career of General James H. Lane,* 127–132; Cornish, "Kansas Negro Regiments in the Civil War," 424.

52. *Leavenworth Daily Conservative,* September 4, 1862, December 24, 1863.

53. Ibid., July 8, 1862.

54. Ibid., July 10, 21, August 22, September 13, October 11, December 24, 1863, January 15, February 4, 10, 1864, October 20, 1866; Thomas C. Cox, *Blacks in Topeka, Kansas 1865–1915: A Social History* (Baton Rouge: Louisiana State University Press, 1982), 16–35.

55. *Leavenworth Daily Conservative,* July 31, August 2, 1864.

Chapter 10: Civil War Kansas and the Negro

1. Quoted in *White Cloud Kansas Chief,* February 8, 1866.

2. *Leavenworth Daily Times,* April 27, 1861, reporting speech by Conway at Topeka.

3. Wallace E. Miller, *The Peopling of Kansas* (Columbia, Ohio, 1906), pp. 67–77.

4. William H. Carruth, "The New England Emigrant Aid Company as an Investment Society," *Kansas Historical Collections,* 6 (1897–1900), 93.

5. Albert D. Richardson, *Beyond the Mississippi* (Hartford, Conn., 1867), p. 43.

6. See *White Cloud Kansas Chief,* November 28, 1861. See also *Kansas Constitutional Convention: A Reprint of the Proceedings and Debates of the Convention Which Framed the Constitution of Kansas at Wyandotte in July, 1859* (Topeka, Kansas, 1920), pp, 56, 272, 299, 324–25, 465–68, for statements and measures indicative of the presence of strong anti-Negro sentiment in Kansas.

7. See *White Cloud Kansas Chief,* April 18, 1861; *Leavenworth Daily Times,* April 14, 1861; *Lawrence Republican,* April 18, 1861; *Topeka Kansas State Record,* April 20, 1861; *Emporia News,* April 27, 1861; *Lawrence Kansas State Journal,* April 18, 1861; *Tuskaloosa Independent,* April 24, 1861; *Olathe Mirror,* June 20, 1861; *Topeka Tribune,* April 20, 27, May 4, 1861.

8. For a detailed analysis of the Kansas radicals, see Albert Castel, "The Jayhawkers and Copperheads of Kansas," *Civil War History,* 5 (September, 1959), 283–93; and Albert Castel, "Kansas Jayhawking Raids into Western Missouri in 1861," *Missouri Historical Review,* 54 (October, 1959), 1–11.

9. For Kansas jayhawking raids into Missouri, see ibid., and Albert Castel, *William Clarke Quantrill: His Life and Times* (New York, 1962), pp. 52–61. The presence of Negro soldiers in Lane's brigade was reported by the *Leavenworth Daily Conservative,* October 8, 9, 1861.

10. Ibid., September 20, 1861.

11. Collamore to Stearns, October 23, 1861, G. L. Stearns Papers, Kansas State Historical Society, Topeka Kansas.

12. John B. Wood to Stearns, November 19, 1861, Stearns Papers.

13. Address to Governor Martin," *Kansas Historical Collections,* 3 (1883–85), 377.

14. See B. W. Lewis, a Glasgow, Missouri, slaveholder, to Governor Thomas Carney of Kansas, August 24, 1863, Governor's Correspondence (Thomas Carney), 1863–64, Kansas State Archives, Topeka, Kansas. See also Atchison *Freedom's Champion,* March 31, 1865. Some Missouri slaveholders took their slaves to Texas at the outbreak of the war in order to safeguard them from jayhawkers. See Castel, *Quantrill,* p. 60.

15. Kansas State Census of 1865, Kansas State Archives, Topeka, Kansas.

16. *Leavenworth Daily Conservative,* July 8, 1862. By 1865 Leavenworth had 3,374 Negro inhabitants—about one-sixth of the town's total population.

17. *Lawrence Kansas State Journal,* November 28, 1861; John B. Wood to George L. Stearns, Lawrence, November 19, 1861, Stearns Papers; Richard Cordley, *A His tory of Lawrence* (Lawrence, Kansas, 1895), pp. 182–85.

18. Kansas State Census of 1865.

19. Samuel J. Reader to "Ella," July 8, 1862, "Samuel J. Reader Letters," *Kansas His torical Quarter,* 9 (May, 1940), 151.

20. *Lawrence Kansas State Journal,* March 13, 1862.

21. *Leavenworth Daily Conservative,* May 27, 1863.

22. Ibid., August 6, 1863.

23. Adela Endorpen, *Memories of the Old Emigrant Days in Kansas, 1862–1865* (Edin burgh and London, 1926), pp. 60–61.

24. C. M. Chase to Sycamore, Illinois, *True Republican and Sentinel,* August 19, 1863, C. M. Chase Letters, Kansas State Historical Society.

25. *Oskaloosa Independent,* September 28, 1861.

26. *White Cloud Kansas Chief,* September 12, November 28, 1861; *Topeka Kansas State Record,* September 7, 1861; *Lawrence Kansas State Journal,* September 26, Decem ber 5, 13, 1861; *Oskaloosa Independent,* October 5, 1861; Atchison *Freedom's Champion,* November 9, December 14, 1861.

27. *Emporia News,* December 21, 1861. At this time the belief was widespread in the North that the Confederate Army was using slaves as soldiers.

28. *Leavenworth Daily Conservative,* July 17, 19, 1862.

29. Ibid., January 21, 1862.

30. *Leavenworth Daily Times,* August 5, 1862.

31. *Leavenworth Daily Conservative,* September 4, 1862, July 10, 1863; John Speer, *Life of Gen. James H. Lane* (Garden City, Kansas, 1896), pp. 261–62.

32. Fort Scott *Bulletin,* July 26, 1862. The exception mentioned is probably the Sev enth Kansas "Jayhawker" Regiment, which had been raised by Jennison and Anthony and contained many abolitionists.

33. *Congressional Globe,* 38th Cong., 1st Sess., pp. 163, 872.

34. *Leavenworth Daily Conservative,* August 6, 1862. See also Dudley T. Cornish, "Kansas Negro Regiments in the Civil War," *Kansas Historical Quarterly,* 20 (May, 1953), 417–20.

35. *Leavenworth Daily Conservative,* July 8, August 6, 27, November 9, 1862.

36. Hoyt to Governor Charles Robinson, August 12, 1862; Jennison to Robinson, August 22, 1862; Montgomery to Robinson, August 3, 1862, Charles Robinson Papers, Kansas State Historical Society. See also *Leavenworth Daily Conservative,* November 9, 1862.

37. Ibid., November 15, 1862.

38. *War of the Rebellion: A Compilation of the Official Records of the Union and Confed erate Armies* (Washington, D.C., 1883–1901), ser. 1, 13, 618–19; A. T. Andreas, comp., *History of the State of Kansas* (Chicago, 1883), p. 1232.

39. "Kansas Regiments," *Report of the Adjutant General of Kansas, 1861–1865* (Topeka, Kansas, 1866), p. 247; *Leavenworth Daily Conservative,* November 10, 1862; Cor nish, "Kansas Negro Regiments," loc. cit., p. 421.

40. "Kansas Regiments," *Report of the Adjutant General,* p. 248.

41. Cornish, "Kansas Negro Regiments," loc. cit., p. 421.

42. *Official Records of the Union and Confederate Armies,* ser. 3, 29–31.
43. George C. Bingham to James S. Rollins and William A. Hall, February 12, 1862, C. B. Rollins, ed., "Letters of George Caleb Bingham to James S. Rollins," *Missouri Historical Review,* 33 (October, 1938), 52. See also *Leavenworth Daily Conservative,* September 21, 1861.
44. Samuel J. Crawford, *Kansas in the Sixties* (Chicago, 1911), pp. 102–104, 116–30; Ira Don Richards, "The Battle of Poison Spring," *Arkansas Historical Quarterly,* 18 (Winter, 1959), 1–12.
45. *Journal of the Kansas House of Representatives, 1865* (Topeka, 1865), p. 395.
46. *Weekly Osage Chronicle* (Burlingame, Kansas), February 6, 1864.
47. C. M. Chase, Sycamore, Illinois, *True Republican and Sentinel,* August 19, 1863, Chase Letters to Anthony as Mayor of Leavenworth employed Negro policemen. See *Leavenworth Daily Times,* March 27, 1864.
48. Manuscript Diary of Samuel J. Reader, September 12, 25, October 10, 1864, Kansas State Historical Society.
49. Edwin C. Manning, "The Kansas State Senate of 1865 and 1866," *Kansas Historical Collections,* 9 (1905–6), 359–75; Daniel W. Wilder, *The Annals of Kansas* (Topeka, 1886), p. 463.
50. *Journal of the Kansas State Senate, 1884* (Topeka, Kansas, 1884), p. 391.
51. John G. Van Deusen, "The Exodus of 1879," *Journal of Negro History,* 20 (April, 1936), 111–29; Glen Schwendemann, "Wyandotte and the First 'Exodusters' of 1879," *Kansas Historical Quarterly,* 26 (Autumn, 1960), 233–54; Glen Schwendemann, "The 'Exodusters' on the Missouri," ibid., 29 (Spring, 1963), 25–40.

Chapter 11: *The Negro in Wisconsin's Civil War Effort*

1. See Appleton (Wisconsin) *Post-Crescent,* December 18, 1966, for a report concerning certain Negro enlistments in four Wisconsin state regiments. Checking by the writer in the 1860 manuscript census reveals that these men were classified as mulattoes, and circumstances surrounding their enlistments indicate that in likelihood their color was undetected.
2. United States Department of Commerce, Bureau of the Census, *Negro Population, 1790–1915* (Washington, 1918), 57 indicates that the Negro population of Wisconsin in 1860 was 0.2% of the state's total population of 775,881. The figure concerning Negro troops credited to Wisconsin is from Wisconsin National Guard Adjutant General Regimental Descriptive Rolls 1861–1865 Unassigned and Miscellaneous, ser. 37/1/29, section 4, unnumbered pages in the Archives Division of the State Historical Society of Wisconsin. Hereinafter materials from the Wisconsin Adjutant General's files will be cited as Adjutant General with title and series number. Approximately 82,000 men were credited to Wisconsin in the Civil War. See William Francis Raney, *Wisconsin: A Story of Progress* (Appleton, 1963, revised edition), 165.
3. The Wisconsin Negro gained the ballot in 1866. For a brief treatment, see Frederick I. Olson, "The Railway Porter Who Wanted To Vote," *Historical Messenger of the Milwaukee County Historical Society* (June, 1960), 6–8. See also O. M. Conover, *Reports of Cases Argued and Determined in the Supreme Court of the State of Wisconsin* (Madison, 1867), 20, 544–561, "Gillespie vs. Palmer et al." For an opinion on the Negro's right to testify in the courts, see State of Wisconsin, Executive Department, Organization and Administration of the Army, ser. 1/1/5–11, Box 20,

Morton to Lewis, December 6, 1864, and Smith to Lewis, December 8, 1864, in Archives Division of the State Historical Society of Wisconsin. In subsequent citations, this source will be cited as Organization and Administration. All correspondence will be referred to by family names.

4. Edward G. Ryan et al., *Address to the People by the Democracy of Wisconsin Adopted in State Convention at Milwaukee,* September 3d, 1862 (n.p., n.d.), 3.

5. Issue of April 11, 1864.

6. United States Census 1860, manuscript, Milwaukee, 1:57 passim; 2:32 passim.

7. John Nelson Davidson, "Negro Slavery in Wisconsin and the Underground Railroad," *Parkman Club Publications* (January 12, 1897), 224.

8. Typical examples may be found in the Milwaukee *Sentinel* May 15 and 16, 1861, *Daily Milwaukee News,* May 20, 1863, letter of "Old Soldier:" *Daily Wisconsin Patriot* (Madison), April 9, 1864. In subsequent citations, the *Daily Wisconsin Patriot* will be designated as Madison *Patriot.*

9. Milwaukee *Sentinel,* September 10 and 11, 1861, provides newspaper coverage of this event.

10. Organization and Administration, Box 15, Bidwell et al. to Salomon, June 17, 1863.

11. *Der Milwaukee See Bote,* November 19, 1862, reveals Deuster's attitude toward Lincoln. For his view of the Negro migrant, see Frank L. Klement, "Peter V. Deuster, the 'See-Bote,' and the Civil War," *Historical Messenger of the Milwaukee County Historical Society* (December, 1960), 4.

12. Issue of October 30, 1862. Newspaper coverage of the Negroes' arrival in Fond du Lac is available in Fond du Lac *Saturday Reporter,* October 25, 1862. See Milwaukee *Sentinel,* October 31, 1862, for a view opposing that of the *News.*

13. Issue of November 1, 1862.

14. Newspaper coverage of the 1862 attempt to stop Negro migration to Wisconsin is available in *Wisconsin Daily State Journal* (Madison), June 7 and 10, 1862, and Milwaukee *Sentinel,* June 9 and 12, 1862. See also State of Wisconsin, *Journal of the Senate* (Madison , 1862), 887–888 and 902. The prohibition was in the form of an amendment to another bill. Events of 1863 are revealed in ibid., *Journal of the Assembly . . .* (Madison, 1863), 286 passim; for petitions, and 529 and 530 for citations from the committee report mentioned in the text. See also ibid., *Journal of the Senate,* 1863, 404, Memorial No. 42, and 633–637. Some petitions in original form are available in State of Wisconsin, Secretary of State, Petitions to the Legislature, ser. 2/3/1/5–7, Box 26 in Archives Division of the State Historical Society of Wisconsin.

15. George T. Williams, *A History of the Negro Troops in the War of the Rebellion Preceded by a Review of the Military Services of Negroes in Ancient and Modern Times* (N.Y., 1888). 18 passim, discusses Negro soldiers in the Revolution; pp. 55–57, in the War of 1812; and p. 146, refers to the Lincoln policy as indicated in the text. Hereinafter, this work will be cited as Williams, *Negro Troops.*

16. See Territory of Wisconsin, *Acts of the Legislature Passed during the Winter Session of 1837–1838, and the Special Session of June, 1838* (Burlington, Iowa, 1838), 276; State of Wisconsin, *General Laws Passed by the Legislature of Wisconsin in the Year Eighteen Hundred and Fifty-Eight; Together with Joint Resolutions and Memorials* (Madison, 1858), 95; and ibid., 1863, 369. Hereinafter, this source will be cited as *Wisconsin Laws.*

17. Reuben Gold Thwaites et al., eds., *Civil War Messages and Proclamations of Wisconsin War Governors* (Madison, 1912), 49.

18. Organization and Administration, Box 1, Noland to Randall, April 18, 1861. Details concerning Noland are available in State of Wisconsin, Executive Department, Administration, Typewritten Copies of Letters to Governor Randall, ser. 1/11–4, Box 1, in Archives Division of the State Historical Society of Wisconsin.

19. E. B. Quiner, *The Military History of Wisconsin; A Record of the Civil and Military Patriotism of the State, in the War for the Union* . . . (Chicago, 1866), 49. Hereinafter, this work will be cited as Quiner, *Military History.*

20. Organization and Administration, Box 1, Horn to Randall, April 18, 1861.

21. Fred Albert Shannon, *The Organization and Administration of the Union Army 1861–1865* (Cleveland, 1928), 2:158. Hereinafter, this work will be cited as Shannon, *Organization.* For the act of July 17, 1862, see George P. Sanger, ed., *The Statutes at Large, Treaties, and Proclamations, of the United States, from December 5, 1859, to March 3, 1863* (Boston, 1863), 12:599. Hereinafter, this source will be cited as *U.S. Statutes.*

22. John C. Rives, comp., *The Congressional Globe: Containing the Debates and Proceedings of the Second Session of the Thirty-Seventh Congress* (Washington, 1862), 32, pt. 4, 3229–3230.

23. For issues of newspapers not dated in the text, see the West Bend *Post,* July 26, 1862 and Madison *Patriot,* August 7, 1862.

24. William B. Hesseltine, *Lincoln and the War Governors* (N.Y., 1948), 202.

25. Issue of August 2, 1862.

26. Organization and Administration, Box 8, Butler to Salomon, July 29, 1862.

27. *The War of the Rebellion: A Compilation of the Official Records of the Union and Confederate Armies* (Washington, 1899), ser. 3, 2, 297, Salomon to Stanton, August 5, 1862. Cited subsequently as *Official Records* with appropriate series designation.

28. Organization and Administration, Box 8, Holmes to Salomon, August 5, 1862.

29. See Shannon, *Organization,* 2:163–164, and Williams, *Negro Troops,* 136–137. For text of the March 3, 1863, law, see *U.S. Statutes,* 12:731. *Official Records,* ser. 3, 3, 215, General Orders 143, and Dudley Taylor Cornish, *The Sable Arm* (N.Y., 1956), 130–131 provide data on the Bureau's origin and functions. Hereafter, the second work will be cited as Cornish, *Sable Arm.*

30. Organization and Administration, Box 17, Pratt to Respected Governer [*sic*], November 22, 1863, Pratt's name appears nowhere on the state service roster.

31. State of Wisconsin, Executive Department, Administration, Letter Books, General, ser. 1/1/1–11, 11, p. 84, Salomon to Pratt, November 27, 1863, in Archives Division of the State Historical Society of Wisconsin. Subsequent citations; Letters Sent.

32. See *Official Records,* ser. 3, 3, 1115, 113, 598, and Adjutant General, Incoming Correspondence, 37/1/1, Box 8, Foster to Salomon, July 31, 1863.

33. For correspondence pertinent to these developments, see Organization and Administration, Box 16, Pirine to Salomon, July 18, 1863; Maxson to Watson, July 29, 1863; Hawley to Salomon, October 10 and 19, 1863; Maxson to Salomon, October 19, 1863; and Salomon to Thomas, August 25, 1863, in Letters Sent, 10:258, and Watson to Hawley, October 12, 1863, in ibid., 538.

34. State of Wisconsin, "Annual Report of the Adjutant General . . .," in *Messages of the Governor of Wisconsin, Together with the Annual Reports of the Officers of the State, for the Year A.D. 1864* (Madison, 1865), 450. Cited subsequently as Governor's Message with short identification of report utilized.

35. U.S. Census, 1860, manuscript, Rock County, 1:31 passim; 2:2 passim; Racine County, 2 passim; and Milwaukee County, 1:19 passim and 2:32, passim. For the Census Director's remark, see *Official Records*, ser. 3, 3, 43–45. Recruitment expectations in terms of Wisconsin's Negro community are defined in *Governor's Message*, "Adjutant General's Report, 1864," 450.

36. Adjutant General, Regimental Descriptive Rolls Unassigned and Miscellaneous 1861–1865, ser. 37/1/29, section 4. Reference to naval recruits among Wisconsin Negroes is found in the *Milwaukee Sentinel*, June 9, 1863. For a history of the Twenty-Ninth U.S.C.T. with which that of Company F is associated, see U.S. Adjutant General, Official Army Register of the Volunteer Forces of the Army for the Years 1861, '62, '63, '64, '65, in 8 parts (Washington, 1867), 8:200, and Frederick H. Dyer, *A Compendium of the War of the Rebellion*, with a new introduction by Bell I. Wiley (N.Y., c. 1959), 3, 1728.

37. These developments are revealed in the Illinois State Archives, Civil War Records, 29th U.S. Colored Troops, Miscellaneous Letters; see Norris to Dear Sir, February 2, Hay to Yates, February 4, Slaughter to Fuller, May 7, W. Bross to Fuller, July 15, undated fragment of letter Isbell to J. Bross [?], and Isbell to Fuller, October 7, 1863; *Official Records*, ser. 3, 3, 838, Foster to Yates, September 25, 1863; Adjutant General, (Wisconsin), Records of Volunteer Regiments, ser. 37/4/1, Box 168, Special Order 13 in folder, 29th U.S. Colored Troops, April 7, 1864; Milwaukee *Sentinel*, April 6, 1864, citing *Wisconsin State Journal*; Williams, *Negro Troops*, 133, and Cornish, *Sable Arm*, 250.

38. Issue of April 11, 1864, editorial, "Col. Bross's Colored Regiment."

39. Adjutant General, Records of Volunteer Regiments, ser. 37/4/1, Box 168, U.S. Colored Troops, Company F Muster Out Roll.

40. *Official Records*, ser. 1, 40, pt. 1, 17, Grant to Halleck, August 1, 1864; and ibid., 134, Grant to Meade, August 1, 1864, and 163, Grant to Halleck, August 22, 1864, for other remarks of Grant's concerning the failure on July 30, 1864.

41. For data covering the text account on the Battle of the Crater, see ibid., 43–44, 59–64, 69, 73, 78, 93, 103, 106, 128, 141, 594–596, and 598–599. See also, George L. Kilmer, "The Dash into the Crater," *The Century Magazine* (September, 1887), 34, 774–776; William H. Powell, "The Tragedy of the Crater," ibid., 760–773; Henry Goddard Thomas, "The Colored Troops at Petersburg," ibid., 774–782. Henry Pleasants Jr. and George H. Straley, *Inferno at Petersburg* (N.Y., c. 1961), 4–169, is undocumented but in addition to discussing the battle, provides details concerning the career and life of Lt. Col. Henry Pleasants who engineered the mine. Cornish, *Sable Arm*, 273–278,, and Joseph T. Wilson, *The Black Phalanx: A History of the Negro Soldiers of the United States in the Wars of 1775–1812, 1861–'65* (Hartford, Conn., 1888), 411–428 are other sources for a discussion of the action. E. B. Quiner, *Military History*, 162, stresses the death of John Bross, Lieutenant Colonel of the Twenty-Ninth, referring to the battle as "one of the numerous charges made upon the enemy's lines . . ." and William de Loss Love, *Wisconsin in the War of the Rebellion; . . .* , (Chicago, 1866), 948, devotes only fragmentary mention to Negro units at the Crater. Wisconsin newspaper coverage is general in reference to Negro units, and reflects views of the editors toward the colored troops. See Madison *Patriot*, August 2, 1864, and Oshkosh *Northwestern*, August 11, 1864, for differing reports on the Negroes' conduct in combat.

42. Vincent J. Esposito, ed., *The West Point Atlas of the Civil War* (N.Y., c. 1962), unnumbered page opposite map No. 139.

43. Cornish, *Sable Arm*, 276 citing George L. Kilmer, "The Dash into the Crater," loc. Cit., 775–776. Casualty figures cited are taken from J. G. Randall and David Donald, *The Civil War and Reconstruction* (second edition, Boston, c. 1961), 424. Tables in *Official Records*, ser. 1, 40, pt. 1, 248, show losses of the Second Brigade with which Company F served at Petersburg to have been 145 enlisted men killed; 339 enlisted men wounded; and 240 enlisted men missing. See also Benjamin Quarles, *The Negro in the Civil War* (Boston, 1953), 205–206 for comments concerning the Negro soldier's treatment if he fell into rebel hands. Cited subsequently as Quarles, *The Negro*.

44. Adjutant General, Records of Volunteer Regiments, ser. 37/4/1, Box 168, U.S. Colored Troops, Company F Muster In and Muster Out Rolls.

45. For the statute of July 4, 1864, see U.S. Statutes, 13, 379. Shannon. Organization, 2:130, is a convenient source for a discussion of the call of July 18.

46. For the remark concerning the call of July 18, 1864, see Organization and Administration, Box 18, J. C. Coon [?] to Lewis, July 22, 1864. Offers to recruit Negroes in the South are in ibid., Hull to Smith, July 21, 1864, Esmond to Lewis, July 28, 1864, Whipple to Firmin, August 4, 1864; Lusk to Lewis, July 21, 1864, is annotated with Lewis's remark relative to no funds for recruitment in the South: see also, Letters Sent, 14, 381, Firmin to Esmond, August 2, 1864. The Milwaukee *Sentinel*, July 23, 25, 26, 1864, reports interest in recruitment of Negroes in the South, and August 3, announces the assessment mentioned.

47. Milwaukee *Sentinel*, July 25, 1864, and July 29, 1864, citing *Wisconsin State Journal*.

48. Organization and Administration, Box 18, Whipple to Firmin, August 4, 1864. See also, Shannon, Organization, 2:77, citing Official Records, ser. 3, 4, 536–537 for a discussion of inducements offered recruits in the South.

49. Organization and Administration, Box 18, Reed to Lewis, July 23, 1864. Reed later became governor of Florida. See The State Historical Society of Wisconsin, *The Dictionary of Wisconsin Biography* (Madison, 1960), 300.

50. Organization and Administration, Box 19, Brockway to Lewis, August 28, 1864, and Milwaukee *Sentinel*, September 1, 1864, citing *Jackson County Banner* (Black River Falls).

51. State of Wisconsin, Executive Department, Letter Books, Special, 1848–1865, ser. 1/1/1/12, 1:247, Lewis to Vincent, August 2, 1864, in Archives Division of the State Historical Society of Wisconsin, and ibid., Correspondence with U.S. and Other Governments, ser. 1/1/1–7, Box 2, Foster to Lewis, August 8, 1864.

52. Milwaukee *Sentinel*, October 12, 1865.

53. Madison Patriot, July 24, 1863, citing letter of J. B. Fry, July 20, 1863, on the earlier status of the Negro as a substitute. See Milwaukee Sentinel, July 21, 1864, editorial, "Important Order Respecting Substitutes," for the Negro's new status.

54. Quiner, *Military History*, 179, 181–182. For the reference to Manual Raynolds, see Adjutant General, Regimental Descriptive Rolls, 1861–1865 Unassigned and Miscellaneous, ser. 37/1/29, section 4, entry for Manual Raynolds.

55. Western Historical Company, History of Milwaukee, Wisconsin, from Prehistoric Times to the Present Date . . . (Chicago, 1881), 731.

56. Milwaukee *Sentinel*, August 23 and 24, 1864.

57. November 14 issue. For examples of substitutes, see Adjutant General, Records of Volunteer Regiments, ser. 37/4/1, Box 168, 29th U.S. Colored Volunteers folder. Muster In Roll No. 25; and ibid., Box 169. Unassigned Colored Troops folder. Muster In Roll No. 66.

58. See State of Wisconsin, *Journal of the Senate*, 1864, 53 and 68; ibid., *Governor's Message*, 1865, 451; and *Wisconsin Laws*, 1866, 35.

59. Shannon, *Organization*, 2:167–168, discusses bounties for Negroes. For text of the law of June 15, 1864, see *U.S. Statutes*, 13, 129–130. Governor Lewis described local bounties in Wisconsin as purely personal agreements. See notation on letter of Luke to Lewis, February 2, 1864, in Organization and Administration, Box. 19.

60. Shannon, *Organization*, 2.166–167, citing *U.S. Statutes at Large*, 12:599. See also J. Hubley Ashton, ed., *Official Opinions of the Attorneys General of the United States* ... (Washington, 1869), 58. The Milwaukee *Sentinel's* observation was made on May 2, 1864. *U.S. Statutes*, 13, 488, provides applicable text of the Enrollment Act of March 3, 1865. Quarles, *The Negro*, 202, remarks that the oath pertaining to freedom was largely up to the individual under terms of the law.

61. Approximately 12,000 Wisconsin men died in the Civil War armed forces. See Raney, op. cit., 165. Desertion figures for Company F are contained on its Muster Our Roll; those for the 34th Wisconsin are listed in Quiner, *Military History*, 820.

62. See Milwaukee Sentinel, January 12 and 19, 1864, citing *Green Bay Advocate;* ibid., June 17, 1864, citing *Wisconsin State Journal;* and ibid., June 18, 1864.

63. L. D. Reddick, "The Negro Policy of the United States Army, 1775–1945," *The Journal of Negro History* (January, 1949), 34, 11–12, remarks that Negroes have had lesser roles assigned them with recognition in non-combat service rather than in combat service.

Chapter 12: *"I Was Always a Union Man"*

1. In some areas of the South, free people of color initially offered their support to the Confederacy. See, for instance, Manoj K. Joshi and Joseph P. Reidy, "'To Come Forward and Aid in Putting Down This Unholy Rebellion': The Officers of Louisiana's Free Black Native Guard During the Civil War Era," *Southern Studies: An Interdisciplinary Journal of the South* 21 (Fall 1982), pp. 326–42; Ira Berlin, Barbara J. Fields, Thavolia Glymph, Joseph P. Reidy, and Leslie Rowland, eds., *Freedom: A Documentary History of Emancipation, 1861–1867, Series 1, Vol. 1, The Destruction of Slavery* (Cambridge: Cambridge University Press, 1985), p. 683.

2. Ira Berlin, Joseph P. Reidy, Leslie Rowland, eds., *Freedom, A Documentary History of Emancipation, 1861–1867, Series 2, Vol. 1, The Black Military Experience* (Cambridge: Cambridge University Press, 1982); Dudley T. Cornish, *The Sable Arm* (Lawrence: University of Kansas Press, 1956); Benjamin Quarles, *The Negro in the Civil War* (Boston: Little Brown, 1959); James McPherson, *The Negro's Civil War: How American Negroes Felt and Acted During the War for the Union* (New York: Pantheon Books, 1965); Hanson B. Hargrove, *Black Union Soldiers in the Civil War* (Jefferson, North Carolina: McFarland Publishers, 1988); Joseph T. Wilson, *The Black Phalanx* (Hartford: Harper Brothers, 1882).

3. For discussion of Southern white Unionism see Carl Degler, *The Other South: Southern Dissenters in the Nineteenth Century* (New York: Harper and Row, 1974), pp. 99–186; Georgia Lee Tatum, *Disloyalty in the Confederacy* (Chapel Hill: University

of North Carolina Press, 1934); Randall C. Jimerson, *The Private Civil War: Popular Thought During the Sectional Conflict* (Baton Rouge: Lousiana State University Press, 1988). Degler indicates that white Southern Unionists were not a monolithic group. They were motivated by a variety of factors, including the beliefs that the South could not win, slavery could be protected more successfully if the South remained a part of the Union, secession was unconstitutional, and slavery was unacceptable.

4. The most significant sources for this essay are the records of the Southern Claims Commission. Established by law in 1871, its task was to accept, investigate, and adjudicate claims filed by persons whose property had been appropriated for use of the Union army. Claimants had to prove ownership of the property taken, provide receipts, and prove loyalty to the Union. Any voluntary aid given to the Confederacy automatically disqualified an applicant. Depositions were taken from neighbors (black and white, Unionist and rebel) in an effort to ascertain the veracity of the claimant. Undoubtedly some claims were exaggerated, but the standard of proof was such that applicants stood little chance of acquiring favorable rulings if they filed fraudulent reports. The Southern Claims records are also useful because they sometimes provide insight into wartime activities and sentiments and postwar prosperity.

5. Virginia's Peninsula lay between the York and James rivers. Six counties were carved from the region, including Elizabeth City, Warwick, York and James City at the southeastern end, and Charles City and New Kent in the northwest.

6. See Luther Porter Jackson, "Rights and Duties in a Democracy: The Brown Family of Charles City County, Virginia," *Norfolk Journal and Guide,* 30 October 1943, p. 8.

7. For a discussion of the limitations of freedom in Charles City, see Edna Green Medford, "It Was a Very Comfortable Place for Poor Folks: Subsistence in a Rural Antebellum Free Black Community," *Locus: An Historical Journal of Regional Perspectives,* 5 (Spring 1993), pp. 131–44. See also Luther Porter Jackson, *Free Negro Labor and Property Holding in Virginia, 1830–1860* (New York: Anthenaeum, 1969).

8. See "List of Free Negroes Returned Delinquent for the Nonpayment of State and Capitation Tax for the Year," 1860, 1861, 1862, File #321, Charles City County Special Court Papers, Manuscript Division, Virginia State Archives, Richmond. See also "Papers of Indenture for Charles City County" in Special Court Papers.

9. Luther P. Jackson, *Free Negro Labor and Property Holding in Virginia, 1830–1860,* pp. 248 and 250.

10. United States, Bureau of the Census, "Manuscript Population Returns," "Household Schedules for Charles City and New Kent Counties," Virginia, 1860. National Archives (microfilm). See also Charles City County, Virginia, "1851 Registry of Free Negroes"; and New Kent County, Virginia, "1856 Registry of Free Negroes," Virginia State Archives, Richmond.

11. Ibid. The "Free Negro Registry" for New Kent clearly bears this out.

12. For discussion of the establishment of Elam Baptist Church see Alexander Q. Franklin, *History of Elam Baptist Church, 1810–1910* (Richmond: Reformer Electric Print, 1910).

13. *Deposition of Joseph Brown, New Kent County, before the Southern Claims Commission,* Southern Claims Case Files, 1877–80, Third Auditor's Office, Virginia, Claim #18499, 2 January 1873. RG 217, National Archives.

14. Robert Engs, *Freedom's First Generation: Black Hampton, Virginia, 1861–1890* (Philadelphia: University of Pennsylvania Press, 1979), pp. 17–22. The fleeing of

fugitive slaves to Fortress Monroe in the spring and summer of 1861 had resulted from General Benjamin Butler's initial acceptance of three such persons who requested asylum there. Word of Butler's decision to declare these men "contrabands of war" and his refusal to return them to their owner spread through the slave community and precipitated a flood of men, women, and children to the safety of the fort.

15. See Berlin et al., *The Destruction of Slavery;* Louis S. Gerteis, *From Contraband to Freedom: Federal Policy Toward Southern Blacks, 1861–1865* (Westport, Conn., 1973); Engs, *Freedom's First Generation.*

16. Frequently, planters who supported the Confederacy, but were not in military service, left their estates just ahead of the arrival of Union troops. They took their most valued and most troublesome slaves with them, leaving the others behind under the supervision of wives and children. Elderly whites sometimes took their chances with the Northern army, gambling that they would not be harassed. Sometimes they lost the gamble.

17. John Spencer Basset, ed., "The Westover Journal of John A. Selden, Esquire: 1858–1862," *Smith College Studies in History,* 6 (July 1921), p. 327.

18. See John M. Gregory to John Armistead, quoted in Mary Ruffin Copeland, ed., *The Confederate History of Charles City County, Virginia* (1957), p. 7. See also, John M. Gregory to Hon. James A. Sedden, 7 March 1863, G142, 1863, Letters Received, Ser. 5, Sec. of War, RG 109, National Archives. A copy of this letter appears in Berlin et al., eds., *The Destruction of Slavery,* pp. 748–54.

19. Deposition of Peyton Harris, Charles City County, Southern Claims Case Files #7592, 6 February 1873; Deposition of Warren Cumber, New Kent County, Southern Claims Case File #19208, 1 February 1873; Deposition of Elias Adkins, Charles City County, Southern Claims Case Files #16642, 20 September 1872.

20. James A. Brewer, *The Confederate Negro: Virginia's Craftsmen and Military Laborers, 1861–1865* (Durham, NC: Duke University Press, 1969), p. 7. See also Berlin et al., *The Destruction of Slavery,* p. 679. Berlin et al. indicate that free black men were "forcibly placed in Confederate service" as early as the summer of 1861.

21. James Brewer, *The Confederate Negro,* p. 7.

22. Deposition of Elizabeth Adkins, Charles City County, Southern Claims Commission Case Files #16642, 11 April 1878. Adkins testified that a Confederate guard came to her farm and impressed her son Joseph and carried him to Jamestown where he built entrenchments with other black men. Joseph was impressed at other times as well. Finally, in May 1864, he tired of eluding the rebels and enlisted in the 37th United States Colored Infantry.

23. Major General J. B. Magruder to General S. Cooper, 22 January 1862, Letters Received, ser. 12, Adjutant and Inspector General, RG 109 [F-272].

24. Major General J. B. Magruder to General S. Cooper, Yorktown, 23 December 1861, #9026, Letters Received, ser. 5, Secretary of War, RG 109, National Archives.

25. US War Department, *The War of the Rebellion: A Compilation of the Official Records of the Union and Confederate Armies,* 1st ser., 51, pt. 2 (Washington, 1891–1902), p. 683.

26. James Brewer, *The Confederate Negro,* p. 135.

27. Ibid., p. 8.

28. See Ira Berlin et al., eds., *The Destruction of Slavery,* pp. 686–7, 748–54.

29. John Spencer Bassett, ed., "The Westover Journal of John A. Selden," p. 318.

30. Deposition of Riley Jones, Charles City County, Southern Claims Commission, Case File #7742, 25 October 1871.

31. Deposition of Edmund Jones of Charles City County, Virginia, Southern Claims Commission, Case File #6473, 29 January 1873.

32. Depositions of Albert Brown and Thomas Cotman (supporting claim of Albert Brown), Charles City County, Southern Claims Commission, Case File #6468, 28 August 1871.

33. Deposition of William Cumber, New Kent County, Virginia, Southern Claims Commission, Case File #19208, 1 February 1873.

34. Deposition of Joseph Brown of New Kent County, Virginia, Southern Claims Commission, Case File #18499, 2 January 1873.

35. Deposition of Warren Cumber, Southern Claims Commission, New Kent County, Virginia, Case File #19208, 1 February 1873.

36. Ibid.

37. James M. Coski, "All Confusion on the Plantations": Civil War in Charles City County, in James P. Wittenburg and John M. Coski, eds., *Charles City County, Virginia: An Official History* (Salem, WV, Don Mills, Inc., 1989), p. 72.

38. *Official Records of the Union and Confederate Armies,* 1st ser., vol. 11, pt. 3, pp. 22–3, 69–70.

39. Ibid., pp. 99–1000.

40. Ibid.

41. For discussion of such relationships see Tinsley Lee Spraggins, "Mobilization of Negro Labor for the Department of Virginia and North Carolina, 1861–1865," *North Carolina Historical Review,* 24 (April 1947), pp. 168–9.

42. See "Depositions" of Thomas Fox, Joseph Brown, Warren Cumber and William Brisby, New Kent County, Southern Claims Commission, Case File #19204, 18 July 1877. Cumber's claim that Brisby was responsible for the escape of at least 100 people seems grossly exaggerated.

43. Deposition of Elias D. Holmes and Mary Adkins for Elias Adkins, Charles City County, Southern Claims Commission, Case File #16642, 20 September 1872. Elias Adkins had filed a claim as representative of his family, since his father had died.

44. Deposition of William Henry Brisby, Southern Claims Commission, New Kent County, Virginia, Case File #19204, 18 July 1877.

45. Deposition of William Charity, Southern Claims Commission, Charles City County, Virginia, Case File #20400, 22 June 1877. Interestingly enough, Charity's mule was taken while he was away laboring for the Union.

46. Deposition of Harris Miles, Southern Claims Commission, Charles City County, Virginia, Case File #20399, 1 August and 25 September 1874.

47. Deposition of Lucy Green, Southern Claims Commission, Charles City County, Virginia, Case File #18854, 21 January 1873.

48. Deposition of Joseph Brown, Southern Claims Commission, New Kent County, Virginia, Case File #18499, 2 January 1873.

49. After the war, the Southern Claims Commission was established. Generally, free blacks were disappointed by the results. William Brisby's $1800 claim was reduced to only $793; Harris Miles was granted $251, despite his request for $600. Perhaps because his claim was so small, William Charity received the full $150 that he asserted was the fair market value for his mule. Lucy Green, who had been told that she "would be paid for everything," saw her claim for $1000 reduced to a mere $105. In

her deposition to the Southern Claims Commission, Green lamented: "I was living there comfortably and the soldiers broke me up entirely . . . I have to live now with one of my sons." The reason for disallowing some portions of these claims seemed to have very little to do with the truthfulness of the claimants (although Lucy Green's claim was viewed with a great deal of suspicion). Instead, the Commission suggested that certain claims would be disallowed because the property was taken for the personal use of an individual soldier, and not for the benefit of the military in general.

50. Berlin et al., eds., *The Destruction of Slavery.*
51. James M. Coski, "All Confusion on the Plantation," p. 72.
52. Deposition of Robert Brown, and deposition of Edmund Waddill (for Robert Brown), Southern Claims Commission, Charles City County, Virginia, Case File #6183, 31 January 1873.
53. Deposition of William Crump, New Kent County, for William Brisby, Southern Claims Commission File #19204.
54. Deposition of Edmund Jones, Charles City County, Southern Claims Commission, Case File #6473, 29 January 1873: "Deposition of Thomas Cotman, supporting the claim of Albert Brown," Charles City County, Virginia, Case File #6486, 28 August 1871.
55. Deposition of Beverly Dixon, New Kent County, Southern Claims Commission, 1 February 1873.
56. Deposition of William Henry Brisby, New Kent County, Virginia, Southern Claims Commission, Case File #19204.
57. Deposition of Riley Jones, Charles City County, Virginia, Southern Claims Commission, Case File #7742, 27 October 18714.
58. See Edna Greene Medford, "Land and Labor: The Quest for Black Economic Independence on Virginia's Lower Peninsula, 1865–1880," *The Virginia Magazine of History and Biography* 100 (October 1992), pp. 567–82.
59. The modest wealth and social status of free people of color in Charles City and New Kent prevented the kind of postbellum separation from the masses that occurred in the Lower South and in certain areas of Virginia. For discussion of such separation elsewhere, see Ira Berlin, *Slaves Without Masters: The Free Negro in the Antebellum South* (New York: Random House, 1974), pp. 386–90.
60. Deposition of William Adkins, statement delivered in defense of claim of Elias Adkins, Southern Claims Commission, Case File #16642, 20 September 1872.

Chapter 13: Humbly They Served

1. The only extensive treatment is in Peter H. Clark's *The Black Brigade of Cincinnati* (Cincinnati, 1864), but this contemporary pamphlet is undocumented and is not based on wide research into newspapers, manuscripts, and monographs. The only modern account is in Charles H. Wesley's *Ohio Negroes in the Civil War* (Ohio Civil War Centennial Publication No. 6, Columbus, 1962), pages 18 to 22.
2. Kenneth P. Williams, *Lincoln Finds a General* (5 vols., New York, 1949–1959), 4, 21–22; John Nicolay and John Hay, *Abraham Lincoln* (10 vols., New York, 1880), 6:121–130; Francis B. Carpenter, *Six Months at the White House* (New York, 1886), pp. 20–24.
3. Williams, op. cit., 1:162–169, 240–241, 251–254, 333–338, 4:1–11, 25–29, 35–46, 50.

4. Dickson to Hassaurek, September 27, 1862, Friedrich Hassaurek Papers, Ohio Historical Society, Columbus.

5. U.S., *8th Census* 1860, 1:xxxi-xxxii; Charles Cist, *Sketches and Statistics of Cincinnati in 1859* (Cincinnati, 1859), pp. 344–345; Henry Cist, "Cincinnati with the War Fever, 1861," *Magazine of American History*, 14 (August, 1885) 144; Lew Wallace, *An Autobiography* (2 vols., New York, 1906), 2:626–628; Cincinnati *Daily Commercial*, September 15, 16, 1862—hereinafter cited as *Commercial*.

6. C. Cist, op. cit., p. 159; H Cist., op. cit., p. 144.

7. H. Cist, op. cit., pp. 138–139; Michael Heintz, "Cincinnati Reminiscences of Lincoln," *Bulletin of the Historical and Philosophical Society of Ohio*, 9 (April, 1951), 117–118; "H. E. B. Stowe," *Dictionary of American Biography*, 18, 116–117; Charles Goss, Cincinnati; *The Queen City* (4 vols., Chicago, 1912), 1:168–170, 192–193, 206.

8. In 1860, Cincinnati had 3,731 Negroes and 157,313 whites (1 out of 42), in 1870 5,904 Negroes and 210,335 whites (1 out of 36). See U.S., *8th Census*, 1:381; Charles Greve, *Centennial History of Cincinnati* (2 vols, Chicago, 1904), 1:868.

9. Carter G. Woodson, *The Negro in Our History* (7th ed., Washington, 1941), pp. 259–261.

10. Goss, op. cit., pp. 167–171, 179–180; C. Cist, op. cit., p. 164; Carter G. Woodson, "The Negroes of Cincinnati Prior to the Civil War," *The Journal of Negro History*, (January 1916), 6–9, 13–16; Clark, op. cit., p. 3.

11. H. Cist, op. cit., pp. 138–144; Clark, op. cit., pp. 4, 7; Goss, op. cit., p. 210.

12. Clark, op. cit., pp. 4–5.

13. Benjamin Quarles, *The Negro in the Civil War* (Boston, 1953), pp. 30–32; Quarles, *Lincoln and the Negro* (New York, 1962), pp. 66–68.

14. Joseph Parks, *Edmund Kirby Smith* (Baton Rouge), pp. 180–187, 200–201, 205–219; *The War of the Rebellion: A Compilation of the Official Records of the Union and Confederate Armies* (70 vols. in 128, Washington, 1880–1901), ser. 1, vol. 16, pt. 1, 909, 936—hereinafter edited as *Official Records;* Joseph Stern Jr., "The Siege of Cincinnati," *Bulletin of the Historical and Philosophical Society of Ohio*, 18 (July, 1960), 166; *Commercial*, September 1, 1862.

15. *Commercial*, September 1, 2, 3, 1862; *Official Records*, ser. 1, vol 16, pt. 2:476, 479, 482, 514. The volunteers who rushed to Cincinnati were labeled "Squirrel-Hunters"; estimates of their number range from 15,000 and 60,000. See Stern, op. cit., p. 175; Robert Harris, *Ohio Handbook of the Civil War* (Columbus, 1961), pp. 25–26; N. E. Jones, *The Squirrel Hunters of Ohio* (Cincinnati, 1898), p. 345.

16. *Official Records*, ser. 1, vol. 16, pt. 2, 470; *Commercial*, September 2, 1862; Wallace, op. cit., 2:607.

17. *Commercial*, September 2, 1862; Wallace, op. cit., 2:607, gives it as "assemble in convenient public places for orders."

18. Cincinnati City Council, Minutes (Manuscript Ledgers, City Hall, Cincinnati), Sep 1, 1862; 35, 297–2300. Hereinafter cited as Minutes.

19. *Commercial*, September 2, 1862.

20. Clark, op. cit., p. 6; Judge Dickson reported that "It was well understood that this order was not intended to, and did not, include colored citizens."—Ibid., p. 15.

21. Ibid., p. 6; *Commercial*, September 2, 1862; Governor Oliver P. Morton of Indiana specifically called for "all able bodied white male citizens . . . who reside in the counties bordering on the Ohio River" to "meet at the places of holding elections in

their respective townships, towns, or wards, and form themselves into military companies. . . ." Order printed in Cincinnati *Daily Enquirer,* September 6, 1862—hereinafter cited as *Enquirer.*

22. *Commercial,* September 22, 1862.

23. Henry Howe, *Howe's Historical Collections of Ohio* (3 vols., Cincinnati, 1902), 1:774; the *Commercial,* September 22, 1862, also reported that "the colored men of the city promptly tendered their services to be used in any manner desired."

24. Born in Cincinnati in 1829, Peter Humphrey Clark was a fiery crusader in journalism and politics, but devoted most of his life to education as an early teacher in the city's colored schools, as their first colored superintendent, as first principal (1866–1887) of the city's only high school for Negroes, and as a trustee of Wilberforce University. His daughter, Consuelo Clark Stewart, was one of the earliest Negro women physicians. See William Simmons, *Men of Mark* (Cleveland, 1887), pp. 374–383; Greve, op. cit., 1:887; Ruth Neely, ed., *Women of Ohio* (3 vols., n., p., n., d.), 1:413.

25. Clark, op. cit., p. 6.

26. *Commercial,* September 4, 1862.

27. *Commercial,* September 22, 1862; Howe, op. cit., 1:774; Clark, op. cit., p. 7.

28. Clark, op. cit., p. 7; *Commercial,* September 22, 1862. Some cite September 2nd, some the 3rd; the round-up began Tuesday night, the 2nd, and continued Wednesday, the 3rd.

29. Clark, op. cit., pp. 7–8. Such colorful reconstructed conversation in Clark's pamphlet could not be verified.

30. *Commercial,* September 4, 1862; *Gazette,* September 4, 1862; Clark errs when he says (p. 8) that "No paper of the city protested against the outrages except the *Gazette*": such inaccuracy and the numerous discrepancies between his quotations and the original sources, as in this quote from the *Gazette,* suggest caution in using Clark's account.

31. William M. Dickson, "The Black Brigade—Its Service in the Siege of Cincinnati: Report to Governor John Brough, January 12th, 1864," in Clark, op. cit., p. 17. A copy of this report could not be located in the state archives. It is reprinted at the end of Clark's pamphlet, pages 14–30, with the last 8 pages (22–30) being a muster roll of the men who served in the Brigade. Hereinafter cited as "Dickson Report."

32. "Dickson Report," p. 17.

33. Dickson to Hassaurek, September 27, 1862, Hassaurek Papers. Similarly, Clark commented on Wallace's role in the cruel round-up: "It may be said that the commanding General had no time, in the press of business, to care for such small matters as the degrees and feelings of colored men. This may be so; but it is the lack of time to attend to such small matters, as mercy and justice, that has involved the nation in this wasteful and bloody contest." Clark op. cit., pp. 6–7.

34. *Commercial,* September 8, 22, 1862; "Dickson Report," pp. 16.

35. "Dickson Report," pp. 15–17, 19, 22–30; Greve, op. cit., 1:769, 2:377–378; *History of Cincinnati and Hamilton County* (n.p., 1894), pp. 183–185.

36. "Dickson Report," p. 17; *Commercial,* September 22, 1862.

37. "Dickson Report," p. 17–18; Wright's order acknowledged that "The negroes of the city so far have turned out and labored very cheerfully when called on to do so." *Official Records,* ser. 1, vol. 16, pt. 2, 504–505. This order, dated September 10th, took official notice of "Col. W. M. Dickson, commanding the negro brigade, loc. cit."

38. "Dickson Report," p. 18; Clark, op. cit., pp. 9–10; *Commercial,* September 4, 1862. The men "had already been accompanied by the engineer in charge for efficient work." "Dickson Report," pp. 16–17.

39. "Dickson Report," pp. 18–19. Howe's depiction (op. cit., 1:774) of "The daily morning march of the corps down Broadway to labor" as a ludicrous procession reminiscent of the march of the beggars, is less fact than fancy since the unit remained in camp.

40. *Commercial,* September 3, 5, 11, 18, 1862, *Official Records,* ser. 1, vol. 16, pt. 2, 487–488; *Enquirer,* September 18, 1862; Goss, op. cit., 1:211.

41. *Commercial,* September 9, 15, 18, 1862. The City Council appropriated $8,400 to pay the laborers but urged the Mayor to seek federal reimbursement—see Minutes, September 18, October 17, 1865, 35:304–305, 341. The total bill for laborers in the siege was $9,405.75. See City of Cincinnati, *Annual Reports* (Cincinnati, 1863), p. 37. The Black Brigade members were paid on the same basis.

42. Goss, op. cit., 1:212; *Gazette,* September 22, 1862. The *Commercial,* September 22, 1862, also praised their work, but the *Enquirer* found nothing good to say and derided efforts to compensate the sable contingent for its first week of labor. See issue of September 22, 1862.

43. "Dickson Report," pp. 19–20; *Commercial,* September 22, 1862; Goss, op. cit., 1:212.

44. *Commercial,* September 18, 1862; "Dickson Report," p. 27.

45. *Commercial,* September 13, 18, 1862; "Dickson Report," pp. 20, 24; Clark, op. cit., p. 10. Clark resented the praise and citations lavished on the noisy "Squirrel-Hunters" while the Black Brigade went unsung. So rowdy were they that one general inquired: "Cannot I get rid of the Squirrel Hunters? They are under no control." Williams, op. cit., 4:61.

46. *Commercial,* September 15, 1862. In his account of the siege, Wallace (*Autobiography,* 2:595–628) never mentions the brutal round-up of the Negroes or their valiant labor; he only refers to the Brigade when listing the officers who helped him, including "Mr. Dickson, in charge of the colored brigade, as he was pleased to denominate it." (p, 615)

47. *Commercial,* September 18, 1862; Williams, op. cit., 4:54, 108–109, 115, 125–126, 135–137; Parks, op. cit., pp. 220–221, 224–226, 228–239, 241–242; *Official Records,* ser. 1, vol. 16, pt. 1, 933. Goss Claims that Smith "afterwards said that he could easily enough have gotten into Cincinnati 'but that all hell could not have gotten him out again.'" Goss, op. cit., 1:212.

48. *Commercial,* September 22, 1862; Clark, op. cit., pp. 11–14; "Dickson Report," p. 20.

49. Goss, op. cit., 1:212; "Dickson Report," p. 20.

50. *Commercial,* September 22, 1862.

51. *Loc. cit.*

52. Quarles, *Negro in the Civil War,* pp. 109–114, 116–120, 184–185; Bell Wiley, *Southern Negroes, 1861–1865* (New Haven, 1938), pp. 147–148, 304; Dudley Cornish, *The Sable Arm* (New York, 1956), pp. 67, 78, 92–93; Thomas W. Higginson, *Army Life in a Black Regiment* (East Lansing, Michgan, 1960, originally, 1870), pp. 211–215.

53. Cornish, op. cit., p. 107; Clark, op. cit., pp. 10–11; "Dickson Report," p. 21; Quarles, *Negro in the Civil War,* pp. 191–193; Whitelaw Reid, *Ohio in the War* (2 vols., Cincinnati, 1868), 2:915–917; *Official Roster of the Soldiers . . . of Ohio . . .*

1861–1866 (12 vols., Akron, 1886–1895), 1:591–593, 625–627. Over 38,000 Negro soldiers died in the war, a mortality rate almost 40 percent higher than for white troops; see John Hope Franklin, *From Slavery to Freedom* (1st ed., New York, 1952), p. 290.

54. Cornish, op. cit., p. x; Abraham Lincoln, *Collected Works*, edited by Roy Basler (8 vols., New Brunswick, N.J., 1953–1955), 8, 2; Quarles, *Lincoln and the Negroes*, p. 180.

55. Dickson to Hassaurek, September 27, 1862, Hassaurek Papers.

Chapter 14: Free Negros and the Freedmen

1. Whitelaw Reid, *After the War: A Southern Tour, May 1, 1865 to May 1, 1866* (New York, 1866), 243–44, 259–60.
2. *Population of the United States in 1860* (Washington, 1864), 194–95. Starting with a list of 240 Negro politicians, David C. Rankin identified the prewar status of 174 of the Crescent City's Reconstruction black leaders; he found that 169 had been free men of color. "The Origins of Black Leadership in New Orleans during Reconstruction," *Journal of Southern History* 40 (August 1974), 419–21. The great majority of the 260,000 free Negroes in the slave states lived in the upper South and in the border states. Ira Berlin, *Slaves Without Masters: The Free Negro in the Antebellum South* (New York, 1974), 136.
3. Berlin, *Slaves Without Masters*, 110–11, 128–30.
4. Helen Tunncliff Catterall, ed., *Judicial Cases Concerning American Slavery and the Negro*, 5 vols. (Washington, 1926–1937), 3:392–92, 447–48, 570–71. In Louisiana 81 percent of free Negroes were mulattoes. *Population of the United States in 1860*, 194.
5. Catterall, ed., *Judicial Cases Concerning American Slavery*, 3:392–93.
6. *Negro Population 1790–1915* (Washington, 1918), 511. See Berlin, *Slaves Without Masters*, 113–14; John W. Blassingame, *Black New Orleans 1860–1880* (Chicago, 1973), 59–61; David C. Rankin, "The Impact of the Civil War on the Free Colored Community of New Orleans," *Perspectives in American History*, 11 (1977–1978), 382; and H. E. Sterkx, *The Free Negro in Ante-Bellum Louisiana* (Cranbury, N.J., 1972), 223–24.
7. In most years during the 1850's Negro veterans of the Battle of New Orleans marched or rode in the annual victory parade. Roland C. McConnell, *Negro Troops of Antebellum Louisiana: A History of The Battalion of Free Men of Color* (Baton Rouge, 1968), 5–8, 15–20, 43–45, 48–54, 69–70, 89–90, 108–15; Berlin, *Slaves Without Masters*, 112–13, 117–30.
8. Berlin, *Slaves Without Masters*, 112–13.
9. Ibid., 108–10, 114–16, 128; McConnell, *Negro Troops of Antebellum Louisiana*, 46–48, 69–70.
10. Charles Barthelemy Roussève, *The Negro in Louisiana: Aspects of His History and His Literature* (New Orleans, 1937), 45; Donald Edward Everett, "Free Persons of Color in New Orleans, 1803–1865" (Ph.D. dissertation, Tulane University, 1952), 250.
11. Everett, "Free Persons of Color in New Orleans," 268–69; Blassingame, *Black New Orleans*, 33–34; Donald E. Everett, "Ben Butler and the Louisiana Native Guards, 1861–1862," *Journal of Southern History*, 24 (May 1958), 202–4; Mary F. Berry,

"Negro Troops in Blue and Gray: The Louisiana Native Guards, 1861–1863," *Louisiana History,* 8 (Spring, 1967), 166–67; Gary B. Mills, "Patriotism Frustrated: The Native Guards of Confederate Natchitoches," *Louisiana History,* 18 (Fall, 1977), 440–41.

12. By the winter of 1862, Louisiana had raised 20,000 regular troops and 15,000 militia (probably including the Native Guards) out of a white population of 357,229. By comparison, free blacks raised 3,000 militia from a population of 18,647, meaning that whereas 10 percent of the white population was under arms, 16 percent of Free Negroes were also arrayed. *Population of the United States in 1860,* 194; John D. Winters, *The Civil War in Louisiana* (Baton Rouge, 1963), 71.

13. James Parton, *General Butler in New Orleans. History of the Administration of the Department of the Gulf in the Year 1862* (New York, 1864), 516–17; Everett, "Free Persons of Color in New Orleans," 273–76; Berry, "Negro Troops in Blue and Gray," 166–73; Mills, "Patriotism Frustrated," 440–41; Berlin, *Slaves Without Masters,* 386–87.

14. This figure is based on statistics in the Adjutant General's Office of the War Department, Joseph T. Wilson, *The Black Phalanx: A History of the Negro Soldiers of the United States in the Wars of 1775–1812, 1861–'65* (Hartford, 1890), 142. Citing an estimate from the Henry Clay Warmoth Papers (Southern Historical Collection, University of North Carolina), C. Peter Ripley maintains that the number of Negro troops from Louisiana was no higher than 18,750. *Slaves and Freedmen in Civil War Louisiana* (Baton Rouge, 1976), 108. I have accepted the War Department figures as the more reliable evidence. The document cited by Ripley does not take into account that the manpower of black units had to be replenished, because soldiers died, deserted, or otherwise left the army.

15. Winters, *Civil War in Louisiana,* 428.

16. James M. McPherson, ed., *The Negro's Civil War: How American Negroes Felt and Acted During the War for the Union* (New York, 1965), 169–70, 281–82.

17. William Wells Brown, *The Negro in the American Rebellion* (Boston, 1867), 186–91.

18. *New Orleans Tribune,* 17 and 24 January 1865. Such evidence as is cited here and directly above reveals the major weakness of John W. Blassingame's *Black New Orleans 1860–1880.* In his preface Blassingame announces his intention to eschew the "often-studied debate over politics" and "examine those areas of life—education, family, religion, social and economic activities—which were of more immediate concern to blacks than politics." The problem with this "new approach" is that the Civil War and Reconstruction demonstrably politicized most aspects of black life in the South. When even the ordinary acts of day-to-day living take on political meaning, the "often-studied debate over politics" cuts to the very heart of peoples' lives.

19. Robert C. Reinders, "The Churches and the Negro in New Orleans," *Phylon,* 22 (Spring, 1961), 242–49, 247; Blassingame, *Black New Orleans,* 148–49.

20. Blassingame, *Black New Orleans,* 148–49; church directory in *New Orleans Tribune,* 1, 2 and 5 February 1865, passim; Everett, "Free Persons of Color in New Orleans," 226–27.

21. *New Orleans Tribune,* 17 February 1865.

22. Ibid., 21 July 1864.

23. Ibid., 31 January, 17 and 26 February, 22 March, 9 April, 18 and 21 May, 7 and 11 June, 1865.

24. Ibid., 24 November (French edition) and 27 December, 1864.

25. Ibid., 14 January 1865.

26. Everett, "Free Persons of Color in New Orleans," 330; Rousseve, *Negro in Louisiana,* 43–44, 118–20.

27. Dr. Roudanez has been one of the backers of the *Union*. Finnian Patrick Leavens, "*L'Union* and the *New Orleans Tribune* and Louisiana Reconstruction" (M.A. Thesis, Louisiana State University, 1966), 12–16; *The Liberator,* 15 April 1864, Rousseve, *Negro in Louisiana,* 118–20. One of the *Tribune* editors was Jean-Charles Houzeau, a white Belgian astronomer and political radical. His autobiographical, "Le Journal Noir, Aux Etats-Unis, de 1863 a 1870" *Revue de Belgique,* 11 (May 1872), 5–28 and (June 1872), 97–122, exaggerates his role as a shaper of *Tribune* editorial policy.

28. Dunn testimony, "New Orleans Riots," *House Report 16,* 39 Cong., 2 sess., 68–69; Dunn testimony, "Louisiana Contested Elections," *House Miscellaneous Document 154,* 41 Cong., 2 sess., pt. 1, 178–81; Marcus B. Christian, "The Theory of the Poisoning of Oscar J. Dunn," *Phylon,* 6 (Fall, 1945), 254–55, nn. 4–10; A. E. Perkins, "Oscar James Dunn," *Phylon,* 4 (Spring, 1943), 105; *New Orleans Tribune,* 30 November 1865.

29. Rankin, "Origins of Black Leadership in New Orleans," 438; Fred Harvey Harrington, *Fighting Politician: Major General N. P. Banks* (Philadelphia, 1948), 112; *New Orleans Tribune,* 25 October 1864. Next to nothing is known about Ingraham's early life. He may have been financially well-off, though, because he maintained two residences before the war, one in New Orleans, the other in St. Tammany parish. Ingraham testimony, "Papers in the case of J. H. Sypher vs. Louis St. Martin," *House Miscellaneous Document 13,* 41 Cong., 1 sess., pt. 1, 42–43.

30. William J. Simmons, *Men of Mark; Eminent, Progressive and Rising* (Cleveland, 1887), 75–80; Anges Smith Grosz, "The Political Career of Pinckney Benton Stewart Pinchback," *Louisiana Historical Quarterly,* 27 (April 1944), 527–28.

31. George H. Devol, *Forty Years a Gambler on the Mississippi* (New York, 1887), 216–17.

32. Simmons, *Men of Mark,* 760–63; Grosz, "Pinchback," 529–31.

33. The notion that blacks constituted a homogeneous class during Reconstruction is dispelled by a number of studies: Donald E. Everett, "Demands of the New Orleans Free Colored Population for Political Equality, 1862–1865," *Louisiana Historical Quarterly,* 38 (April 1955); Rankin, "Origins of Black Leadership in New Orleans" and "Impact of the Civil War on the Free Colored Community of New Orleans"; Leon F. Litwack, *Been in the Storm So Long: The Aftermath of Slavery* (New York, 1979); Thomas Holt, *Black Over White: Negro Political Leadership in South Carolina during Reconstruction* (Urbana, 1977); Peter Kolchin, *First Freedom: The Responses of Alabama's Blacks to Emancipation and Reconstruction* (Westport, Conn., 1972); and Gary B. Mills, *The Forgotten People: Cane River's Creoles of Color* (Baton Rouge, 1977). Holt, in particular, emphasizes that the interests of propertied blacks leaders and the interests of landless freedmen often differed significantly.

34. Appleton's *Annual Cyclopaedia and Register of Important Events, 1863* (New York, 1864), 589–90; *New Orleans Times,* 6 November 1863.

35. The petition bore the signatures of twenty-seven free Negro veterans of the Battle of New Orleans and the additional signatures of over one thousand men of color. Thomas J. Durant and twenty-one other white Unionists also signed the appeal. *The Liberator,* 1 and 15 April 1864; McPherson, ed., *Negro's Civil War,* 278–79.

36. Lincoln to Hahn, 13 March 1864, Abraham Lincoln Papers, Library of Congress.
37. Peyton McCrary, *Abraham Lincoln and Reconstruction: The Louisiana Experiment* (Princeton, 1978), 237–70; Ted Tunnell, "Anvil of the Revolution: The Making of Radical Louisiana 1862–1877" (Ph.D. dissertation, University of California at Berkeley, 1978), 57–74.
38. *New Orleans Tribune*, 28 July 1864.
39. *Debates in the Convention for the Revision and Amendment of the Constitution of the State of Louisiana* (New Orleans, 1864), 142, 156, 165–66, 182–83, 210–11, 224, 394, 501–2, 602–6.
40. For example, *The Union*, 1 December 1863. Most of the surviving copies of the *Union* are in French. Some excellent excerpts have been translated in McPherson, ed., *Negro's Civil War.*
41. *New Orleans Tribune*, 25 August 1864.
42. Ibid., 13 August (see also 9 and 16 August) 1864.
43. The senate tabled indefinitely Smith's first bill by a vote of twenty to four. *Journal of the Senate of the State of Louisiana* (New Orleans, 1864), 56–59; *Debates in the Senate of the State of Louisiana* (New Orleans, 1864), 45–50; New Orleans *Daily True Delta*, 16 November 1864. The Smith bills constituted the basis of the *New Orleans Tribune*'s misleading discussion of a "Quadroon Bill," 10 November (French edition, 12 November, 16 November 1864, passim.
44. Herman Belz, *Reconstructing the Union: Theory and Policy during the Civil War* (Ithaca, 1969), 190–94; McCrary, *Lincoln and Reconstruction*, 207–10, 232–33.
45. Belz, *Reconstructing the Union*, 267–72; James M. McPherson, *The Struggle for Equality: Abolitionists and the Negro in the Civil War and Reconstruction* (Princeton, 1964), 308–10; McCrary, *Lincoln and Reconstruction*, 293–302.
46. The description is James H. Ingraham's, *New Orleans Tribune*, 18 March 1865.
47. An interesting division occurred among the Protestant clergy. Despite initial support, the AME and AME Zion pastors ended up against the petition while the African Baptist ministers lined up solidly with the pro-petition minority. *New Orleans Tribune*, 14 January, 5, 9, and 15 February 1865, and the *Black Republican*, 15, 22, and 29 April 1865.
48. *New Orleans Tribune*, 14 January, 5 February 1865, passim.
49. Ibid., 9 December 1864, but see also 11 August 1864, and 22 March, 2 April, 19 May, and 30 June 1865.
50. Ibid., 24 January 1865.
51. *Senate Debates, 1865*, 158.
52. *New Orleans Tribune*, 13 August, 10 and 24 September, 1, 4, and 8 December 1864.
53. *The War of the Rebellion: A Compilation of the Official Records of the Union and Confederate Armies*, 130 vols. (Washington, 1880–1902), ser. 1, 47, pt. 1, 1146–48.
54. *New Orleans Tribune*, 14 and 18 March 1865.
55. Ibid., 18, 28, 29 and 30 March 1865. The ultra profederal editorials of the *Black Republican* leave no doubt as to the source of its income.
56. *New Orleans Tribune*, 23 and 28 March 1865.
57. Ibid., 20 January 1865.
58. Ibid., 15 March 1865.
59. Ibid., 20 January (but see also 1 February, 7 March, and 25 April) 1865.
60. Ibid., 27 December 1864.

61. Ibid., 29 December 1864. In this same editorial the *Tribune* claimed that "The emancipated shall really be free only when we will see him associated with the educated and intelligent [free Negroes] who can better appreciate the value of freedom." See also "Our Duty," 16 December 1864.

62. *New Orleans Tribune*, 21 July 1864.

63. Ibid., 30 November 1864, but see also 28 and 29 January 1865.

64. Ibid., 31 March 1865.

65. Ibid., 21 January 1865.

66. Ibid., 14, 21, February and 17 March 1865.

67. Ibid., 31 January, 4, 17, 25 February, 22 and 28 March 1865.

68. Ibid., 28 March 1865.

69. Ibid., 17 and 25 February 1865.

70. Parton, *Butler in New Orleans*, 526; William F. Messner, "The Federal Army and Blacks in the Gulf Department 1862–1865" (Ph.D. dissertation, University of Wisconsin, 1972), 113–14.

71. George H. Hepworth, *The Whip, Hoe, and Sword: or, The Gulf-Department in '63* (Boston, 1864), 163–68.

72. Roger A. Fischer, *The Segregation Struggle in Louisiana 1862–1877* (Urbana, 1974), 48–55; Tunnell, "Anvil of the Revolution," 128–60.

Chapter 15: Union Chaplains and the Education of the Freedmen

1. This bill had been introduced originally by his colleague, Thaddeus Stevens. *Congressional Globe*, 37 Cong., 3 Sess., pt. 1, 557 (1862).

2. For an excellent treatment of the continuing concern for the Negro on the part of anti-slavery leaders see James M. McPherson's *The Struggle for Equality: Abolitionists and the Negro in the Civil War and Reconstruction* (Princeton, New Jersey, 1964). A more detailed study of a specific application of anti-slavery principles is found in Willie Lee Rose's *Rehearsal for Reconstruction: The Port Royal Experiment* (New York, 1964).

3. Negroes were at first so designated by Benjamin F. Butler in May, 1861, while he was commanding the Union garrison at Fortress Monroe, Virginia. When Butler was informed that three fugitives who had come through Union lines had been used by the Confederates to construct fortifications, he reportedly remarked, "These men are contraband of war; set them to work," Quoted in George W. Williams, *A History of the Negro Troops in the War of the Rebellion, 1861–1865* (New York, 1888), 70. The name persisted and was used in every theater of the war. There is an interesting discussion of the practicality of the term "contraband" for use by conservative Northerners, sensitive to property rise and ownership, in Rose, *Rehearsal for Reconstruction*, 14–15.

4. Richard F. Fuller, *Chaplain Fuller: Being a Life Sketch of a New England Clergyman and Army Chaplain* (Boston, 1864), 198–208; James B. Rogers, *War Pictures, Experiences and Observations of a Chaplain in the U.S. Army in the War of the Southern Rebellion* (Chicago, 1863), 122–24; James M. McPherson, *The Negroes' Civil War* (New York, 1965, 211–13.

5. Quoted in Chester Forrester Dunham, *The Attitude of the Northern Clergy Toward the South* (Toledo, 1942), 207.

6. Rogers, *War Pictures*, 131, 217–19.

7. George Whitfield Pepper, *Personal Recollections of Sherman's Campaigns in Georgia and the Carolinas* (Zanesville, Ohio, 1866), 236–37, 250.

8. Fuller, *Chaplain Fuller*, 193, 198–99. The chaplain, who was a brother of Margaret Fuller, of Brook Farm, was killed at Fredericksburg, Virginia, by Confederate sharp-shooters. Service Record, Files of the Adjutant General's Office, National Archives, Record Group 94.

9. Monthly Report, dated September 30, 1864, Letters Received, Files of the Surgeon General's Office, National Archives, Record Group 679.

10. Monthly Report, dated October 31, 1864, and February 28, 1865, Letters Received, Files of the Adjutant General's Office, National Archives, Record Group 679.

11. Rev. Frederic Denison, *Shot and Shell: The Third Rhode Island Heavy Artillery Regiment in the Rebellion, 1861–1865* (Providence, 1879), 131–32; Rose, *Rehearsal for Reconstruction*, 88.

12. Special Order No. 15, dated November 11, 1862, reads as follows:

"Chaplain Eaton of the 27th Ohio Infantry Vols. Is hereby appointed to take charge of the Contrabands that come into camp in the vicinity of this Post (LaGrange, Tennessee), organizing them into suitable Companies for working, see that they are properly cared for, and set them to work picking, ginning, and Baleing [*sic*] all cotton now cut and ungathered in fields.

"Suitable Guards will be detailed by commanding officers nearest where the parties start work to protect them from molestation.

"For further instructions the Officer in charge of these Laborers will call at these Hd. Qrs."

Manuscript copy filed with Eaton's Service Record, Files of the Adjutant General's Office, National Archives, Record Group 94. In December, 1862, to facilitate the chaplain's work by outlining more specifically the areas in which Eaton's authority was final, Grant issued the following order:

"Chaplain John Eaton Jr., of the 27th Regiment Ohio Volunteers, is hereby appointed General Superintendent of Contrabands for the Department.

"He will designate such Assistant Superintendents as may be necessary for the proper care of these people, who will be detailed for their duty by the Post or District Commander.

"All Assistant Superintendents will be subject to the orders of the Superintendent. . . ." *The War of the Rebellion: A Compilation of the Official Records of the Union and Confederate Armies* (Washington, 1880–1901), ser. 1, vol. 18, pt. 2, 395–96. Hereafter cited as *Official Records*.

13. John Eaton, *Grant, Lincoln, and the Freedmen* (New York, 1907), 13–15; Martha Mitchell Bigelow, "Freedmen of the Mississippi Valley, 1862–1865," *Civil War History*, 8 (March, 1862), 39.

14. Eaton, *Grant, Lincoln, and the Freedmen*, 192–93.

15. Ibid., 195–96.

16. Special Order No. 63 from the War Department, dated September 29, 1863, read in part as follows:

"VI. Transportation will be furnished for persons and goods, for the benefit of these people [the Negroes] on Government Transports and Military Railroads within the Department on the order of the General Superintendent [Eaton].

"VII. Citizens voluntarily laboring for the benefit of these people, saving as they do to the government, cost of labor in providing for their care, will, when properly accredited by the General Superintendent, be entitled to rations, quarters, and transportation on Government Transports and Military Railroads within the Department."

Quoted in Eaton, *Grant, Lincoln, and the Freedmen,* 194.

17. Eaton had been appointed to this position on December 17, 1862. General Order No. 13 read, in part, as follows:

"Chaplain John Eaton Jr., of the 27th Regiment Ohio Volunteers, is hereby appointed General Superintendent of Contrabands for the Department."

Official Records, ser. 1, vol. 18, pt. 2, 395–96; Eaton, *Grant, Lincoln, and the Freedmen,* 26–27.

18. Order No. 26, dated September 26, 1864, read in part as follows: "To prevent confusion and embarrassment, the General Superintendent of Freedmen will designate officers, subject to his orders as Superintendent of Colored Schools, through whom he will arrange the location of all schools, teachers, and the occupation of houses and other details pertaining to the education of Freedmen. All officers commanding, and others, will render the necessary aid." Printed copy filed with Eaton's Service Record, Files of the Adjutant General's Office, National Archives, Record Group 94.

19. Eaton's authority as General Superintendent was greatly enhanced when he was commissioned as Colonel of the 9th Louisiana Native Guards (later the 63rd United States Colored Infantry). His resignation from the chaplaincy of the 27th Ohio was accepted on October 9, 1863, and he was mustered out of service. The next day he received his appointment as Colonel of the 9th Louisiana.

Service Record, Files of the Adjutant General's Office, National Archives, Record Group 94.

20. These were the Reverend L. H. Cobb, Superintendent of the Colored Schools in the Memphis District; the Reverend James A. Hawley and a Reverend Mr. Buckley, both superintendents in the large Vicksburg District; C. S. Crossman, a former teacher of the Toledo public schools, Superintendent in Natchez; Reverend Joel Grant, Superintendent of the Arkansas District; W. F. Allen, Superintendent of the Helena District; and J. L. Roberts, Superintendent at Columbus, Kentucky. Eaton, *Grant, Lincoln, and the Freedmen,* 196.

21. Eaton, *Grant, Lincoln, and the Freedmen,* 197.

22. Eaton, *Grant, Lincoln, and the Freedmen,* 197–201.

23. Printed copy filed with Eaton's Service Record, Files of the Adjutant General's Office, National Archives, Record Group 94.

24. Eaton, *Grant, Lincoln, and the Freedmen,* 215–16.

25. Charles Francis Adams Jr. to Charles Francis Adams, November 2, 1864, in Worthington C. Ford., ed., *A Cycle of Adams Letters* (Boston, 1920), 2:218.

26. Dudley Taylor Cornish, *The Sable Arm: Negro Troops in the Union Army, 1861–1865* (New York, 1966), 49.

27. John Eaton to Edwin Stanton, October 20, 1864. Copy filed with Eaton's Service Record, Files of the Adjutant General's Office, National Archives, Record Group 94.

Chapter 16: Black Education in Louisiana, 1863–1865

1. See William Ivy Hair, *Bourbonism and Agrarian Protest: Louisiana Politics, 1877–1900* (Baton Rouge, 1969), pp. 107–141, for a discussion of the decline in public education in Louisiana after Reconstruction.

2. For a general discussion of black education in Louisiana during the Civil War and Reconstruction, see Roger A. Fischer, *The Segregation Struggle in Louisiana*

1862–1877 (Urbana, 1974); John W. Blassingame, *Black New Orleans, 1860–1880* (Chicago, 1973), pp. 107–122; Robert S. Bahney, "Generals and Negroes: Education by the Union Army, 1861–1865," (Ph.D. dissertation University of Michigan, 1965), pp. 201–220; Howard Asley White, *The Freedmen's Bureau in Louisiana* (Baton Rouge, 1970), pp. 166–200. The term "Gulf Department" was used by the federal army to denote those portions of southern Louisiana under Union control during the Civil War. Although the boundaries of the department shifted with the fortunes of the Union army, for the purposes of this study the Gulf Department includes those parishes in southern Louisiana which President Lincoln excluded from the operation of the Emancipation Proclamation. These parishes are Saint Bernard, Plaquemines, Jefferson, Saint John, Saint Charles, Saint James, Ascension, Assumption, Terrebonne, Lafourche, Saint Mary, Saint Martin, and Orleans.

3. The most complete discussion of the war in Louisiana is John D. Winters, *The Civil War in Louisiana* (Baton Rouge, 1963). A recent study of Reconstruction in Louisiana is Joe G. Taylor, *Louisiana Reconstructed, 1863–1877* (Baton Rouge, 1974).

4. Lincoln chose Banks to head the Gulf Department primarily as a result of the General's reputation as a political moderate who had scrupulously avoided extremes in his pre-war career as a Massachusetts Congressman and Governor. Banks' political career both before and after the war followed a torturous path between political parties, all in an attempt at remaining in the mainstream of public political sentiment. Despite his vacillations in party membership, Banks consistently adhered to a belief in free labor thought and the necessity for American expansion. Fred Harvey Harrington, *Fighting Politician: Major-General Nathaniel P. Banks* (Philadelphia, 1948), p. 86. Banks' initial address to the people of Louisiana stressed the unparalleled affluence which Louisiana would experience if they acquiesced to the state's reconstruction. *New York Times,* December 29, 1862. For further elaboration in regard to Banks' emphasis upon increased staple production see William F. Messner, "The Federal Army and Blacks in the Gulf Department, 1862–1865," (Ph.D. dissertation University of Wisconsin, 1972), pp. 108–111.

5. President Lincoln excluded slaves in the Gulf Department from the effect of his Emancipation Proclamation and as a consequence these blacks did not receive their formal emancipation until January, 1864. By early 1863, however, both department officials and planters generally recognized the fact that the slaves assumed they were free and demanded to be treated accordingly. Messner, "Federal Army and Blacks," pp. 117–130.

6. See ibid., chaps. 4 and 5, for a discussion of the federal army's institution of a plantation labor program in Louisiana.

7. Banks' regulations stipulated a three dollar per month wage, before deductions, for first class hands. In 1864 first class hands received eight dollars per month with three dollars deducted for clothing.

8. Thomas Conway to Nathaniel Banks, June 1, 1863, Nathaniel Banks Papers, Library of Congress.

9. Thomas Hooper to N. Banks, August 27, 1863, ibid.

10. Nathaniel Banks, *Emancipated Labor in Louisiana* (New York, 1864), p. 7.

11. *The Liberator,* January 8, 1864. See also: Silas Fales to his family, May 31, 1863, Silas Fales Papers, Southern Historical Collection, University of North Carolina; M. Gonzalves to S. Jocelyn, December 31, 1863, American Missionary Association

Archives, Amistad Research Center, Dillard University (cited hereafter as AMA Archives); M. Gonzales to Lewis Tappan, February 9, 1864, ibid.; John Tucker to G. Whipple, March 22, 1864, ibid.

12. N. Banks to Gardner Banks, August 26, 1864, *OR*, Ser. 1, 51, pt. 2, 869.

13. Headquarters, Dept. of the Gulf to Parish Provost Marshals, June 27, 1864, Banks Papers

14. *National Anti-Slavery Standard,* January 23, 1864; *Second Annual Report of the New England Freedmen's Aid Society* (Boston, 1864), pp. 46–48.

15. Report of Superintendent of Schools William Stickney, October 19, 1863, Banks Papers.

16. *National Anti-Slavery Standard,* January 23, 1864; *Second Annual Report of the New England Freedmen's Aid Society,* pp. 46–8.

17. Ibid., *New York Tribune,* October 17, 1863; Hanks to Banks, September 26, 1863, Banks Papers; *New York Times,* October 26, 1863.

18. Report of W. Stickney, October 13, 1863, Banks Papers; *Second Annual Report of the New England Freedmen's Aid Society,* pp. 46–8; Report of State Auditor A. P. Dostie, March 9, 1864, Abraham Lincoln Papers, Robert Todd Lincoln Collection, Library of Congress.

19. General Orders, No. 23, February 3, 1864, *OR*, Ser. 1, 34, pt. 2, 227–31.

20. General Orders, No. 38, March 22, 1864, *OR*, Ser. 3, 4, 193–94; Bahney, "Negroes and Generals," 215; Charles Kassel, "Educating the Slave—A Forgotten Chapter of Civil War History," *Open Court,* 16 (April, 1927), 241.

21. Ibid., J. V. Smith to Banks, October 15, 22, 1864, Banks Papers; C. Taubling to Simeon Jocilyn, April 9, May 11, 1864, AMA Archives; T. Conway to G. Whipple, October 4, 1864, ibid.; Special Orders No. 280, October 11, 1864, ibid.; I. Hubbs to G. Whipple, October 13, 1864, ibid.; Benjamin Plumly to the Firm of Barnes and Burr, October 20, 1864, Records of the Bureau of Refugees, Freedmen, and Abandoned Lands, Louisiana Records, Superintendent of Education, vol. 38, Record Group 105, National Archives (cited hereafter as LFB, RG 105, NA); B. Plumly to J. Tucker, October 20, 1864, ibid.

22. Bahney, "Negroes and Generals," 224–28; John C. Gregg, *Life in the Army* (Philadelphia, 1868), pp. 225–26.

23. B. Plumly to Banks, June 24, 1864, Banks Papers; J. V. Smith to Banks, October 29, 1864, ibid., George Denison to Salmon Chase, October 8, 1864, Salmon Chase Papers, Library of Congress. See Messner, "Federal Army and Blacks," chap. 4 for a discussion of the struggle between the military and Treasury agents for supremacy in Louisiana's Republican party.

24. Mac Heyman, *Prudent Soldier: A Biography of Major General E. R. S. Canby* (Glendale, Calif., 1959), pp. 265–66; Bahney, "Negroes and Generals," 219–21.

25. Wheelock to Banks, April 1, 1864, LFB, Superintendent of Education, 5, 38 RG 105, NA.

26. White, *Freedmen's Bureau in Louisiana,* pp. 174–75; Carl Schurz, *Speeches, Correspondence and Political Papers of Carl Schurz* (New York, 1913), 1:32; Deer Range Plantation Record, October 16, 1865, Maunsel White Papers, Southern Historical Collection.

27. Wheelock to Banks, April 1, 1864, LFB, Superintendent of Education, 5, 38, RG 105, NA. A similar plan for taxing black soldiers to pay the salaries of their teachers was suggested by Thomas Conway to Daniel Ullman, March 16, 1864, Records of

the United States Continental Army Commands, 1821–1920, Department of the
Gulf, Office of the Adjutant General, Box 38, Record Group 94, National Archives.
Cited hereafter as AGO, RG 94, NA.

28. Bahney, "Negroes and Generals," 221; Hurlbut to C. T. Christensen, October 25,
   1864, *OR,* ser. 1, 41, pt. 4, 223–34.

29. *Memorial Record of the New York Branch of the United States Christian Commission*
   (New York, 1866), 31–33; *Forty-Ninth Report of the American Bible Society* (New
   York, 1871), 167–68; *New York Tribune,* February 27, 1864; G. K. Eggleston,
   "The Work of Relief Societies During the Civil War," *Journal of Negro History,* 91
   (July, 1929), 272–99.

30. *Eighteenth Annual Report of the American Missionary Association* (New York,
   1864), 26–7; *New York Times,* April 24, 1864; Winters, *Civil War in Louisiana,*
   397–98; C. Taubling to S. Jocelyn, April 22, 1864. AMA Archives.

31. *Second Annual Report of the Northwestern Freedmen's Aid Commission* (Chicago,
   1865), p. 15. The Northwestern Commission sent nine teachers to the Gulf Department. The other two freedmen's organizations which operated in the Mississippi
   Valley were the Western Freedmen's Aid Society and the Western Sanitary Commission. Both concentrated their work in the upper portion of the valley.

32. See James McPherson, *The Struggle for Equality: Abolitionists and the Negro in the
   Civil War and Reconstruction* (Princeton, 1964), pp. 154–77; Willie Lee Rose,
   Rehearsal for Reconstruction: The Port Royal Experiment (New York, 1964), pp.
   29–30, 85–89, 229–235; and Joel Williamson, *After Slavery: The Negro in South
   Carolina During Reconstruction* (Chapel Hill, 1965), pp. 210–13, for discussion of
   the work of freedmen's aid societies in educating blacks in various areas of the South
   during Reconstruction.

33. Hanks to Banks, February 24, 1864, Banks Papers.

34. General Orders, No. 38, March 22, 1864, *OR,* Ser. 3, 4, 193–94.

35. Julius H. Farmlee, "Freedmen's Aid Societies, 1861–1871," *Negro Education,* Bureau
   of Education Bulletin, No. 38 (2 vols., Washington, D.C., 1917), 1:293. Of the more
   than 200 teachers involved in freedmen's education in the Gulf Department, fewer
   than one-quarter were supplied by northern philanthropic organizations.

36. See Messner, "The Federal Army and Blacks," 201–257, 270–80.

37. Israel Hubbs to S. Jocelyn, January 8, 1864, AMA Archives; Charles Strong to
   S. Jocelyn, February 19, 1864, ibid.

38. I. Hubbs to S. Jocelyn, January 8, February 16, 1864, AMA Archives; C. Strong to
   S. Jocelyn, February 19, May 7, 1864; ibid.; F. Green to G. Whipple, February 16,
   1865, ibid.; E. Wheelock to S. Jocelyn, May 3, 1864, ibid.; I. Hubbs to G. Whipple,
   September 23, 1864, ibid.; W. Knowles to G. Whipple, September 28, 1864, ibid.;
   B. Plumly to N. Banks, June 16, 1864, Banks Papers; J. V. Smith to Banks, October
   15, 1864, ibid.

39. Wheelock to Banks, May 25, 1864, LFB, Superintendent of Education, V, 38 RG
   105, NA.

40. Bowen to all Parish Provost Marshals, February 5, 1864, Dept. of Gulf, Office of
   the Provost Marshal, 5, 298, RG 393, NA.; Wheelock to "Government Teachers in
   Saint Charles Parish," September 28, 1864, LFB, Superintendent of Education, 5,
   38, RG 105, NA.

41. B. Plumly to S. Holabird, May 30, 1865, LFB, Superintendent of Education, Box
   52, RG 105, NA.; E. Wheelock to Henry Stuart, June 11, 1865, ibid.

42. J. V. Smith to Banks, January 21, 1865, Banks Papers.
43. L. H. Birge to Wheelock, June 10, 1864, LFB, Superintendent of Education, Box 52, RG 105, NA.
44. Wheelock to Banks, June 20, 1864, ibid.; Wheelock to Hurlbut, February 7, 1865, Ibid., 5, 38, W. Stickney to Plumly, May 10, 1864, ibid., Box 52.
45. George Darling to Banks, July 15, 1864, Banks Papers.
46. Banks to Parish Provost Marshals, June 27, 1864, ibid.; Banks to T. D. Chickering, August 12, 1864, LFB, Superintendent of Education, Box 52, RG 105, NA.
47. Banks to Lincoln, December 30, 1863, Roy P. Basler, ed., *The Collected Works of Abraham Lincoln* (New Brunswick, 1953), 7:123–25; Lincoln to Banks, January 13, 1864, ibid., 123–24; Banks to Lincoln, January 22, 1864, ibid., 162–63.
48. G. Denison to Chase, April 1, June 17, 1864, Chase Papers, LC.
49. *Debates in the Convention for the Revision and Amendment of the Constitution of Louisiana . . . ,* 1864 (New Orleans, 1864), p. 72.
50. Ibid., pp. 142–44.
51. Ibid., pp. 158, 181, 494.
52. Ibid., pp. 476–499.
53. Ibid., p. 502.
54. Ibid., pp. 601, 641.
55. Banks to Lincoln, July 25, 1864, R. T. Lincoln Coll., Lincoln to Banks, August 9, 1864, ibid.
56. *Convention Debate,* p. 601
57. *New Orleans Tribune,* October 23, 1864.
58. *Louisiana House Debates,* 1864 (New Orleans, 1865), p. 150.
59. *New Orleans Tribune,* February 17, 1865.
60. The military supported its school system during the war by drawing upon the Corps D'Afrique fund which had been accumulated by the sale of cotton confiscated by the army after the Port Hudson campaign. The failure of the army to make the freedmen's schools self-supporting during Reconstruction was the prime reason for the system's decline. By October of 1865 the Freedmen's Bureau had been able to collect only $32,000 out of the $228,000 owed it in school taxes. White, *Freedmen's Bureau in Louisiana,* p. 174.
61. *New Orleans Times,* September 17, December 27, 1865; *New York Tribune,* July 25, 1865; Plumly to William Taylor, September 21, 1864, LFB, Superintendent of Education, 5, 38, RG 105, NA; Plumly to Banks, October 20, 1864, Banks Papers.
62. *Eighteenth Annual Report of the American Missionary Association* (New York, 1864), pp. 17–20.
63. *Eighteenth Annual Report of the AMA,* pp. 17–20.
64. *Nineteenth Annual Report of the AMA* (New York, 1865), pp. 32–33. See also: F. Greene to G. Whipple, July, 1864, AMA Archives; E. Birge to G. Whipple, June 2, 1864, Ibid.
65. *Forty-ninth Annual Report of the American Bible Society,* pp. 140–41.
66. Plumly to William Taylor, September 21, 1864, Superintendent of Education, 5, 38, RG 105, NA.
67. Banks, *Emancipated Labor,* p. 21.
68. G. Darling to Hanks, July 18, 1864, Banks Papers.
69. R. Wilkinson to his wife, February 11, 1864, Robert F. Wilkinson Papers, New York Historical Society.

70. Hanks to James Tucker, May 27, 1864, Banks Papers.
71. Banks, *Emancipated Labor,* p. 11.
72. Plumly to Chase, June 20, 1863, Chase Papers, LC; Plumly to James Tucker, November 18, 1864, R. T. Lincoln Coll.
73. *Eighteenth Annual Report of the AMA,* pp. 17–20.
74. Ibid.
75. Eric Foner, *Free Soil, Free Labor, Free Men: The Ideology of the Republican Party Before the Civil War* (New York, 1970), p. 296.
76. *Eighteenth Annual Report of the AMA,* 17–20; *The Liberator,* January 8, 1864.

Chapter 17: Notes on the Education of Negroes at Norfolk and Portsmouth, Virginia During the Civil War

1. Luther P. Jackson, *Free Negro Labor and Property Holding in Virginia, 1830–1860* (New York, 1942), p. 70 and John H. Russell, *The Free Negro in Virginia, 1619–1865* (Baltimore, 1913), p. 70.
2. Russell, op. cit., p. 145.
3. *American Missionary* (New York: American Missionary Association, 1863), 6:104.
4. Thomas J. Wertenbaker, *Norfolk, Historical Southern Port* (A history written under contract with the "city fathers"; Durham, North Carolina, 1931), chaps. 9 and 10.
5. Bell I. Wiley, *Southern Negroes* (New York, 1953), p. 263.
6. Frank Moore, *Rebellion Record* (New York, 1871), 8, doc. 263.
7. W. H. Woodbury, *Letter to the AMA,* June 1, 1865 (AMA Collection, Fisk University Library).
8. G. Greene, *Letter to the AMA,* May 13, 1863 (AMA Collection, Fisk University Library).
9. *American Missionary,* 7:137.
10. Wertenbaker, op. cit.
11. John Oliver personal letter, February 17, 1863 (AMA Collection, Fisk University Library).
12. Harriet Taylor, *Letter to the AMA,* February 24, 1863 (AMA Collection, Fisk University Library).
13. Josephine Strong, *Letter to the AMA,* January 21, 1865 (AMA Collection, Fisk University Library).
14. Luther P. Jackson, "Religious Development of the Negro in Virginia from 1830–1860," *Journal of Negro History,* 16, no. 2 (April, 1931).
15. *American Missionary,* 8 (1865), 138.
16. G. M. Trevelyan, *British History in the Nineteenth Century: 1782–1901* (London, 1922), p. 160.
17. Samuel Dill, *Roman Society, From Nero to Marcus Aurelius* (New York, 1956), pp. 266–67.
18. Ibid., p. 259.
19. "Never was I so grateful for life, as now: for amidst these pressing cares around the infant cradle of this nation, 'born in a day,' I feel how good it is to be here, forgetful of self. Lately, after the cares of the school-room have passed away, our labors for these people extend far into the night. But never was rest more sweet; and when morning calls again to toil, we greet freedom, at every breath. Do you know, dear brother, how many delightful circumstances cluster around this world. I can not go

through this city, on a bright morning without having a hundred little hands touch mine, with a right smart 'howdy' breaking from their grateful lips. And when we bent in morning prayer at school, within the circle of larger children, more repeat with me, 'Our Father, which art in heaven'." From H. S. Beals, Portsmouth, Virginia, December 14, 1863 (AMA Collection, Fisk University Library). This is one of the numerous "sentimental" expressions of missionary teachers during this period. About Beals himself there will be reference in the third section of this paper.

20. *American Missionary,* 7 (1864), 108.
21. Dill, op. cit., p. 261.
22. H. S. Beals, *Letter to the AMA,* February 19, 1862 (AMA Collection, Fisk University Library).
23. W. Niles, *Letter to the AMA,* January 25, 1861 (AMA Collection, Fisk University Library).
24. Beals personal letter, March 26, 1864 (AMA Collection, Fisk University Library).
25. S. L. Daffin, *Letter to the AMA,* March 14, 1864 (AMA Collection, Fisk University Library).
26. Mary E. Burden, *Letter to the AMA,* June 14, 1864 (AMA Collection, Fisk University Library).
27. William L. Coan, *Letter to the AMA,* March 17, 1864 (AMA Collection, Fisk University Library).
28. Coan, *Letter to the AMA,* March 29, 1864 (AMA Collection, Fisk University Library).
29. Coan, *Letter to the AMA,* March 12, 1864 (AMA Collection, Fisk University Library).
30. Coan, *Letter to the AMA,* June 26, 1864 (AMA Collection, Fisk University Library).
31. Woodbury, *Letter to the AMA,* February 26, 1864 (AMA Collection, Fisk University Library).
32. Daffin, *Letter to the AMA,* March 14, 1864 (AMA Collection, Fisk University Library).
33. Daffin, *Letter to the AMA,* September 7, 1864 (AMA Collection, Fisk University Library).
34. Mary Reed, *Letter to the AMA,* July 18, 1864 (AMA Collection, Fisk University Library).
35. Coan, *Letter to the AMA,* July 27, 1864 (AMA Collection, Fisk University Library).
36. *American Missionaries,* 8 (1865), 284.
37. H. C. Percy, *Letter to the AMA,* January 26, 1865 (AMA Collection, Fisk University Library).
38. Percy, *Letter to the AMA,* February 10, 1869 (AMA Collection, Fisk University Library).
39. Ibid.
40. Luther P. Jackson, "The Origin of Hampton Institute," *Journal of Negro History,* 10, no. 2.
41. A. Drummond, *Letter to the AMA,* July 1, 1864 (AMA Collection, Fisk University Library).
42. W. S. Bell, *Letter to the AMA,* October 31, 1864 (AMA Collection, Fisk University Library).
43. *American Missionary,* 8 (1865), 292.
44. Bell, *Letter to the AMA,* June 22, 1864 (AMA Collection, Fisk University Library).

Chapter 18: The American Missionary Association and Black Education in Civil War Missouri

1. For a detailed study of prewar activities of the American Missionary Association see Clifton H. Johnson, "The American Missionary Association, 1846–1861: A Study of Christian Abolition" (unpublished Ph.D. dissertation, University of North Carolina, Chapel Hill, 1959).

2. Augustus Field Beard, *A Crusade of Brotherhood: A History of the American Missionary Association* (Boston, 1909), 97.

3. Absalom Gardiner to Dear Brother, April 8, 1856, American Missionary Association Archives, Amistad Research Center, Dillard University, New Orleans, Louisiana. Hereafter cited as AMAA.

4. *American Missionary,* 2 (March, 1858), 61.

5. Ibid. (July, 1858), 164.

6. G. H. Pool to S. S. Jocelyn, February 7, 24, April 20, 1859, AMAA.

7. Ibid., April 20, 1859, AMAA.

8. Ibid., May 4, 1859, AMAA.

9. Mrs. Amos B. Hill to G. Whipple, August 29, 1859, AMAA.

10. S. Blanchard to S. S. Jocelyn, September 27, 1859; and A. B. Hills to Lewis Tappan, February 9, 1860, AMAA.

11. S. Blanchard to S. S. Jocelyn, January 8, 1860, AMAA; *American Missionary,* 4 (July, 1860), 161–192.

12. S. Blanchard to S. S. Jocelyn, April 23, 1860, AMAA.

13. Ibid.

14. Ibid. May 17, June 6, 1860, AMAA; *American Missionary,* 4 (April, 1860), 88–89; ibid., 5 (January, 1861), 20; ibid., 5 (February, 1861), 44.

15. Ibid., 6 (July, 1862), 164; S. Blanchard to S. S. Jocelyn, January 14, 1861, May 12, June 6, October 9, December 10, 1862; and A Free Soil Resident to S. S. Jocelyn, February 1, 1861, AMAA.

16. G. Candee to S. S. Jocelyn, March 26, 1863, AMAA.

17. Fugitive slaves before Lincoln's Emancipation Proclamation were commonly called contrabands of war, a designation first used by General Benjamin F. Butler at Fortress Monroe, Virginia, in 1861. Butler referred to escaped slaves as contraband to avoid having to return them to their rebel masters.

18. J. L. Richardson to S. S. Jocelyn, April 7, 10, July 4, 1863, AMAA.

19. Ibid., April 30, May 12, 16, 22, June 5, July 4, 1863, AMAA; *American Missionary,* 7 (July, 1863), 158.

20. Ibid., 5 (August, 1861), 178–179; Lewis Tappan to A. Pearson, October 27, 1863; Tappan to T. Tucker, October 27, 1863; Tappan to Mrs. F. E. G. Stoddard, November 20, 1863; Tappan to M. Hamilin, March 10, 1864, all in Lewis Tappan Papers, Library of Congress, Washington, D.C.; J. L. Richardson to S. S. Jocelyn, November 7, 1863, AMAA.

21. Lewis Tappan to Charles Sumner, February 13, 1865; Tappan to D. Baldwin, June 3, 1865, both in Tappan Papers; *American Missionary,* 7 (July, 1863), 158.

22. J. L. Richardson to S. S. Jocelyn, June 5, 27, July 4, 1863, AMAA; *American Missionary,* 8 (January, 1864), 18.

23. Lydia A. Hess to S. S. Jocelyn, May 4, 1863; J. L. Richardson to S. S. Jocelyn, November 7, 1863; S. Sawyer to S. S. Jocelyn, April 21, 1863, all in AMAA.

24. J. L. Richardson to S. S. Jocelyn, November 7, 28, December 18, 1863, AMAA.

25. R. I. Brigham, "Negro Education in Ante Bellum Missouri," *Journal of Negro History*, 30 (October, 1945), 412–414; William E. Parrish, *Missouri Under Radical Rule, 1865–1870* (Columbia, Mo., 1965), 118; *American Missionary*, 7 (May, 1863), 111; J. L. Richardson to S. S. Jocelyn, December 19, 1863, AMAA.

26. J. L. Richardson to S. S. Jocelyn, March 1, 5, 14, 1864; Teachers Monthly School Report, April, 1864; L. A. Montague to S. S. Jocelyn, March 30, 1864, all in AMAA.

27. An Appeal by the St. Louis Board of Education for Free Colored Schools" (Flyer), AMAA; G. Candee to G. Whipple, June 1, 1864, AMAA.

28. Ibid., June 1, 22, 1864; L. A. Montague to S. S. Jocelyn, April 26, 1864, all in AMAA.

29. G. C. Booth to Secretaries of the AMA, October 20, November 18, 26, 1864; M. M. Clark to G. Whipple, November 17, 1864; G. Wilkerson to M. E. Striby, January 20, 1864, all in AMAA.

30. Richardson, Hess, Montague and Booth taught in the free schools. Candee, whose merits ended with his good intentions, was a missionary. Harriet E. Townsend, Katherine A. Dunning and Reverend D. N. Goodrich worked in Benton Barracks which housed ill and homeless freedmen who had migrated from the South.

31. C. A. Briggs to Miss Dodge, January 4, 1864; Helen J. Ward to G. Whipple, May 17, 1864, both in AMAA; C. A. Briggs to J. W. Alvord, March 17, 1867, Missouri, Letters Received by the Chief Disbursing Officer, Record Group 105, National Archives, Washington, D.C.

32. C. A. R. Briggs to Dear Friend, March 4, 1865; Briggs to G. Whipple, February 2, 1865; Briggs to G. Whipple and M. E. Strieby, May 1, 1865; W. Baker to G. Whipple, February 25, March 9, 1865; D. N. Goodrich to M. E. Strieby, February 25, 1865, all in AMAA.

33. The AMA paid Miss Baker's salary (ten dollars a month) but the local black community paid her board. L. M. Pinney to G. Whipple, September 1, 1864; A. Baker to G. Whipple, November 3, 30, 1864, both in AMAA.

34. Ibid., January 10, February 22, March 1, 1865; Baker to S. Hunt, November 18, 1865, AMAA.

35. A. Baker to G. Whipple, March 24, 1865; Baker to S. Hunt, January 31, 1866, both in AMAA.

36. L. A. Montague to M. E. Strieby, June 20, 1864; William Porter to M. E. Strieby, October 14, 1865, both in AMAA.

37. L. A. Montague to M. E. Strieby, June 20, 1864; Montague to S. S. Jocelyn, July 28, 1864; Teachers Monthly School Report, July 1864, all in AMAA.

38. A. Baker to S. Hunt, May 17, November 18, 1865, AMAA.

39. Carondelet, Warrensburg, Kansas City, Jefferson City, Independence and St. Louis.

40. In 1869–1870 the AMA operated schools at Fulton, Ironton, Lebanon, Osceola, Palmyra, Richmond, Spring Valley, Warrensburg and Westport. See *American Missionary*, 14 (June, 1870), 126.

Chapter 19: Black Churches and the Civil War

1. Clarence Walker, *A Rock in a Weary Land: The African Methodist Episcopal Church During the Civil War and Reconstruction* (Baton Rouge: Louisiana State University Press, 1982) in booklength form offers a very good treatment of the role of the AME Church in the Civil War and Reconstruction.

2. Sources on the history of the AME and the AMEZ include: William J. Walls, *The African Methodist Episcopal Zion Church: Reality of the Black Church* (Charlotte, NC: AME Zion Publishing House, 1974); Harry V. Richardson, *Dark Salvation: The Story of Methodism as it Developed Among Blacks in America*. C. Erick Lincoln Series on Black Religion (Garden City, NY: Anchor Press/Doubleday, 1976); Carol V. R. George, *Segregated Sabbaths: Richard Allen and the Emergence of Separate Black Churches, 1760–1840* (New York: Oxford University Press, 1973).

3. Richard R. Wright Jr., comp., *The Encyclopedia of the African Methodist Episcopal Church*, 2d ed. (Philadelphia: The Book Concern of the AME Church, 1947), 603.

4. Durman Malone, ed., *Dictionary of American Biography*, vol. 5 (New York: Charles Scribner's Sons, orig. 1932/1933, copyright renewed 1960–61), 192–193; William J. Simmons, *Men of Mark: Eminent, Progressive and Rising* (Cleveland, Ohio: George M. Revell & Company, 1887), 133–143.

5. *The Christian Recorder,* June 13, 1863, 97. Also see Clarence Walker, *Rock*, 39–40, and Leon F. Litwack, *Been in the Storm So Long: The Aftermath of Slavery* (New York: Vintage Books, A Division of Random House, 1980), 64–103.

6. *The Christian Recorder,* July 18, 1863, 117.

7. See Litwack, *Storm*, 64–103, and *The Christian Recorder,* July 18, 1863, 117.

8. *The Christian Recorder,* September 26, 1863, 153.

9. *The Christian Recorder,* July 25, 1863, 121.

10. *The Christian Recorder,* July 18, 1863, 118.

11. *The Christian Recorder,* May 30, 1863, 89, and *The Christian Recorder,* November 28, 1863, 189–190.

12. Walls, *AMEZ,* 185–187. *Star of Zion* (Charlotte, NC), October 31, 1918, 1, 4, 5, 8; and Edward L. Wheeler, *Uplifting the Race: The Black Minister in the New South, 1865–1902* (New York: University Press of America, 1896), 13.

13. Walls, *AMEZ,* 185–187.

14. Walls, *AMEZ,* 187–189.

15. Wheeler, *Uplifting,* 14.

16. Albert J. Raboteau, *Slave Religion: The "Invisible Institution" in the Antebellum South* (New York: Oxford University Press, 1978), depicts the depth, vitality, commitment, and creativity in the religion of southern black Christians.

17. Walls, *AMEZ,* 188–189.

18. James W. Hood, *Sketch of the Early History of the African Methodist Episcopal Zion Church* (N.p., 1914), 24.

19. William B. McClain, *Black People in the Methodist Church: Whither Thou Goest?* (Cambridge, Massachusetts: Schenkman Publishing Company, 1984), 75–82.

20. *The Christian Recorder,* July 9, 1864, 109.

21. See Walls, *AMEZ,* 459–471.

22. Othal Hawthorne Lakey, *The History of the CME Church* (Memphis: The CME Publishing Couse, 1985, 101–223.

Chapter 20: Sherman Marched—and Proclaimed "Land for the Landless"

1. *The War of the Rebellion: Official Records (Armies),* ser. 1, 39(pt.3):222, 576–77, 594. Citations hereafter to the ORA are to ser. 1, except where otherwise noted.

2. *ORA,* 39 (pt. 3):660–61.

3. *ORA,* 39 (pt. 3):713, 44:7–14, 114, 147–48, 212.

4. *ORA,* 44:10–12, 700–02, 855.

5. *ORA,* 44:10, 12, 727, 728, 771, 786, 959.

6. *ORA,* 44.0, 13 14, 114, 147–48, 152, 159, 700–02, 726–27.

7. *ORA,* 44:727–28, 741–43, 797–800.

8. *ORA,* 38 (pt. 1):36; 44:636, 726, 728–29, 740–43, 797–800, 820–21.

9. *ORA,* 44:700–02, 727, 786, 797, 817–18, 841 42; 47(pt 2):18.

10. *ORA,* 39 (pt. 3):222.

11. *ORA,* 39 (pt. 3):713–14; 44:59, 159, 166, 212. It was later implied that Sherman might have armed blacks had he been granted his request for assignment of a Union colonel who was experienced in organizing black soldiers, a request not granted. *New York Tribune,* December 24, 1864, p. 4.

12. *ORA,* 39(pt.3):701.

13. *ORA,* 44:13, 75, 159, 166–67, 203–05, 211–12; 47(pt.2):36.

14. *ORA,* 44:701–02, 727, 729–30, 817–18; ser.3, 2:152–53; 4:118–19, 1022–31. A thorough account of the genesis and evolution of the Port Royal Experiment is Willie Lee Rose, *Rehearsal for Reconstruction* (New York, 1964).

15. *ORA,* 44:787.

16. *ORA,* 44:836–37.

17. Lloyd Lewis, *Sherman—Fighting Prophet* (New York, 1932), pp. 478–79; Earl Schenck Miers, *The General Who Marched to Hell* (New York, 1951), pp. 272–73; Paul M. Angle, ed., *Three Years in the Army of the Cumberland: The Letters and Diary of Major James A. Connolly* (Bloomington, 1959), p. 373; William Saxton Diary, v. 26, p. 33, Saxton Family Papers, Yale Univ. Library.

18. Ezra J. Warner, *Generals in Blue* (Baton Rouge, 1964), pp. 115–16.

19. Angle, *Three Years in the Army of the Cumberland,* pp. 354–55; Burke Davis, *Sherman's March* (New York, 1980), pp. 91–94.

20. *ORA,* 44:186–87, 502.

21. *ORA,* 44:663, 674; Angle, *Three Years in the Army of the Cumberland,* pp. 349–56.

22. Angle, *Three Years in the Army of the Cumberland,* pp. 354–55; Davis, *Sherman's March,* pp. 91–94.

23. *ORA,* 44:699; *New York Tribune,* December 15, 1864, p. 1.

24. *ORA* 47(pt.2):36–37.

25. *ORA* 47(pt.2):37–41.

26. W. T. Sherman to President Johnson, February 2, 1866, Andrew Johnson Papers, Library of Congress, ser. 1, Reel 20.

27. *ORA,* 47(pt.2):44.

28. *ORA,* 47(pt.2):60–62.

29. *ORA,* 39(pt.3):701; 47(pt.2):37.

30. *ORA,* 47(pt.2):835.

31. *ORA,* ser. 3, 4:1024–26.

32. Saxton to E. D. Townsend, AAG, U.S. Army, January 15, 1865, accepting promotion to major general by brevet, to rank from January 12, 1865, in Rufus Saxton file, Letters Rec'd by Appointment, Commission and Personal Branch of the Adj. Gen., File No. 1302, ACP 1879, RG 94, National Archives; Willard Saxton Diary, v. 26, pp. 25–26, 33–40; William S. McFeelin, *Yankee Stepfather* (New Haven, 1968), pp. 47–48.

33. Saxton to O. O. Howard, June 4 and September 5, 1865, Nos. S-14 and S-83, Letters Rec'd & Registers by the Commr., Bureau of Refugees, Freedmen and Abandoned Lands, RG 105, National Archives, M 752, Roll 17; Claude F. Oubre, *Forty Acres and a Mule* (Baton Rouge, 1978), pp. 46–47.

34. Circular No. 4, April 22, 1865, Orders of Asst. Commr. for S.C., Bureau of Refugees, Freedmen and Abandoned Lands, RG 105, National Archives, M. 869, Roll 37.

35. 13 U.S, Stat:507.

36. McFeely, *Yankee Stepfather*, pp. 45–48, 62–64; Howard to Saxton, May 22, 1865, Letters Sent, Endorsements and Circulars by the Commr., Bureau of Refugees, Freedmen and Abandoned Lands, RG 105, National Archives, M. 742, Roll 1.

37. James D. Richardson, *Messages and Papers of the Presidents,* H. Rep. Misc. Doc. 210, pt. 6, 53d Cong., 2d Sess. (1897):310–12.

38. George R. Bentley, *A History of the Freedmen's Bureau* (Philadelphia, 1955), p. 74.

39. Howard to Saxton, June 8, 1865, Letters Sent, Endorsements and Circulars by the Commr., Bureau of Refugees, Freedmen and Abandoned Lands, RG 105, National Archives, M. 742, Roll 1.

40. Saxton to Howard, June 4, 1865, No. S-14, Letters Rec'd and Registers by the Commr., Bureau of Refugees, Freedmen and Abandoned Lands, RG 105, National Archives, M. 752, Roll 17; Oubre, *Forty Acres and a Mule,* p. 68.

41. Bentley, *Freedmen's Bureau,* pp. 97–98; Oubre, *Forty Acres and a Mule,* pp. 51–52.

42. Bentley, *Freedmen's Bureau,* pp. 69, 98–100; McFeely, *Yankee Stepfather,* pp. 126–29; Oubre, *Forty Acres and a Mule,* p. 51; Saxton to Howard, September 5, 1865, No. s-83, Letters Rec'd and Registers by the Commr., Bureau of Refugees, Freedmen and Abandoned Lands, RG 105, National Archives, M. 752, Roll 17.

43. Bentley, *Freedmen's Bureau,* pp. 99–100; McFeely, *Yankee Stepfather,* pp. 130–48, 195–200.

44. Sen. Ex. Doc. No. 25, 39th Cong., 1sr Sess. (1866): 8–10. The measure also included a section authorizing rental and sale to "freedmen and loyal refugees" of public lands in Florida, Mississippi, Alabama, Louisiana, and Arkansas in plots not exceeding forty acres and another section authorizing the Bureau, if Congress were to provide appropriations therefor, to acquire land "for refugees and freedmen dependent on the government for support" which the Bureau later could sell, presumably to the occupants, at cost. Neither such section made particular provision for Sherman "title" holders, and the latter section was most ambiguous. Ibid., p. 9.

45. Resolution of September 18, 1865, Committee on Ordinances and Resolutions, Reports and Resolutions, South Carolina Convention (1865), 11–12, S.C. Archives; W. H. Trescot to Gov. Benjamin F. Perry, October 24, 1865, Leters Rec;d and Sent, September 20—December 21, 1865, Benjamin F. Perry Papers, S.C. Archives; Trescot to Gov. James L. Orr, February 4, 1866, Letters Rec'd, October 11, 1865—April 3, 1866, James L. Orr Papers, S.C. Archives; W. H. Trescot to President Johnson, January 31, 1866 (two letters—Letters Rec'd by Pres. Johnson Relating to Bureau Affairs, Bureau of Refugees, Freedmen and Abandoned Lands, RG 105, National Archives; Johnson to Sherman, February 1, 1866, Andrew Johnson Papers, Library of Congress, ser. 2, v. 3, p. 77, Reel 42; Sherman to Johnson, February 2, 1866, ibid., ser. 1, Reel 20. Trescot had been prominent in South Caroina affairs for years. R. Nicholas Olsberg, "A Government of Class and Race: William Henry Trescot and the South Carolina Chivalry 1861–1865" (Ph.D. Diss., Univ. of S.C., 1972), Lib. Of Cong. microflim.

46. Sen. Ex. Doc. No. 25, 39th Cong. 1st Sess. (1866): 1–8; Richardson, *Messages and Papers of the Presidents*, pt. 6: 398–405; Cong. Globe, 39th Cong., 1st Sess. (1866): 936–43.

47. Willard Saxon Diary, v. 26, pp. 218–19, v. 27, pp. 22–23, 51, 59–61, 68–69; purported copy of letter of December 1 1865, from Trescot to Johnson, Saxton Family Papers, Letterbook 7 (among loose papers); Brief Sketch of the Military Service of Rufus Saxton, p. 3, in Rufus Saxton file, Letters Rec'd by Appointment, Commission and Personal Branch of the Adj. Gen., File No. 1302, ACP, RG 94, National Archives; McFeely, *Yankee Stepfather*, pp. 226–28; Oubre, *Forty Acres and a Mule*, p. 59.

48. Trescot to Orr, February 28 and March 4, 1866, Letters Rec'd, October 11, 1865—April 3, 1866, James L. Orr Papers, S.C. Archives; Howard to Johnson, February 22, 1866, Andrew Johnson Papers, Library of Congress, ser. 1, Reel 20.

49. Trescot to Orr, March 4, 1866, Letters Rec'd, October 11, 1865–April 3, 1866, James L. Orr Papers, S.C. Archives; Trescott [*sic*] to Johnson, February 22, 1866, Andrew Johnson Papers, Library of Congress, ser. 1, Reel 20.

50. Bentley, *Freedmen's Bureau*, pp. 123–24; Martin Abbott, *The Freedmen's Bureau in South Carolina* (Chapel Hill, 1967), pp. 60–62; Oubre, *Forty Acres and a Mule*, pp. 61–67; Trescot to Johnson, March 12, 1866, and copies of Howard to R. K. Scott, Asst. Commr. For S.C., March 8, 1866, and of Scott's General Orders No. 9, March 7, 1866, Letters Rec'd by Pres. Johnson Relating to Bureau Affairs, Bureau of Refugees, Freedmen and Abandoned Lands, RG 105, National Archives.

51. 14 U.S. Stat.: 173; Richardson, *Messages and Papers*, pt. 6:422–265; Bentley, *Freedmen's Bureau*, pp. 133–34. In June Congress had adopted the Southern Homestead Act opening for homesteading some public lands in Florida, Mississippi, Alabama, Louisiana, and Arkansas. It was assumed that blacks could acquire land under that act. It made no particular provision for Sherman "title" holders. Such lands were of inferior quality; for that and other reasons the act had little practical consequence. Bentley, *Freedmen's Bureau*, pp. 134, 144–46.

52. Probably it will never be known precisely how many "titles" were issued, and when, throughout the Sherman order area from Charleston into Florida because of inadequacy of record keeping at the time, loss of records since, and sheer difficulty in finding what records remain. The most specific effort to tell the story is Oubre, *Forty Acres and a Mule*, pp. 46–71. See also Abbott, *Freedmen's Bureau in S.C.*, pp. 7–16, 54–63; Carol K. Rothrock Bleser, *The Promised Land* (Columbia, 1969), pp. 7–12.

53. Heads of Families Certificate Books, Direct Tax Comm. S.C., Nos. D-3 through D-6, Records of Internal Rev. Serv., RG 58, National Archives. Books D-1 and D-2 contain copies of certificates of tax land sales to blacks, numbered 1 through 800, from December 10, 1863, through November 24, 1865. There is a gap between Book D-2 and Book D-3. The latter begins with certificate number 836 on September 21, 1866, the first reciting issuance pursuant to the July 1866 statute. Each certificate thereafter, consecutively numbered, so recites. The last such certificate is in Book D-6, number 2234 of September 23, 1871. The 1866 statute provided that the lands to be sold were to be in St. Helena's and St. Luke's Parishes. The certificates recited, for the earlier years, that they were for land in Beaufort District and, for the later years, in Beaufort County. The District was changed to County in 1868; each contained the two Parishes referred to in the 1866 statute. Letter of June 12,

1981, to the author from William L. McDowell, Deputy Director, S.C. Department of Archives and History.

Chapter 21: Lincoln and Black Freedom

1. This essay is based upon my *Lincoln and Black Freedom: A Study in Presidential Leadership* (Columbia: University of South Carolina Press, 1981) and my essay "From Emancipation to Segregation: National Policy and Southern Blacks," in *Interpreting Southern History: Essays on the Recent Historical Literature in Honor of S. W. Higginbotham,* ed. John B. Boles and Evelyn T. Nolen (Baton Rouge: Louisiana State University Press, 1986).
2. For citations to the quotations from Randall, Hofstadter, Stampp, and Current, and their views generally, see "From Emancipation to Segregation," notes 42, 43, 44. The last quotation is from Vincent Harding, *There Is a River: The Black Struggle for Freedom in America* (New York: Harcourt Brace Jovanovich, 1981), p. 236.
3. Benjamin P. Thomas, *Abraham Lincoln: A Biography* (New York: Alfred A. Knopf, 1952), p. 407.
4. Robert W. Johannsen, "In Search of the Real Lincoln, or Lincoln at the Crossroads," *Journal of the Illinois State Historical Society* 61 (1968): 237.
5. Richard N. Current, *The Lincoln Nobody Knows* (New York: McGraw Hill, 1958), p. 236.
6. Wendell Phillips to Ann Phillips, March 31, 1862, Blagden Papers, Houghton Library, Harvard University, printed in part in Irving H. Bartlett, *Wendell and Ann Phillips: The Community of Reform, 1840–1880* (New York: W. W. Norton, 1982), pp. 52–53.
7. Roy P. Basler, ed., Marion Dolores Pratt and Lloyd A. Dunlap, asst. eds., *The Collected Works of Abraham Lincoln,* 9 vols. (New Brunswick, N.J.: Rutgers University Press, 1953–55), 5: 146. Any subsequent Lincoln quotation from the *Collected Works of Lincoln* that is readily located by date or occasion will not be noted.
8. Flanders to Lincoln, January 16, 1864, Abraham Lincoln Papers, Library of Congress, Microfilm edition, 1959.
9. Basler, *Collected Works of Lincoln* 6: 364–65.
10. Richard Nelson Current, *Speaking of Abraham Lincoln: The Man and His Meaning for Our Times* (Urbana: University of Illinois Press, 1983), p. 164.
11. Basler, *Collected Works of Lincoln,* 8:248.
12. Ibid., 2:501.
13. Ibid., 2:256.
14. Ibid., 5:537.
15. Frederick Douglass, *Life and Times of Frederick Douglass Written by Himself* (reprint of 1892 rev. ed., New York: Crowell-Collier, 1962), pp. 360–61.
16. Basler, *Collected Works of Lincoln,* 5:372.
17. Ibid., 7:483.
18. Ibid., 7:243; Hahn to W. D. Kelley, June 21, 1865, *New York Times,* June 23, 1865, reprinted from the *Washington Chronicle.*
19. Basler, *Collected Works of Lincoln,* 7:486.
20. *New Orleans Tribune,* May 23, 1865.
21. Clipping of an address at Tremont Temple, Boston, in Nathaniel P. Banks Papers, Library of Congress.

22. *New Orleans Tribune,* April 25, 1865.
23. Banks to Preston King, May 6, 1865, Andrew Johnson Papers, Library of Congress.
24. From a headline in the *Maryland Union,* October 20, 1864, quoted in Charles Lewis Wagandt, *The Mighty Revolution: Negro Emancipation in Maryland, 1862–1864* (Baltimore: Johns Hopkins University Press, 1964), p. 260.
25. LeRoy P. Graf and Ralph W. Haskins, eds., *The Papers of Andrew Johnson,* 7 vols. to date (Knoxville: University of Tennessee Press, 1967–), 1:136; 2:477; 3:319–20, 328:5:231, 233, 328: for the veto message, see the documentary collection LaWanda Cox and John H. Cox, eds., *Reconstruction, the Negro, and the New South* (Columbia: University of South Carolina Press, 1973), p. 59.
26. Richard E. Neustadt, *Presidential Power: The Politics of Leadership from FDR to Carter* (New York: John Wiley and Sons, 1980), p. 135.

Chapter 22: Lincoln and Race Relations

1. William Hanchet, *The Lincoln Murder Conspiracies* (Urbana and Chicago: 1983) 37.
2. Hans L. Trefousse, *Andrew Johnson: A Biography* (New York: 1989).
3. *Congressional Globe,* 28th Congress, 1st Sess., App. 95–98.
4. Leroy P. Graf, ed., *The Papers of Andrew Johnson* (Knoxville: The University of Tennessee Press, 1967–) 7:251–53.
5. 9 April 1868, W. G. Moore, Diary, Johnson Papers, LC.
6. Thomas R. Turner, *Beware of the People Weeping: Public Opinion and the Assassination of Abraham Lincoln* (Baton Rouge: Louisiana State University Press: 1982).
7. C. Vann Woodward, ed., *Whitelaw Reid, After the War: A Tour of the Southern States, 1865–1866* (New York: 1965) 44.
8. Roy P. Basler, ed., *The Collected Works of Abraham Lincoln* (New Brunswick: 1953) 1:74–75..
9. Ibid., 2:20–22.
10. Ibid., 2:461–69.
11. James McPherson, *Battle Cry of Freedom: The Civil War Era* (New York: Oxford University Press, 1988) 284.
12. Basler, ed., *Collected Works,* 2:263, 439.
13. James McPherson, *The Political History of the United States During the Great Rebellion, 1860–1865* (Washington: 1865) 195–96.
14. Basler, ed., *Collected Works,* 5:28–31, 144–46.
15. *Great Rebellion,* McPherson, 212–13, 254–55, 196–98.
16. Ibid., 245–47, 251.
17. Hans L. Trefousse, *Lincoln's Decision for Emancipation* (Philadelphia: 1975) 35–38, 44–46, 89–91.
18. Basler, ed., *Collected Works,* 5:388–89.
19. Ibid., 5:503; 6:28–31, 281, 406–10.
20. Trefousse, *Lincoln's Decision for Emancipation,* 53–54; Basler, ed., *Collected Works,* 7:53–56.
21. J. G. Randall and Richard N. Current, *Lincoln the President: Last Full Measure* (New York: 1955) 302ff.; *Great Rebellion,* 237, 406.
22. Hans L. Trefousse, *The Radical Republicans: Lincoln's Vanguard for Racial Justice* (New York: 1969) 28–33; James Brewer Stewart, *Holy Warriors: The Abolitionists*

and American Slavery (New York: 1976) 105; Oscar Sherwin, *Prophet of Liberty: The Life and Time of Wendell Phillips* (New York: 1958) 272; Fawn Brodie, *Thaddeus Stevens, Scourge of the South* (New York: 1959) 109.

23. Cf. LaWanda Cox, *Lincoln and Black Freedom: A Study in Presidential Leadership* (Columbia S.C.: 1981) 20 ff.

24. Basler, ed., *Collected Works*, 1:259–61; Richard N. Current, *The Lincoln Nobody Knows* (New York: 1958) 218.

25. Basler, ed., *Collected Works*, 1:222–23.

26. Ibid., 2:322–33, 405, 498, 3:146; 2:501.

27. Ibid., 3:145–46; 3:105 (Douglas' remarks); Don E. Fehrenbacher, "Only His Stepchildren: Lincoln and the Negro," *Civil War History*, 20 (1974): 298.

28. Basler, ed., *Collected Works*, 5:370–75.

29. Benjamin P. Thomas, *Abraham Lincoln* (New York: 1952) 363.

30. Frederick Douglass, *Autobiographies* (New York: 1994) 785, 797, 802ff.

31. Basler, ed., *Collected Works*, 7:101, 243.

32. Cox, *Lincoln and Black Freedom*, 142–84.

33. Frederick Bancroft and William A. Dunning, *The Reminiscences of Carl Schurz* (New York: 1908) 3:222–23.

For Further Reading

Berlin, Ira, et al., eds. *The Destruction of Slavery* Series 1, volume 1 of *Freedom: A Documentary of Emancipation, 1861–1867*. New York: Cambridge University Press, 1985.

———. *Slaves No More: Three Essays on Emancipation and the Civil War.* New York: Cambridge University Press, 1992.

Brewer, James H. *The Confederate Negroes: Virginia's Craftsmen and Military Laborers, 1861–1865.* Durham: Duke University Press, 1969.

Cox, LaWanda. *Lincoln and Black Freedom: A Study in Presidential Leadership.* Columbia: University of South Carolina Press, 1981.

Dyrden, Robert F. *The Gray and the Black: The Confederate Debate on Emancipation.* Baton Rouge: Louisiana State University Press, 1972.

Franklin, John Hope. *The Emancipation Proclamation.* New York: Doubleday, 1963.

Gerteis, Louis. *From Contraband to Freedman: Federal Policy Toward Southern Blacks, 1861–1865.* Westport, Conn.: Greenwood Press, 1973.

Jordan, Ervin. *Black Confederates and Afro Yankees in Civil War Virginia.* Charlottesville: University of Virginia Press, 1995.

Litwack, Leon. *Been in the Storm Too Long: The Aftermath of Slavery.* New York: Knopf, 1979.

Quarles, Benjamin. *The Negro in the Civil War.* Boston: Little, Brown, 1953.

———. *Lincoln and the Negro.* New York: Da Capo, 1990.

Wiley, Bell I. *Southern Negroes, 1861–1865.* New Haven, Conn.: Yale University Press, 1938.

Index

Abbott, James B., 125
Adams, Charles Francis, Jr., 229
Adkins, William, 180
African Methodist Episcopal Church
    (AME), 34, 207, 272, 275, 276, 278,
    279, 280, 282
African Methodist Episcopal Zion Church
    (AMEZ), xiv, 207, 272, 276–79, 280,
    281, 282
Aglar, S. F., 66
Allen, Edward S., 36
American Baptist Home Missionary
    Society, 238
American Baptist Missionary Union, 226
American Bible Society, 243
American Free School, 263
American Missionary Association, xiii, 34,
    35, 227, 238, 239, 248, 249, 252,
    255, 259–67
American Tract Society, 252
Anderson, Bill, 67
Anderson, Osborne Perry, 7, 9
Anderson, R. C., 136, 137
Andrew, John Albion, 110
Andrew, John, 198
Anglo-African Educational Society, 250
Anthony, Daniel R., 136, 146
Antoine, Caesar C., 202
Arnold, Richard, 30, 32
Ashley, James, 304
Ayers, James T., 40

Baker, Alma, 266, 267
Baker, William, 265, 266
Banks, Nathaniel P., 118, 204, 232, 233,
    237, 242, 244, 303, 304, 307, 308,
    309
Barrow, Robert R., 53
Bass, Eli, 67
Bass, Paris, 67
Batson, Francis, 96

Baunzhaf, Charles, 62
Beals, H. S., 252
Beebe, George M., 124
Beecher, Henry Ward, 187
Beecher, Lyman, 186
Bell, W. S., 254, 256, 257
Bertonneau, Arnold, 210
Bingham, George Caleb, 152
Birney, James G., 186
Blanchard, Stephen, 260, 261
Blow, Henry, 266
Blunt, James G., 139
Booth, George C., 265
Booth, John Wilkes, 13, 317
Bowles, J., 125
Boyd, Henry, 187
Breckinridge, John Cabell, 110
Briggs, C. A., Mrs., 265, 266
Brisbin, James, 24
Brisby, William Henry, 180, 181, 183
Broadhead, James O., 66
Brockway, E. L., 164
Bross, John, 162
Bross, William, 162
Brown, Albert, 177
Brown, B. Gratz, 308, 309
Brown, Edmund Collier, 178
Brown, John, 7, 46, 121, 136, 137, 146,
    260
Brown, John, Jr., 60
Brown, Joseph, 178
Brown, O., 254
Brown, Robert, 182, 183
Brown, Samuel, 173
Brown, William O., 68
Brown, William Wells, 7
Bryan, Alexander, 34
Buchanan, James, 46
Buckingham, William A., 324
Buell, Don Carlos, 94, 95
Burbridge, S. G., 24

Bureau of Colored Troops, 161
Bureau of Refugees, Freedmen and
    Abandoned Lands (Freedmen's
    Bureau), 77
Burgoine, Robert, 173
Burns, George MacGregor, 305
Burton, E. P., 30
Butler, Benjamin F., 12, 51, 53, 110,
    126, 198, 204, 218, 248, 252, 303
Butler, Cornelius, 160
Butler, W. F., 276

Cailloux, André, 205
Caldwell, George, 64
Caldwell, Robert, 136
Campbell, Rex, 74
Candee, George, 262, 263, 264
Carney, Thomas, 130
Carter, Rachel, 97
Casey, Julius, 96
Chase, Salmon P., 37, 113, 114, 116,
    201, 237, 303, 307
Cheatham, John L., 97
Cheatham, William S., 97
Chester, Thomas Morris, 12
Christian Commission, 226
Christian Methodist Episcopal Church
    (CME), 278, 280, 281, 282
Clark, M. M., 264, 265
Clark, Peter H., 190, 196
Clay, Henry, 323
Clayton, Powell, 64
Clinton, Joseph Jackson, 276, 278
Coan, William L., 254, 255, 257
Coffin, Charles, 40
Coffin, Levi, 186
Cohen, Fanny, 29, 31
Collamore, George W., 147
Colored Union League, 35
Committee on Public Education, 241
Committee on the Conduct of the War,
    163
Confiscation Act, 150, 320
Conkling, James C., 320
Contraband Relief Association, xiii
Contraband Relief Society, 262
Conway, Martin F., 126, 145
Conway, Thomas W., 212, 233

Cooper Institute, 7
Cordley, Richard, 124, 133
Cornish, Dudley Taylor, 140
Corps d'Afrique, 204, 236
Cotman, Thomas, 183
Cox, LaWanda, 325
Crane, Mary, 21
Crawford, Samuel J., 139, 152
Cumber, Warren, 178, 183
Cunningham, Charles E., 62

Daniels, Edward, 62
Davidson, John Nelson, 156
Davis, Annie, 13
Davis, Jefferson, 46, 52, 103
Davis, Jefferson C., 286–88
Denison, Frederic, 226
Denison, George S., 114
Deuster, Peter V., 157
Dickson, William Martin, 186, 192, 193,
    196, 197, 199
Doolittle, James R., 159
Dostie, Anthony P., 212
Douglass, Frederick, 5, 6, 7, 9, 11, 14,
    261, 300, 306, 323, 324
Dove, William A., 207, 208
Du Bois, W. E. B., 253
Duff Green's Row, xiii
Dumas, Francis E., 202
Dunham, Edward A., 64
Dunn, Oscar J., 202, 208
Dupré, Lucien J., 53
Durant, Thomas J., 201, 212, 303
Eastman, A. M., 256
Eaton, John, 226, 227, 228, 229
Eaton, William, 226
Ebenezer Creek, 286–87, 288, 296
Ellis, Franklin, 179
Ellis, J. H., 59
Emancipation Proclamation, xii, 5, 8, 9,
    11, 12, 13, 14, 21, 22, 27, 52, 59, 81,
    126, 128, 135, 152, 199, 273, 299,
    302, 303, 305, 310, 320, 323
Emery, Agnes, 134
Emory, William Helmsby, 117
Enrollment Act (1864), 161
Escort, Paul D., 79, 80
Evans, William N., 264

Fanon, Frantz, 55
Fee, John, 23
54th Massachusetts, 13, 38, 198, 199
55th Massachusetts, 198
1st S.C. Volunteers (33d USCT), 38
Fisher, Hugh Dunn, 127
Flanders, Benjamin F., 303
Fletcher, Thomas C., 265
Forrest, Nathan Bedford, 94, 97
Fort Negley (Nashville, Tenn.), 93–105
Fort Wagner (S.C.), 13, 198, 199
Foster, John G., 33, 284, 285, 288, 289
Fowley, Joseph, 98, 104
Fox, George, 173
Frazier, Garrison, 38
Freedman's Department, 229
Freedmen's Bureau, 29, 43, 44, 77, 82,
    98, 106, 225, 227, 238, 255, 292, 293
Freedmen's Bureau Act (1865), 291,
    292, 296
Freedmen's Relief Society (Quincy, Ill.), 63
Frémont, John C., 60, 147, 149, 320
French, Mansfield, 41
Friends Association for the Relief of
    Colored Freedmen, xiii
Frisbie, H. N., 236
Fugitive Slave Law (1850), 26, 62, 126,
    211, 321
Fuller, Arthur B., 225

Gaiter, Daniel, 49
Gamble, Hamilton F., 126
Gamble, Hamilton R., 60
Garfield, James A., 18
Garnet, Henry Highland, 7, 10
Garret, Angie, 13
Gilmer, J. F., 93
Glover, Richard, 64
Gordon, Nellie Kinzie, 33
Gordon, Robert, 187
Gordon, Sarah, 33
Gordon, William Washington, 33, 38
Gould, John, 30
Grant, Ulysses S., 37, 84, 94, 163, 185,
    226, 227, 228, 283, 284, 285, 294, 310
Greeley, Horace, 301, 320
Green, Louis F., 65
Green, Lucy, 181

Gregory, John M., 182
Guitar, Odon, 59
Gutman, Herbert, 75

Hahn, Michael, 210, 212, 303, 307, 308,
    324
Haiti, 83, 324
Hall, James D. S., 275
Halleck, Henry W., 114, 116, 286, 288, 290
Hamilton, Thomas, 10
Hampton, Samuel, 173
Hanks, George, 117, 239, 244
Hardee, Charles, 30
Hardee, William J., 284
Hardin, Judson, 48
Harpers Ferry raid, 7
Harris, Isham G., 93
Harrison, Isaac, 48
Haskell, John G., 122
Hawes, Richard, 196
Hayes, Margaret J., 66
Helper, Hinton, 260
Henderson, J. B., 66
Hepworth, George H., 218
Herold, David, 317
Hess, Lydia A., 262, 263, 264
Heth, Henry, 196
Hickman, John, 223
Higginson, Thomas W., 198
Hill, David, 276
Hills, Amos B., 260
Hinton, Jim, 97
Hinton, Richard J., 136
Holmes, Dan, 60
Holt, Joseph, 22
Honer, William, 191
Hood, James Walker, xiv, 272, 276–79
Hood, John Bell, 103, 104
Hooper, Thomas, 234
Horn, Frederick W., 157, 158
Houston, Ulysses L., 42
Houx, Fanny, 68
Howard, Jane Wallace, 36, 39
Howard, O. O., 29, 42, 43, 292, 293, 295
Howe, Henry, 190, 191
Hoyt, George, 151
Hubbs, Isaac, 236
Human Aid Society, 250

Hunt, Ralph, 98
Hunter, David, 152, 198, 320
Hyde, Patsy, 103

Île la Vàche, Haiti, 83, 324
Ingraham, James H., 202, 207, 208, 213, 215

Jackson, Claiborne F., 126
Jackson, James H., 66
Jacobs, Harriet, xiii
Jennison, Charles R., 60, 124, 146
Jess, Mary, 36
Jinnings, Thomas, 47
Jocelyn, S. S., 260
Johns, Joseph, 195
Johnson, Andrew, 35, 42, 43, 94–95, 100, 201, 292, 293, 294, 309, 311, 314, 315, 316, 317–18, 319, 325
Johnson, Daniel, 74
Johnson, Hannah, 13, 14
Johnson, James, 63, 64
Johnson, Sarah, 83
Jones, Edmund, 177
Jones, Marshall P. H., 190, 191, 193, 196, 197
Jones, Riley, 177, 183

Kagi, John Henrie, 136
Kansas Emancipation League, 136, 141
Kansas State Colored Convention, 141
Kelley, William D., 308
Kendrick, W., 259
Kenner, Duncan F., 53
Kilpatrick, H. Judson, 283
Kolchin, Peter, 74
Kollock, George J., Mrs., 31, 43
Krekel, Arnold, 61
Kutzner, Edward A., 61

Lakey, Othal, 281
Lamar, Caroline A. N., 30
Lamar, Charles A. L., 30
Lane, James Henry, 121, 122, 126, 137, 145, 146, 148, 150, 151, 198
Langston, Charles H., 136
Langston, John M., 198
Lathrop, Stanley, 62

LeGrand, Julia, 53
Levine, Lawrence, 75
Lewis, B. W., 130
Lewis, Carter, 173
Lewis, James, 164, 165
Lincoln, Abraham, xii, 5, 6, 7, 8, 9, 10, 11, 12, 13, 14, 19, 21, 22, 26, 27, 38, 45, 52, 59, 60, 63, 94, 110, 118, 126, 127, 128, 134, 135, 138, 139, 147, 149, 150, 151, 157, 158, 160, 163, 164, 165, 185, 186, 188, 199, 206, 210, 211, 212, 232, 237, 242, 273, 291, 296, 299, 300–316, 317–25
Litwack, Leon, 75, 79
Loan, Benjamin, 61
Lockett, Frank, 49
Lockwood, C. L., 248, 254
Louisiana National Equal Rights League, 207
Lupton, James, 194
Lynch, James, 275
Lyon, Nathaniel, 127

Magill, S. W., 35, 41
Magruder, John Bankhead, 176
Mann, Horace, 252
Marrs, Elijah, 16
Mars, J. L., 257
Martin, George J., 138
Maslowski, Peter, 98
Mathews, William D., 136, 141
Maxson, Orrin T., 161
McCary, Robert, 207, 208
McRoberts, A. J., 61
Mercer, George, 31
Methodist Episcopal Church North, 207
Methodist Episcopal Church, South (ME, S), 272, 279
Middleton, John, 33
Miles, Harris, 181, 183
Miles, William H., 281
Miller, Charley, 48
Miller, John F., 95
Mitchell, C. J., 46
Mongomery, James, 124, 146, 151
Montague, L. A., Mrs., 263, 264, 267
Montague, John S., 34
Moore, H. H., 224

Moore, J. J., 279
Moore, Thomas O., 54, 114, 204
Moore, W. G., 318
Morgan, James L., 65
Morton, James Sinclair, 94, 95, 102
Morton, Samuel G., 95

National Enrollment Act (1863), 160
National Equal Rights League, 207
National Freedmen's Relief Association, 238
National Union Brotherhood Association, 207
Native Guards, 114, 115, 119, 198, 204, 205, 208, 209, 210
Negley, James S., 94
Nell, William C., 7
New Orleans, 8, 9, 47, 50, 51, 53, 107, 108, 109, 110, 111, 114, 152, 172, 201–10, 235, 236, 238, 239, 240, 244, 303, 307, 308–9
Nichols, George W., 31
Nichols, John, 63
Niles, William, 252
Noland, W. H., 158
Norfolk, Va., 8, 9, 79, 80, 245, 248–49, 253, 254–55, 256
North Carolina Annual Conference, 278
Northwestern Freedmen's Aid Commission, 238

Overton, Lewis, 136

Paine, E. A., 16
Painter, Nell Irwin, 74
Palmer, John, 24, 25
Payne, Lewis, 317
Payton, Ed, 65
Pearman, Thomas, 173
Peck, Solomon, 226
Pennsylvania Freedman's Aid Commission, 226
Pepper, George, 224
Percy, H. C., 255
Phelps, John Wolcott, 51, 112
Phillips, Timothy, 64, 64
Phillips, Wendell, 145, 187, 302, 321
Pierce, Edward, 254
Pile, James A., 64

Pinchback, Pickney Benton Stewart (P. B. S.), 202, 208, 209
Pinkerton, Alan, 16
Pinney, Laura M., 266
Plumly, Benjamin Rush, 212, 236, 244
Polk, Elias, 94
Pollard, Edward, 183
Pomeroy, Samuel C., 126, 145
Pool, G. H., 260
Postlewaite, Bill, 50
Pratt, Andrew, 161
Price, J. C., 276
Price, Jacob A., 68
Price, Sterling, 126, 127
Proclamation of Amnesty and Reconstruction, 304

Raymond, C., 254
Reader, Samuel J., 153
Reed, Mary, 255
Reid, Whitelaw, 34, 201, 202
Remond, Charles Lenox, 7
Revels, Hiram R., 263
Reynolds, William C., 66
Rice, Spottswood, 67
Richardson, J. L., 262, 263
Richardson, W. J., 34
Roberts, J. R., Mrs., 63
Robinson, Armstead L., 50
Robinson, Charles, 126, 145
Robinson, James F., 187, 189
Rock, John S.
Rogers, James B., 224
Rose, Willie Lee, 231
Rosecrans, William S., 24, 67
Roudanez, Jean Baptiste (J. B.), 202, 208, 210
Roudanez, Louis, 202, 208
Round, J. E., 277
Ruggles, Daniel, 52, 53
Rush, Christopher, 277
Ryan, Edward G., 156

Salomon, Edward, 160, 161
Sanborn, Franklin S., 125
Saxton, Rufus, 40, 41, 42, 43, 198, 285–86, 289–90, 291, 292, 293, 294, 295, 296

Schermerhorn, Isaac, 199
Schofield, John, 103
Schurz, Carl, 325
Scott, Harry, 49
Scott, Winfield, 50
Seaman, H. C., 151
Seddon, James, 54
Selden, John, 177
Seward, William H., 304
Shaffer, John Wilson, 118
Shaw, Robert G., 198
Shepley, George F., 210
Sherman, William T., xiv, 29, 30, 32, 34,
   36, 37, 38, 39, 40, 41, 42, 100, 101,
   164, 283–96
Shurtleff, Giles W., 199
Siebert, Wilbur, 125
Simms, James, 29
Simpson, S. N., 134
Singleton, Marrinda Jane, 80
Slidell, John, 46
Smith, Charles, 211
Smith, Gerrit, 321
Society of Friends, 227
Southern Methodist Episcopal Church,
   207
Speed, Joshua, 321
Stanton, Edwin M., 38, 94, 113, 160,
   227, 286, 288, 289, 308
State Central Committee of Colored Men
   (Michigan), 11
Stearns, George L., 137, 147
Steele, Frederick, 304
Stephenson, Wendell Holmes, 127
Stevens, Thaddeus, 321
Stickney, William, 235
Stiles, Elizabeth Mackay, 30
Stowe, Calvin, 186
Stowe, Harriet Beecher, 186
Strong, W. G., 276
Sumner, Charles, 210, 212, 321

Talbot, William K., 225
Taney, Roger Brooke, 45
Tattnall, Josiah, 39
Taylor, John R., 195
Temperance Society, 250
33d USCT (1st S.C. Volunteers), 38

Thomas, George H., 100, 101, 102
Thomas, Lorenzo, 161
Tod, David, 189, 196
Tower, Z. B., 103
Trego, Joseph H., 64
Trescot, William Henry, 294, 295
Trevigne, Paul, 208
Turner, Henry M., 272–76
Turner, Nat, 107, 174
Turner, William, 173

Ullmann, Daniel, 120
Underground Railroad, 123, 125, 131,
   140, 186
United African Methodist Episcopal
   Church in America, 280
U.S. Christian Commission, 238

Vanderhorst, Richard H., 281
Vaughan, Richard C., 66

Wade, Benjamin, 23
Wadsworth, James, 324
Wall, O. S. B., 198
Wallace, Lew, 189, 192, 194, 196
Weed, Charles, 117
Wells, James Madison, 213
Western Freedman's Aid Committee, 227
Wheeler, Joseph, 165, 283, 296
Wheelock, Edwin, 236, 237, 239, 245
Wilcox, Samuel T., 187
Wilkerson, Green, 265
Williams, James H., 151
Williams, John, 195
Wilson, Ephraim J., 61
Wilson, Henry, 23
Witherspoon, Andrew, 164
Wood, John B., 133
Woodbury, W. H., 255
Woodson, Carter G., 74
Woodward, William E., 15
Works Progress Administration, 104
Wright, Horatio, 189

Yancey, William L., 187

Zion Baptist Association, 34